Lecture Notes in Computer Science

Edited by G. Goos and J. Hartmanis

89

Computer Aided Design Modelling, Systems Engineering, CAD-Systems

CREST Advanced Course
Darmstadt, 8.–19. Sep

T0222304

Edited by J. Encarnacao

Springer-Verlag
Berlin Heidelberg New York 1980

Editor

Jose Encarnacao
Technische Hochschule Darmstadt
Institut für Informationsverwaltung
und Interaktive Systeme
Steubenplatz 12
6100 Darmstadt
Germany

AMS Subject Classifications (1979): 68-06, 68 A05, 68 B15,
68 J10, 68 K05
CR Subject Classifications (1974): 3.2, 4.33, 6.35, 8.1, 8.2

ISBN 3-540-10242-6 Springer-Verlag Berlin Heidelberg New York
ISBN 0-387-10242-6 Springer-Verlag New York Heidelberg Berlin

Printing and binding: Beltz Offsetdruck, Hemsbach/Bergstr.
2145/3140-543210

INTRODUCTION

by

Jose   Encarnacao

Technische Hochschule Darmstadt
Fachgebiet Graphisch-Interaktive Systeme
Institut für Informationsverwaltung und Interaktive Systeme
Steubenplatz 12; 6100 Darmstadt

Introduction

This Advanced Course on Computer Aided Design, held at the
Technical University of Darmstadt from September 8th to 19th 1980,
is financed by the Ministry for Research and Technology of the
Federal Republic of Germany and by the Commission of the
European Communities.

The lecturers of this Advanced Course are the internationally
well-known technical experts on the area of CAD:

K. Bo, University of Trondheim, Trondheim, Norway

T. Neumann, Technical University of Darmstadt, Darmstadt, Germany

H. Nowacki, Technical University of Berlin, Berlin, Germany

A. Requicha, University of Rochester, Rochester, N.Y., USA

T. Sancha, Cambridge Interactive Systems, Cambridge, U.K.

E.G. Schlechtendahl, Kernforschungszentrum Karlsruhe, Germany

H. Tucker, CAD Center, Technical University of Denmark, Lyngby, DK

M.A. Wesley, IBM Watson Research Center, Yorktown Heights, USA

We would like to thank all the lecturers for their contributions
to the Advanced Course, and especially H. Tucker who kindly agreed
to participate at very short notice.

The Course addresses the following topics:

> Scope and purpose of CAD
> CAD system architecture
> Design of CAD systems
> Design optimisation in CAD
> Aspects of CAD methodology
> The resource aspect in CAD systems
> Graphics for presentation of data
> Geometric modelling
> 3 D-Graphics
> Surface generation and fairing
> Data base design for CAD

> Case studies
> Ergonomics
> Economics

The objective is to have these topics presented by outstanding technical experts; these lecturers are supposed to prepare for the course a
set of lecture notes. These lecture notes, as a whole, should - in a
first approach - serve as some sort of a CAD text book. A Lecturers'
Seminar took place in March 1980 in Seeheim in order

> 1) to discuss and agree on the topics
>   and contents of all lectures   and
>
> 2)·to decide upon some common terminology and
>   common understanding of the technical objectives
>   for the course and for the course proceedings.

The result of this coordination seminar was to structure the content
of the course in

> I   Modelling in CAD (Requicha, Wesley, Nowacki)
> II   CAD System Engineering (Bø, Neumann, Schlechtendahl)
> III CAD Systems - Architecture, Design, Justification -
>   (Bø, Sancha, Tucker, Schlechtendahl)

The first part is concerned with the problems of object representation,
geometric models, curves, surfaces and the modelling of design decisions for CAD. In this part the fundamental methods and algorithms
are presented, which can be seen as a design methodology for CAD applications. The second part discusses different functions of a CAD system
(data base, graphics, man-machine interaction) from a system engineering point of view. The last part presents the CAD system aspect, including application system architectures and CAD system justification.

It was decided in Seeheim to have July !st as the deadline for the
lecture notes (camera ready). All lecturers, but one, have accomphlished
with this deadline. It is their merit, that it was possible to have
the course proceedings printed before the beginning of the course. We
would like to express our sincere gratitude to all lecturers for their
fantastic spirit of cooperation and for the high level standard of
the lecture notes they produced.

No Advanced Course like this one, can be organized without assistance.
Mrs. Deubner, Frenk and Kalbfuß were a great help in all organizational

matters; Mrs. R. Kimeswenger was always a safe and efficient support in all secretarial aspects. Last not least, the editor would like to express his gratitude and appreciation to his associates

Norbert Baron and

Walter Klos

for their advice and invaluable assistance in preparing, organizing and running this Advanced Course.

Darmstadt, July 1980

J. Encarnacao

CONTENTS   PAGE

*This chapter did not arrive in time for printing.   461

Chapter 1

Representations of Rigid Solid Objects

by

Aristides A. G. Requicha

Production Automation Project
The University of Rochester
Rochester, New York 14627

1.1 INTRODUCTION

Most mechanical products are collections of rigid solids ("parts") which are manufactured and assembled via processes whose effects are primarily geometrical. Geometrical information -- for specifying parts and products, and for controlling processes -- obviously is of crucial importance in the mechanical industries, and computational means for handling such information therefore are required for automatic or computer-aided design and production.

This chapter discusses the specification of object geometry in the context of Computer Aided Design (CAD) systems. Figure 1.1 provides a high-level, functional view of a CAD system. Observe that--

1) The paramount goal is the creation of representations (symbol structures) which designate (define) physical solids. While some of the information required to define a solid mechanical part is non-geometrical (e.g. material, hardness, ...) the bulk of it is geometrical.

2) Representations are the sources of data for programs. Some programs may be regarded as CAD-system components because they generate displays or compute other important properties of objects, while other programs (e.g. for manufacturing planning) are properly external to the CAD system.

The Geometric Modelling (sub)System (GMS) shown in Fig. 1.1 provides facilities for entering, storing, and editing representations of the geometry of solid objects. At present most of the geometric information contained in a GMS's representations must be supplied by human users of the CAD system in which the GMS is imbedded, because the available automatic-design procedures (e.g. for selecting quasi-optimal parameters for gear trains or heat exchangers) are very specialized. Powerful automatic design systems driven from functional specifications are coming into use in the electronic industries, but analogous systems for the mechanical industries cannot be developed until reasonably general means are found to specify formally the function of mechanical artifacts, and to relate function to geometry. (Automatic design procedures are not shown in Fig. 1.1.)

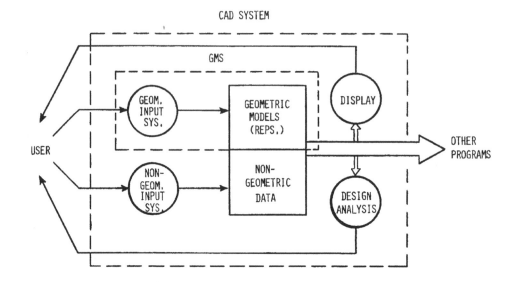

Fig. 1.1   A Functional View of a Mechanical
CAD System

In this first chapter we shall be concerned with the characterization and design of representations for solids, because the properties of the representations in a GMS determine its ultimate capabilities and limitations. The creation (entry) and use of object representations are discussed in Chapter 2.

We attack the representation problem in the two stages shown in Fig. 1.2. First we define a mathematical modelling space (shown at the center of Fig. 1.2) by replacing the real-world entities under study (physical solids) with mathematical entities which we call mathematical models of solids (or simply abstract solids); we then associate representations, i.e. symbol structures constructed over a finite alphabet, to the mathematical models. The choice of an abstract modelling space is discussed in [58] where it is argued that the appropriate mathematical models are subsets of E3 (three-dimensional Euclidean space) which are bounded, closed, regular and semi-analytic. We call such sets <u>r-sets</u>. Intuitively, r-sets may be viewed as "solid curved polyhedra bounded by well-behaved surfaces".

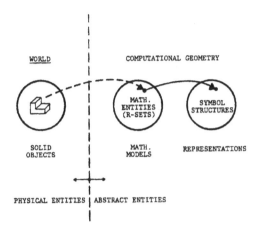

Fig. 1.2 A Two-Stage Approach to
Geometric Modelling

This Chapter focusses on the problem of associating representations to r-sets. The main goals of the Chapter are to establish a precise framework for characterizing schemes for representing rigid solid objects (Section 1.2), and to describe the known schemes in terms of the framework (Section 1.3). While a discussion of specific GMS's is beyond the scope of this Chapter, we shall provide brief comments on a wide range of illustrative extant systems.

The Chapter deals directly only with the representation of <u>nominal</u> (i.e. untoleranced) objects; the practically important problem of representing tolerancing information is addressed elsewhere [57] [34]. Tolerance specifications define classes of solids which are functionally equivalent and interchangeable in assembly. Therefore, to represent toleranced objects one must design representation schemes for <u>equivalence</u> <u>classes</u> of solids. This involves representing a nominal solid plus allowable variations. The characterization of representation schemes developed in Section 1.2 applies equally to the representation of (single) nominal objects or of classes of solids, but Section 1.3 deals exclusively with nominal objects and does not cover the representation of variations.

We have endeavored to make the Chapter understandable to a spectrum of readers, without sacrificing mathematical rigor, by providing intuitive interpretations for all of the concepts discussed. Thus, readers who are familiar with the elementary concepts of sets, relations and mappings, but not with r-set theory [58] [60], should be able to follow the main lines of reasoning simply by ignoring technical mathematical details and focussing on the intuitive meanings of technical terms.

1.2 CHARACTERIZATION OF REPRESENTATION SCHEMES

This section defines representation schemes and discusses some of their important formal and informal properties.

1.2.1 Definitions

A mathematical modelling space enables us to define and study the properties of generic elements of the space, but provides us with no direct means for "talking about" or for computing properties of specific elements of the space. It is representations that provide means for designating (referring to, "naming") individual elements of a mathematical modelling space, and they constitute the raw material on which algorithms operate.

Representations are finite structures constructed with symbols from a finite alphabet according to syntactical rules. Such symbol structures are equivalent to strings of symbols, and therefore a set of syntactically admissible (i.e. syntactically correct) representations may be viewed as a language. Section 1.2.2 below discusses briefly the means we use for describing sets of admissible representations. Our main concern is the meaning or semantics of representations, which we define below by means of representation schemes. In essence, a representation scheme associates representations (symbol structures) with the entities (models) they designate in a mathematical modelling space.

Before defining representation schemes formally we shall review briefly some elementary mathematical concepts. A (binary) <u>relation</u> z between two sets X and Y is simply a set of ordered pairs (x,y) where x is an element of X and y is an element of Y. We use z : X --> Y to denote a relation z from X to Y. The set of all x which occur as first elements in a pair is the <u>domain</u> D of the relation, and the set of all y which occur as second elements in a pair is the <u>range</u> V of the relation. Generally, D and V are proper subsets of X and Y, i.e. the relation need not be defined for all points in the spaces X and Y. The inverse of a relation z, denoted z^{-1}, is the relation obtained by inverting the order of the elements in each pair. Finally, a function (also called a mapping, transformation, etc.) is a single-valued relation, i.e. a relation in which no element x of X occurs more than once as the first element of a pair.

A <u>representation scheme</u> is defined as a relation s : M --> R, where M is a mathematical modelling space and R is a <u>representation space</u>, i.e. a set of syntactically correct symbol structures over some

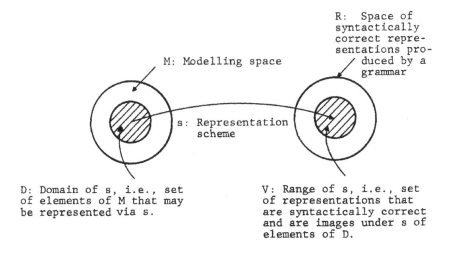

R: Space of syntactically correct representations produced by a grammar

M: Modelling space

s: Representation scheme

D: Domain of s, i.e., set of elements of M that may be represented via s.

V: Range of s, i.e., set of representations that are syntactically correct and are images under s of elements of D.

Fig. 1.3 Domain and Range of a Representation Scheme

finite alphabet. We denote the domain of s by D, and the image of D under s, i.e. the range of s, by V. Any representation in the range V is said to be valid. Valid representations must be both syntactically and semantically correct, i.e. they must have corresponding elements in M (see Fig. 1.3).

Observe in Fig. 1.3 that we neither assume that all objects are representable (i.e. D need not equal M) nor that all syntactically correct representations are valid (i.e. V need not equal R). Our rationale is the following. The range V may be viewed as a language, but the ranges of practical representation schemes seldom may be defined by "reasonable" (e.g. context-free) grammars. Therefore it is more useful to consider representation spaces R that may be defined easily by formal means, with the understanding that not all elements of R are valid representations. This implies that the syntax of representations is not an essential property of a representation scheme s because any syntax that defines a superset of V leads to a scheme that differs from s only in a trivial formal sense. In the remainder of the Chapter we shall use the terms "syntax" and "semantics" somewhat informally, and we shall assume that the syntax is chosen sensibly so that R is not unnecessarily larger than V.

A "syntactical variant" R' of a representation space R may be obtained by establishing a one-to-one correspondence between R and R' via a mapping v' that does not depend on the space M being represented. The correspondence between elements of R and R' must be independent of the meaning of the representations. For example, if representations in R are tree structures one may construct a syntactical variant R' by a mapping v' which replaces each tree structure of R by its postfix string equivalent. Observe in this example that the mapping v' is indeed independent of the meaning of the representations. While syntactical variants may be useful for certain purposes (e.g. to increase readability by humans), they will be ignored in this Chapter because the properties of representation schemes discussed in the Chapter are essentially independent of the schemes' syntax.

We conclude by defining two formal properties of representations and representation schemes: completeness and uniqueness. A representation r in V is unambiguous or complete if it corresponds to a single object, i.e. if the set $s^{-1}(r)$ is a single-element subset {m} of M. It is unique if its corresponding objects do not admit representations other than r in the scheme, i.e. if $s(s^{-1}(r))=\{r\}$.

A representation scheme s : M --> R is complete or unambiguous if all its valid representations are unambiguous, i.e. if the inverse relation s is a function. A scheme is unique if all its valid representations are unique, i.e. if s is a function. Note that completeness does not imply nor is implied by uniqueness. An unambiguous and unique representation scheme establishes a one-to-one correspondence between its domain and its range. (In the mathematical literature the term "representation" is used mainly to denote such one-to-one mappings, and representations are not restricted to finite-length symbol structures.)

We shall discuss the importance of these notions in Section 1.2.4 below, but first we shall introduce a useful methodology for defining representation spaces and schemes, and present examples to illustrate what these almost trivial but abstract definitions mean in concrete terms.

1.2.2 A Methodology for Defining Specific
       Representation Schemes

We introduce the required notions informally, mainly by means of an example, because they are quite simple and may be familiar to many readers.

Consider a family of solid squares in E2 having the following properties. Each square has sides of unit length, each side is parallel to either the X or the Y axis, and each vertex has integer coordinates. Figure 1.4 shows several members of the family. Each member may be characterized by the coordinates of (say) its left lower corner, and therefore the family depends on two parameters. (Parametric families of entities often are called "entity schemata" or generic entities.)

A member of a family of entities is called an entity instance. The process of instancing (or instantiating), i.e. of selecting a

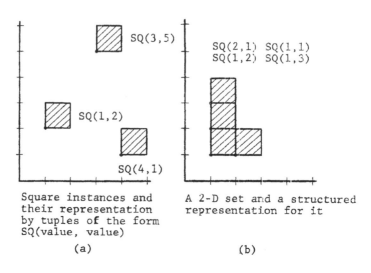

Square instances and
their representation
by tuples of the form
SQ(value, value)

(a)

A 2-D set and a structured
representation for it

(b)

Fig. 1.4   A Simple Scheme for Representing a
Particular Class of 2-D Sets

specific member of the family, corresponds to assigning specific
values to the family's parameters. The square instances in Fig. 1.4a
may be represented by the strings SQ(1,2),... shown in the figure.
Such strings are called instances of a generic tuple SQ(x,y), where x
and y are (integer) variables. Observe that a tuple instance in our
example (and in common practice) contains a "family name" or "type
code" which designates a specific family, and a set of parameter
values which designates a specific member of the family.

We may devise a scheme for representing more complex 2-D sets by
constructing structured representations which contain tuple instances,
each of which represents a square instance. For example, we may
define structured representations to be ordered sets of tuple
instances. Fig. 1.4b shows an L-shaped 2-D set and its corresponding
representation in such a scheme.

The example illustrates the basic technique we shall use for
defining specific representation schemes:

1) Define families of entities -- called generic primitives -- whose
   elements are called primitive instances. (When no confusion is
   likely to arise we shall use "primitive" to refer both to generic

primitives and their instances; "tuple" will be used similarly.) A representation scheme must possess a <u>finite</u> number of generic primitives.

2) Associate with each primitive for representational purposes a <u>generic</u> <u>tuple</u>, and with each primitive instance a <u>tuple</u> <u>instance</u> (q0,q1,...qN), where q0 is an integer or character string usually called a <u>type</u> <u>code</u>, and q1,...,qN are numeric parameter values, which often are real numbers. (We shall ignore the difficulties associated with representing real numbers, and use as a model of computation a real random access machine whose registers can store real numbers [63].) The type codes for distinct generic primitives in a representation scheme must be distinct. The "length" N+1 of a tuple is fixed for each generic tuple, but may vary among generic tuples.

3) Define <u>structuring</u> <u>rules</u> for constructing <u>structured</u> <u>representations</u> from tuple instances. Structured representations generally have "variable length", i.e. they may contain an arbitrary but finite number of tuple instances.

4) Define the semantics of structured representations by exhibiting a mathematical rule that associates geometric entities to such representations (or conversely).

We note in passing that one may define representation schemes in which single tuple instances are the only admissible representations. Such schemes -- called "pure primitive instancing schemes" or "trivially structured schemes" -- are discussed further in Section 1.3.3 below.

Observe that the relation t : T --> T', where T is a generic primitive (a family of geometric entities), and T' is the corresponding set of tuple instances, is a representation scheme in its own right and therefore the definitions of Section 1.2.1 apply. In particular, it follows that tuple instances that correspond to certain values of the parameters q1, ..., qN may be invalid. In practice, the validity of tuple instances may be verified easily because the primitives usually are simple geometric entities.

Generic tuples provide convenient means for representing

parameterized families of geometric entities, regardless of whether such entities are primitives in a scheme. Therefore it is useful to consider <u>generic</u> <u>structured</u> <u>entities</u> (variously called macro-, procedure- or parametric-entities, or entity schemata) representable by tuples whose semantics are defined by structures with non-instantiated parameters.

1.2.3 <u>Examples</u>

Suppose we wish to represent simple planar polygons. Let M be the space of all simple polygons in E2, where by a simple polygon we mean precisely a subset of E2 that is homeomorphic (topologically equivalent) to a disc and whose boundary is the union of a finite number of bounded line segments. (Intuitively, a homeomorphism is an "elastic deformation".) The polygon's vertices are the boundary's "corners", i.e. the points where the tangent to the boundary is not single-valued. This definition of simple polygon coincides with the usual notion of a polygon with no holes and no self-intersecting sides. Simple polygons are "2-D solids" containing all of the points "inside" and "on" the polygonal boundary.

The acknowledgement of a modelling space M enables us to define general properties of polygons. For example we may define convexity: a polygon is convex if it contains every line segment whose endpoints belong to the polygon. We may also define the diameter ("maximal dimension") of the polygon as the maximal distance between any two points of the polygon. Note that these are "representation-free" (representation-independent) properties of polygons because they do not depend on the particular means chosen to designate specific polygons.

A representation scheme for polygons -- which we shall call Scheme I for later reference -- may be defined as follows. Let the domain D be M, and let the syntactically correct representations in R be <u>ordered</u> sets of points in E2, each represented by a 2-tuple of Cartesian coordinates.

Let us first rephrase the definition of the scheme's syntax to illustrate the notions introduced in Section 1.2.2 above. Consider a single generic primitive which is the family of E2 points, and a single generic tuple (q1,q2), where q1 and q2 are real variables. (Because there is but one primitive, the type code q0 is unnecessary and will be omitted.) Primitive instances are individual points of E2, and therefore the space T of primitive instances coincides with E2. The space T' of tuple instances is the space of all pairs of real numbers. The relation t : T --> T' is simply the one-to-one and onto function which assigns to each point of E2 its coordinates in a fixed Cartesian coordinate system. It is clear that all of the tuple instances are valid with respect to t since a pair (x,y), where x and y are arbitrary real numbers, always corresponds to some point of E2. The structuring rule amounts simply to constructing ordered sets of tuple instances.

To complete the definition of Scheme I we must specify the meaning of structured representations. We define the relation s : M --> R by the rule: construct an ordered set of points by listing in arbitrary order the vertices of the polygon, ensuring that each vertex appears once and only once in the list. Figure 1.5 shows a polygon and three representations constructed according to the above rule.

POLYGON

Vertex Lists
(1) P1 P2 P3 P4 P5
(2) P2 P3 P4 P5 P1
(3) P2 P5 P1 P3 P4

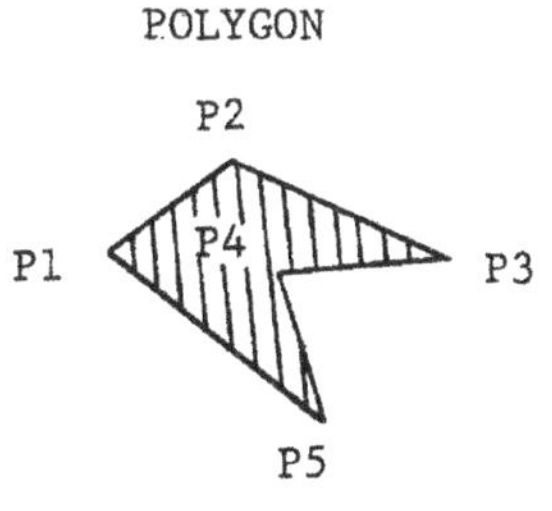

Fig. 1.5 A Polygon and Three Admissible
Vertex Lists

Clearly, s is mathematically well defined. The range V is defined implicitly since both D and the association rule are known. It is easy to see that V is a proper subset of R, i.e. there are syntactically correct representations that are not (semantically) valid. For example, a list of collinear points cannot represent a polygon. But is any finite set of isolated non-collinear points in E2 the vertex set of a simple polygon? A "constructive" answer to this question -- which we leave as a non-trivial exercise for the reader -- implies a test for determining the validity of our representations.

Figure 1.5 shows that the representations are not unique, since a single polygon has several representations which correspond to different vertex permutations.

Figure 1.6 shows that the representation scheme also is not complete: the polygons in Fig. 1.6a and 1.6b are different and yet they have the same vertices (and hence the same representations).

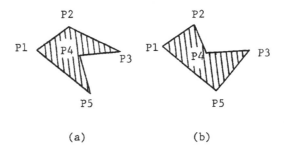

Fig. 1.6   Two Polygons that Admit Under Scheme I
the Representation P1 P2 P3 P4 P5

We conclude that Scheme I is neither complete nor unique. We shall discuss two exemplary modifications that achieve completeness.

Scheme II: We restrict the domain to the class of convex polygons, and keep our initial association rule. The modified representation scheme is complete because (1) the represented polygon is the convex hull of its vertices and (2) a set of points has a unique convex hull. Note, however, that we have decreased the "coverage" (the domain) of our representation scheme.

Scheme III: We revert to the domain of Scheme I but add information to the representations. Suppose specifically that we modify the association rule by requiring that vertices be listed in the order they are encountered when one traverses the polygon's boundary without backtracking. The modified scheme is complete because ordering the vertices is equivalent to defining the polygon's edges (and hence its boundary), and by Jordan's curve theorem [2] [32] the boundary defines a unique polygon.

The three schemes for representing planar polygons warrant a few final remarks.

1) All three have the same representational syntax. Schemes I and II differ only in their domain, while Schemes I and III differ only in their association rules. This should convince readers that representation schemes must be defined fully, i.e. both syntactically (the properties of elements of R) and semantically (the M, R pairings), if one is to assess their properties in a meaningful way.

2) We defined the schemes by defining their domains and association rules; we shall see later that it is often convenient to define representation schemes "backwards", i.e. to define the association rule and the range, rather than the domain.

3) One could represent polygons in many other ways. The formal properties developed below provide one basis for comparing alternative schemes, and the intended applications provide a second, complementary basis -- as we shall show in Section 1.3.

1.2.4 Formal Properties of Representation Schemes

This section discusses the practical implications of some important formal properties of representation schemes that follow from the earlier definitions.

1.2.4.1 Domain

The domain of a representation scheme characterizes the descriptive power of the scheme, i.e. the set of entities representable in the scheme.

1.2.4.2 Validity

The range of a representation scheme is the set of representations which are valid. Representational validity is of obvious importance in ensuring the (syntactic as well as semantic) integrity of data bases, in that data bases should not contain symbol structures which correspond to "nonsense objects". (M. C. Escher's well-known prints provide examples of graphical representations of nonsense 3-D objects.) Evoking algorithms for computing object properties on invalid object representations usually has unpleasant effects which may range from system crashes to seemingly reasonable but meaningless results.

In the past, the responsibility for ensuring the validity of representations in a GMS has rested with humans. Typically, a human creates an object representation and then checks visually that the object "makes sense" by examining graphic displays. This is an error-prone procedure. More importantly, if representations of solids are created by automata (programs) rather than by humans as a step in the algorithmic solution of a problem, visual checking is usually impossible. Programs that create such representations for "internal purposes" already exist, as the following examples show.

1) The PADL-1.0/2 system generates section views of objects by creating a "new" sectioned solid and displaying it. Interference between parts in an assembly is handled similarly [70], [71].

2) A part-program verification system operating in the PADL-1 environment synthesizes solids from cutter path and cutter shape data [39].

Program-created object representations undoubtedly will proliferate in future systems. For example, systems for automatic manufacturing planning will need to deal with partially finished workpieces not specified by humans, and in due course humans will be able to specify the mechanical function of (non-aesthetic) objects to programs which will synthesize automatically the objects' geometry.

These considerations lead us to believe that future GMS's cannot rely on human validation, and must ensure representational validity by automatic (algorithmic) means. Validity may be ensured automatically either by testing syntactically correct representations after they are constructed, or by embedding validity constraints in the procedures which create object representations. The cleanest way of ensuring validity is to design representation schemes such that all syntactically correct representations are valid (see Section 1.3.6 for an example).

Validity is also important when families of objects -- "generic objects" or "object schemata" -- are defined via representations which contain uninstantiated symbolic parameters. (The primitives of Section 1.2.2 are an important special class.) Representations of object schemata are akin to procedures or macros in algorithmic languages, and appear to be very useful in GMS's.

The two general approaches for ensuring validity cited earlier also apply to generic objects. Thus, validity may be tested after numeric values are bound to a schema's parameters, or (preferably) validity constraints may be built into the facilities for defining object schemata.

We shall illustrate the issues by means of our Scheme II for representing convex polygons via arbitrarily ordered vertex lists. Suppose that we want to deal with a family of 4-sided convex polygons having three fixed vertices and a variable vertex, as shown in Fig. 1.7. (This is a contrived example. Natural examples may be found in mechanical engineering, e.g. counterbored and countersunk holes, keyways, and standard fasteners, all of which may be defined generically in terms of symbolic parameters.) We may represent the family by a generic tuple $Q(a,b)$ which is defined by ("macro-expands" into) the vertex list

$$(0,0) \quad (0,1) \quad (1,0) \quad (a,b).$$

Figures 1.7a and 1.7b show the polygons which correspond to $Q(2,2)$ and $Q(0.5,-0.5)$; Fig. 1.7c shows that $Q(0.5,0.2)$ is not a valid representation of a convex polygon in the scheme because the point (a,b) is not a vertex of the convex hull of the four points. We conclude that validity constraints are not built automatically into our definition of $Q(a,b)$, and that to ensure it one must find the appropriate constraints on the parameters (this may be difficult in less trivial examples) and embody them in conditionals within the schemata definitional facility.

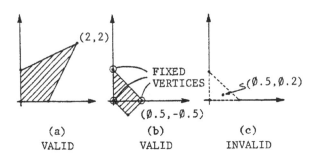

Fig. 1.7 Instances of Polygons in a Convex Polygon
Schema that Admits One Variable Vertex

1.2.4.3 Completeness

Completeness (as defined in Section 1.2.1) is probably the most important characteristic of representation schemes because it captures precisely the intuitive notion of "informational completeness". Specifically, each representation in a complete scheme corresponds to exactly one entity in the mathematical modelling space M, and hence contains enough information to distinguish that entity from all other entities in the domain D of the scheme. Representations in incomplete schemes generally correspond to several modelling-space entities, i.e. do not contain enough information to distinguish single elements in D.

The importance of completeness is best understood in the context of applications, where one must compute properties of represented entities. An example will illustrate the issues. Suppose that one wishes to compute (1) the diameters and (2) the areas of possibly concave polygons in the domain D = M of Schemes I and III. Earlier arguments show that polygons' diameters can be computed correctly from representations in the incomplete Scheme I, whereas polygons' areas cannot (see Fig. 1.6). On the other hand, representations in the complete Scheme III suffice for both calculations -- and indeed for the calculation of any mathematically defined property of any polygon representable in Scheme III -- because each representation designates exactly one polygon-entity in M. (We ignore here properties defined by functions that are not computable at all.)

It should be evident that incomplete representations can be adequate sources of data for specific applications, but that completeness should be sought when there is a wide range of applications to be supported by a practical modelling system, and especially when the range of applications is not known in advance.

1.2.4.4 Uniqueness

The importance of representational uniqueness derives mainly from the role of uniqueness in assessing the equality of two objects. Equality assessment is important in a number of applications. An example: repeated representations may be culled from a data base only if one can determine that two representations (in the same scheme) correspond to the same object. A second example: automatic planning algorithms which search a space of alternatives must be able to recognize previously encountered situations ... or else the search may loop indefinitely.

Representation schemes which are both unambiguous and unique are highly desirable because they are one-to-one mappings. This implies that distinct representations in such schemes correspond to distinct objects, and therefore object equality may be determined by algorithms which compare object representations "syntactically". Equality assessment in schemes which are unambiguous but not unique requires more elaborate techniques.

Unambiguous but non-unique representations of r-sets may be tested for equality as follows. Given two r-sets A and B, construct the regularized symmetric difference $S = (A -^* B) \cup (B -^* A)$, and determine if S is the null set. (The operator $-^*$ above denotes regularized set difference [59], [58].) It is easy to see that $S = 0$ if and only if A = B. This method of determining equality requires a capability for deciding whether a regularized set composition is null.

An example will illustrate two types of non-uniqueness which are quite common in schemes for representing geometric entities. We shall modify our earlier polygon schemes as follows.

Scheme IV: The elements of the domain D are equivalence classes of congruent convex polygons rather than single polygons. A representation of a congruence class is an arbitrarily ordered list of the vertices of an arbitrary member of the class, with each vertex represented by its cartesian coordinates as in Section 1.2.3. The modification implies that we view all polygons of the same "shape" (i.e. congruent polygons) as the same single object regardless of the polygons' positions in the cartesian coordinate system. The representation scheme is not unique for two reasons.

1) Vertices in a list may be permuted.

2) Vertices may correspond to different members of a congruence class which differ only by the member-polygons' positions (see Fig. 1.8).

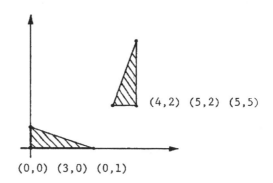

(4,2) (5,2) (5,5)

(0,0) (3,0) (0,1)

Fig. 1.8 Positional Non-Uniqueness of Congruent
Polygons Represented by Vertex Lists

"Permutational" non-uniqueness (case 1 above) is relatively trivial; nevertheless, determining whether two lists contain the same elements may be computationally expensive when the lists are large.

"Positional" non-uniqueness is more pernicious because generally it is not easy to design algorithms for deciding whether two geometric entities are congruent.

1.2.5 Informal Properties of Representation Schemes

This section discusses several properties of representation schemes which are practically important but which cannot be formalized readily in a useful way.

1.2.5.1 Conciseness

Conciseness refers to the "size" of representations in a scheme. Concise representations are convenient to store and to transmit over data links whereas "verbose" representations are not. Concise representations contain relatively few "redundant" data. The validity of such representations is usually easy to ensure because non-redundancy implies that the entities which constitute the representation are largely independent, and therefore need satisfy few constraining relations.

It is important to realize, however, that selectively imposed redundancy may have practical advantages. Specifically, it may be used to detect and correct "syntactic" errors in representations, and to improve (often dramatically) computational efficiency by storing, rather than computing, often-needed data derivable from a concise representation.

The notions of conciseness and redundancy have a strong information-theoretic flavor, and probably can be formulated precisely in terms of information theory. However, it is not clear that such a formalization is practically useful.

1.2.5.2 Ease of Creation

The ease with which (valid) representations may be created by users of modelling systems is of obvious importance, especially if the users are human. Concise representations generally are easier to create than verbose ones, because conciseness implies that fewer data need be specified and that the individual data items are largely independent.

Modelling systems based on verbose representations usually must contain powerful input sub-systems to help users with the creation of representations. Such modelling systems also should possess automatic validity-ensuring mechanisms to relieve users of the burden of ensuring "manually" the validity of representations.

1.2.5.3 Efficacy in the Context of Applications

Representations of objects (e.g. solids) should be viewed for practical purposes as sources of data for algorithms. Algorithms are computational embodiments of mathematical functions which associate values (e.g. diameter, volume,...) with objects. An unambiguous representation is guaranteed to be a sufficient source of data, but may not support some specific application efficaciously because it may not be a "convenient" or "efficient" source of data for any algorithm that computes the value of some specific function.

For each mathematical function it is often possible to design several representation schemes for elements of the function's domain and range, and several algorithms which "evaluate" the function, i.e. which map representations of elements in the function's domain into representations of corresponding elements in the function's range (see Fig. 1.9). The design of representation schemes that permit the use of "good" algorithms for evaluating practically useful functions is a central issue in the design of modelling systems. Good algorithms should be correct, efficient, and should also exhibit subtler but important characteristics such as robustness in the presence of numerical errors, and extensibility.

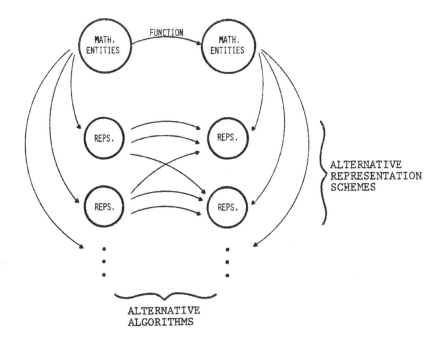

Fig. 1.9 Alternative Representations and
Algorithms for Evaluating a Single Function

The correctness of an algorithm can be assessed only if precise algorithm specifications are available. In the realm of geometry an algorithm specification consists of the definition of a mathematical function (including its domain and range) to be "evaluated" by the algorithm, together with definitions of the representation schemes for the domain and range. The proper specification of geometric algorithms has not received the attention it deserves. For example, published algorithms for computing set-theoretical intersections of "polygons" or "polyhedra" do not agree with the algorithms' specifications (see [67] for further discussion).

The classical methods for analyzing and comparing algorithms (see e.g. [3] and recent work on geometric algorithms, e.g. [63] and [43]) ignore the issues of robustness and extensibility, and apply mainly to algorithms which operate on a fixed pair of input (domain) and output (range) representation spaces. The larger problem of comparing alternative "function-evaluation triples" consisting of algorithms and input and output representation schemes (see Fig. 1.9) is not well understood.

In summary, little is known in an abstract sense about representational efficacy. We lack not only formal means for characterizing the class of functions which may be evaluated efficiently by algorithms operating on representations in a particular scheme, but also insight into the interplay between representations and algorithms.

The experience accumulated to date in geometric modelling indicates that no single object representation is uniformly "best" when many applications must be accommodated, and that (as cited earlier) redundant data often play a pivotal role in achieving efficiency. We conclude that "general purpose" GMS's are likely to contain multiple representations of objects, in different schemes, with each representation tailored to a specific class of applications [20].

1.2.6 Multiple Representations: Consistency,
      Equivalence, and Conversion

The presence of multiple representations (in different schemes) to support a diversity of applications introduces a strong form of redundancy in a modelling system and raises the issue of consistency (defined formally below). In essence, one must ensure that the various symbol structures which allegedly represent the same object (or objects) in different schemes do not carry contradictory information. Mechanisms for ensuring consistency usually involve the ability to convert the representation of an object in one scheme into its representation in another scheme. The design of algorithms for representation conversion is a topic of current research in geometric modelling (see e.g. [72]).

Consistency may be defined formally as follows. Let s and s' in Fig. 1.10 be representation schemes for entities in a mathematical

modelling space M. We shall say that a representation r in R and a
representation r' in R' are <u>consistent</u> if there exists an element m of
M such that r belongs to the set s(m) and r' belongs to s'(m).
Therefore consistency requires the existence of (at least) one object
m having representations r and r' in the two schemes. The dashed
lines in Fig. 1.10 indicate that m may have several representations in
R and R' (when the schemes are not unique), and that other elements of
M may correspond to r and r' (when the schemes are not complete).

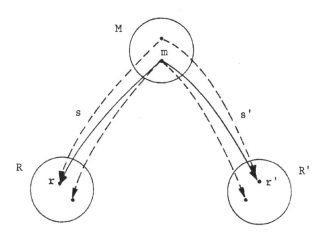

Fig. 1.10   Representational Consistency

Consistency generally is not an equivalence relation between
valid representations in schemes s and s' because, while reflexive (a
valid representation is consistent with itself) and symmetric (if r is
consistent with r' then r' is consistent with r), it is generally not
transitive (i.e., r consistent with r' and r' consistent with r" need
not imply r consistent with r").

We define representational equivalence as follows. Two
representations r and r' in schemes s and s' are <u>equivalent</u> if the
sets $s^{-1}(r)$ and $s'^{-1}(r')$ are equal. Observe that consistency
requires only that $s^{-1}(r)$ and $s'^{-1}(r')$ have a non-empty
intersection, and therefore equivalence is a strong form of
consistency. It is easy to see that representational equivalence is
an equivalence relation, and that two <u>unambiguous</u> representations are

equivalent if and only if they are consistent.

The definition of representational equivalence may be extended as follows to cater for entire representation schemes. Two representation schemes s and s' are equivalent if each representation r of s possesses an equivalent r' of s', and conversely. It follows from the definition that equivalent representation schemes have the same domain, and that two unambiguous representation schemes are equivalent if and only if they have the same domain.

Consistency, not equivalence, is the practically important concept when dealing with ambiguous representations. In geometric modelling, for example, it is important to require that the top and front views of an object be consistent (both are ambiguous graphic representations of solids). It would be unreasonable to require that all solids exhibiting a common top view also exhibit a common front view -- that is, that the top and front views be equivalent.

Representation conversion algorithms provide the basic means for enforcing representational consistency. A conversion algorithm is a specification of a sequence of operations for computing a symbol mapping a : Ra --> Ra'. The domain Ra and range Ra' of 'a' are subsets of two representation spaces R and R' which correspond to representation schemes s and s' for entities in a modelling space M. We shall distinguish between consistent (theoretically exact) and approximate conversions. Loosely, a consistent conversion produces a representation of the original entity while an approximate conversion produces a representation of an entity which approximates the original one. Consistent conversions between unambiguous representations are lossless (theoretically invertible). Formal definitions follow; the conditions in the definitions apply for all valid representations r within Ra.

A conversion is consistent (or theoretically exact) when a(r) is consistent with r. A conversion is approximate when it is not theoretically exact but satisfies the following condition: there exist two elements m and m' of M such that r $\in$ s(m), a(r) $\in$ s'(m'), and m' approximates m. (An entity m' approximates another entity m when their distance d(m,m') in an appropriate metric is less than a positive number δ .) For example, a representation of any polygon in Scheme III may be converted into a representation of a "cellular" approximation to the polygon in the scheme illustrated in Fig. 1.4.

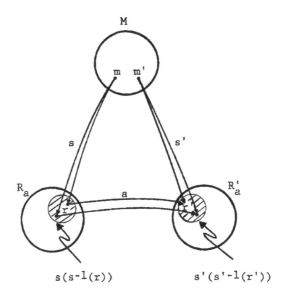

Fig. 1.11 Lossless Conversion Between Complete
but Non-Unique Representations

A conversion is <u>lossless</u> (or <u>theoretically invertible</u>) when the
set $s(s^{-1}(r))$ is the inverse image under 'a' of $s'(s'^{-1}(r'))$, where
$r'=a(r)$. Figure 1.11 illustrates the definition when s and s' are
unambiguous but non-unique representation schemes (this is the
practically interesting case). Observe that $s(s^{-1}(r))$ is the set of
all representations of a single m in scheme s. The definition implies
that 'a' maps all of the representations of m in Ra into
representations of m' in Ra', and that representations of objects
other than m are not mapped into representations of m'. Essentially
'a' establishes a one-to-one, and hence invertible, correspondence
between m and m'. Therefore "no information is lost", i.e. m is
"recoverable" from (representations of) m'. Note that m' need not
equal m; for example, m' may be the result of applying to m a known
deformation to make m' easily representable in s'. This implies that
a lossless conversion need not be a consistent conversion. On the
other hand, a consistent conversion between equivalent unambiguous
schemes is always lossless. It should be clear also that a conversion
from an unambiguous representation to an ambiguous one cannot be

lossless because $s'(s'^{-1}(r'))$ is "too large".

The interplay between representational consistency and representation conversion arises in practical systems in two slightly different guises.

1) When given a representation, it may be necessary to construct another consistent representation in a different scheme (e.g. to enable some property of a represented object to be computed efficiently).

2) When given several consistent representations, it may be necessary to update (consistently) all when one is edited.

Experience in the practical solution of these problems is limited because most existing modelling systems are strongly biased towards particular applications, and therefore do not contain multiple representations. The PADL-1 system, which possesses representations for solids in three unambiguous schemes and one ambiguous scheme, approaches the problem of consistency maintenance as follows [71].

1) A complete representation (in one scheme) for each object is considered fundamental.

2) All other representations are derived from the fundamental representation by conversion algorithms.

3) Only the fundamental representation may be edited; algorithms propagate changes to the other representations.

This approach is safe but relatively inflexible. Some of the difficulties that arise when one attempts to provide more flexible means for maintaining consistent multiple representations are listed below.

1) It is usually impossible to update consistently an unambiguous representation to correspond to modifications made to an ambiguous representation. Direct editing of ambiguous representations therefore should be prohibited.

2) Conversion between representations in two unambiguous schemes is

always possible theoretically <u>provided</u> that the schemes are equivalent. When the two schemes have different domains it is possible that editing a representation in one scheme will create an object not representable in the other. Note that the theoretical possibility of conversion does not imply that algorithms to effect such conversions are known. In practice one may be able to convert representations from a scheme s into a scheme s' but not vice-versa. (Later sections provide examples.)

1.2.7 Representation Hierarchies

It is useful to consider representations at various levels of abstraction. Figure 1.12 illustrates the notion; observe that the single representation space of Fig. 1.2 has been replaced by a hierarchy of representation spaces linked through mathematical relations (usually mappings) which we call representation <u>sub-schemes</u>. Formal properties of representation sub-schemes analogous to those of representation schemes may be defined easily.

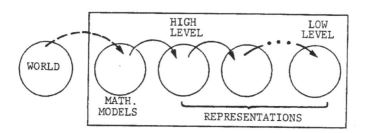

Fig. 1.12 A Representational Hierarchy

The lower-level representations in Fig. 1.12 may be viewed as "implementations" or as "refinements" of their higher-level counterparts, and thus Fig. 1.12 merely formalizes the widely accepted notion that various levels of abstraction are useful at different stages in the design and implementation of systems.

An exemplary hierarchy for representing polygons via Scheme II may be constructed as follows. Let representations at the highest level be ordered sets of real numbers; for example

$$(0.0, 0.0) \quad (0.0, 1.0) \quad (1.0, 0.0)$$

represents a triangle. At the second level let the ordered sets be represented by arrays containing the x and y coordinates of the vertices. (Alternatively, one could use a linked list of records, each having two fields for the point coordinates and a link field.) Finally, at the third level the arrays (or linked lists) are represented by bit patterns in certain memory locations.

The discussion in the remainder of this Chapter is couched in terms of high-level representations. The computational implementation of such representations is largely a straightforward programming exercise.

1.3 SURVEY OF REPRESENTATION SCHEMES FOR RIGID SOLIDS

The following sections discuss the known methods for representing classes of r-sets that model physical solids. First we study the various methods by discussing the properties of "pure" schemes, each based on a single method, and then we focus on hybrid schemes which combine several methods, and on the conversion between schemes.

1.3.1 Preview

Ambiguous schemes for representing solids are discussed briefly in Section 1.3.2, but the bulk of Section 1.3 is devoted to the study of unambiguous schemes. We distinguish seven basic methods that may be used to construct unambiguous representation schemes for solids.

1) Pure primitive instancing.

2) Spatial occupancy enumeration.

3) Cell decomposition.

4) Constructive solid geometry (CSG).

5) Sweeping.

6) Interpolation.

7) Boundary representation.

Pure template instancing is based on the principles discussed in Section 1.2.2. All of the other methods above lead to structured schemes whereby solids are represented by aggregates of representations of primitive entities. The following is a brief description of each of the methods 2-7 and of their theoretical foundations.

Spatial occupancy enumeration. Space is divided into a grid of 3-D cells (usually cubes), and a solid is represented by a list of the cells which it occupies, i.e., of the cells which contain "material".

Cell decomposition. A solid is decomposed into simple solid cells with no holes and whose interiors are pairwise disjoint. A solid is the result of "glueing" component cells that satisfy certain "boundary-matching" conditions discussed in Section 1.3.5. Cell decomposition may be viewed as a generalization of spatial occupancy enumeration in that cells need neither lie on a fixed grid nor have pre-specified size and shape. Cell decomposition methods are based on the theory of triangulation and its extensions discussed in [58] and elementary textbooks in combinatorial (algebraic) topology (e.g. [2] and [32]).

CSG. Solids are defined as combinations of solid "building blocks" via operations akin to volumetric addition and subtraction. CSG may be viewed as a generalization of cell decomposition; the "glueing operator" of cell decomposition methods is replaced by the more powerful CSG operators which need not satisfy "boundary-matching" conditions, may be applied to solids whose interiors are not disjoint, and may add as well as remove volume. CSG is based on the mathematics of regular sets and regularized set operators [59], [60], [58].

Sweeping. A solid or a bounded surface moving along a trajectory sweep a "volume". Therefore a solid may be represented by a pair (moving body, trajectory). Sweeping is unrelated to the methods 2-4 above; it may be studied formally by using the mathematical notion of set product or through set operations on an infinite number of sets.

Interpolation. A solid may be defined (for example) as the union of all the line segments PQ whose endpoints P and Q lie, respectively, in two given 2-D sets A and B. Therefore the solid may be represented by the pair (A,B). Interpolation rules other than the "lofting" rule just described are possible. Interpolation schemes for solids will not be discussed further because they have neither been studied theoretically nor used practically in a geometric modelling context.

Boundary representation. While all of the methods above represent solids directly, boundary representations are indirect, in that they represent explicitly (directly) the solid's topological boundary rather than the solid itself. The theoretical basis for boundary representation lies on certain separation theorems which generalize the E2 Jordan's curve theorem to more general spaces [58].

Observe that 2-6 above essentially are standard mathematical methods for building sets from other sets. Such methods are not restricted to E3 solids; with trivial modification they may be applied also (e.g.) to surfaces and curves. Boundary representation replaces the problem of representing a set with that of representing another set of reduced dimensionality; the initial set may be a solid, as suggested above, but it may also be (e.g.) a surface or a curve. Therefore one can design schemes for representing solids which use a combination of the methods above. Such "hybrid" or "nonhomogeneous" schemes will be discussed in Section 1.3.9 below.

1.3.2 Ambiguous Representations

We shall discuss, following semi-historical lines, a few widely-used ambiguous representations.

The traditional means for specifying mechanical parts -- engineering drawings -- are best viewed as informal means of communication among humans. Humans make liberal use of "common sense" to interpret drawings; sometimes they make errors of interpretation, and occasionally they interpret "correctly" drawings which contain geometric errors (e.g. extraneous lines) without noticing that such errors exist.

We know of no formal definition of drafting as a representation scheme; usually drafting textbooks state that a "sufficient" number of views, section views, details, and "notes" should be supplied in a drawing to avoid "ambiguity". This "definition" is too informal for a precise study of drafting as a representation scheme; it also makes it virtually impossible to specify and design reliable algorithms for computing properties of solids represented by drawings. Nevertheless, drawings are an effective means of communication among humans and have been the major medium for geometric specification used by industry until recently. The first computer aided drafting systems, some of which are still in use, represented drawings (2-D entities) rather than 3-D solids. In such systems changes made to a view of an object are not propagated automatically to other views because the system does not "know" that the various views are projections of a single object.

One may move beyond drafting toward more formal schemes in one or both of the following directions.

1) The essential notion in drafting is the representation of solids by a collection of projections of solids on planes. If one wishes to retain this basic notion and seek drafting-like unambiguous representation schemes one must either

(a) define a domain D of solids, a rule s which associates solids in D to drawings (i.e. collections of projections), and prove that s^{-1} is a function, or

(b) define a range V of valid drawings, and exhibit a mapping s^{-1} between drawings and solids.

Both alternatives involve proving that a single solid corresponds to each drawing. Establishing such a correspondence is a difficult problem, closely related to scene analysis studies which attempt to infer 3-D shape information from 2-D projections. It is known, for example, that it is possible to construct unambiguously the set of edges of any rectilinear (i.e. plane-faced) polyhedron (see [58] for a precise definition of rectilinear polyhedron) given a sufficiently large set of its planar projections [64], but we do not know of any results which show that reasonably general classes of curved objects can be represented <u>unambiguously</u> by a finite set of projections.

2) Abandon the use of projections as representations, and seek suitable collections of 3-D entities. Drafting practice suggests the use of "edges" (whose projections are the lines and curves which constitute drawings). This leads to the so-called wireframe representations wherein a solid is represented by a collection of "edges". It can be shown by counter example (see [70]) that wireframes are ambiguous representations even for the domain of rectilinear polyhedra; an interesting algorithm for finding all the rectilinear polyhedra which have a given wireframe is reported in [46]. (Representations of rectilinear polyhedra by vertex lists also are ambiguous -- see [70].) The majority of the commercially available "3-D" geometry systems are based on (curved) wireframe representations, although some include a capability for defining certain types of "faces". Such systems cannot support reliably (for example) a fully automatic elimination of hidden lines or computation of section views.

If one goes further and associates "edges" with "faces" that cover completely an object's boundary, then one can get an unambiguous representation...as we shall see later. Thus ends a line of development which may be termed the graphics approach to solid representation.

Another line of development has led to a distinct type of ambiguous representations. The development was motivated by the following practical problem: given a <u>physical</u> solid, such as a human head or a clay model of an automobile body, construct a "reasonably accurate" computer representation of the solid. The usual approach to solving this problem consists in measuring the coordinates of a large number of points lying on the boundary of the object or in the object's interior, and using the finite set of measured points as a representation of the object. The measuring operation is a "3-D digitization" that may be performed in various ways; to obtain data points in the interior of an object may involve physically slicing the object or using X-ray or ultrasonic scanning techniques.

It is clear that such finite collections of points generally are

not complete representations of r-sets. In pratice one may construct
an unambiguous representation of an r-set such that the measured
points belong to the set, but distinct construction methods may lead
to distinct r-sets because of the ambiguity of the initial
representation. An interesting algorithm for constructing boundary
representations from finite sets of boundary points is described in
[27].

The remainder of Section 1.3 is devoted to a study of unambiguous
schemes for representing solids.

1.3.3 Pure Primitive Instancing Schemes

An independent approach to solid object representation has been
used in the manufacturing world, mainly in the context of so-called
Group Technology. It is based on the notion of families of objects,
each member of a family being distinguishable by a few parameters.
Such schemes are pure primitive instancing schemes (see 1.2.2) whose
primitive instances are r-sets (i.e. solids).

Figure 1.13 provides an example: a scheme possessing three
families of objects. The parameters of the family of toothed wheels
having type code 1 (Fig. 1.13a) are the wheel's diameter D and the
number N of equally spaced teeth. Family 2 (Fig. 1.13b) has an
additional parameter D'. Family 3 (Fig. 1.13c) has two parameters:
the overall pin's length L, and the pin's diameter Dp. All of the
other characteristics of the objects are not specified explicitly
because either (1) they are constant throughout the family (e.g. the
height and the diameter of the wheels' shafts), or (2) they depend on
the specified parameters (e.g. the diameter of the pin's head is
proportional to the pin's diameter Dp). Figure 1.13 also shows
equivalent but more readable representations in which the type codes
have been replaced by family string identifiers.

The distinguishing characteristic of pure primitive instancing
schemes is the impossibility of "combining" existing representations
to create new and more complex ones. Such schemes are akin to

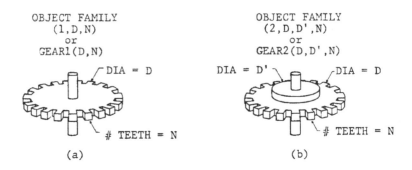

OBJECT FAMILY
(1,D,N)
or
GEAR1(D,N)

DIA = D

TEETH = N

(a)

OBJECT FAMILY
(2,D,D',N)
or
GEAR2(D,D',N)

DIA = D'   DIA = D

TEETH = N

(b)

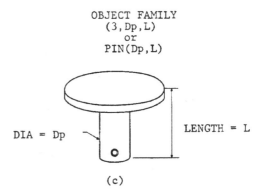

OBJECT FAMILY
(3,Dp,L)
or
PIN(Dp,L)

DIA = Dp   LENGTH = L

(c)

Fig. 1.13   A Pure Primitive Instancing Scheme

languages defined by grammars in which it is not possible to combine
words to form sentences. Pure primitive instancing schemes therefore
have relatively small domains, because large domains require an
inordinate number of families and/or parameters.

The validity of representations may be checked trivially when the
objects in a family are relatively simple. Thus, for example, any
representation in the scheme illustrated in Fig. 1.13 is valid
provided that the parameters are positive. (Note, however, that one
might want to restrict the domain by requiring e.g. that D' < D in
Fig. 1.13b; this would add another condition to be satisfied for
validity.)

Pure primitive instancing schemes may be defined so as to be both complete and unique. The scheme of Fig. 1.13, however, is not unique because GEAR1(D,N) = GEAR2(D,D',N) when D' is the value of the diameter of the shaft.

In principle, pure primitive instancing schemes are concise and easy to use, and they promote standardization of components. In practice, however, such advantages obtain only for domains small enough to be covered by a small catalog of families each having a small number of parameters. When the catalog is large the schemes become unwieldy for both humans and machines.

The other main drawback of pure primitive instancing schemes is the difficulty of writing algorithms for "processing" representations, i.e. for computing properties of the solids represented. A considerable amount of knowledge specific to object families must be built into such algorithms, and this leads to algorithms which treat each object family as a special case. Algorithms for processing "structured" representations can seek to exploit structural knowledge in order to process structured representations "uniformly", rather than on a case by case basis.

We suspect that the pure primitive instancing schemes now used in industry will be replaced by the more powerful structured schemes discussed below, because these latter provide the same "part family" capabilities through "generic" or "macro" structured object representations (see Sections 1.2.2 and 1.2.4.2).

1.3.4 Spatial Occupancy Enumeration

A representation of a solid in a spatial occupancy enumeration scheme is essentially a list of spatial cells occupied by the solid. The cells, sometimes called voxels (an abbreviation of "volume elements"), are cubes of a fixed size which lie on a fixed spatial grid. Each cell may be represented by the coordinates of a single point, e.g. the cell's centroid. (For simplicity we shall discuss only the cubical grid, although others can be used, because the type of grid does not affect the basic properties of the schemes.)

A representation in a spatial occupancy enumeration scheme is simply a (possibly unordered) set of three-tuples. A specific spatial scanning order is convenient for a variety of practical reasons, and therefore spatial enumerations usually are ordered sets, called spatial arrays. The semantics of such representations is the obvious one: a cell corresponds to each three-tuple, and the solid represented is the union of all such cells. The representation scheme is defined fully since we defined its range and its association rule.

The domain D is a subset of the space of rectilinear polyhedra. A representation is valid provided that the three-tuples correspond to centroids of cells, and therefore validity may be established trivially.

It is clear from the definitions that the representation schemes are unambiguous. They also are unique except for permutational and positional non-uniqueness (see Section 1.2.4.4). Spatial arrays do not exhibit permutational non-uniqueness because of the implied spatial scanning rule.

Spatial arrays are potentially quite verbose, but verbosity depends largely on how well the class of physical objects of interest matches the domain of polyhedra representable by spatial occupancy enumeration. Thus, in certain architectural applications buildings are sufficiently "modular" for one to use relatively short spatial array representations based on a coarse spatial grid [45]. Spatial arrays also appear to be a reasonable representation for r-sets which provide approximate models for "irregular" biological objects such as those encountered in computed tomography; the representations may be created directly by measuring equipment operating on the physical objects. (Spatial occupancy enumeration is one of the methods for constructing an unambiguous representation from a finite-set-of-points ambiguous representation -- see Section 1.3.2.) For such objects as mechanical parts, spatial occupancy enumeration is too verbose for practical use as a "master" definitional medium. (Ponder, for example, the problem of representing an r-set that approximates, to within 0.001", a cylindrical pin with a diameter of 0.5" and a length of 2".) However, spatial-array representations of objects which are coarse approximations of mechanical parts can be used effectively, e.g. to improve the average performance of geometric algorithms.

Spatial occupancy enumeration shares certain interesting properties with other schemes that are based on the decomposition of solids into cells with non-intersecting interiors. These properties will be discussed at the end of Section 1.3.5 in the context of cell decomposition schemes.

Schemes have been proposed which are hybrid combinations of a restricted form of CSG and spatial occupancy enumeration [56]. Such schemes are similar to the "quad-tree" representations (see e.g. [23]) used in image processing. They avoid some of the verbosity of pure spatial occupancy enumeration and have other practical advantages as well.

1.3.5 Cell Decompositions

A solid triangulation of a rectilinear polyhedron is a decomposition of the polyhedron into tetrahedra which are bounded by triangles, which in turn are bounded by edges whose endpoints are the vertices of the triangulation. (Triangulations are discussed in precise mathematical terms in [58], and in topology texts such as [2] and [32].) The decomposition must satisfy the following condition: any two tetrahedra in the triangulation must either be disjoint or must meet precisely at a common triangle, edge or vertex. The condition implies that tetrahedra must not interpenetrate, and that they be "glued" only at common triangles, edges, or vertices. Curved polyhedra also may be triangulated by decomposing them into "curved tetrahedra" which satisfy a condition analogous to that above.

Cell decompositions are a generalization of triangulations wherein cells may have an arbitrary number of "faces". The definitions are similar, but tetrahedra and triangles are replaced by 3-cells and 2-cells, respectively. A 3-cell is a set topologically equivalent to a convex rectilinear 3-D polyhedron (e.g. an octahedron); 3-cells are bounded by an arbitrary but finite number of 2-cells. A 2-cell is a set topologically equivalent to a simple polygon (as defined in Section 1.2.3); 2-cells are bounded by an arbitrary but finite number of edges. Note that cells may not have "holes"; thus, for example, a solid torus is not a 3-cell. Cell decompositions are more convenient than triangulations for practical purposes because the number of cells in a cell decomposition usually is much smaller than the number of tetrahedra in a triangulation of a solid.

A solid may be represented by decomposing it into cells and by representing each cell in the decomposition. Clearly, spatial occupancy enumeration schemes are a particular case of cell decomposition schemes in which all of the cells must be cubical and lie on a fixed grid.

Cell decomposition schemes are potentially capable of representing any domain of r-sets because all r-sets are triangulable [58] [36]. The domain represented by a specific cell decomposition scheme is determined by the types of cells allowed by the scheme.

The validity of cell-decomposition representations of solids is difficult to establish. The problem is essentially the 3-D analog of the validity problem for cell decompositions of boundaries which will be discussed in Section 1.3.8.2 below.

Cell decompositions (and hence triangulations) are obviously unambiguous representations of r-sets, but they are not unique because each r-set admits many distinct cell decompositions.

Cell decomposition representations generally are neither concise nor easy to create. Valid cell decompositions of curved solids are hard to construct directly by humans, and algorithms for constructing such representations from others are a topic of current research [5].

Cell-decomposition representations provide convenient means for computing certain topological properties of objects. For example, there are known algorithms for determining whether a solid is "one-piece" (i.e. connected), whether it has "voids", "holes", and so forth [58].

Cell decompositions, spatial arrays (Section 1.3.4), and certain restricted forms of CSG (Section 1.3.6) are based on decomposing a solid into components whose interiors are pairwise disjoint. Because objects are defined as unions of cells, an object is null if and only if all cells correspond to empty sets. (As noted in 1.2.4.4 tests for object nullity are helpful for establishing object equality.) Cell disjointness facilitates the computation of a solid's volume, moments of inertia, and other properties which involve volume integrals over the solid [44]. (Because the cells have disjoint interiors the contribution of each cell may be computed separately.) Finally, disjointness plays a key role in the modelling of non-homogeneous objects -- an important topic (e.g. in finite element analysis) that is beyond the scope of this Chapter.

Solid triangulation schemes have been used for the internal representation of rectilinear polyhedra in the GMS described in [37], and also in an algorithm for computing the volume of convex rectilinear polyhedra [22]. Cell decompositions are the primary representations used in 3-D (solid) finite element analysis.

1.3.6 Constructive Solid Geometry

Constructive solid geometry (CSG) connotes a family of schemes for representing rigid solids as "constructions" or "combinations" (via the regularized set operators) of solid components [59]. CSG and boundary representations (Section 1.3.8) are the best understood and currently most important representation schemes for solids, and therefore are treated in this survey more thoroughly than the other known schemes. Section 1.3.6.1 discusses the tree structures characteristic of CSG representations, and section 1.3.6.2 discusses the primitives which correspond to some of the CSG tree leaves. Formal and informal properties of CSG schemes are discussed in Sections 1.3.6.3 and 1.3.6.4. We conclude by discussing briefly the use of CSG-related representations in GMS's.

1.3.6.1 CSG Trees

CSG representations of objects are (ordered) binary trees whose non-terminal nodes represent operators, which may be either rigid motions (translations and/or rotations) or regularized set operators

(regularized union, intersection and difference, denoted respectively
by U*, ∩*, and −*), and whose terminal nodes (leaves) may be either
primitive leaves which represent subsets of E3, or transformation
leaves which contain the defining arguments of rigid motions. CSG
trees may be defined by the following BNF.

```
<CSG tree> ::= <primitive leaf> |
               <CSG tree> <set-operator node> <CSG tree> |
               <CSG tree> <motion node> <motion arguments>.
```

(In certain CSG schemes, e.g. that embodied in PADL-1 [71], subtrees
may be shared and therefore representations are acyclic graphs rather
than trees; data sharing is unimportant for the purposes of this
Chapter and will be ignored.)

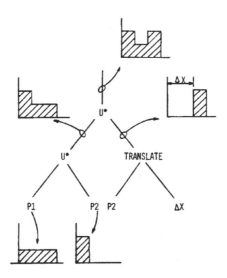

Fig. 1.14 A CSG Tree and the Solids Represented
by its Subtrees (Solids are shown in
orthographic projection.)

The semantics of CSG-tree representations is obvious (see
Fig. 1.14): each subtree that is not a transformation leaf represents
a set which is the result of applying the indicated motional and
combinational operators to the sets represented by the primitive
leaves. (An ordering convention is needed for associating a meaning
to nodes which contain non-symmetric operators such as −*.) Rigid

motions are well understood and therefore motion nodes and transformation leaves need not be discussed further. Regularized set operators are modified versions of their usual counterparts; they are discussed at length in [59], [58], and [60]. Primitive leaves are dealt with in the following section.

1.3.6.2 Primitive Leaves

The primitive leaves of a CSG tree are tuples which represent subsets of E3. Each CSG scheme has a fixed set of generic primitives (see Section 1.2.2) whose instances are represented by primitive leaves. The generic primitives are called (generic) half-spaces. It is useful to distinguish two types of half-spaces, simple and composite, defined as follows.

Let $F(Q,p)$, where $Q = (q1,q2,...,qN)$ is a parameter vector and $p = (x,y,z)$ is a generic point of E3, be a real-valued analytic function in E3 for each value of the parameter vector Q in some set Dq. The parameters $q1,q2,...$ are called configuration parameters, Q is a configuration vector and Dq is a configuration domain. For each fixed value of Q in Dq the set

$$I(Q) = ki\{p : F(Q,p) < 0\},$$

where k and i denote closure and interior in the usual E3 topology, is a regular semi-analytic set [58]. Now let us construct a family of sets as follows. For each value of Q in Dq apply to $I(Q)$ a rigid motion that belongs to a set Dp of motions called a position domain. The family S of sets which results when the construction above is repeated for all values of Q in Dq, and for all motions in Dp is called a generic simple half-space, and the members of the family are called simple half-space instances.

Because a rigid motion of E3 may be defined by a position vector $P = (dX,dY,dZ,aX,aY,aZ)$, where dX, dY, and dZ are displacements that define a translation, and aX, aY, and aZ are angles that define a rotation, a simple half-space instance corresponds to a specific choice of values for the configuration and position vectors Q and P.

Instancing may be viewed as a two-step process. Firstly one
"configures" the half-space by assigning values to the configuration
vector Q, and then one "positions" the configured half-space by
assigning values to the position vector P. The configuration and
position vectors, together with their respective domains, are said to
provide a parameterization for the family of sets which constitute a
generic half-space.

An example:

$$F(R,p) = x**2 + y**2 - R**2,$$

where R is the single-component configuration vector, is an algebraic
(and hence analytic) function for R in the configuration domain Dq
defined by R>0. The set

$$I(R) = ki\{(x,y,z) : x**2 + y**2 - R**2 < 0\}$$

is an unbounded solid cylinder of radius R whose axis coincides with
the z-axis of E3. If we let Dp be the set of all rigid motions of E3,
F(R,p) together with Dq and Dp defines a cylindrical simple half-space
as the collection of all unbounded solid cylinders of E3. Each
instance is a cylinder with a specific radius placed at a specific
location in E3.

Simple half-spaces may be combined via regularized set operators
and used to construct generic composite half-spaces by a procedure
analogous to that described above. Figure 1.15 illustrates the
notion. A generic bounded cylindrical composite half-space is the
family of sets congruent to sets of the form

$$H = S1 \cap* S2 \cap* S3,$$

where S1 and S2 are instances of a planar simple half-space and S3 is
an instance of a cylindrical simple half-space, in the relative
positions shown in the figure.

A generic composite half-space can also be parameterized in terms
of configuration and position parameters. The following is an
adequate parameterization for the example shown in Fig. 1.15: the
configuration vector is (R,H) with a configuration domain defined by

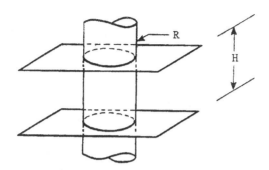

Fig. 1.15 An Instance of a Cylindrical Composite
Half-Space Defined as the Intersection of Three
Simple Half-Space Instances

R>0 and H>0, and the position vector is a 6-tuple that defines a rigid
motion in the position domain of all rigid motions of E3. Observe
that the configuration and position parameters of the simple
half-spaces used to define a composite, together with appropriate
domains, provide a (perhaps non-minimal) parameterization for the
composite.

Half-spaces are primitives of CSG schemes. Each CSG scheme
possesses an associated finite collection {Hi}, i=1,...,M, of (simple
or composite) generic <u>primitive</u> <u>half-spaces</u>. Instances of half-spaces
in {Hi} are represented by tuples which contain a type code that
designates a particular Hi, and contain also the values of
configuration and position vectors Qi and Pi. (The discussion above
shows that such a parameterization is always possible.)

We shall distinguish two types of CSG schemes. The first type --
called <u>CSG</u> <u>based</u> <u>on</u> <u>general</u> <u>primitive</u> <u>half-spaces</u> -- has unrestricted
{Hi}, some of which may be unbounded. The second type -- called <u>CSG</u>
<u>based</u> <u>on</u> <u>primitive</u> <u>solids</u>, or simply CSG because it is the most common
and useful of the two -- possesses a set of Hi which are <u>bounded</u> and
therefore are r-sets. The second type is a particular case of the
first but has different properties, as we shall see below.

1.3.6.3 Formal Properties

The domain of CSG representation schemes is determined by the following.

1) The specific set of primitive half-spaces {Hi}. (Recall that a generic half-space definition includes a specification of its configuration and position domains.)

2) The available motional operators.

3) The available regularized set operators.

The domain of a CSG scheme with primitive half-spaces {Hi} is always a subset of the regularized Boolean class defined by {Hi}. The regularized Boolean class contains all of the sets definable by a finite number of motions and regularized set operations (complement excluded) on arbitrary instances of the half spaces Hi. (Observe that such a class of sets is mathematically well defined and independent of the means used to represent the sets.) The domain of a CSG scheme equals the regularized class defined by its {Hi} when (1) the motional operators are general, i.e. any rigid motion of E3 is allowable, (2) the three regularized set operators U*, ∩* and -* are available, and (3) both the motional and combinational operators are general, i.e. applicable to any object representable in the scheme. When the primitives are composite rather than simple half-spaces usually the

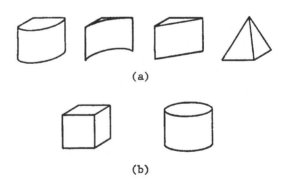

(a)

(b)

Fig. 1.16 Two CSG Schemes Having Different
Primitives but the Same Domain

domain is determined by the set of <u>simple</u> half-spaces {Sj} which underlie the {Hi} (see Section 1.3.6.2). Thus the two representation schemes with general motional and combinational operators and primitives depicted in Figs. 1.16a and 1.16b have the same domain, which is the regularized Boolean class defined by planar and cylindrical simple half-spaces.

Every CSG tree whose primitive leaves are valid representations of half-spaces is guaranteed to define a single regular semi-analytic subset of E3. (This follows immediately from the algebraic closure of regular semi-analytic sets [58].) Primitive validity is ensured when the configuration and position vectors are within their specified domains Dq and Dp. For example, a cylindrical half-space instance in our earlier example is valid if and only if the half-space's radius is positive.

The primitives of CSG schemes based on general half-spaces need not be bounded, and therefore a set defined by a CSG tree may be unbounded (and hence not an r-set). It follows that primitive validity does not suffice to ensure validity of a composition in such schemes. Boundedness of compositions is difficult to verify. The only viable approach known to us involves re-representing the set via its boundary (see Section 1.3.8), and testing for "face" boundedness. This is computationally expensive and requires non-trivial algorithms.

Because primitive solids are bounded, and hence r-sets, the algebraic properties of r-sets guarantee that <u>any</u> CSG tree on primitive solids is a <u>valid</u> representation of an r-set when the primitive leaves are valid. Because in practice primitive leaf validity is satisfied trivially as noted earlier, the validity of CSG representations based on solid primitives may be ensured essentially at the syntactical level. Thus any representation that satisfies the syntactical rules described by the BNF of Section 1.3.6.2 is valid if its leaves are valid.

It is important to realize that the "guaranteed validity" of CSG schemes based on solid primitives applies only to CSG schemes in which the combinational operators are <u>general</u> regularized set operators which may be applied to any objects in the domain of the representation scheme. CSG-like schemes in which the operators are not general have validity properties akin to those of cell decompositions (Section 1.3.5); expensive computations may be required to ensure that the conditions for operator applicability are not violated. It is worth noting that, in practice, restrictions are placed on operators largely to facilitate "boundary evaluation", i.e. the computation of the boundaries of the objects represented in the scheme; this goal is defeated if one seeks to provide automatic validity testing because the computations required for validity testing and (general) boundary evaluation have comparable complexities.

CSG representations are obviously unambiguous since both rigid motions and regularized set operations produce single well-defined sets.

CSG representations are not unique because generally it is possible to construct the same solid in many ways. For example, the solid of Fig. 1.14 may be defined alternatively as the difference of two blocks.

To determine whether two objects are equal one may represent in the CSG scheme the regularized symmetric difference of the two objects, and test the difference for nullity (see Section 1.2.4.4). However, null tests appear to be expensive, as do approaches based on re-representing the difference object via its boundary.

It is worth remarking that operators in a CSG tree provide non-redundant information: generally they may not be inferred from a knowledge of the half-space instances, as the following discussion will show.

Consider a collection of pairs (bHi, Ni) satisfying the following conditions.

1) bHi is the boundary of an instance of a primitive half-space Hi.
2) Each bHi has a subset Gi which is a 2-D polyhedron (i.e. has an "area") and lies on the boundary of an object S.
3) The union of all of the Gi is the object's boundary.
4) Ni indicates the "material side" of bHi with respect to the object. (Ni could be, for example, an inward unit normal vector.)

A collection {(bHi, Ni)} with such properties does not suffice to define an r-set unambiguously: see Fig. 1.17, which shows two distinct solids possessing the same collection of pairs (bHi, Ni). Therefore a list of (possibly unbounded) "oriented surfaces" does not suffice to define solids unambiguously, and a fortiori neither does a list of "un-oriented surfaces".

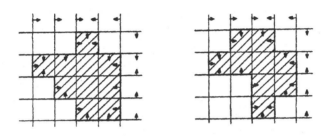

Fig. 1.17   Two Solids Possessing the Same "Oriented Surfaces"

Work reported in [52] shows that a collection of pairs (bHi, Pi), where Pi is a point which belongs to both bHi and the object's boundary, also does not define a solid unambiguously. We conclude that approaches based on lists of "surfaces", oriented or not, augmented or not with "points on the object's boundary" lead to ambiguous representations of solids. We shall see in Section 1.3.8 below that boundary-based unambiguous representations of solids require that the boundary itself be represented unambiguously.

1.3.6.4 Informal properties

CSG schemes whose primitives are well matched to the domain of objects to be represented are very concise. Schemes based on primitive solids usually are more concise than those based on general half-spaces, because the latter usually have "lower-level" primitives. For example, the object represented via three primitive "blocks" in Fig. 1.14 would require eight primitive instances in a scheme whose primitives are planar simple half-spaces.

The limited experience accrued to date in implemented CSG schemes indicates that humans create easily CSG representations of certain types of objects, such as unsculptured (functional) mechanical parts.

CSG representations are not efficient sources of geometric data for producing line drawings of objects, and certain types of graphic interaction operations (e.g. "pick an edge") are difficult to support directly from CSG representations. However, simple and extensible algorithms are known for other interactions (e.g. "pick a face"), for generating shaded displays, and for computing integral properties (e.g. the volume) of objects [29] [30] [44]. Some of these algorithms are slow in sequential machines but are inherently parallel, and therefore are promising candidates for hardware implementation. It appears that CSG representations will be of considerable importance for manufacturing automation, e.g. in the study of rough machining operations.

CSG is a powerful and general descriptive medium. The majority of GMS's implemented or designed recently use some form of CSG, as we shall see in the following section.

1.3.6.5 Use of CSG and Related Schemes in GMS's

Spatial arrays (Section 1.3.4), cell decompositions (Section 1.3.5), and certain schemes used in architecture which are based on "block" primitives [47] may be viewed as particular cases of CSG possessing a single "glue" operator. ("Glue" is a restricted form of union that applies only to sets with disjoint interiors.)

CSG schemes possessing a single but general union operator and a single primitive have been used in computer graphics and computer vision. Specifically, the scheme described in [33] has a single ellipsoidal primitive while the scheme described in [6] has a single spherical primitive. Schemes possessing a single associative operator (e.g. union) obviously do not need to represent the operator explicitly, and thus CSG trees in such schemes may be collapsed into lists or sets of primitive leaves.

Many GMS's which use a boundary representation scheme as their primary or "archival" definitional medium also offer CSG-like input facilities. For example, there may be a "union command" which, when executed, produces a boundary representation of the union of two boundary-represented solid arguments. The majority of such systems, at their present stage of development, cater only for rectilinear polyhedra. Systems with these characteristics (insofar as we know) include EUCLID [9], EUKLID [26], GEOMAP [38], GEOMED [8], GLIDE [24], 3DFORM [74], a system developed at the University of Michigan [12], and two systems developed at Ohio State University [53], [75]. Systems which cater also for curved objects having certain types of quadric surfaces are BUILD-1 [16] [17], BUILD-2 [18], COMPAC [65], [66], GIPSY [61] and PROREN-2 [62].

Several GMS's use a CSG-related representation as their primary definitional medium. SHAPES [41] [42] and TIPS-1 [50] [51] are based on generally unbounded primitive half-spaces, while GDP [31] [73], GMSOLID [13] [15], PADL-1 [69] [71], and Synthavision [29] [30] are based on bounded solid primitives. GMSOLID and PADL-1 use CSG representations of the form discussed in Sections 1.3.6.1-1.3.6.4; the other systems just listed use somewhat different representations. For example, TIPS-1 uses 3-level structures rather than binary trees; TIPS-1 representations are of the form

OBJECT = (A1 U A2 U ...) - (B1 U B2 U ...),

where the Ai and Bi are intersections of primitive half-spaces or their complements.

Set operator generality has a strong impact on the characteristics of CSG schemes (e.g. validity -- see Section 1.3.6.3), and is important also in the context of manufacturing automation applications [70]. GMSOLID, PADL-1, and (apparently) BUILD-2 possess regularized set operators which are applicable to any object representable in the systems. The literature on the other systems cited in this Section does not allude to regularity issues, and therefore many of the systems are likely to contain operators that either cannot be applied to certain objects or yield non-solid (invalid) results. (Non-solid objects may be created when, for example, non-regularized intersection is applied to two solids having partially coincident, overlapping boundaries [59].)

1.3.7 Sweep Representations

The basic notion embodied in sweep representation schemes is very simple: a set moving through space may sweep a "volume" (a solid) that may be represented by representing the "moving object" plus the "trajectory".

Sweeping may be formulated rigorously in terms of either set products or unions of an infinite number of sets, as we shall see below. Readers are warned, however, that much less is known about sweep representations than about the other schemes discussed in this paper. The underlying theory has not been worked out fully, but there is no doubt that the conclusions below apply for "well-behaved" sets.

The following section studies two simple and useful forms of sweeping. Section 1.3.7.2 deals with a type of sweeping important in manufacturing automation. Finally, general sweeping is discussed briefly in Section 1.3.7.3.

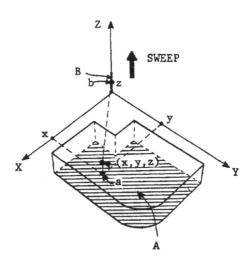

Fig. 1.18 Translational Sweeping

1.3.7.1 Translational and Rotational Sweeping

Firstly we consider a translational sweeping scheme illustrated in Fig. 1.18. Let A be a well-behaved bounded set lying on a plane (A is a "solid curved polygon" which may contain "holes"), and let B be a bounded straight line segment normal to the plane of A and having an endpoint on the plane. Construct the set product C = A x B. (Recall that the elements of of C are ordered pairs (a,b), where 'a' is an element of A and 'b' is an element of B.) C is an abstract space; to obtain a solid S we must immerse (or place) C in E3 by constructing a mapping, called an immersion, i : C --> E3. The solid is the image of C under 'i', i.e. S = i(C).

The immersion used by translational sweeping schemes is the natural one illustrated in Fig. 1.18. Assuming, for simplicity, that B lies on the Z axis and A lies on the XY plane, the immersion mapping is defined per i(a,b) = (x,y,z), where (x,y,0) are the coordinates of 'a' and (0,0,z) are the coordinates of 'b'. (Sweeps along a direction oblique to the plane of A may be defined in a similar manner, and have essentially the same properties as orthogonal sweeps.) S is the volume swept when all points of A are translated along a trajectory parallel to B. Alternatively, and equivalently, S may be defined as the union, for all 'b' in B, of the sets $A_b = T_b(A)$ where T_b is a translation by 'b' along the direction of the segment B.

Clearly S may be represented by a pair (representation of A, representation of B); the latter is trivial and therefore the problem of representing a 3-D solid S is reduced to that of representing a 2-D set A. This is done usually by means of a 2-D boundary representation scheme, i.e. by representing the bounding edges of A.

The domain of a translational sweeping scheme is restricted to solids exhibiting "translational symmetry". A representation of S is valid when A's representation is valid, and therefore validity may be tested in 2-D. A representation is unambiguous when A is represented unambiguously. Translational sweep representations usually are not unique; Figs. 1.19b and 1.19c show two translational sweeps which correspond to the parallelepiped shown in Fig. 1.19a.

The definition of rotational sweeping schemes is similar to that

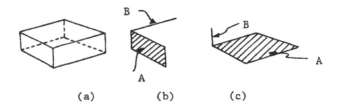

Fig. 1.19   Non-Uniqueness of Translational
Sweep Representations

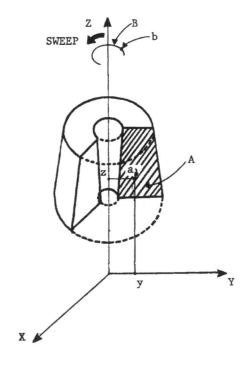

Fig. 1.20   Rotational Sweeping

of translational sweeping schemes. Fig. 1.20 illustrates the notion.
A set S is defined as S = i(A x B), where 'i' is the "natural"
immersion, A is a 2-D set as before, but B is an arc of a circle
rather than a line segment. The solid S is the volume swept when A is
rotated about the Y axis through an angular interval defined by the
arc B. Usually A is represented by its bounding edges. (The
rotational sweeping scheme described in [11] is an exception: the 2-D
set is represented by a cell decomposition.)

The domain of rotational sweeping schemes is restricted to solids
having "rotational symmetry". The properties of rotational sweeping
schemes are essentially those of translational sweeping schemes.

Rotational sweeping is used by many GMS's which deal exclusively
with turned (lathe) parts. Translational sweeping is used in systems
for describing flat sheet metal parts. Both types of sweeping are
used as a means to enter object descriptions in GMS's based on
boundary representations (e.g. in the CADD system marketed by
McDonnell-Douglas, St. Louis, MO, and in the ROMULUS system marketed
by Shape Data, Cambridge, U.K.). The representation of 2-D sets by
bounding edges leads to convenient interfaces for
traditionally-trained draftsmen.

1.3.7.2 Volumes Swept by Motions of a Solid

Sweep representations provide natural means for describing the
solid volume swept by a rigid solid in motion through space. Such
swept volumes are important in the context of design and production
automation, as the following examples indicate.

1) Dynamic interference: A solid S1 moving through space collides
   with another solid S2 if the volume swept by S1 intersects S2
   [14].

2) Material removal: The effect of a machining operation is to
   remove from a workpiece the solid volume swept by the cutter when
   it moves along a specified trajectory [68] [70].

A representation scheme based on "solid sweeping" may be
constructed as follows. Let A be an r-set that models a rigid solid.
It is well-known from Classical Mechanics that a rigid solid has six
degrees of motional freedom. The coordinates (x,y,z) of the solid's
centroid (or another agreed point of the solid) plus three orientation
angles (a1,a2,a3) measured in some agreed manner (e.g. the Euler
angles) suffice to describe completely the position (location plus
orientation) of the solid at each instant of time. Therefore a
solid's position corresponds to a six-tuple of parameters
(x,y,z,a1,a2,a3), i.e. to a point in 6-D space. The motion of any
specific solid is completely determined by the temporal evolution of
its representative point in 6-D space. To define a swept volume we
let B be a curve in 6-D space, and we construct the product A x B.
Finally we immerse the 9-D space A x B in E3 by a mapping 'i' defined
as follows. Let 'a' be a point of A, and let b = (x,y,z,a1,a2,a3)) be
a point of B. Observe that to each point 'b' corresponds a set
A congruent to A but at a position defined by the six-tuple 'b' (see
Fig. 1.21); denote by T a rigid transformation of E3 which takes A
onto A , i.e., such that A = T (A). Then i(a,b) = T (a), i.e., a
point 'a' is mapped onto its "corresponding" point when the solid is
in the position defined by 'b'. Note that the immersion 'i' is not
one-to-one. S = i(A x B) equals the union of the A sets for all 'b'
in B, i.e., S is the union of of all of the volumes which the moving
object occupies at each instant of time during its motion.

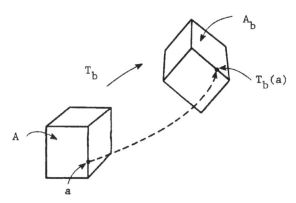

Fig. 1.21 Mapping the Points of A Onto Points of
the Volume Swept by the Motion of A

The domain of solid sweeping schemes depends on the solids and trajectories available and is difficult to characterize in other terms. The formal properties of solid sweeping schemes are essentially those of translational and rotational sweeping schemes, but validity may not be tested in 2-D since A is a 3-D solid.

The completeness of solid sweeping schemes implies that a cutter trajectory specified by a part program written in a language such as APT [40], together with a representation of the cutter or its "envelope" and a representation of the initial workpiece, is an unambiguous representation of the workpiece which results from a specified machining operation. Such a representation might be termed "operational" or "procedural" since it defines a solid by describing a method for manufacturing it. The major disadvantage of such a representation is the lack of known algorithms for computing properties of represented solids.

1.3.7.3 General Sweeping

Very little is known about general sweep representations. Figure 1.22 shows that sweeping a homogeneously 1-D polyhedron along another may produce a set which is not homogeneously 2-D. (Similar examples may be constructed in 3-D.) Mathematical conditions on the "component" sets A and B, and on the the immersion mapping 'i' for ensuring that the resulting set i(A x B) is an r-set do not appear to be known.

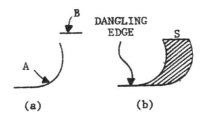

Fig. 1.22 General Sweeping May Produce
Non-Regular Sets

The three examples of sweeping discussed in Sections 1.3.7.1 and 1.3.7.2, as well as the example depicted in Fig. 1.22 amount to moving a rigid object (not necessarily a solid) through space. General sweeping may involve also the motion of a non-rigid object which undergoes deformations as it travels through space. Non-rigid sweeping schemes may be defined as in Section 1.3.7.2 by using transformations T that are not rigid motions. Binford and others have implemented modelling systems which use so-called "generalized cylinders" or "generalized cones" [1] [10]; such systems are based on non-rigid sweeping schemes. Generalized cones appear to be quite useful for describing objects such as airplanes, animals and dolls which may be naturally decomposed into a few "tube-like" components.

General sweep representations also are used extensively in a recent proposal for an ANSI standard representation of solid objects [4].

1.3.8 Boundary Representations

Boundary representations of solids are familiar to most computer scientists because they are used extensively in computer graphics [28] [29]. A solid is represented by segmenting its boundary into a finite number of bounded subsets usually called "faces" or "patches", and representing each face by (for example) its bounding "edges" and "vertices".

Figure 1.23 provides an example of a boundary representation for a rectangular pyramid. The representation is a directed graph containing object, face, edge and vertex nodes. The scheme illustrated in the figure is based on boundary triangulation, i.e. the segmentation of an object's boundary into non-overlapping triangles. It is clear that any rectilinear polyhedron may be represented in such a scheme.

The remainder of this section discusses issues which arise in the design of boundary representation schemes, and the properties of such schemes.

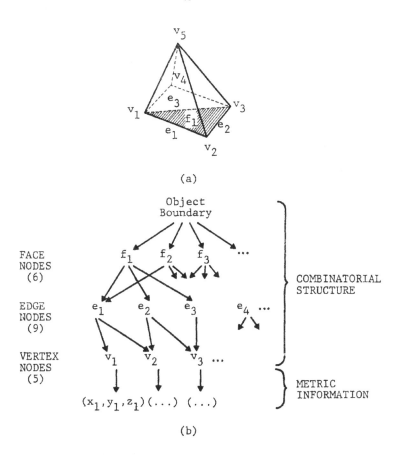

(a)

(b)

Fig. 1.23   A Boundary Representation for a
Rectangular Pyramid

1.3.8.1 Design Issues

Most people have the same intuitive notion of "face" for
rectilinear polyhedra.   Observe, however, that the faces in the
representation of Fig. 1.23 do not agree with the intuitive notion
because the pyramid's rectangular bottom has been segmented into two
triangles.   Furthermore, it is not intuitively clear what are the
faces of <u>curved</u> objects: see Fig. 1.24.   The examples of Figs. 1.23
and 1.24 show that faces are representational artifacts which may or
may not correspond to one's intuitive notion of "face"; in any event

the entity "face" must be defined by the designers of boundary representation schemes. We shall propose certain characteristics which reasonable definitions of "face" should possess.

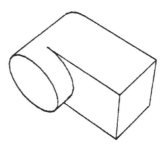

Fig. 1.24 What are the Faces?

Firstly we shall assume that each boundary representation scheme has a finite number of generic <u>primitive</u> <u>surfaces</u> bHi which are the boundaries of regular semi-analytic half-spaces Hi. (To avoid certain mathematical subtleties we shall assume in the sequel that the bHi are 2-manifolds without boundaries [2].) Faces should satisfy the following conditions.

1) A face of an object is a subset of the object's boundary.
2) The union of the faces of an object equals the object's boundary.
3) Each face is a subset of some primitive surface bHi.
4) A face must be a homogeneously 2-D topological polyhedron [2], i.e., it must have "area" and must not have "dangling edges" or "isolated points".

In particular schemes, faces may be required to satisfy additional, non-essential conditions such as connectedness, simple connectedness, maximality (in the set inclusion sense) or quasi-disjointedness. Thus, in most boundary schemes used in computer graphics faces must be quasi-disjoint, connected and maximal while in the boundary scheme used in PADL-1 [71] none of these properties are required. An additional condition often imposed on faces is that each face possess a "constant normal". Figure 1.25 shows that faces with non-intuitive properties may result if this condition is ignored. Faces are defined in the scheme illustrated in the figure as maximal subsets which satisfy conditions 1-4 above; the (disconnected) hatched face of Fig. 1.25a exhibits "opposing normals", and so do the (connected) hatched faces of Fig. 1.25b. (These last exhibit another anomaly: they intersect on a line which is not a bounding edge of either face.)

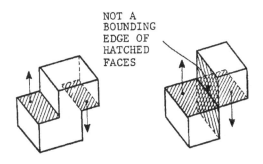

Fig. 1.25   Subsets of a Single Surface May
Possess opposing Normals

Faces must be represented unambiguously if a boundary representation scheme is to be unambiguous. Planar faces may be represented by their bounding edges, as in Fig. 1.23, but non-planar faces require that their "host surface" bHi also be represented, typically by primitive instancing. Figure 1.26 shows that additional information may be needed to represent unambiguously faces which lie in certain surfaces. (To distinguish between the shaded spherical triangle of Fig. 1.26 and the remainder of the sphere typically one orients the bounding edges of the face according to some convention.)

Specialized techniques exist for representing the doubly-curved ("sculptured") faces usually called "patches"; see [7] for an entry into the extensive literature on the subject, and see also Chapter 3 below. Some of the techniques amount to defining the patches' edges together with an interpolation rule, while other techniques are based on approximating sets of curves with specific types of curved surfaces. Surface patches also may be defined via a collection of cross-sections plus an interpolation rule [48], or by sweeping a curve

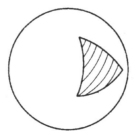

Fig. 1.26   A Face Lying in a Spherical Surface

along another [35].

Face representation via edges is the 2-D analog of solid representation via faces, and edges are representational artifacts in the same sense that faces are representational artifacts. Thus the entity "edge" must be defined mathematically and appropriate edge-representation schemes must be designed.

Figure 1.27 illustrates some of the issues raised by edge representation. The entire intersection of the two cylindrical surfaces may be represented unambiguously by "pointing" to the surfaces, i.e. as a pair (Surf1,Surf2). However, subsets of the intersection generally are not represented unambiguously by their end points together with the surface pair. A common solution to this problem involves segmenting the intersection. Observe in the figure that removal of the "critical points" where the two ellipses intersect separates the intersection of the two cylinders into four connected components, each homeomorphic to an open line segment and representable unambiguously by a triple (Surf1,Surf2,P) where P is some point in the interior of the component. If one defines edges as curve segments that are homeomorphic to closed line segments and lie entirely within the closure of an intersection-curve component, it is clear that edges can be represented unambiguously by their endpoints together with the triple which represents its "host" component.

The various extant boundary representation schemes differ in the redundant data they provide to speed-up specific algorithms. A simple

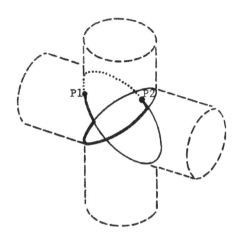

Fig. 1.27 Endpoints P1 and P2 Bound Four Curved
Segments of the Intersection of Two Cylindrical
Surfaces

example: although surface normals are not required to define
completely a solid's boundary (and hence the solid), most schemes
store with each face the direction of an outward normal to the face
because such information is easy to store and is useful for generating
graphic displays.

Other redundant information takes the form of adjacency relations
between faces, edges, and vertices; such information sometimes is
stored to avoid expensive searches that otherwise would be required by
certain algorithms. One of the most elaborate schemes containing
explicit adjacency information is that described in [8]. The
trade-off between the complexity of the algorithms which construct and
maintain elaborate boundary representation structures and the
efficiency of algorithms which use such representations (e.g. to
produce displays with hidden lines removed) is not well understood.

In summary, a designer of a boundary representation scheme must
address the following questions:

1) What is a face?
2) How are faces represented?
3) What is an edge?

4) How are edges represented?

5) What redundant data are maintained?

Each question has important implications, but a discussion of such matters would take us too far afield.

1.3.8.2 Formal Properties

Boundary representation schemes are potentially capable of covering domains as rich as those of cell-decomposition or CSG schemes. Indeed, given a CSG scheme with primitive half-spaces {Hi} it is always possible to design a boundary representation scheme with the same domain whose primitive surfaces are (a subset of) {bHi}.

Boundary representation schemes are unambiguous (complete) if faces are represented unambiguously, but generally they are not unique. Completeness follows from deep mathematical theorems which ensure that an r-set is defined unambiguously by its boundary [58]. (General (non r-set) subsets of E3 are not defined unambiguously by their boundaries.) Uniqueness, except for permutational and positional non-uniqueness, may obtain in particular schemes. For example, faces that are maximal and have properties 1-4 lead to unique representations in schemes whose primitive half-spaces have the following "non-overlap" property: when bHi & bHj is a 2-D polyhedron then either Hi = Hj or Hi = c*Hj.

The validity of boundary representations raises interesting issues which we shall discuss in the remainder of this section. To study validity one proceeds "bottom-up", e.g. by investigating conditions for vertex nodes to represent points of E3, for edge sub-graphs (i.e. edge nodes plus their corresponding vertex nodes) to represent line segments, and so on. Validity conditions may be classified into two generic categories, "combinatorial" and "metric". We shall present the validity conditions for two exemplary schemes. (Such conditions follow directly from elementary algebraic topology [58] [2].)

Scheme A: the triangulation scheme illustrated in Fig. 1.23.

The following are the combinatorial conditions.

1) Each face must have precisely three edges.
2) Each edge must have precisely two vertices.
3) Each edge must belong to an even number of faces.
4) Each vertex in a face must belong precisely to two of the face's edges.

Conditions 1 and 2 are obvious. Conditions 3 and 4 ensure, respectively, that the faces form a 2-cycle and that each face's edges form a 1-cycle [58] [2]; intuitively, they imply that the surface "closes" and that the edges form "loops". It is not difficult to write efficient algorithms for testing the combinatorial conditions above, or to imbed such conditions in the procedures which construct and update the representations. The so-called "Euler operators" which are used in some of the GMS's based on boundary representations schemes more elaborate than Scheme A [8] [19] [25] appear to play the role of ensuring that combinatorial validity conditions analogous to those above are met. (An exemplary Euler operator: 'SplitEdge' divides an edge into two by introducing a new vertex in the interior of the original edge.)

Satisfaction of the foregoing combinatorial conditions does not ensure that representations in Scheme A are valid. Mathematically, the problem is the following. A combinatorial structure (as in Fig. 1.23) that satisfies conditions 1-4 defines a combinatorial entity called an "abstract complex". Metric information associated with the entities of the representation must be compatible with the combinatorial structure in the following sense: there must exist a sub-polyhedron of E3 with a triangulation whose faces, edges, and vertices may be put in a one-to-one correspondence with those of the abstract complex. Therefore, the problem is that of constructing a realization of an abstract complex in E3. The following metric conditions must be satisfied.

5) Each three-tuple of vertex coordinates must represent a distinct point of E3.
6) Edges must either be disjoint or intersect at a common vertex.
7) Faces must either be disjoint or intersect at a common edge or vertex.

Conditions 6 and 7 are computationally unpleasant because they require face/face comparisons and other expensive calculations.

Combinatorial structure and metric information have been called, respectively, "topology" and "geometry" by other authors [8], [18], [24], who advocate the "separation of topology from geometry" in GMS's. Such a separation is sometimes convenient in that one may (for example) represent a translated rectilinear polyhedron simply by translating all of its vertex coordinates without altering its combinatorial structure. It should be obvious, however, that combinatorial structure and metric information are not independent. Observe in Fig. 1.28 that a change of coordinates of the vertex P converts a valid representation in Scheme A which corresponds to the object of Fig. 1.28a into an invalid representation, because the faces of the object of Fig. 1.28b intersect in lines which have no corresponding edge nodes in the combinatorial structure. (For clarity, triangulations of the rectangular faces in Fig. 1.28 are not shown.) Of course the solid indicated in cross-section in Fig. 1.28c could be represented in Scheme A in a valid manner by segmenting the "self-intersecting faces" of Fig. 1.28b, but this would alter extensively both the combinatorial structure and the metric information of the initial representation.

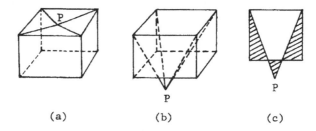

(a)   (b)   (c)

Fig. 1.28 Illustration of the Interdependence of Combinatorial Structure and Metric Information

Scheme A may be generalized in several directions. The following is a simple generalization whose validity conditions follow directly from existing mathematical results [58].

Scheme B: Faces are simple planar polygons without holes (see Section 1.2.3) rather than triangles, but otherwise the definition of

Scheme B coincides with that of Scheme A. This leads to cell-decompositions rather than to triangulations of the boundary. Validity condition 1 does not apply, but conditions 2-7 are applicable and the following additional conditions are required.

4a) The union of the edges in a face must be a connected set. Together with condition 4 this ensures that a face's edges form a "single loop" and therefore (by Jordan's curve theorem [2]) that the face is a cell if the metric conditions 5-8 are satisfied.

8) All of the vertices in a face must lie in a plane.

Schemes A and B cover only rectilinear polyhedra. Curvature introduces a variety of interesting and delicate validity issues. For example, it is no longer sufficient to show that the edges associated with a face node form a loop (1-cycle) to prove that they, together with host surface information, represent a face unambiguously. Figure 1.29 shows that closed curves lying in a torus need not bound a face. Such curves are called "non-bounding cycles" in algebraic topology. (The number of distinct types of non-bounding cycles -- two for the torus as shown in the figure -- is a topological invariant which equals twice the number of "handles" or "holes" of the (orientable) surface [58] [2].) The known algorithms for determining whether a 1-cycle bounds a 2-D subset of a surface are non-trivial; they require the generation of a cell decomposition of the whole surface such that the 1-cycle's edges also are edges of the decomposition.

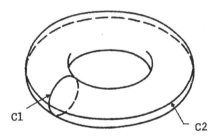

Fig. 1.29 Two Closed Curves Which Do Not
Bound Subsets of a Toroidal Surface

Clearly we have not exhausted boundary representation schemes. (For example, Scheme B may be further generalized by allowing faces to have "holes".) We shall not study validity conditions for additional examples because those above suffice to reach the following conclusions.

-- Standard results from elementary algebraic topology lead directly to validity conditions.
-- Boundary representation schemes have a complex set of validity conditions.
-- Validity conditions of a combinatorial nature are usually easy to test but metric conditions are complex and computationally expensive to test.

Validity conditions for solid triangulations and cell decompositions are 3-D generalizations of the validity conditions discussed above. It is worth noting that the "verification of finite element meshes" essentially amounts to checking the validity of cell decompositions [55].

1.3.8.3 Informal Properties

Boundary representations are verbose, e.g. an order of magnitude longer than corresponding CSG representations. The sheer volume of required data and the delicate validity conditions make it difficult for humans to construct, without computer assistance, boundary representations of even moderately complex objects. Essentially all of the known GMS's that rely on boundary representations attempt to provide such assistance via a user-oriented input language (see the references cited in Section 1.3.6.5).

The main virtue of boundary representations lies in the ready availability of representations for faces, edges, and relations between such; these data are important for generating line drawings and graphic displays, and for supporting certain types of graphic interactions. Thus it is not surprising that boundary representations have been used extensively in computer graphics.

We noted in Section 1.2.4.4 that object equality may be detected in non-unique schemes by testing for null symmetric differences. Because boundaries are represented as unions of faces, a boundary is null (and hence the object is null) if and only if it has no faces. Therefore testing for nullity is trivial in boundary representation schemes. (However, computing the symmetric difference of two objects represented by their boundaries is not trivial.)

The majority of boundary representation schemes use methods closely related to cell decomposition of object boundaries. This implies that it is relatively easy to compute from such representations "homological properties" of objects, i.e. connectedness, number of "holes", and other properties which can be inferred from the homology groups of an object [58] [2].

1.3.9 Hybrid Schemes

Hybrid, or non-homogeneous, representation schemes may be designed by combining the approaches discussed in the preceding sections. Three examples follow.

1) A CSG/boundary hybrid: representations are CSG-like trees whose leaves are either tuples which represent primitive solids or boundary representations of non-primitive solids.

2) A CSG/solid-sweep hybrid: representations are CSG-like trees whose leaves may be solid-sweep representations of non-primitives.

3) A CSG/general-sweep hybrid: representations are CSG-like trees whose leaves are general-sweep representations (e.g. generalized cylinders).

Scheme 1 is used as the basis for the input language of some GMS's (see Section 1.3.6.5); systems such as BUILD-2 [18] and GLIDE [24] can store such representations. Scheme 2 is useful for the verification of programs for numerically-controlled machine tools [39]. Scheme 3 is the major representation scheme used by ACRONYM

[10], a system designed for applications in computer vision and manipulation.

Hybrid schemes pose a serious practical problem: it is difficult to design algorithms for computing properties of objects represented in such schemes. For example, an algorithm for computing the volume of objects represented in scheme 1 would have to be able to deal with pure CSG representations, pure boundary representations, and combinations of the two. Usually it is preferable to homogenize hybrid representations via conversion algorithms because application algorithms then may be designed to operate on a single (pure) scheme.

1.3.10 Conversion Between Representations

The previous sections show that none of the extant schemes for representing solids has properties that are uniformly better than those of other schemes. The ability to convert representations in a scheme into corresponding representations in other schemes therefore is of great practical importance for well-engineered modelling systems. (The homogenization of representations in hybrid schemes is a particular case of representation conversion.)

Figure 1.30 summarizes the current state of knowledge about algorithmic conversion between representations of solids. There are two main reasons for the lack of algorithms for bidirectional exact conversion. The first is of a fundamental nature: schemes such as spatial enumeration or simple (translational or rotational) sweeping generally have domains which are smaller than those of CSG, boundary representations or cell decompositions. The second reason is practical rather than fundamental: algorithms for effecting certain conversions are not known at present.

Cell decompositions (and therefore also spatial enumerations) may be converted exactly into boundary representations via simple algorithms which compute modulo 2 combinatorial boundaries [2]; this amounts to selecting those cell faces which belong to only one cell in the decomposition. Algorithms for converting exactly translational and rotational sweeps into boundary representations also are simple

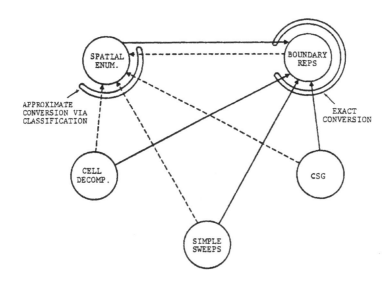

Fig. 1.30   Representation Conversion: Current
State of Knowledge

because there is a straightforward correspondence between the bounding
edges of the 2-D "moving set" and the faces in a boundary
representation of the swept solid.   Exact conversion of CSG to
boundary representations (called "boundary evaluation" in Rochester
jargon) requires non-trivial algorithms.   Boundary evaluation
algorithms used in the PADL-1 processor [71] are based on the notion
of "set membership classification" discussed in [67] and a forthcoming
report [72].   Work related to "inverse boundary evaluation",
i.e. conversion of boundary representations into CSG, is described in
[54].

Approximate conversion into spatial enumeration may be
accomplished via algorithms which compute the so-called point
membership classification function [67] [59], i.e. which determine
whether a point of E3 is in the interior, on the boundary, or in the
outside of a solid. (For restricted domains of rectilinear polyhedra
the conversions are exact rather than approximate.)

The relative paucity of known conversion algorithms poses

significant constraints on the GMS's that can be built today.

1.4 SUMMARY AND CONCLUSIONS

This Chapter focusses on the representational issues that arise in the design and analysis of GMS's. The distinguishing feature of the present treatment is the clear distinction between physical solids, abstract (and representation-independent) mathematical models of solids, and representations for (abstract) solids. The distinction has several advantages. Specifically, (1) mathematical models can be studied essentially independently of computational considerations, (2) such important concepts as representational validity and ambiguity can be defined mathematically, and (3) a rich body of mathematical knowledge can be applied to the study of geometric modelling (e.g. to derive conditions for representational validity).

The formal aspects of representation-scheme theory currently are reasonably well understood, although much remains to be learned about sweeping and interpolation schemes. Many of the major gaps in our present knowledge are centered on applications, which cover a broad spectrum. Our brief discussions of applications uncovered a fact that has important implications for GMS design: none of the known representation schemes has characteristics that are uniformly better than all of the others. Therefore a GMS that is intended to support a broad and open-ended range of applications should contain multiple representations of each object, in different schemes, to achieve flexibility and versatility. The first industrially viable GMS's that maintain multiple object representations are currently being implemented [13] [20] [21]. Careful consideration of validity and consistency issues in the design of such GMS's has yielded designs capable of ensuring automatically the integrity of representations. This is a major advance over earlier modelling systems which relied on user validation.

The design, analysis and implementation of industrially useful geometry systems raise a variety of issues in addition to those addressed in this Chapter. The following is a non-exhaustive list of such additional issues.

-- The representation and use of tolerancing information [57] [34].
-- The design of congenial user interfaces.
-- The use of (geometric) representations for practical applications in automatic manufacturing, robotics, and so forth.
-- The archiving and management of object representations.
-- Implementation issues and hardware/software support.

The discussions in the following Chapters are relevant to several of these topics.

ACKNOWLEDGEMENTS

I would like to thank all of my colleagues in the Production Automation Project, and especially H. B. Voelcker and R. B. Tilove, for the many helpful discussions on representational issues that we have had over the past few years.

The work reported in this Chapter was supported primarily by the National Science Foundation under grants GI-34274X, APR76-01034 and DAR78-17064.

A shortened, less technical version of portions of this Chapter has been submitted to a professional journal for publication; some of the figures and portions of the text are reproduced here by permission of the journal publisher.

REFERENCES

1. G. J. Agin and T. O. Binford, "Computer descriptions of curved objects", IEEE Trans. on Computers, C-25: 439 (1976).

2. M. K. Agoston, Algebraic Topology, Marcel Dekker, Inc., New York, 1976.

3. A. V. Aho, J. E. Hopcroft and J. D. Ullman, The Design and Analysis of Computer Algorithms, Addison-Wesley Publishing Co., Reading, Mass., 1976.

4. "Digital representation of physical object shapes", Proposed Standard ANSI Y14.26.1, American Society of Mechanical Engineers, New York (1978).

5. D. Arnon, "A cellular decomposition algorithm for semi-algebraic sets", Tech. Report No. 353, Computer Science Dept., Univ. of Wisconsin (1979).

6. N. Badler, J. O'Rourke and H. Toltzis, "A spherical representation of a human body for visualizing movement", Proc. IEEE, 67: 1397 (1979).

7. R. E. Barnhill and R. F. Riesenfeld, Eds., Computer Aided Geometric Design, Academic Press, New York, 1974.

8. B. G. Baumgart, "Geometric modelling for computer vision", Report STAN-CS-74-463, Stanford Artificial Intelligence Lab., Stanford Univ. (1974).

9. Y. J. Bernascon and J. M. Brun, "Automated aids for the design of mechanical parts", Tech. Paper MS75-508, Society of Manufacturing Engineers (1975).

10. T. O. Binford, R. A. Brooks and R. Greener, "Progress report on a model-based vision system", Workshop on the Representation of Three-dimensional Objects, Univ. of Pennsylvania, Philadelphia, Pa. (1979).

11. O. Bjorke, "Topological characteristics of product definitions", CIRP Journal--Manufacturing Systems, 1: 33 (1972).

12. H. J. Borkin, J. F. McIntosh and J. A. Turner, "The development of three-dimensional spatial modeling techniques for the construction planning of nuclear power plants", Computer Graphics, 12: 341 (1978).

13. J. W. Boyse, "Preliminary design for a geometric modeller", Research Publication GMR-2768, Computer Science Dept., General Motors Research Laboratories (1978).

14. J. W. Boyse, "Interference detection among solids and surfaces", Communications of the ACM, 22: 3 (1979).

15. J. W. Boyse, "Data structure for a solid modeller", Research Publication GMR-2933, Computer Science Dept., General Motors Research Laboratories (1979).

16. I. C. Braid, "Designing with volumes", Ph.D. Dissertation, Univ. of Cambridge, U.K. (1973).

17. I. C. Braid, "The synthesis of solids bounded by many faces", Communications of the ACM, 18: 209 (1975).

18. I. C. Braid, "New directions in geometric modelling", Proc. Geometric Modeling Project Mtg., CAM-I, Inc., St. Louis, Mo. (1978).

19. I. C. Braid, R. C. Hillyard and I. A. Stroud, "Stepwise construction of polyhedra in geometric modelling", C. A. D. Group Document No. 100, University of Cambridge, U.K. (1978).

20. C. M. Brown, A. A. G. Requicha and H. B. Voelcker, "Geometric modelling systems for mechanical design and manufacturing", Proc. 1978 Ann. Conf. ACM, Washington, D.C., p. 770 (1978).

21. C. M. Brown and H. B. Voelcker, "The PADL-2 project", Proc. 7th NSF Conf. on Production Research and Technology, Ithaca, N.Y., p. F1 (1979).

22. J. Cohen and T. Hickey, "Two algorithms for determining volumes of convex polyhedra", Journal of the ACM, 26: 401 (1979).

23. C. R. Dyer, A. Rosenfeld and H. Samet, "Region representation: boundary codes from quadtrees", Communications of the ACM, 23: 171 (1980).

24. C. Eastman and M. Henrion, "GLIDE: a language for design information systems", Computer Graphics, 11: 24 (1977).

25. C. M. Eastman and K. Weiler, "Geometric modelling using the Euler operators", Research Report No. 78, Institute of Physical Planning, Carnegie-Mellon Univ. (1979).

26. M. E. Engeli, "A language for 3D graphics applications", in International Computing Symposium (A. Gunther et al., eds.), North-Holland, Amsterdam, 1973, p. 459.

27. H. Fuchs, Z. M. Kedem, and S. P. Uselton, "Optimal surface reconstruction from planar contours", Communications of the ACM, 20: 693 (1977).

28. W. K. Giloi, Interactive Computer Graphics, Prentice Hall, Englewood Cliffs, N.J., 1978.

29. R. A. Goldstein and R. Nagel, "3-D visual simulation", Simulation, 16: 25 (1971).

30. R. Goldstein and L. Malin, "3D modelling with the Synthavision system", Proc. 1st Ann. Conf. on Computer Graphics in CAD/CAM Systems, Cambridge, Mass., p. 244 (1979).

31. D. D. Grossman, "Procedural representation of three-dimensional objects", IBM J. Research and Development, 20: 582 (1976).

32. M. Henle, A Combinatorial Introduction to Topology, W. H. Freeman and Co., San Francisco, 1979.

33. D. Herbison-Evans, "NUDES 2: A numeric utility displaying ellipsoid solids, version 2", Computer Graphics, 12: 354 (1978).

34. R. C. Hillyard, "Dimensions and tolerances in shape design", Ph.D. Dissertation, Univ. of Cambridge, U.K. (1978).

35. J. K. Hinds and L. P. Kuan, "Surfaces defined by curve transformations", Proc. 15th Ann. Mtg. NC Society, Chicago, Ill., p. 325 (1978).

36. H. Hironaka, "Triangulations of algebraic sets", in Algebraic Geometry, ARCATA 1974, Proc. of Symposia in Pure Mathematics, American Mathematical Society, Providence, R.I. (1975).

37. M. Hosaka, F. Kimura and N. Kakishita, "A unified method for processing polyhedra", in Information Processing '74, North-Holland, Amsterdam, 1974, p. 768.

38. M. Hosaka and F. Kimura, "An interactive geometrical design system with handwriting input", in Information Processing '77 (B. Gilchrist, ed.), North-Holland, Amsterdam, 1977, p. 167.

39. W. A. Hunt and H. B. Voelcker, "Toward automatic verification of programs for numerically controlled machine tools", Tech. Memo. No. 34, Production Automation Project, Univ. of Rochester (1980).

40. IIT Research Institute, APT Part Programming, McGraw-Hill, New York, 1967.

41. J. H. Laning, D. A. Lynde, and V. Moreggia, "SHAPES User's Manual", Charles Stark Draper Lab., Cambridge, Mass. (1973).

42. J. H. Laning and S. J. Madden, "Capabilities of the SHAPES system for computer aided mechanical design", Proc. 1st Ann. Conf. on Computer Graphics in CAD/CAM Systems, Cambridge, Mass., p. 223 (1979).

43. D. T. Lee and F. P. Preparata, "Location of a point in a planar subdivision and its applications", Proc. 8th ACM Symposium on the Theory of Computing, Hershey, Pa., p. 231 (1976).

44. Y. T. Lee and A. A. G. Requicha, "Algorithms for computing the volume and other integral properties of solid objects", Tech. Memo. No. 35, Production Automation Project, Univ. of Rochester (1980).

45. L. March and P. Steadman, The Geometry of Environment. M.I.T. Press, Cambridge, Mass., 1974.

46. G. Markowsky and M. A. Wesley, "Fleshing out wireframes", Research Report No. RC 8124, IBM Thomas J. Watson Research Center, Yorktown Heights, N.Y. (1980).

47. W. J. Mitchell and M. Oliverson, "Computer representation of three-dimensional structures for CAEADS", Report CERL-TR-P-86, Construction Engineering Research Lab., U.S. Army Corps of Engineers (1978).

48. R. B. Morris and D. B. Welbourn, "Computer graphics and numerically controlled machine tools for pattern, mould and die production", Proc. 16th Int. Machine Tool Design and Research Conf., Manchester, U.K., p. 137 (1975).

49. W. M. Newman and R. F. Sproull, Principles of Interactive Computer Graphics, McGraw-Hill, New York, 1979.

50. N. Okino, Y. Kakazu, and H. Kubo, "TIPS-1: technical information processing system for computer-aided design, drawing and manufacturing", in Computer Languages for Numerical Control (J. Hatvany, ed.), North-Holland, Amsterdam, 1973, p. 141.

51. N. Okino et al., "TIPS-1", Institute of Precision Engineering, Hokkaido University, Sapporo, Japan (1978).

52. I. Oyake, "Parts representation in CAD/CAM", Proc. of National Computer Conference, Anaheim, Cal., p. 801 (1975).

53. R. E. Parent, "A system for sculpting 3-D data", Computer Graphics, 11: 138 (1977).

54. R. J. Popplestone, C. M. Brown, A. P. Ambler and G. F. Crawford, "Forming models of plane-and-cylinder faceted bodies from light stripes", Proc. 4th Int. Joint Conf. on Artificial Intelligence, Tbilisi, Georgia, USSR, p. 664 (1975).

55. K. Preiss, "A procedure for checking the topological consistency of a 2-D or 3-D finite element mesh", Proc. 16th Design Automation Conf., San Diego, Cal., p. 200 (1979).

56. D. R. Reddy and S. Rubin, "Representation of three-dimensional objects", Report CMU-CS-78-113, Computer Science Dept., Carnegie-Mellon Univ. (1978).

57. A. A. G. Requicha, "Part & assembly description languages I: Dimensioning & tolerancing", Tech. Memo. No. 19, Production Automation Project, Univ. of Rochester (1977).

58. A. A. G. Requicha, "Mathematical models of rigid solid objects", Tech. Memo. No. 28, Production Automation Project, Univ. of Rochester (1977).

59. A. A. G. Requicha and H. B. Voelcker, "Constructive solid geometry", Tech. Memo. No. 25, Production Automation Project, Univ. of Rochester (1977).

60. A. A. G. Requicha and R. B. Tilove, "Mathematical foundations of constructive solid geometry: General topology of regular closed sets", Tech. Memo. No. 27, Production Automation Project, Univ. of Rochester (1978).

61. R. Schuster, "System und Sprache zur Behandlung graphischer Information im rechnergestutzten Entwurf", Report KFK-2305, Kernforschungszentrum, Karlsruhe, W. Germany (1976).

62. H. Seifert, N. Bargele, and B. Fritsche, "Different ways to design three-dimensional representations of engineering parts with PROREN2", Proc. Conf. Interactive Techniques in Computer Aided Design, Bologna, Italy, p. 335 (1978).

63. M. I. Shamos, "Computational geometry", Ph.D. Dissertation, Yale Univ. (1978).

64. R. Shapira, "A technique for the reconstruction of a straight-edge, wire-frame object from two or more central projections", Computer Graphics and Image Processing, 3: 318 (1974).

65. G. Spur and J. Gausemeier, "Processing of workpiece information for producing engineering drawings", Proc. 16th Int. Machine Tool Design and Research Conference, Manchester, U.K., p. 17 (1975).

66. G. Spur, "Status and further development of the geometric modelling system COMPAC", Proc. Geometric Modeling Project Mtg., CAM-I, Inc., St. Louis, Mo. (1978).

67. R. B. Tilove, "Set membership classification: A unified approach to geometric intersection problems", IEEE Trans. on Computers, C-29 (1980).

68. H. B. Voelcker et al., "Discrete part manufacturing: Theory & practice", Part I of Tech. Report No. 1, Production Automation Project, Univ. of Rochester (1974).

69. H. B. Voelcker et al., "An introduction to PADL: Characteristics, status, and rationale", Tech. Memo. No. 22, Production Automation Project, Univ. of Rochester (1974).

70. H. B. Voelcker and A. A. G. Requicha, "Geometric modelling of mechanical parts and processes", Computer, 10: 48 (1977).

71. H. B. Voelcker et al., "The PADL-1.0/2 system for defining and displaying solid objects", Computer Graphics, 12: 257 (1978).

72. H. B. Voelcker et al., "Boundary evaluation procedures for objects defined via constructive solid geometry", Tech. Memo. No. 26, Production Automation Project, Univ. of Rochester (1980).

73. M. A. Wesley, T. Lozano-Perez, L. I. Lieberman, M. A. Lavin, and D. D. Grossman, "A geometric modelling system for automated mechanical assembly", IBM J. Research and Development, 24: 64 (1980).

74. T. C. Woo and R. F. Poshadlo, "A feature oriented design modification system", Proc. 1st Ann. Conf. on Computer Graphics in CAD/CAM Systems, Cambridge, Mass. (1979).

75. C. I. Yessios, "A notation and system for 3-D constructions", Proc. 15th Design Automation Conf., Las Vegas, Nev., p. 125 (1978).

Chapter 2

Construction and Use of Geometric Models.

Michael A. Wesley,

IBM Thomas J. Watson Research Center,
Yorktown Heights,
New York.

The material presented in this chapter draws heavily on the work of my colleagues at the Thomas J. Watson Research Centre and I gratefully acknowledge their permission to use their work.

2.1 INTRODUCTION.

The concept of a unified engineering data base containing full descriptions of the geometric and physical properties of objects and relationships among them is very appealing. Consider the following hypothetical scenario of the use of a comprehensive engineering data base in the future:

The mechanical engineer generates his initial design interactively, performing engineering calculations, and describing the properties and shape of each part. The properties may include such things as the material type, heat treatment parameters, and surface finish. The shape constitutes a complete description of the geometry of a part, where completeness is the ability to answer all relevant questions that may occur.

The engineering data base is now available for the simulation and validation of the design. Engineering properties, such as the strength, stiffness, vibrational characteristics, heat transfer, aerodynamics, etc. can be derived and fed back into a design modification process. In addition, the geometric relationships among the surfaces, holes, and other features of a part can be verified.

As the design development extends from a single part to multiple parts making up an assembly or mechanism, the relationships among parts can be investigated. Static interferences can be checked, dynamic interferences occuring as parts move along trajectories can be detected, mechanisms can be simulated, etc..

As the design moves into the manufacturing stage, the same engineering data base is used again. If a part is to be machined, the numerical control (NC) programs are generated automatically; if a part is to be cast or moulded, the dies are designed and the NC programs generated. If the part is to be formed, the process is simulated for input to later stages in the manufacturing process.

With the parts manufactured, assembly takes place. Fixtures are designed and manufactured, and robot programs for assembly, painting, inspection and quality control are generated.

As the product is released to the customer, documentation in terms of illustrations for instruction and service manuals is generated automatically.

Throughout this process the ability to feed back information and make design alterations exists. These changes may be as early as the initial design process before any real parts have been built, or as late as engineering changes towards the end of the life of the product.

The central ingredient in this scenario of the future is the engineering data base with its descriptions of the physical and geometric properties of objects; this data base is generated initially at the design stage and is updated and transformed as the manufacturing process unfolds. In this chapter the requirements of the data base are derived, and the role of the data base in the various stages of the scenario outlined above are discussed; algorithms and examples are presented indicating the potential for realisation of the scenario. The use of the data base in an overall information management system, such as inventory control or production scheduling, will not be considered explicitly, though the potential for such extensions exists.

2.2 THE DESIGN PROCESS.

The universal tool of design is the drawing [1]. Through drawings, which have been developed into a stylized art form, the designer is able to describe geometric properties by drawing outlines, generally in an abbreviated form, of a number of two dimensional views or projections of a three dimensional object. This shape information may be augmented by metric information in the form of dimensions, and auxiliary information such as material types, tolerances, and manufacturing processes to be used. This extra design information may be embedded in the drawing itself (e.g. dimensions), may be in the form of special symbols (e.g. welding specifications), and may be added as textual footnotes on the drawing sheet (e.g. manufacturing processes). Although drawing standards exist, the designer has considerable freedom in selecting the nature of the views provided, the level of detail included (or, more important, omitted in order to prevent the drawing becoming too confusing), whether to include auxiliary detail views in complex areas, and whether to draw external or cross section views.

When humans view a design expressed as a set of 2-D drawings they interpret the design using a vast amount of experiential knowledge about drawings and about the nature of the objects being represented. Thus humans are able to correlate sets of complex drawings (which may be incomplete or ambiguous in a mathematical sense) with textual information embedded in the drawings, and visualize the 3-D properties of the object being represented.

From the point of view of generating and using an engineering data base as postulated in Section 2.1 above, it is clear that the nature and content of the information provided in the design process will have to be changed. In many ways the design process can be expected to be greatly simplified, though in other areas it may become more demanding because of the demand of computer based systems for exactness. The input of geometric information can be expected to be greatly simplified; the dimensions of objects are part of the object input data and separate dimensioning is no longer needed; unlike conventional drawings, the model *is* to scale, to accuracies far higher than those encountered in normal engineering practice. The declarative textual information will have to be entered in a form more directly related to the processes involved and the sub-components of the objects concerned. If the relative placement of parts is specified symbolically in terms of surfaces in contact, holes in alignment, etc., assembly drawings and exploded views can be generated automatically. It is important to note that although after the initial input many stages of the manufacturing process will take place automatically, pictorial information will still be necessary for the human to understand and verify the process.

2.2.1 The Data Base.

The comprehensive engineering data base introduced in Section 2.1 above contains all the information necessary to enable real objects to be simulated at the various stages of the manufacturing process[2,3]. The data base therefore contains not only descriptions of the geometric and physical properties of objects, but also contains information about the relationships between objects. These relationships may be geometric, for example the relative spatial positions of objects, and may be physical, for example the manner in which other objects constrain the motion of an object. In this section the design of a data base which allows representation of objects and their inter-relationships is presented. The design is based on the World Model of the Geometric Design Processor (GDP) [4]. The World Model was derived originally for use in the assembly environment of the AUTOPASS robot programming language[5]. It is readily extensible to meet the requirements of the comprehensive engineering data base and the simulation of the real physical world through the various stages of the production process.

The World Model is a graph structure in which each vertex represents a volumetric entity - a *part*, *sub-part*, or an *assembly*- and the edges are directed and labelled to indicate four kinds of relationships: *part-of*, *attachment*, *constraint*, and *assembly-component*. Figure 2.1 shows an example of a World Model graph structure.

An *object vertex* may represent one of three types of entities:

83

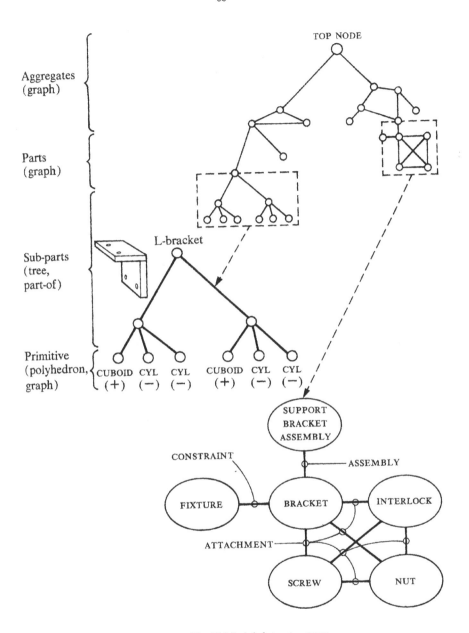

Figure 2.1 World Model data structure.

* A 3-dimensional *part* (e.g., a machine screw or L-bracket), whose shape is fixed but whose position and orientation may be changed.

* A *sub-part* (e.g., a screw-head or bore-hole), a volumetric entity out of which parts are composed.

* An *aggregate* (e.g., piston and crankshaft, or a model of a manipulator) whose constituent assemblies or parts bear a fixed functional relationship but whose internal geometry can change.

The role of a particular object vertex is determined by its context in the World Model structure and the value of its volume class attribute (described below). The attributes of a vertex are as follows:

Name - a symbolic name provided by the user.

Class - a list of classes to which the object belongs. These classes provide semantic information to the various planning components of the manufacturing system compiler. Examples of object classes are: *general object*, *fastener*, *assembly*, *hole*, *rotor*, and *locking device*. In the example the *L-Bracket* is a non-primitive, general object (see below for a discussion of primitive and non-primitive). Some of these classes are further qualified by type and may have associated geometric information. An example is *fastener* which may have type qualifiers such as *clip*, *bolt*, *nut*, etc..

Volume Class - defines the interpretation of the object vertex: A value of "PART" means this vertex is a part, in the sense described above. A value of "AGGREGATE" means this vertex is an assembly or aggregate. Values of "SOLID" or "HOLE" indicate that this vertex is a sub-part which adds or subtracts a volumetric component to/from the part or sub-part to which it belongs. (See below for a description of how positive and negative volumes are combined).

Geometric description - The general problems of the representation of solid objects have been considered in Chapter 1. The key point to be appreciated is that the geometric description must be expressed in terms of *volumetric* properties of objects (e.g which 3-D points are in material and which are in space), and how the component sub-parts of an object fit together (e.g. the surface topology). For algorithmic, programming, and computational reasons, the representation used here is polyhedral. Although many engineering objects rely on curved surfaces, particularly for bearings, the simplifications from restricting the representation to polyhedra are significant, and any object may in theory be represented to any desired degree of accuracy by increasing the number of facets in the polyhedral approximation. The polyhedral description is a set of point, edge, and surface list structures (Figure 2.2) accessed by a

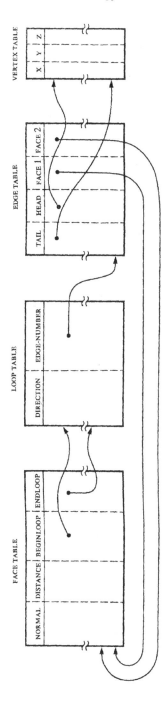

Figure 2.2 Data structure of a GDP polyhedron.

pointer at the object vertex. Individual elements of the polyhedron may be accessed, thus allowing the user to refer to *spatial features* of the object. The choice of representing shapes in terms of polyhedra results in closure under the set operations of union, intersection, and difference. This property provides a uniform geometric representation of primitive volumes, complex objects, and assemblies. The set operations are provided by the MERGE algorithm (see below).

Coordinate transformation - a 4x4 homogeneous transformation matrix which, when applied to a point in the object's coordinate frame, yields the point's coordinates in a world reference frame.

Physical properties - for example, material and weight, used in such calculations as centre of gravity and object stability.

Primitive parameters - If the object vertex represents an instance of one of the primitive volumes (see below), the arguments passed to the primitive object procedure are stored in the object vertex. For example, for a CUBOID, the X, Y and Z side-lengths would be stored.

An object vertex also contains a list of pointers to relational descriptors. These descriptors define physical relationships that the object has with other objects in the World Model. The relationships provided are:

Part-of - the part-of relation represents the logical containment of one object in another; it has several interpretations:

* A *part* may be *part-of* an *aggregate*. An *aggregate* can also be *part-of* another *aggregate*.

* A *sub-part* (represented by an object vertex with volume class "SOLID" or "HOLE") may be *part-of* a *part*, or of another *sub-part*.

Attachment - There are three types of *attachment relationships*: *rigid*, *non-rigid*, and *conditional*. Each descriptor indicates the type of attachment, the two objects related, and relative coordinate transforms between the two objects. In addition, non-rigid and conditional attachment descriptors contain information to qualify the particular relation. An important research topic is the derivation of attachment (and constraint) relationships from object properties in the data base; until this becomes feasible, most relationships must be declared by the user.

Rigid attachment occurs when no relative motion is possible between the frames of objects; the relationship may have a force qualifier that defines ranges of thrusts and torques over which the rigid attachment holds.

Non-rigid attachment occurs when objects cannot be separated by an arbitrarily large distance but relative motion between their frames is possible. Non-rigid attachments are the basis of the system's model of mechanisms and are classified on the basis of the type of mechanical joint they model. The representation of non-rigid attachment enables the system to analyze the kinematics of mechanisms. At present two joint types, linear and rotational, are permitted, though this may be extended later to include other types such as ball joint; both types may be qualified with force and spatial limits.

Conditional attachment is the representation of objects being supported by gravity (but not strictly attached). The relationship enables the system to move a part supporting another part. Qualifiers in the command define the range of orientations over which the support relationships will hold, so that, for example, the supported part is not allowed to fall off. These qualifiers form a condition list, each element of which is a spatial position, orientation, or velocity condition expressed parametrically as a linear inequality. The intent is that the attachment holds only as long as the constraints are met.

Constraint relationships - represent physical constraints of one object on another. A constraint is described by a type, a direction vector, a force threshold, and a pointer to the constraining object. A *translational constraint* specifies that the object cannot move in the given direction unless the force threshold is exceeded. A *rotational constraint* describes limits of rotation of an object about a given vector. Constraint relationships need to be updated whenever an object is moved to reflect newly created or removed physical constraints resulting from that movement, and may become attachments.

Assembly component - A type of aggregate called an *assembly* has special meaning in the World Model. It may be dynamically created during high level language compilation and represents a set of objects which is closed under *attachment* and *assembly*. An assembly vertex is created when an assembly naming statement is encountered in an AUTOPASS program [5]. This type of statement assigns a name and a coordinate frame to a vertex, and establishes the *assembly-component* relationship between that vertex and an object (specified in the statement). The programmer is thus dynamically declaring a new structure that can then be used like any other object in subsequent statements. Such an object does not have a polyhedral representation of its own but implicitly acquires the descriptions of the (transitively) attached chain of objects. Thus, an *assembly* allows grouping of assembled parts under one name for future reference.

2.2.2 Construction of Geometric Models.

The potential for application of computers to mechanical design has been recognized for at least 20 years [6]. Since that time much work has been done on the development of production systems both for the entry of a design into a computer data base and for the use of a mechanical design data base in design analysis and in manufacturing.

In the field of data base entry, computer draughting systems allow a designer to interact with a display or tablet to produce drawings of objects, generally in the classic manner of two dimensional projections of the edges of the three dimensional object. Some systems also provide the capability of representing data in three dimensions; for example, depth coordinates may be added to the elements of a two dimensional view, corresponding features in each of several views may be related, and isometric views may be constructed. These computer draughting systems have been engineered to very high levels of performance and can greatly enhance the productivity of a designer. As well as producing drawings of the edges of objects, computer draughting systems exist which allow the description of the surfaces of objects as smooth curves or patches splined together at their boundaries; in general these surfaces are represented by means of a discrete mesh superimposed on the surface.

However, for the most part, these systems do not deal in terms of volumetric descriptions, and the volumetric form of the data base is considered rather expensive to acquire. In the long term, the aim is to generate the World Model as part of the overall design process, with volumetric properties entered by means of an interactive design and draughting system, and relational properties entered by declaration statements. At present, the process of constructing geometric models is under development from both the representational and human factors points of view. In this section three methods of constructing geometric models are described:
- procedural description,
- interactive graphics, and
- data base conversion.

2.2.2.1 Procedural Description.

In the procedural description approach, an object is described by creating a program; execution of the program produces an instance of the object. The approach allows a structure that is meaningful to the user to be imposed on the object description. GDP allows the user to create such World Models by executing *procedural representations* of aggregates, parts, and subparts.

The specification which is used to create a World Model reflects the hierarchical structure defined by the *part-of* relation in the model itself. The user defines aggregates by listing the parts and aggregates from which they are composed. Similarly, parts (and sub-parts) are defined by grouping together collections of sub-parts:

Several other features are required to produce a complete description of the World Model: first, the user must be able to define the geometrical relationships among a set of entities which are *part-of* another entity. This amounts to being able to define the positions and orientations of those sub-entities in some suitable coordinate frame. Second, it is necessary to specify more exactly the relation between an entity and another entity which it is *part-of*. Specifically, the user must be able to indicate that one entity is a *part* and is *part-of* an *aggregate*. Also the user must be able to indicate that an entity is a *sub-part* which is *part-of* a *part* (or another *sub-part*) and in addition, whether the *sub*-part contributes a positive ("SOLID") or negative ("HOLE") volume to its super-part. Complex shapes can be formed by "gluing together" simpler shapes (formally, taking the union of polyhedral point sets). Conversely, one can use negative sub-parts ("HOLES") as "machine tools" that can cut and drill sections out of parts (taking the set difference of polyhedra). This ability greatly reduces the burden of describing all the points, lines, and surfaces which define a complex part's polyhedral representation; it is possible because of the MERGE algorithm for combining general polyhedra (see below).

The final feature needed to complete the hierarchical description process is a basis set of objects from which others can be defined. GDP supplies a set of seven *primitive objects* (see Figure 2.3). The primitive objects are "parameterized" in the sense that the user may invoke instances which vary in size, aspect ratio, fineness of polyhedral approximation (for curved objects), etc. Because the user-supplied object descriptions use the same procedural representation as the system-supplied primitive objects, the user can effectively "customize" and extend the set of primitives.

Defining Objects with Procedures

Following the work of Grossman [7], GDP implements the hierarchical object descriptions in the form of a procedural representation, in which aggregates, parts and sub-parts are represented by *object procedures*. An object procedure represents a "template" for an object. An activation of an object procedure corresponds to creating an *instance* of the object in 3-D space. An object procedure may have parameters, which change the form of

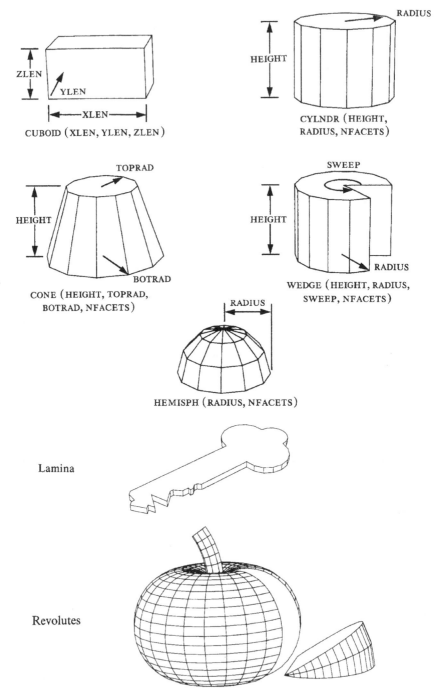

CUBOID (XLEN, YLEN, ZLEN)

CYLNDR (HEIGHT, RADIUS, NFACETS)

CONE (HEIGHT, TOPRAD, BOTRAD, NFACETS)

WEDGE (HEIGHT, RADIUS, SWEEP, NFACETS)

HEMISPH (RADIUS, NFACETS)

Lamina

Revolutes

Figure 2.3 Primitive objects.

the *instance* of the object resulting from an activation of that procedure. Such a procedure may represent a generic object; for example:

```
SCREW: PROCEDURE (LENGTH,DIAMETER,THREADSPERINCH,NSECTORS);
    /* OBJECT PROCEDURE DEFINING A MACHINE SCREW.
       NSECTORS IS THE NUMBER OF FACETS IN THE POLYHEDRAL
       APPROXIMATION OF THE CYLINDER THAT MODELS THE
       SHAFT OF THE SCREW.   */
    DECLARE (DIAMETER,HEADRADIUS,HEADTHICKNESS,LENGTH,
      NSECTORS SLOTDEPTH,SLOTTHICKNESS,THREADSPERINCH) FLOAT;
    CALL SOLID(SHAFT,'SHAFT',LENGTH,DIAMETER,THREADSPERINCH,
               NSECTORS);
    CALL ZTRAN(LENGTH);
    HEADTHICKNESS=DIAMETER;
    HEADRADIUS=DIAMETER;
    CALL SOLID(CYLNDR,'HEAD',HEADTHICKNESS,HEADRADIUS,NSECTORS);
    SLOTDEPTH=0.4*HEADTHICKNESS;
    SLOTTHICKNESS=0.5*SLOTDEPTH;
    CALL XYZTRAN(-HEADRADIUS,-SLOTTHICKNESS/2.0,
                 HEADTHICKNESS-SLOTDEPTH);
    CALL HOLE(CUBOID,'SLOT',2.0*HEADRADIUS,SLOTTHICKNESS,
              SLOTDEPTH);
END SCREW;
```

Activating this procedure with parameters (0.5, 0.25, 20, 16) will create an instance of a 1/4-20 screw of length 0.5, and, in the internal representation, will approximate the curved portions of the screw by 16 facets (Figure 2.4). Object procedures may call other object procedures, which corresponds to building an object up out of sub-objects, as described above. In the machine screw example the threaded shaft of the screw is defined and generated by another procedure SHAFT (not shown here). Object procedures are always called through one of four "generic" procedures: Calls to PART and AGGREGATE generate "PART" and "AGGREGATE" object vertices; calls to HOLE or SOLID generate object vertices corresponding to positive and negative sub-parts (The set of primitive object procedures are listed in Figure 2.5). In the example the slot in the head of the screw is formed by subtraction of the primitive CUBOID, in the statement that begins "CALL HOLE (CUBOID...". The actual parameters used in creating a primitive are always saved in the World Model data structure. By use of union and difference operators on pairs of volumes (primitive or not) very complex objects may be realized. While not all possible shapes can be realized, the domain of parts for mechanical assembly and most other tasks can be adequately approximated. Note that in this example another parameter "HEADTYPE" could have been included; in contrast to the other parameters which were

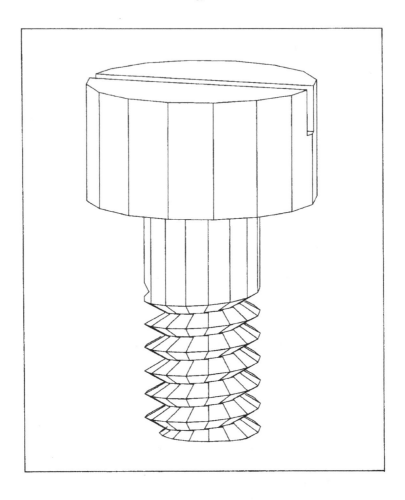

Figure 2.4 Result of procedure SCREW.

used to achieve essentially changes of scale, this parameter could be used for conditional selection of screw head types which are totally different topologically and geometrically. Thus the ability to pass parameters to a procedure allows very general representation of families of parts.

So far, objects have been described only by their shape; their locations and orientations in 3-D space must also be established. Associated with the object procedure interpreter is a *position cursor*, a current reference frame having a 3-D location and orientation. Any activation of an object procedure causes the reference frame to be passed to it. The procedure defines the object with respect to the reference frame. The user can manipulate, store, and retrieve the position cursor through a number of PL/I procedures supplied with the system. In the example the call to ZTRAN moves the reference frame from one end of SHAFT to the end where the HEAD is to be positioned. (The frame manipulation and other auxiliary procedures are listed in Figure 2.6).

In addition to calling other object or frame manipulation procedures, an object procedure can perform arbitrary computations to the limit of the base language (PL/I). This is illustrated by the line:

SLOTDEPTH = 0.4 * HEADTHICKNESS;

This, together with the ability to pass parameters between object procedures, greatly increases the power and flexibility of object definitions.

Interpreting Procedural Descriptions

The procedural representation is converted into a World Model by compiling and executing the object procedures in a context where the GDP primitives are defined. Executing the object procedures builds the World Model data structure as follows:

Any invocation of one of the generic object procedures (HOLE, SOLID, PART, or AGGREGATE) results in the allocation of an object vertex in the World Model. The volume-class for that vertex is specified by the called procedure ("HOLE", "SOLID", etc.). If a name for the object vertex was supplied, it is stored in the vertex. If the "called object" is one of the GDP-supplied primitives, a polyhedral representation of the primitive object, based on the object parameters and the position cursor, is bound to the object vertex.

In the case of non-primitives, the user-supplied object procedure (e.g., SCREW) is then invoked; usually it will invoke other user-supplied or primitive object procedures. Except for the case of *aggregates*, the next step is to create a polyhedral representation of the

```
                          (CUBOID,"name",XLEN,YLEN,ZLEN);

                          (CYLNDR,"name",HEIGHT,RADIUS,NFACETS);

        HOLE              (WEDGE,"name",HEIGHT,RADIUS,SWEEP,NFACETS);

        SOLID             (CONE,"name",HEIGHT,TOPRAD,BOTRAD,NFACETS);
CALL
        PART              (HEMISPH,"name",RADIUS,NFACETS);

        AGGREGATE         (LAMINUM,"name",DATA-ARRAY);

                          (REVOLUTE,"name",DATA-ARRAY);

                          (user supplied object procedure,parameter-list);
```

Figure 2.5 Primitive object procedures.

```
        X

        Y
CALL        TRAN  (DIST);   /*Translate position cursor*/
        Z

        XYZ


        X

CALL    Y ROT      (ANGLE); /*Rotate position cursor*/

        Z


        X

CALL    Y MIRROR;           /*Reflect position cursor about axis*/

        Z


        STORE
CALL              (COORDINATE-FRAME);
        RECALL
```

Figure 2.6 Auxiliary World Model definition procedures.

non-primitive part or sub-part. To do this, it is necessary to combine the polyhedral representations of the sub-parts according to their specified polarity ("HOLE" or "SOLID"). This task is performed by the MERGE algorithm, which realizes the complete range of set operations on arbitrary polyhedra. The algorithm takes two polyhedra, described by lists of points, lines, and surfaces, and yields a new polyhedron which is either the union, intersection, or difference of its arguments (see Figure 2.7 for definitions of these operations).

As the procedural representations are interpreted, successive applications of the MERGE algorithm are used to build up quite complex shapes, as illustrated in Figure 2.8. The MERGE algorithm can also be invoked directly in GDP, allowing the World Model to be altered and subsequently re-merged. Systems that do not have this operation are unable to generate explicit forms of composite objects. Without explicit representation of the objects at higher nodes of the tree, it is relatively difficult to perform operations that depend on the volume properties of the composite object, for example robot path planning or even finding the volume of an object, without putting strong constraints on the structure of the tree.

2.2.2.2 Interactive Graphics.

A natural alternative to the compiled procedural descriptions discussed in Section 2.2.2.1 is the construction of the procedure interactively at a graphics terminal. The designer interacts with a 2-D display screen using a keyboard, a cursor, and perhaps a light pen to indicate position and parameter values. As each sub-object is entered, be it a system primitive or a user-defined macro object, the new model component is added to the display in suitable form. The model component parameters and positions may be specified symbolically as relationships between *spatial features* of objects, for example as alignments between edges and faces, or user defined auxilliary coordinate frames, or may be entered numerically at the keyboard. The screen may contain multiple views from any viewpoint, with perspective or orthographic projections. The rendering may be according to selected drawing standards with hidden lines suppressed or dashed, variable line thicknesses, etc.. Dimensions may be generated and overlaid automatically.

The designer is therefore now able to express a design directly in 3-D rather than as multiple 2-D projections. The issue is to determine whether designing in 3-D, or at least a representation of 3-D on a 2-D screen, is a function that humans can perform well. The amount of specification needed from the designer is certainly reduced significantly; for example, a single cuboid entered in terms of its origin and extents (i.e. four points) will automatically appear correctly as rectangles in three orthographic views. The results so far

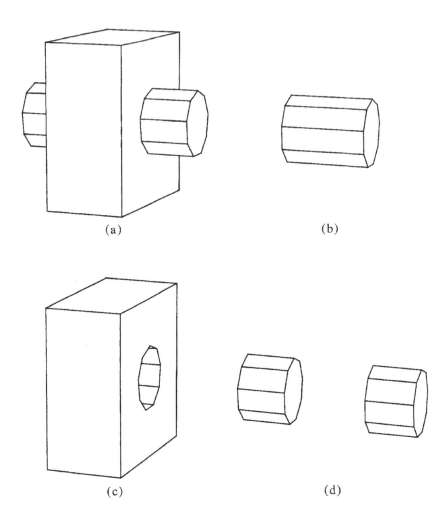

(a)   (b)

(c)   (d)

Figure 2.7 MERGE operations: (a) union; (b)intersection; (c) and (d) difference.

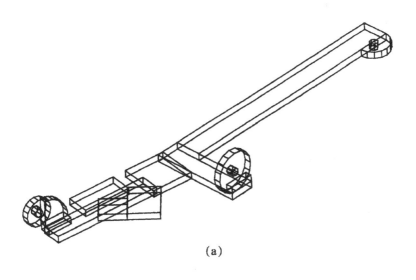

(a)

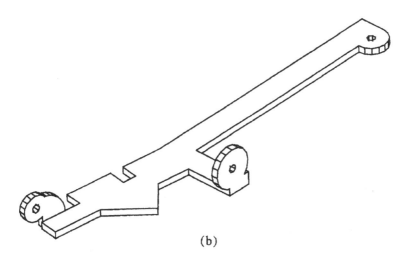

(b)

Figure 2.8 MERGE example: (a) components before merging; (b) resulting object.

on the human factors of interactive solid design are very encouraging[8], particularly in the case of objects that are hard to visualize from 2-D projections.

2.2.2.3 Data Base Conversion.

As mentioned above, many existing computer based design systems emulate the old-fashioned manual draughting process and describe objects in terms of 2-D projections of edges and vertices. Further, there is a large existing data base of designs that have been generated in this format. At present, the volumetric form of the data base is considered to be rather difficult and expensive to acquire, and design analysis data are generated in a computer assisted manner. For example, in the case of numerically controlled machine tools, the path of the cutter may be input over a drawing at a graphics terminal. This section presents an algorithm, due to Markowsky and Wesley [9], for automatically bridging the gap between these two computer representations of object geometry, i.e. from an object described in terms of its edges (a *Wire Frame*), to a volumetric description in terms of solid material, empty space, and the topology of surfaces and edges. In its present form, the algorithm is restricted to objects whose surfaces are planar. However, since the algorithm is a topological algorithm, it could be adapted to non-planar surfaces.

Quite apart from its practical applications, the problem is of some theoretical interest. An edge description does not necessarily represent a unique object, and an algorithm should be able to detect ambiguities, enumerate solutions, and accept user decisions as to which solution is required. As with many geometrical problems, the simple cases are straightforward and the complex cases are extremely difficult; for example, many patholog-ical cases can exist - vertices and edges contacting faces, and coplanar opposing faces meeting with edge contact.

Although the literature on geometric modeling is extensive and growing rapidly [10], few authors have chosen to represent objects formally. They are therefore generally unable either to prove the correctness of their methods, to handle the full range of patho-logical cases and ambiguities that occur in practice, or even to describe objects precisely. However, the PADL project [11] has based its work on point set topology and is able to prove the correctness of algorithms for computing the set operations of union, intersection and difference between polyhedra. In the fuller description of this Wire Frame algorithm [9] polyhedra are defined formally, and the algorithm is described in terms of algebraic topology. Idesawa [12,13] describes a wire frame reconstruction scheme as part of the general problem of constructing solids from many 2-D projections. The method used is based on finding sets of co-planar edges and fitting them together to form solid objects; however, the reconstruction method is not based on a formal description of objects and does not handle ambiguities or many of the pathological cases. Experience in modeling has shown that even though pathological relationships among faces, edges, and vertices may not be physically realizable, they do occur frequently in the stylized world of geometric modeling, and a general purpose modeling system should be able to handle them. Lafue [14] also describes a program for generating solids from 2-D projections, but requires that objects be described in terms of faces rather than edges; further, faces are described in a stylized manner with extra edges to permit description of holes.

Other authors have considered the machine vision problem of recognizing polyhedral objects from incomplete edge descriptions [15-17]. In this situation local ambiguities can exist and are resolved, if possible, by global propagation. The propagation is performed by labeling areas, whereas the algorithm described in this paper handles ambiguities in terms of volume regions. The use of volumes rather than areas leads to a much simpler handling of the process of labeling.

The goal of the Wire Frame Algorithm is to construct all objects which have a given wire frame. It is a fairly elaborate algorithm with quite a few distinct stages. The key stages of the algorithm are outlined below.

Stages of the Algorithm

1. *Checking Input Data*: The input data are assumed to be a valid Wire Frame, that is the ordered pair of vertices and edges $(V(\mathcal{O}), E(\mathcal{O}))$. In this stage the input data may be checked for various kinds of errors such as non-distinct vertices and edges. The choice of actual tests performed is based on the source of the input data and the expected types of errors.

2. *Finding Planar Graphs*: All planes which contain at least two intersecting edges are found. A canonical normal is defined and a graph of coplanar edges formed for each distinct plane. For each vertex lying in a plane a circular list of edges meeting that vertex in the plane is created and ordered counter-clockwise with respect to the canonical normal.

3. *Calculation of Virtual Faces*: In each planar graph the set of partitioning cycles is uncovered (bridges are ignored). The nesting relationships among these cycles are then determined, and all candidates for faces found. These candidates are called *virtual faces*.

4. *Checking for Illegal Intersections between Virtual Faces*: Two virtual faces can intersect illegally, i.e. so that both cannot be faces of the real object, in only two ways. These intersections are detected in this stage and appropriate action taken:
   -A type I intersection occurs an when interior point of an edge of one face pierces an interior point of the other face. The former virtual face is deleted.

-A type II intersection occurs when there is no type I intersection, yet a vertex of one face is in the plane of the other and there exists a point that is interior to both faces. A decision on the faces cannot be made at this stage, and temporary additional edges called *cutting edges* are introduced. These cutting edges cut some of the virtual faces discovered in Stage 3 into new, smaller, virtual faces.

5. *Calculation of Virtual Blocks*: For each edge a circular list of the virtual faces containing that edge is created. This list is ordered radially around the edge. These lists are used to find all partitioning cycles of the virtual face graph; the nesting relationships among these cycles are found and used to uncover all candidates for solid regions. These candidates are called *virtual blocks*. Virtual blocks are bounded by virtual faces and partition $\mathbb{R}^3$. Any virtual face which does not belong to two different virtual blocks is dropped.

6. *Constructing All Solutions for the Wire Frame*: A decision tree, based on virtual blocks and using a few basic tests, assigns solid or hole state to all virtual blocks and thereby constructs all possible objects having a given wire frame. In this decision process, edges and cutting edges are treated separately; cutting edges are subsequently removed.

A number of examples chosen to illustrate particular features of the algorithm and taken from [9] are shown in Table 2.

Table 2a shows a double tetrahedron. Seven triangular virtual faces are found, being the six outside faces and the internal area bounded by the waist of the figure. Three virtual blocks are found; the decision process assigns solid state to (1) and (2); block (3) is the unbounded virtual block; (1) and (2) are combined to produce the output object.

Table 2b shows an object with 1-D bridges on the faces containing abcd and kmnp. The plane graphs contain three bridges ef, kl and op, none of which appear in the virtual faces for the planes shown. Two virtual blocks are found, one the output object, and one the unbounded virtual block.

Table 2c shows four cubes positioned on two levels with four shared vertices enclosing a rectangular area abcd; abcd is found to be a virtual face, but in the virtual block building process is detected to be a 2-D bridge (i.e., it is assigned opposite directions in the same virtual block to become a zero thickness sheet), and is not used in the output objects.

Table 2d contains an octohedron extended by a cube and pierced by a vertical square prism. The two plane graphs containing abcd and efgh have Class I intersections with the vertical sides of the hole and therefore are not virtual faces. Six virtual blocks are found and assigned states as shown.

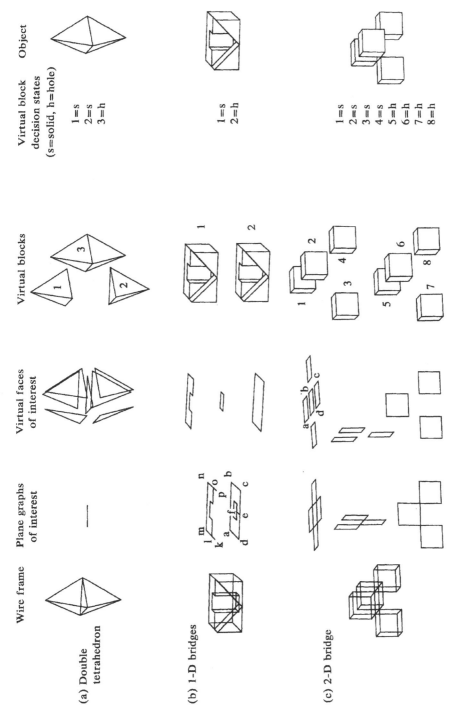

Table 2. Examples of the Wire Frame algorithm.

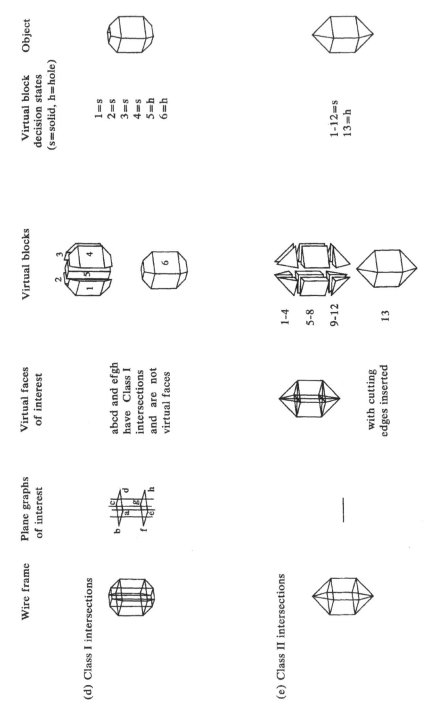

Table 2. Examples of the Wire Frame algorithm - continued.

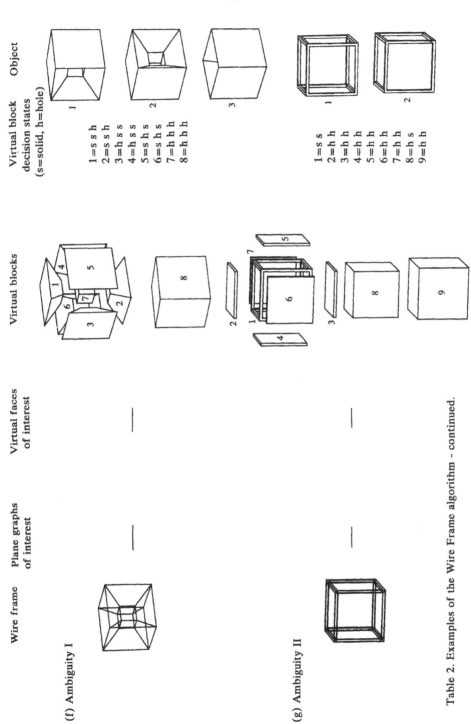

Table 2. Examples of the Wire Frame algorithm - continued.

Table 2e shows the object of Table 4.1d without the piercing hole. Four face graphs with Class II intersections occur and are shown as virtual faces with cutting edges inserted. Thirteen virtual blocks are found and assigned states as shown.

Table 2f shows a well known ambiguous wire frame [18]; eight virtual blocks are found and the decision process enumerates three valid solutions: one pair of opposing blocks ((1,2), (3,4), or (5,6)) must have hole state, the centre block (7) always has hole state.

Table 2g shows another ambiguous wire frame that could well occur in practice. Nine virtual blocks are formed; the decision process finds that block (8) can have hole or solid state.

Figure 2.9a, also taken from [9], shows a more complicated wire frame with 1256 edges and 850 vertices. In the course of the reconstruction process the Wire Frame algorithm finds 93 virtual blocks, most of them being window holes and enclosed volumes inside tubular members of the structure, and generates the volumetric representation shown in Figure 2.9b. This example shows that the Wire Frame algorithm can handle problems of realistic engineering complexity.

2.3 THE DESIGN ANALYSIS PROCESS.

At any stage of the initial design and subsequent refinement process, the designer may perform design analysis studies appropriate for the level of detail of the design entered thus far. These studies may be for individual objects, or for study of interactions between objects in an assembly. The results of the analysis may be used to confirm the validity of the design or to provide guidance for corrective actions to be taken. The analysis tools covered in this section are:
  - computation of basic engineering properties such as surface area, volume, centre of gravity, etc.,
  - generation and use of finite element models for analysis of properties expressed by two or three dimensional partial differential equations, for example heat flow and elastic deformation,
  - study of design correctness in terms of relationships between parts, for example:
    - whether parts fit correctly,
    - whether parts move freely,
    - whether mechanisms move correctly,
    - whether tolerance distributions are correct.

Figure 2.9 Wire Frame algorithm: (a) Input Wire Frame with 1256 edges and 850 vertices; (b) Output volumetric representation of Wire Frame.

2.3.1 Basic Engineering Properties.

Given a geometric model with the attributes discussed in 2.2.1 above, basic engineering properties such as edge length, surface area, volume, centre of gravity, and moments of inertia may readily be calculated by appropriate integration of the model elements[19]. The results given in this section are based on a polyhedral model representation, similar results may be derived for models with higher order surfaces.

The above properties may be expressed in terms of integrals - a single integral for edge length, a double integral for area, and triple integrals for the volume moments. As a single integral, the total edge length L of an object $\mathcal{O}$ may be expressed directly as:

$$L_e = \sum_{\text{edge}_i \in \mathcal{O}} l_i$$

where l_i is the length of edge$_i$ and is given by:

$$l_i = ((v_{hi} - v_{ti}) \bullet (v_{hi} - v_{ti}))^{1/2}$$

where $\bullet$ represents the scalar or dot product of two vectors.

The higher order integrals may be derived by projection from a projection point P. When P is at infinity, the projection is parallel and is onto a line for double integrals, and onto a plane for triple. The treatment here will be in terms of finite P.

The total surface area of an object $\mathcal{O}$ is given by:

$$A_s = \sum_{\text{face}_i \in \mathcal{O}} a_i$$

where a_i is the area of face$_i$, which has the plane equation (n_i, d_i). To compute a_i, choose a convenient projection point in the plane of face$_i$ say one of the vertices v_1 of face$_i$, then the area a_i is the sum of the signed areas of the triangles formed by P and each directed edge in the face in sequence:

$$a_i = \frac{1}{2} n_i \bullet \left\{ \sum_{j=2, \, v_j \in \mathcal{O}}^{n-1} (v_j - v_1) \times (v_{j+1} - v_1) \right\}$$

where $\times$ represents the vector or cross product of two vectors.

The triple integrals may be evaluated by choosing a convenient projection point in three space, say the origin O, and evaluating the integral for the tetrahedron formed by O and, in each face, each set of three vertices formed by a fixed vertex and each of the directed edges in sequence. The signed volume of a tetrahedron with vertices O, v_1, v_i, v_{i+1} is given by:

$$v = \frac{1}{6}\{(v_1 - O) \times (v_i - O)\} \bullet (v_{i+1} - O)$$

The centre of gravity is given by:

$$G = \frac{O + v_1 + v_i + v_{i+1}}{4}$$

The signed moment of inertia may be derived as follows:

1. - Let r be a unit vector through O;
   the moment of inertia I_b of a uniform bar of length a about an axis through its mid-point and parallel to r, and making an angle α with the bar is:

$$I_b = \int_{-a/2}^{a/2} \sin^2\alpha \, x^2 dx = \frac{\sin^2\alpha \, a^3}{12}$$

2. - The moment of inertia I_Δ of a triangle $v_1v_2v_3$ about an axis through its centroid, parallel to r, making an angle α with the base of the triangle, and making an angle β with the median to the base is:

$$I_\Delta = \sin\gamma \int_0^c \left\{ \left(\frac{\lambda b}{c}\right)^3 \frac{\sin^2\alpha}{12} + \frac{\lambda b}{c}\left(\lambda - \frac{2c}{3}\right)^2 \sin^2\beta \right\} d\lambda$$

$$= \sin\gamma \frac{bc}{12}\left(\frac{b^2 \sin^2\alpha}{4} + \frac{c^2 \sin^2\beta}{3}\right)$$

$$= \frac{A_\Delta}{6}\left(\frac{b^2 \sin^2\alpha}{4} + \frac{c^2 \sin^2\beta}{3}\right)$$

where b is the length of the base,
   c is the length of the median to the base,
   γ is the angle between the base and the median to the base, and
   A_Δ is the area of the triangle.

3. - The signed moment of inertia $I_{\Delta r}$ of a tetrahedron $Ov_1v_2v_3$ about r may be found by integration along the axis of centroids of slices parallel to face $v_1v_2v_3$:

Let **G** be the centroid of the face $v_1v_2v_3$:
$$G = \frac{v_1 + v_2 + v_3}{3},$$
d be the length of the axis of centroids: $d=|G|$,

e be the perpendicular distance from **G** onto **r**: $e = |G \times r|$, and

δ be the signed angle between the axis of centroids and the normal to the plane of v1v2v3,

Then

$$I_{\Delta r} = \left(I_\Delta + A_\Delta e^2\right)\frac{\cos\delta}{d^4}\int_0^d \lambda^4 d\lambda$$

$$= \left(I_\Delta + A_\Delta e^2\right)\frac{d\cos\delta}{5}$$

The total volume of $\mathcal{O}$ is given by:

$$V_\mathcal{O} = \sum_{face_i \in \mathcal{O}}\left\{\sum_{edge_j \in face_i} v_{ij}\right\}$$

The overall centre of gravity of $\mathcal{O}$ is given by:

$$G_\mathcal{O} = \frac{1}{V_\mathcal{O}}\sum_{face_i \in \mathcal{O}}\left\{\sum_{edge_j \in face_i} G_{ij}v_{ij}\right\}$$

The overall moment of inertia of $\mathcal{O}$ about **r** is given by:

$$I_{\mathcal{O}r} = \sum_{face_i \in \mathcal{O}}\left\{\sum_{edge_j \in face_i} {}^rij\right\}$$

2.3.2 Finite Methods for Higher Level Engineering Properties.

A wide range of physical properties of volumetric objects can be expressed by 3-dimensional partial differential equations with boundary conditions. The equations are often Laplacian of the form $\nabla^2\theta = \phi(x,y,z,t)$, and the boundary conditions are generally at the surface of the object. Such equations may be used to represent many important physical properties, for example, heat flow in semi-conductor chips, and plastic deformation of an object under load.

Such problems may be solved by means of finite difference or finite element numerical methods. In the finite difference approach a solution may be generated, possibly by relaxation, over a mesh of discrete points distributed through the body of the object and positioned so that the equation and boundary conditions may readily be expressed and evaluated. Given a mesh of well chosen points, numerical methods are generally available for the solution of the equation. The outstanding problem is the one of generation of the discrete element mesh. At present this is done in a largely manual manner, building, say, hexahedra to fill the object, and possibly using an interactive graphics system.

The finite element approach, which was intended originally for problems in structural analysis, and has been generalized to field problems such as heat flow, represents objects by finite area or volume elements interacting at their boundaries[20]. Again, numerical methods exist for solution once a discrete finite element form of the problem has been defined, and have been embedded in extensive program packages, for example NASTRAN[21]. In both finite element and finite difference methods an important step forward will come when the mesh can be generated automatically from a geometric model [22].

2.3.3 Design Validation.

Design validation here is concerned with investigating geometric interference relationships between parts. The aim is to be able to answer questions of the form:

- do parts fit together correctly in a static sense, or do they interfere?
- do parts interfere in a dynamic sense as they are moved, either individually, or as components of a mechanism?
- what is the smallest distance or the closest approach between parts?
- what is the effect of tolerances on the above questions?

In contrast to the standard draughting methods of showing the relationships between objects by means of an assembly drawing, an interactive geometric graphics system allows the designer to "fly" objects into the correct relative positions. However, a much more powerful technique with advantages when an assembly is the subject of design reviews, and the positioning has to be simulated many times, is the use of a symbolic descriptions of placement. A symbolic description may express geometric relationships (for example, co-planarity and co-linearity) between *spatial features* of objects (for example, faces, edges, vertices, and axes of holes, etc.). The significance of the approach is that it allows a procedural description of an assembly sequence; execution of an assembly procedure causes models of the parts to be fetched from a parts library and a scene composed with the objects in their correct relative positions. If the designs of objects are changed so that the positions of features are changed, then re-execution of the procedure allows the scene to be re-composed with the parts positioned automatically in their new relative positions. If the assembly is purely sequential, then a single stream procedure suffices; if the assembly requires parallel operations (e.g. parta-A must be held in position whilst part-B is inserted) then parallel processes can be used. However, since no test of physical realisability is being postulated for the part placement process (that is, no test is being made on whether it is physically possible for the parts to reach the desired position), the parallel process can be implemented in an interleaved sequential manner.

The problem of determining whether an assembly is physically realisable, that is whether there is a collision-free path for a part to its final position, is another use for the collision-free trajectory generator described below (Section 2.6.1.2). In this case the supposition is that if no valid, i.e. collision-free, path can be found for the object alone to reach the final position, then no such trajectory exists and the assembly cannot be built.

In performing design validation on scenes containing complicated arrangements of complex parts, the limitations of a 2-D display screen become very apparent, and the user may easily mis-interpret the view on the screen and fail to recognize error and collision situations. The recommended approach is therefore to perform overall global checks, for example for interference, to view highlighted results on an overall view of the scene, and then to zoom in and examine regions of interest in greater detail.

Interference tests between polyhedral objects will only be meaningful when the accuracy of any polyhedral approximation to curved surfaces is less than the minimum intended distance between parts. Although a polyhedral approximation may be made arbitrarily accurate by introducing more faces, the computational load may also become arbitrarily large. Thus interference testing with polyhedral models is not seen to be viable in situations with very small clearances between curved surfaces, for example high precision mechanisms such as occur in a mechanical watch or clock.

2.3.3.1 Static Design Validation.

When simulating the spatial positions of solid objects, it is readily possible to generate physically unrealisable situations with objects or components of objects occupying the same region of space. Tests for interference are therefore based on simulating the objects in their desired positions and testing for various types of interference between them.

In testing for static mechanical interference between two objects A and B, a system should be able to detect the following situations:

1- A and B disjoint. There is no interference.

2- A and B touch externally; no interior point of A is interior to B, and vice versa. This is a normal, correct, condition in mechanical assembly, and there is no interference.

3- A is partially inside and partially outside B, or vice versa. This is a condition that may arise through minor errors in part positioning or tolerances.

4- A and B touch internally, with interior points of A interior to B, or vice versa. This situation usually occurs through orientation errors in the positioning of the parts.

5- A is totally contained within the interior of B, or vice versa.

These cases are illustrated in Figure 2.10.

In general, tests for interferences involving the boundaries of objects, that is cases 2,3, and 4 above are implemented by investigating the relationships between pairs of faces, one from each object. In the case of polyhedral models, it is necessary to test only for a point of an edge of one face being contained in the interior or boundary of the other. Computationally this may be achieved by using utility functions provided internally in GDP. These utilities include such operations as INFACE, which determines whether a given point is in the material, boundary, or outside of a face, INOBJ, which performs a similar function for an object, and INDIRN, which determines whether moving from a given point in a given direction is in the exterior, surface, or interior of an object.

The algorithm proceeds as follows:

for each edge (e_{Ai}) of face$_i$ (f_{Ai}) of object A:
  for each face$_j$ (f_{Bj}) of object B:
    if a point P of e_{Ai} is contained in the plane of f_{Bj} then:
      test for P being contained in f_{Bj} (this is an INFACE test)
        if P is an interior point of both e_{Ai} and f_{Bj}, then case 3 has occurred; P is entered into a list of new interference points (NIP).

        else if P is a boundary point of either e_{Ai} or f_{Bj}, then one of cases 2,3, or 4 exists. Which of these cases exists may be determined by investigating whether moving along e_{Ai} away from P is entering material of B (this is an INDIRN test). If P is a vertex of A or B, then P is entered into a list of old interference points (OIP).

repeat for edges of B against faces of A.

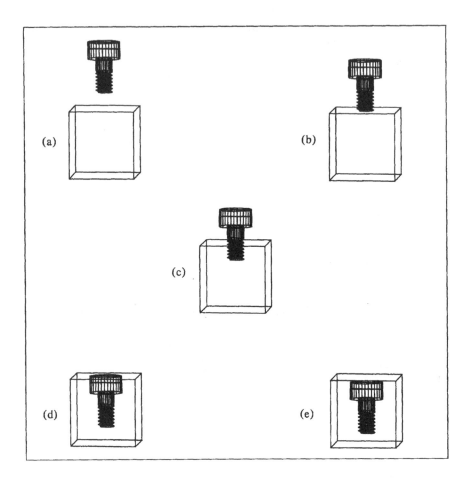

Figure 2.10 Classes of static interference: (a) disjoint; (b) external contact; (c) interpenetration; (d) internal contact; (e) total containment.

If no contact between faces is detected, then one or both cases 1 and 5 exist. A and B are partitioned into their sets of disjoint edge sub-graphs. One vertex from each subgraph of A is tested for containment in each subgraph of B, and vice-versa.

The above tests are sufficient to decide amongst the five classes of interferences (note that the classes are not mutually exclusive). Suitable response messages, together with the ability to display the lists of points NIP and OIP overlaid on views of the objects, enable the user to investigate the nature of interferences.

An important extension to the static interference tests discussed above is the ability to determine the minimum distance between two objects. Assuming that the two objects are disjoint (case 1 above), the minimum distance between them may be derived as the minimum distance between their boundaries (faces), which in turn may be investigated by determining the minimum distance between a boundary of one face (an edge or vertex) and the other face.

The minimum distance between an edge of object A (e_{Ai}) and a face of object B (f_{Bj}) may occur at either an interior or a boundary point of of f_{Bj}. To test for a minimum at an interior point of f_{Bi}, the minimum distance between e_{Ai} and the plane of f_{Bj} is found; this occurs at one or both ends of e_{Ai}. The vertex (or vertices) of e_{Ai} are projected orthogonally onto the plane of f_{Bj}. If this projection point is interior to f_{Bj} (INFACE test), then this is the minimum distance between e_{Ai} and f_{Bj}. Otherwise the minimum distance occurs at the boundary of f_{Bj}, and is found as the minimum distance between e_{Ai} and $e_{Bk} \in f_{Bj}$.

2.3.3.2 Dynamic Design Validation.

In the case of dynamic interference, that is, interference and contacts generated as objects move relative to each other, it is assumed that objects do not penetrate (i.e. not classes 3,4,or 5 above) at the start of a motion. The problem then becomes one of testing for new collisions between boundaries as objects move. Following the approach of Boyse [23], faces of two polyhedral objects may collide, as one moves in a trajectory relative to the other, in only two ways:

    1 -a vertex of one object may pierce a face of the other; this test must be performed for A moving past B and vice versa,

    2 -an edge of one may cut an edge of the other; this test need be performed only once.

These cases hold true for all trajectories; solutions are discussed below for two types of trajectories: translation or rotation of one object past a stationary object for both classes of collision. Since translations may be added vectorially, the case of both objects translating simultaneously is also covered; other cases, many of which are interesting (e.g. two doors opening, and general motions of mechanisms and manipulators with many joints in series), remain to be solved.

In the solutions to be discussed below, it is important to note that although the objects themselves are polyhedral, and may be approximations to objects with curved surfaces, the trajectories are analysed in terms of continuous motion; the computation is therefore both fast and accurate.

A vertex of an object translating or rotating moves in either a straight line or a circle in a plane perpendicular to the axis of rotation. The test for a point on the vertex trajectory being in the plane of a face, followed by an INFACE test is straightforward and lists of interference points are generated.

An edge moving under a general translation sweeps out a parallelogram, and under a rotation sweeps out a hyperboloid of revolution. In both cases the penetration point of the swept surface by an edge of the other object may be derived.

The penetration information in both the edge and vertex cases may be presented to the user in terms of lists of vertices of the original objects (OVL) and new interference points (NIP); the points in these lists may be referred to both objects in their original positions. They may also be stored with a measure of the distance along the trajectory at which the collision point was found. Thus the distance sequence of collisions may be established, and in particular, the distance to first collision determined. This latter is the basis of the "move until touch" operation operation used in the simulation of robot programs below.

An example of the investigation of dynamic interference is shown in Figure 2.11. At (a) a gate is shown with its hinges. At (b) the gate is shown with its gate post. At (c) the result of a rotational interference test about the axis of the hinges is shown - the system has responded that the first collision occurred at 126.3° rotation, and has highlighted the collision points on both the gate and the gate post. At (d) the gate has been rotated by 126.3° and is seen to be just colliding with the gate post.

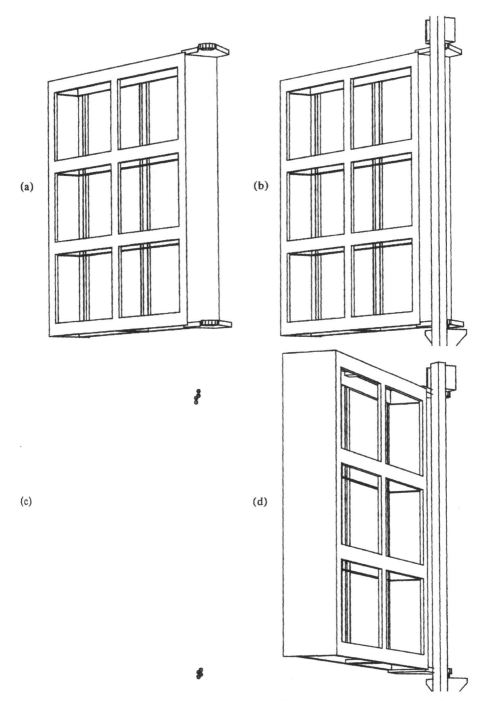

Figure 2.11 Dynamic interference: (a) Card gate; (b) Gate on gatepost; (c) Interference points at 126°; (d) Gate rotated 126°.

2.3.3.3 Analysis of Tolerances.

All parts are subject to variability in the manufacturing process. In cases where size deviation from the nominal is important or even critical, tolerances are specified as part of the design process and embedded in the engineering data base.

Variability in the dimensions of parts can be derived from the part design tolerance specifications, assuming that the manufactured part is within design tolerance. An overall design analysis system should be able to ensure that design dimensions and tolerances are specified consistently and completely at design time. This may be done analytically in some cases [24,25], though the full treatment of interacting tolerances appears to be rather complicated (e.g. simultaneous tolerances on dimensions, parallelism, and surface finish), particularly if mean and worst case statistics are required. Monte Carlo methods offer quick results with the least intellectual effort but may require large amounts of simulation time to generate reliable statistics [26].

From the point of view of representation of objects, design tolerances may cause severe problems if the tolerances are sufficiently large to change the topology of the object, that is, different instances of the part may have different topologies. Modeling systems that build explicit topological representations of objects may have considerable difficulty with this phenomenon.

2.3.4 Simulation of Mechanisms.

Application packages are commercially available for the simulation of the kinematics of certain classes of mechanisms; a geometric modeling system allows many opportunities for simulation of both the kinematics and dynamics of mechanisms.

Cases of mechanisms involving simple translation and rotation have already been covered in Section 3.3.2; the analysis there could be extended to handle some more complex motions. The approach to be described here is based on discrete simulation of the kinematics of mechanisms of arbitrary complexity.

An interactive modeling system such as GDP allows the components of a scene to be manipulated interactively by translation and rotation of objects; the extent of the motion may be either specified explicitly, or be determined by *move until touch* qualifiers. Thus by appropriate manipulation a mechanism can be exercised, and when critical positions are reached, further tests, for example, for closest approach, or verification of a cam rotation-displacement curve may be investigated in detail.

A more powerful approach is obtained with a macro instruction capability where a pre-stored file of commands is executed. A program can be written to analyze a mechanism of arbitrary complexity in arbitrarily fine discrete steps; this program can generate a file of modeling system commands (a macro instruction file) which, when executed with a model of the mechanism loaded, will cause the mechanism to step through its operating sequence. If desired, each sequential position of the mechanism may be drawn and may be photographed with a single frame motion picture camera for subsequent playback of a film of the animated mechanism.

Since the basic engineering properties of the components of a mechanism (i.e. the volume, mass, centre of gravity, and moments of inertia) may be derived for arbitrarily complex objects, these properties are also available to a program to analyse the dynamic properties of mechanisms.

Another approach to the analysis of mechanisms, which is still at the research stage, is the automatic generation of the kinematic properties of mechanisms from the assembly specification [27]. This approach is based on an understanding of the motion constraints imposed between objects by their geometries and relative placements.

2.4 THE GRAPHIC DOCUMENTATION PROCESS.

The engineering data base can be the source of all graphic documentation throughout the life of a design. In the short term, the documentation can be expected to continue to be in hard copy format, preferably on film rather than paper, but in the longer term the aim will be to do away with hard copy entirely and rely instead on soft copy graphics output devices. Thus, the main component of the documentation process is the ability to produce 2-D representations of 3-D objects; this will be in terms of real and contour edges of the object.

Algorithms exist to produce 2-D representations of 3-D objects according to many rules and specifications. In general, if the drawing process can be specified algorithmically, then it can be implemented automatically. Thus the following can readily be produced:
  - any projection, e.g axonometric or perspective,
  - any viewpoint, e.g. front, top, and side, or stereo pairs,
  - full dimensioning,
  - cross sections,

- selection of line types:
  - visible edges solid,
  - contour edges calculated,
  - occluded edges:
    omitted,
    dashed,
    etc..

Difficulties arise in areas which cannot be specified algorithmically, for example, those generally left to the discretion of the designer in order to make a drawing clearer. For the most part this involves decisions on what to leave out of the drawing, and algorithms attempting to imitate this process will be rather heuristic, may fail to produce acceptable output in some instances, and will need human guidance.

The computation of projection views, be they orthogonal or perspective, etc. with a given gaze point and eyepoint or gaze direction, is well established in interactive computer graphics [28]. In common with systems for depicting architectural scenes, it is necessary to allow for a viewpoint being surrounded by objects, for example in the view from the driver's cab of a vehicle.

In principle, every dimension may be included on a drawing; alternatively graph processing techniques may be used to prune the set of dimensions so that the drawing has just sufficient dimensions; however, there may be many ways of dimensioning a drawing, in terms of both drawing standards and and manufacturing processes, and operator guidance may be necessary to obtain a meaningful representation.

Cross sections may be produced explicitly by first producing a sectioned model. This may be done with MERGE DIFFERENCE operations, or a direct sectioning algorithm to cut an object at a surface. The explicitly sectioned model may then be drawn directly in the same manner as any other solid object model.

The choice of line representation has been extensively studied. The most important problem is that of determining occlusion in an efficient manner and many algorithms are available [29]. In general, numerical errors do not cause problems in producing drawings since it is relatively easy to preserve computational accuracy to the level of the finest resolvable detail on the graphic device. This is quite different from the situation that exists with a MERGE type of operation, where the output of one operation may be the input to another computational operation, and errors can propagate. Having determined that a line segment is indeed occluded, it may be omitted entirely (full hidden line suppression), or may be drawn with a special line type, for example dashed; this latter case leads to an interesting drawing problem in ensuring that dashed lines overlay each other in a sensible manner, i.e. that the line segments overlay line segments and the blank segments overlay blank segments. Since the full occlusion test can be very expensive in scenes with large numbers of edges (e.g.>5000), other techniques can be used to give approximate rendering, for example, omit all faces that point away from the viewer. In most situations the human is able to recognize errors in the drawing (extra lines have been drawn) but the potential for mistaken perception exists.

The techniques discussed above apply to scenes composed of multiple objects, though the occlusion algorithm needs to handle cases where an edge of one object is in contact with the surface of another object. Thus assembly drawings may be produced and, with suitable operations to move component objects along axes, exploded views may be produced. An example of an exploded view of an assembly is shown in Figure 2.12. As well as producing overall assembly views, detail views of localized regions may also be produced. All of these techniques may be used in the production of maintenance documentation as well as for use in the manufacturing process.

2.5 THE MANUFACTURING PROCESS.

The areas of application of geometric modelling to manufacturing operations considered here are cutting, forming, and joining.

2.5.1 Cutting Processes.

In cutting operations, numerically controlled (NC) machine tools represent a well established technology, though the current level of use and rate of installation of new equipment remain surprisingly low, due largely to the high cost of controls and, in particular, programming. Both of these costs can be expected to drop significantly in the near future. Languages exist for the specification of tool paths (e.g. APT [30]) and are generally used by specialized part programmers; these language processors often have graphics simulation capability for tool path verification. Another method of generating NC programs is available on some computer aided draughting systems and allows the designer to input a tool path over a drawing, with the system checking that with the specified tool the cutting path is indeed tangent to the surface. These computer assisted NC programming systems are generally 2 or 2.5-D in nature and can therefore handle only rather simple cases.

Figure 2.12 An exploded view of an assembly.

The advantages of being able to generate NC programs for both milling machines and lathes directly from geometric models has been recognized for some time [31,32], though the results so far are limited. The basic approach is to generate the surface which represents the locus of the reference coordinate frame for a specified cutter size and type such that the cutting action is tangential to the desired surface. A path is then found in this tool frame surface which generates the desired object surface to specified accuracy without making erroneous cuts into material. The first problem, that of surface generation is essentially a simplified form of the "growing" operation used in Section 2.6.1.2 for robot path planning, and is essentially solved for polyhedral objects[33]. The second problem, that of surface filling, is difficult and unsolved except for rather simple cases.

Another level of application of geometric models in cutting operations is the validation of an existing program. Although graphics simulation is already available, it is generally not based on volumetric models, and the role of the human is an essential and error-prone part of the process. In principle, geometric modelling can be used in either of two ways:

1. - to verify that only surface contact takes place between the volume swept out by a tool in its path and the model (class 2 interference as described in Section 2.3.3.1) [34].

2. - to subtract the swept volumes from the original block and see if the remaining object is indeed the desired object. A very simple example of this approach with an APT program is shown in Figure 2.13.

2.5.2 Forming processes.

The general problems of computer based modeling of the plastic flow of objects under load has been discussed in Section 2.3.2. These methods, although technically feasible, are currently expensive in both human and computer time. A simple case that is amenable to a simple though approximate solution is the bending of sheet metal parts [35].

2.5.3 Joining Processes.

Joining processes include such operations as gluing and welding. Two aspects are of interest: representation of the effects of the process, and execution of the process.

The concept of rigid attachment has already been covered in Section 2.2.1 and allows the basic idea of joining as a relationship between objects in the data base. Analysis of the strength of the joint, that is the *force qualifier*, must be performed in terms of the amount

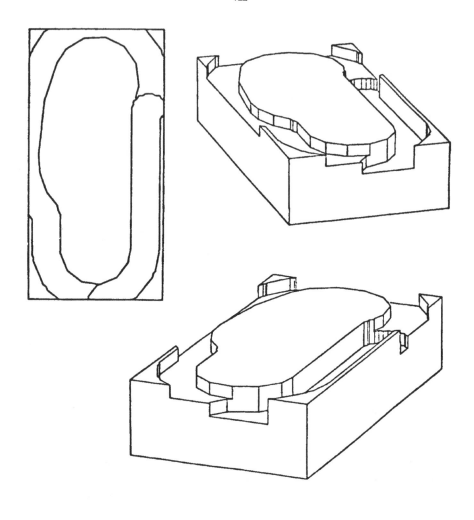

Figure 2.13 Simulation of an APT program.

of material deposited; this is particularly significant in welding where the cross section of the weld must be known.

The execution of the joining process is in principle an application area for industrial robots; in fact resistance spot welding of car bodies is the largest single application of industrial robots to date[36]. The problems are in the area of understanding the semantics of the tool, be it a glue gun or a welding torch, and the ability to execute and control suitable trajectories.

2.6 THE ASSEMBLY PROCESS.

Mechanical assembly is of major economic importance. Historically, all mechanical assembly operations were performed manually. As the requirements of assembly have grown, both in terms of complexity and volume, so has the desire to automate the process. One approach to the automation of the assembly process is the use of computer controlled industrial robots. Such machines have a number of motions that can move a gripping mechanism around the work space and use it to pick up parts and perform assembly operations on them. Machines of this class are already widely accepted in industry. However a major ingredient in the economic justification of such installations is the cost of applications programming. Further, programming is becoming more complex as efforts are made to increase the generality and reliability of applications by use of sensory feedback from the assembly world. This feedback takes the form of tactile and force sensors from the gripping mechanism and the work area, and may be extended to include video and other remote sensing techniques.

Two main approaches to simplification of the programming of general purpose mechanical assemblers are in evidence. One is programming by showing, in which the machine is led through the assembly motions by the programmer, perhaps using a pushbutton control box, and the motions stored for repetetive replay. The other approach is through the use of textual programming. At a very high level, such as the natural language statement:
screw the bracket and the interlock together
the system must recognize the items *bracket* and *interlock*, and interpret the *screw* action to be performed on them. The system must then generate a plan to achieve the desired goal. This problem could be approached by the use of Artificial Intelligence problem solving systems such as [37-39], which would attempt to break the problem down into a series of sub-goals to be achieved in sequence. This is a very complex problem which is not generally solvable by any existing AI techniques.

Consider now the description of the same example shown in Figure 2.14 taken from an existing industrial assembly instruction sheet. In this case the problem has already been broken down into a sequence of sub-goals which are recognizable assembly steps. The assembly sequence has been specified together with the parts, tools, and fixtures to be used. However, there is still explicit information missing, such as how the bracket is to be placed in the fixture, which hole in the bracket is to be used, and what is to be done with the screw. Since this form of high level language exists, and applications have already been written and optimized, it is clearly an attractive candidate for a formalized assembly language.

At a lower level of assembly programming the code is *manipulator directed*, that is, it is concerned with specification of manipulator motions to achieve the desired assembly goal. The programmer must visualize the three dimensional nature of the assembly operation, specify motions in terms of geometric variables, and analyze symbolic sensors. At an even lower level of manipulator control language, such as ML[40], the user programs directly in the manipulator's motor space and interprets absolute sensor data.

From the point of view of a user, the higher the level of language used, the easier the human programming process becomes. In the examples of four programming levels introduced above, the natural language level is deemed infeasible to implement at present, and the lowest (ML) is an extremely difficult level at which to program. The essential difference between the assembly instruction sheet of Figure 2.14 and the lower levels described is that the former describes the assembly operations to be performed, while the latter describe manipulator motions to achieve an assembly operation. The manipulator-level user must be prepared to program the necessary motions to accomodate the geometry of the assembly operations, and the interpretation of sensor data. Even with the assistance of subroutines for performing common operations, the complexity of the coding task will require that he be an experienced programmer as well as one skilled in the art of manipulator control.

The assembly instruction sheet approach requires that the system understand the geometry of the assembly world. An assembly programming system working at this level will also have to include a means for specification of the geometry of parts, fixtures, manipulators, and other items of the assembly world. In both the case of specifying the geometry and of writing the assembly code, it is desirable that the user be a designer or an assembly engineer rather than a programmer.

2.6.1 Off-line Programming of Industrial Robots.

In the following sections the role of geometric modeling in the off-line programming of industrial robots is considered. Two application areas are covered: the verification of an existing robot program, and the generation of a new robot program from a high level description of the assembly operations.

2.6.1.1 Emulation of Existing Robot Programs.

A geometric modeling system makes it possible to emulate certain parts of an existing robot program in which motions are specified in manipulator rather than goal terms. The modeling system can readily simulate the deterministic parts of the program including, in particular, the motions that are known explicitly at emulation time. Unfortunately, the real problems in robot programming, and hence those areas of a program most in need of testing, arise from uncertainty in the assembly environment - parts are never exactly the same size, robot motions are subject to error, and some assembly operations require adaptive motions (for example, putting a peg in a hole with very small clearance). Work on the emulation of robot programs that emulate sensory data is in progress[34]. In a purely deterministic situation an operation of the form *move until touch*, that is the *guarded move* of [40], allows realistic emulation of the gross motion stages of a robot program. However, a useful general solution appears to be rather difficult. To some extent this difficulty represents a lack of understanding at the algorithm level of how best to interpret sensory data, and this in turn induces difficulties in incorporating sensory data features in a robot programming language.

2.6.1.2 Execution of Very High Level Robot Programs.

Assembly directed programming is a level of programming language in which the user specifies an operation in terms of the assembly rather than the robot motions necessary to execute it. A compiler converts assembly directed statements into manipulator language statements for a particular manipulator configuration using a geometric data base to simulate the assembly world at compile time. Assembly directed programming enables the user to specify assembly operations in a familiar manner, but it is also necessary that he be able to refer to assembly objects, such as parts, fixtures, and tools, in a familiar and natural manner.

Natural language, because of its ambiguity and use of context to complete descriptions, is not a suitable form for stating assembly operations with adequate precision, but the assembly instruction sheet is. A workable approach is to use a formalized syntax with an English like appearance, as proposed for the AUTOPASS language[5]. In this language the user specifies the overall assembly operation as a sequence of high level statements, each involving operations on the level of positioning one part or inserting one screw. The statements enable the user to communicate the assembly process to the system in a natural and convenient manner. The statements have verbs such as PLACE, TURN, INSERT, qualifiers such as UNTIL TORQUE IS *5 ft-lb*, and objects and features of objects with user defined names such as *10-32 screw* and *side-bracket-top-surface*. However, the statements are not in a natural language but have a formalized syntax with precisely defined semantics for all permissible verbs and qualifiers. The problem domain has been sufficiently constrained so that each assembly statement can invoke a pre-stored template which describes a sequence of utility routines to be used in the generation of the implementation plan. The calling of some of these routines may be optional depending on the state of the assembly world, and the individual routines may require a process similar to problem solving in a restricted domain, for example trajectory planning routines. In the event that the compiler is unable to find solutions to one or more of the basic steps as specified by the template for the command, the user would be asked to re-specify the operation.

The workspace and manipulator are represented by a World Model data base. The representation of both geometric information, such as the shape of an object and its location in the assembly world, and physical information such as stability of objects and support relationships (for example, will a part fall over if another part is removed), attachment relationships between objects (for example, if the *interlock* is removed from the *fixture*, will the *bracket* be removed also) is conceptually straightforward. However, major differences arise between the recognition of changes in the geometric and physical states of the system as a result of manipulator actions. Changes in the geometry are readily understood, but changes in physical relationships are much harder to recognize. For example, in the program given in Figure 2.14, how does the system recognize that inserting a screw into a hole attaches all four objects together? The AUTOPASS approach is to place on the user the responsibility for specifying physically realizable operations, for example, that parts are placed in stable positions, for informing the system of changes in attachment relationships, and for declaring new relationships such as attachment.

At the start of compilation of an AUTOPASS statement the World Model represents the current state of the assembly world. During the course of compilation of the statement the data base is used to provide information for such operations as choice of the grasp point on an object and generation of manipulator trajectories. At the end of compilation of the statement the Model is updated to reflect the changes that would occur with successful execution of the statement. The overall structure of the AUTOPASS system is shown in

9 1.ASM SUPPORT BRACKET
10 P/U AND POSITION THE NUT IN THE NEST OF THE FIXTURE
11 1090037 NUT, CAR RET TAB   QTY 01
12 P/U, ORIENT AND POSITION THE BRACKET INTO THE
   FIXTURE WITH ITS TAB OVER THE NUT
13 1115191 BRACKET ASM. RAIL SUPPORT   QTY 01
14 P/U SCREW AND LOAD DRIVER
15 1107378 STUD, CR TAB INTERLK   QTY 01
16 P/U, ORIENT AND POSITION THE INTERLOCK OVER THE
   BRACKET HOLE, WITH THE NOTCHED LUG UP
17 1117637 INTERLOCK, CR + TAB   QTY 01
18 P/U AIR DRIVER
19 DRIVE SCREW TIGHT
20 TORQUE 12.0 IN/LBS
21 ASIDE AIR GUN

Figure 2.14 Support bracket assembly
taken from an assembly sheet.

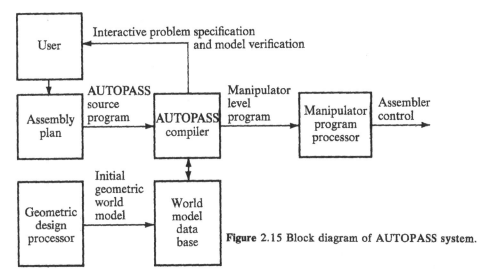

Figure 2.15 Block diagram of AUTOPASS system.

1. OPERATE *nutfeeder* WITH *car-ret-tab-nut* AT *fixture-nest*
2. PLACE *bracket* IN *fixture* SUCH THAT *bracket.bottom*
          CONTACTS *car-ret-tab-nut.top*
          AND *bracket.hole* IS ALIGNED WITH *fixture.nest*
3. PLACE *interlock* ON *bracket* SUCH THAT
          interlock.hole IS ALIGNED WITH *bracket.hole*
          AND *interlock.base* CONTACTS *brbacket.top*
4. DRIVE IN *car-ret-intlk-stud* INTO *car-ret-tab-nut*
          AT *interlock.hole*
          SUCH THAT TORQUE IS EQ *10 in-lbs* USING *air driver*
          ATTACHING *bracket* AND *interlock*
5. NAME *bracket interlock car-ret-intlk-stud car-ret-tab-nut*
          ASSEMBLY *support bracket*

Figure 2.16 AUTOPASS program for support bracket assembly.

Figure 2.15. The user generates an assembly plan, codes it as an AUTOPASS source program and also provides an initial geometric model of the assembly world using a Geometric Design Processor. The AUTOPASS compiler processes the source program one statement at a time. The compiler interacts with the World Model data base for information on the geometric and physical relationships involved in the assembly operations, and with the user to ensure correctness of specification of the assembly plan. The target code consists of procedures in manipulator level language. AUTOPASS is embedded in a subset of PL/1 and offers the user many of the control and data type facilities of that language.

As an illustration of the use of the language Figure 2.16 shows the AUTOPASS program to perform the *bracket* and *interlock* assembly operation of Figure 2.14. The example shows the closeness of the level of the AUTOPASS representation to that of the assembly instruction sheet, and that, within the restricted domain and rigid semantics of the language, the problem specification is sufficiently complete for the compiler to generate correct manipulator code. Consider now the semantics of the two PLACE statements:

Statement no.2: PLACE is the general movement statement of a state change class of assembly statements. The general sequence of operations that it generates is: move the hand to a position that permits pickup of the object, grasp the object, move along a clear trajectory to an approach position for putting the object in the target place, put it in place.

The spatial position and orientation of the object in the target place is determined by the combination of final conditions listed in the SUCH THAT phrases. The qualifiers indicate which way up the *bracket* should be (*bracket.bottom* contacts *car-ret-intlk-nut.top*), and the alignment of two axes (*interlock.hole* WITH *fixture.nest*). In this case the alignment is not be measured directly but is inferred from the dimensions of the objects. Depending on the geometry of *fixture* and *bracket*, the compiler may find the final condition specification incomplete (orientation about the axis is not specified), and would then ask for more qualifiers. Note that *interlock.hole* and *fixture.nest* are both assumed to have natural axes; if this proves to be false, the compiler asks for further specification. In general a library of force feedback routines is used to ensure that spatial final conditions have been met.

In addition to the general operations of trajectory calculation and collision avoidance, the PLACE command also requires a functional module to find possible pickup points on the object. This module must interact with the trajectory calculator since the hand orientation at pickup may render a predicted trajectory infeasible at its final position. After this state change the transform for *bracket* is updated and the *bracket* vertex now has constraint edges showing its relations relative to its new location in the *fixture*.

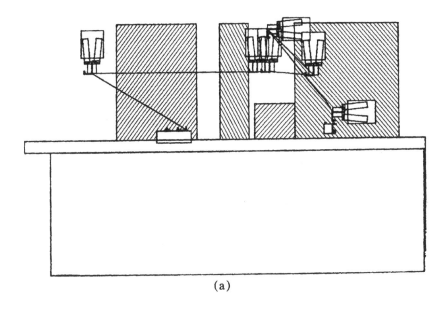

(a)

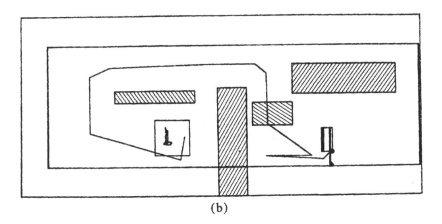

(b)

Figure 2.17 Path-finding application: (a) side view of calculated trajectory; (b) top view of trajectory (gripper not shown).

Statement no.3: In PLACE *interlock* ON *bracket*, ON indicates to the compiler that this is a placement operation in open surroundings, whereas in Statement no.2 IN indicated some measure of enclosure. This information is used by the compiler in analyzing the required final position of an object and the approach trajectory. Again, if orientation is not specified, the compiler queries the user to see if it is important and, if not, is free to choose any orientation that enables it to meet other conditions. Removal of a requirement such as orientation makes the task of selecting a pick up point and trajectory easier, as the extents of the required manipulator motions are less likely to reach the allowable limits in motor space, as defined in a table of motor constraints.

Algorithms for the generation of collision-free trajectories have been developed [41,42,33]. Of these [33 and 42] are rather general but rely on the use of polyhedral models.; [42] has been used successfully for planning paths for a 7 degree of freedom manipulator(Figure 2.17). The basic goals of the trajectory generator are to find safe paths even in a cluttered environment (i.e. it may be necessary to go close to obstacles), and to guarantee that these paths are near optimum in terms of a specified objective function (e.g. time or distance). The central problem is to allow for the finite extent of the moving manipulator and the objects it is holding, that is the volume swept out during a motion. Search methods based on postulating a trajectory, generating the swept volume, and testing for interferences as in Section 2.3.3 are computationally expensive and algorithmically inefficient. The approach used is to finesse the swept volume problem by working in a state space corresponding to the degrees of freedom of the manipulator. The obstacles are represented as *forbidden regions* in the manipulator state space, where the boundaries of the forbidden regions are made up of the locus of points where the moving and fixed objects are in contact. The collision-free path planning problem now becomes one of finding a line path between the start and goal points outside the forbidden regions in the manipulator state space. In practice the path planning is performed in a 3 degree of freedom sub-space, with the shape of the forbidden regions incorporating locally fixed values of remaining degrees of freedom.; full degree of freedom capability is provided by switching between automatically selected sub-spaces.

The path planning process may be regarded as one of *shrinking* moving objects to a point, and of *growing* fixed obstacles by a suitable inverse transformation. This process is illustrated for a 2 degree of translational freedom case in Figure 2.18): (a) shows the initial state of a problem to move object A from **start** to **goal**; (b) shows the desired minimum distance path; (c) shows an intermediate stage with A shrunk to half size and the obstacles grown accordingly; (d) shows the shrinking completed and a line path to **goal**. More correctly, the boundary of a forbidden region is the locus of the frame origin of the moving object as it moves in contact around the boundary of a fixed object; a choice of a

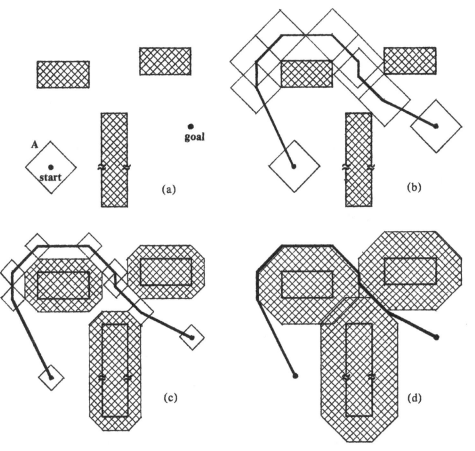

Figure 2.18 Two degree of freedom example of growing and shrinking operation.

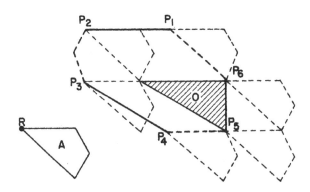

Figure 2.19 An exact growing algorithm.

different frame for the moving object results in a different grown object. An example is shown for two convex objects **O** and **A** in Figure 2.19. Note that the dashed segments of the locus of **R** (the origin of **A**) represent the edges of **A** taken in reverse order; this operation is known as *mixing* [43].

The shrinking and growing operations are basic to a range of path planning operations; as well as collision-free trajectories for robots, they include NC tool path generation, wire routing both at the wire harness and integrated circuit level, and paint spray path determination.

2.6.2 Model Driven Industrial Vision.

As an example of the use of polyhedral models in vision[44], algorithms have been developed to determine the stable orientations of parts on a plane and then generate the 2-D outlines and extract features from them. The program STABLE takes as input a polyhedron and returns a list of support planes defining "stable" orientations of that polyhedron. The method used first calculates the convex hull of the object by applying a "gift-wrapping" algorithm to the polyhedron's vertices. Figure 2.20b shows the convex hull computed for the part shown in Figure 2.20a. Next, the object's centre of mass is found; the centre of mass is projected onto each of the convex hull faces, thus hypothesizing that the face is a stable support plane. If the projected point lies within the bounds of the face polygon, then it is tentatively declared a stable plane. A test is made for the degree of stability by calculating the energy needed to "tip" the object by rotating over the edge in the support plane nearest the projected centre of mass. If the energy is large enough, i.e., exceeds a user-set threshold, then the convex face is a support plane. All the faces are checked and those passing the tests are ranked in decreasing order of stability (i.e., "tipping" energy) and returned in a list to the calling program. Figure 2.20c shows the stable positions found for the interlock.

The object model can be manipulated so that it rests on any of the stable support faces of the convex hull. An imaginary camera viewpoint is set to simulate the real camera's placement in the workstation and a program then calculates the outer boundary of the object's projection into the display plane. The vector list may be displayed or passed to application programs for feature analysis. Figure 2.20d shows the outlines for each of the three stable orientations of the interlock as viewed from directly above a block platform.

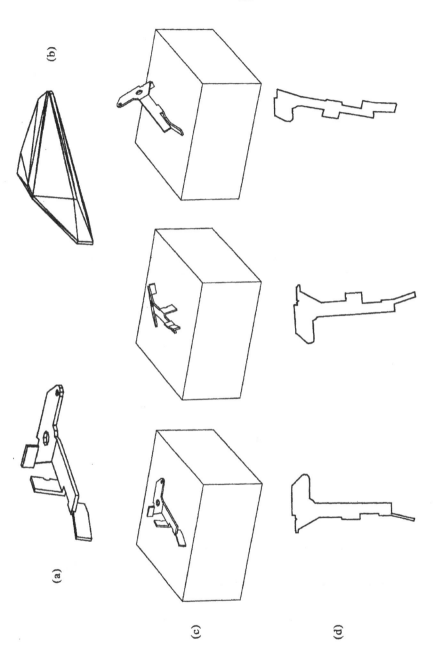

Figure 2.20 An example of model driven vision.

2.7 PRODUCT TEST.

After manufacture and assembly, products may be subjected to quality control inspection, either in terms of individual components or complete assemblies. Automated inspection is based on the correlation of sensory data with information embedded in the engineering data base. The correlation operations may be geometric, that is comparison of measured dimensions or behaviour with information derived from the geometric model and its dimension and tolerance specifications, or may in terms of physical properties such as weight, stiffness, torque, etc. which may be derived from the data base. Other types of inspection information will be specified in the data base by explicit declaration at design time.

A general purpose means of gathering sensory data is an industrial robot. Such a device can move around the inspection area and can read in tactile, video, and other sensory data synchronized in space and time. Many of the remarks made above about using a geometric data base for programming robots for assembly, e.g. planning and simulating collision-free paths, apply also to inspection.

2.8 CONCLUSIONS.

In this chapter the role of a comprehensive engineering data base in design, manufacture, assembly, and inspection has been developed. By means of examples and references to the literature it has been shown that many of the ingredients are already technically feasible. It remains to be seen whether the outstanding problems are solvable, and which areas are or will become economically feasible.

2.9 ACKNOWLEDGEMENTS.

The material presented in this chapter draws heavily on the work of my colleagues at the Thomas J. Watson Research Centre and I gratefully acknowledge their permission to use their work. Roger Evans collaborated on the MERGE algorithm. Bill Fitzgerald, Franklin Gracer, and Bob Wolfe have worked on interactive graphics for geometric modeling. David Grossman provided the concept of procedural representation, provided the examples in Figures 2.12, 2.13 and Table 2g, and has given me continuing encouragement to work on geometric modeling. Mark Lavin worked on the initial implementation of GDP. Larry Lieberman worked on the AUTOPASS language, built the basic interactive system, worked on the MERGE algorithm, generated many of the semantic routines, and has used GDP in his work on industrial vision. Tomàs Lozano-Perez built the command processor for GDP and worked on the collision avoidance algorithm. George Markowsky worked on the Wire Frame algorithm. Jeanine Meyer worked on emulation of robot languages. Michael Wesley worked on the AUTOPASS language, the MERGE algorithm, the path planning algorithm, mechanical design validation, and the Wire Frame algorithm. Peter Will originated the work on geometric modeling at Yorktown. Bill Fitzgerald, Mark Lavin, Larry Lieberman, and Russell Taylor read early drafts of this chapter and contributed many valuable comments.

2.10 REFERENCES.

[1] J. C. Jones, "Design Methods", Wiley-Interscience, 1970.
[2] R. N. Wolfe, "3D Geometric Data Bases for Mechanical Engineering", Proceedings of conference on Data Base Techniques for Pictorial Applications, held in Florence, June 20-22, 1979; Lecture Notes in Computer Science, No. 81, Springer-Verlag, 1980, pp 253-261.
[3] M. A. Wesley, "High Level Languages and Modeling", Research Report RC8195, IBM Thomas J. Watson Research Center, P.O. Box 218, Yorktown Heights, NY 10598, March 1980.
[4] M. A. Wesley, T. Lozano-Perez, L. I. Lieberman, M. A. Lavin, D. D. Grossman, "A Geometric Modelling System for Automated Mechanical Assembly", IBM Journal of Research and Development, vol. 24, no. 1, pp. 64-74 (January 1980).
[5] L. I. Lieberman and M. A. Wesley, "AUTOPASS: An Automatic Programming System for Computer Controlled Mechanical Assembly", IBM Journal of Research and Development, Vol. 21, No. 4, 321-333, July 1977.
[6] I. E. Sutherland, SKETCHPAD: "A Man-Machine Graphical Communication System", Proceedings SJCC, vol. 23, p. 329 (1963).
[7] D. D. Grossman, Procedural Representation of Three Dimensional Objects, IBM Journal of Research and Development,Vol. 20, No. 6, 582-589, Nov. 1976.
[8] R. N. Wolfe, private communication.
[9] G. Markowsky and M. A. Wesley, "Fleshing Out Wire Frames", Research Report RC 8124, IBM Thomas J. Watson Research Centre, Yorktown Heights, New York, February 1980; to be published in the IBM Journal of Research and Development, September 1980.
[10] A. Baer, C. Eastman, M. Henrion, "Geometric Modelling: a Survey", Computer Aided Design, vol. 11, no. 5, pp.253-272 (September 1979).
[11] A. G. Requicha, R. B. Tilove, "Mathematical Foundations of Constructive Solid Geometry: General Topology of Closed Regular Sets", Tech. Memo. No. 27, Production Automation Project, Univ. of Rochester, March 1978.
[12] M. Idesawa, "A System to Generate a Solid Figure from a Three View", Bulletin of the JSME vol. 16, no. 92, pp. 216-225 (Feb. 1973).
[13] M. Idesawa, T. Soma, E. Goto and S. Shibata, "Automatic Input of Line Drawing and Generation of Solid Figure from Three-View Data", Proceedings of the International Joint Computer Symposium 1975, pp. 304-311.
[14] G. Lafue, "Recognition of Three-Dimensional Objects from Orthographic Views", Proceedings 3rd Annual Conference on Computer Graphics, Interactive Techniques, and Image Processing ACM/SIGGRAPH, pp. 103-108 (July 1976).
[15] D. A. Huffman, "Impossible Objects as Nonsense Sentences", Machine Intelligence 6, B. Meltzer and D. Michie (eds.), Edinburgh Univ. Press, Edinburgh, 1971, pp. 295-324.
[16] M. B. Clowes, "On Seeing Things", Artificial Intelligence, Vol. 2, pp. 79-116 (1971).
[17] D. Waltz, "Understanding Line Drawings of Scenes with Shadows", The Psychology of Computer Vision, P. H. Winston (ed.) McGraw-Hill, New York, 1975, pp. 19-91.
[18] H. B. Voelcker and A. A. G. Requicha, "Geometric Modeling of Mechanical Parts and Processes", Computer, December 1977, pp. 48-57.
[19] Y. T. Lee, "Algorithms for Computing the Volume and other Integral Properties of Solid Objects", Technical Memorandum TM-35, Production Automation Project, University of Rochester, Rochester, New York, February 1980.
[20] K-J. Bathe, and E. L. Wilson, "Numerical Methods in Finite Element Analysis", Prentice-Hall, 1976.
[21] R. H. MacNeal, Editor: "NASTRAN Theoretical Manual", NASA Sp-221, Scientific and Technical Information Office, Washington, D.C. 1972.
[22] B. E. Brown, "Modeling of Solids for Three-Dimensional Finite Element Analysis", Ph.D. dissertation, Department of Computer Sciences, University of Utah, Salt Lake City, Utah, June 1977.
[23] J. Boyse, "Interference Detection among Solids and Surfaces", Comm. ACM. vol.22, no. 1, pp. 3-9 (Jan. 1979).
[24] A. A. G. Requicha, "Dimensioning and Tolerancing", Report no. TM-19, Production Automation Project, University of Rochester, 1974.
[25] R. C. Hillyard and I. C. Braid, "Analysis of dimensions and Tolerances in Computer Aided Mechanical Design", Computer Aided Design, vol. 10, pp. 161-166 (May 1978).
[26] D. D. Grossman, "Monte Carlo Simulation of Tolerancing in Discrete Parts Manufacturing and Assembly", Stanford Artificial Intelligence Laboratory Memo AIM-280, Stanford University, Palo Alto, Ca., May 1976.
[27] R. H. Taylor, "A Synthesis of Manipulation Control Programs from Task Level Specifications", Stanford Artificial Intelligence Laboratory, Computer Sciences Department, Report No. STAN-CS-76-560, Palo Alto, California, July 1976.
[28] W. M. Newman, and R. F. Sproull, "Principles of Interactive Computer Graphics", McGraw-Hill 1973.
[29] I. E. Sutherland, R. F. Sproull, and R. A. Schumacker, "A Characterisation of Ten Hidden-Surface Algorithms", Computing Surveys, Vol. 6, No. 1, March 1974.
[30] IIT REsearch Institute Staff, "APT Part Programming", Mc-Graw-Hill, 1967.
[31] T. C-H. Woo, "Computer Understanding of Design", Ph.D. Thesis, University of Illinois at Urbana-Champaign, 1975.

[32] A. R. Grayer, "The Automatic Production of Machined Components Starting from a Stored Geometric Description", C.A.D. Group Document No. 88, University of Cambridge Computer Laboratory, Corn Exchange Street, Cambridge, England.

[33] T. Lozano-Perez, "Spatial Planning with Polyhedral Models", Ph.D. Thesis, Massachusetts Institute of Technology, Cambridge, Mass., June 1980.

[34] J. M. Meyer, private communication.

[35] M. A. Wesley, private communication.

[36] W .R. Tanner, editor, "Industrial Robots", Volume 2: Applications, Society of Manufacturing Engineers, Dearborn, Michigan, 1979.

[37] D. G. Bobrow and B. Raphael, "New Programming Languages for Artificial Intelligence Research", Computing Surveys, Vol. 6,No. 3, 153-174, Sept. 1974.

[38] C. Hewitt, "Description and Theoretical Analysis (Using Schemata) of Planner: A Language for Proving Theorems and Manipulating Models in a Robot", AI Memo No. 251, MIT Project MAC, Cambridge, MA, April 1972.

[39] S. E. Fahlman, "A Planning System for Robot Construction Tasks", Artificial Intelligence 5, 1-49, 1974.

[40] P. M. Will and D. D. Grossman, "An Experimental System for Computer Controlled Mechanical Assembly", IEEE Trans. on Computers, Vol. C-24, No. 9, 879-888, September 1975.

[41] S. Udupa, "Collision Detection and Avoidance in Computer Controlled Manipulators", Ph.D. Thesis, California Institute of Technology, Pasadena, California, 1977.

[42] T. Lozano-Perez, M. A. Wesley, "An Algorithm for Planning Collision-Free Paths Among Polyhedral Objects", Comm. ACM. vol. 22, no. 10, pp. 560-570 (Oct. 1979).

[43] L. A. Lyusternik, "Convex Figures and Polyhedra", Dover Publications, N.Y. 1963. (Translated from the Russian by Smith T.J., original copyright Moscow 1956).

[44] L. I. Lieberman, "Model Driven Vision for Industrial Automation", presented at the IBM International Symposium on Advances in Digital Image Processing, Bad Neuenahr, Germany, September 1978.

Chapter 3

Curve and Surface Generation and Fairing

by

Horst Nowacki

Technische Universität Berlin
Institut für Schiffstechnik
Berlin 10, Salzufer 17-19

Chapter 3: Curve and Surface Generation and Fairing

3.1 INTRODUCTION

In computer-aided design curves and surfaces, expressed in some suitable mathematical form, principally serve the purpose of describing
the shape of technical objects. Our interest in this context lies in
the entire process of developing the description of such shapes with
the aid of computers, from initial concept formulation to final definition (Fig. 3.1).

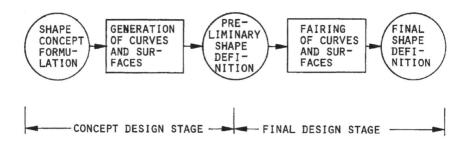

Fig. 3.1 : Development of shape description

The development of a shape description, whether by conventional manual
methods or by computer, will normally evolve through several stages of
refinement, unless a direct analytical description of the shape is immediately at hand. It is important to distinguish primarily between two
principal stages of development with different objectives and rules:
The concept design stage, where the generation of curves and surfaces
takes place and results in a preliminary shape definition, and the final design stage, which leads to a final shape definition of appropriate quality, for instance for fabrication purposes, by means of a fairing process.

This two-stage process corresponds to traditional design practice in
many branches of industry where "free-form" design, that is, design of
curves and surfaces by non-analytical means, especially drafting me-

thods, is employed. In the automotive industry, for example, a clay model of the car body shape is normally produced from a draft of the
shape design, modified according to the stylist's instructions, until
eventually the form can be digitized and faired to toolmaking tolerances. In ship design, similarly, a preliminary lines plan on a smaller
scale is initially developed and used as a basis for evaluating the
design functionally; later, in former practice, the lines of the ship
were faired full scale on the mold loft to improve the quality of the
lines to manufacturing tolerances. Today, in both industries, computer
methods are heavily used at the fairing stage, almost eliminating conventional lofting procedures, whereas corresponding methods for initial shape design are adopted much more hesitantly. Similar tendencies
may be observed in the aerospace industry and in the design of complicated machine parts.

Generation and fairing of curves and surfaces are thus two distinct
processes with different objectives. These will be discussed in more
detail in the following section. Our goal is to review different types
of problem formulations in curve and surface development as they arise
at certain stages in engineering applications, and then to examine how
the solution of these problems may be approached by means of available
computer-based methods.

3.2 PROBLEM FORMULATIONS

To derive more precise problem statements for the two principal stages
of shape description development let us examine more closely the definitions and steps in Fig. 3.1. Prior to designing a curve (or surface)
a concept of its intended shape must be developed. The desired properties of the shape are normally derived from technical, physical, even
aesthetical, or other functional requirements, which must be translated
into geometric requirements by the designer. In the following we will
assume that this thought process has been completed so that we may limit ourselves strictly to sets of geometric functional requirements on
the shape.

The problem of curve (surface) design from geometric requirements may
then be stated as follows:

"<u>Given</u>: A set of geometric requirements such as:
Offsets, slopes, second derivatives, ... ,
areas, (volumes), centroids, ... ,
sufficient to characterize the intended shape.

<u>Find</u>: A curve (surface) meeting these requirements."

The linear flow chart in Fig. 3.1 is not intended to convey that a single generation step will be sufficient to guarantee an adequate result for the preliminary shape definition. On the contrary, this design process is usually highly iterative because the design tends to proceed from few, rather tentative requirements to a more and more concrete and comprehensive set. Initial contradictions or conceptual conflicts in the requirements must be removed, usually by trial and error. However, the basic problem of shape design stated above repeats itself for every modified set of requirements. Any method that solves this curve (surface) generation problem will assist the designer in eventually achieving a satisfactory preliminary shape definition.

The process of curve (surface) generation aims at agreement between shape and some intended specific geometric properties, but does not automatically ensure a sufficient quality in the "fairness" of the curve (surface). Fairness is a somewhat elusive property whose more precise definition will be discussed in section 3.4. For the moment it should be sufficient to associate fairness loosely with the absence of undesired local shape deficiencies, in particular, oscillations. It is evident that the curve (surface) generation procedure does not explicitly measure fairness so that its results may not be adequately fair for production purposes or by other standards. This is why a separate fairing process is generally required.

The objective of the <u>fairing problem</u> may be formulated as follows:

"<u>Given</u>: A curve (surface), or a corresponding set of offset points, approximating an intended shape.

<u>Find</u>: A fairer curve (surface) according to some fairness criterion (section 3.4) without deviating too far from the given shape."

This formulation is still qualitative, but it may convey the general goal of the fairing process.

A few examples may serve to further illustrate the different orientations in shape generation and fairing. A curve may be designed strictly
from given offset points, which may have been lifted off from a hand
sketch. If all offset data are treated as "hard constraints" so that
the curve must pass through all points, the design problem is reduced
to an interpolation problem.

If, by contrast, the hand sketch is regarded only as a preliminary
shape definition so that the offset data for the most part are acting
only as "soft constraints", then a new curve may be faired through the
data points improving the fairness relative to the given curve.

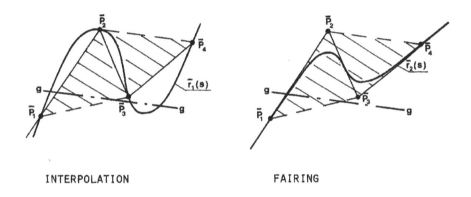

INTERPOLATION   FAIRING

Fig. 3.2 : Comparison between interpolation and fairing

A comparison between the contrasting results of these two formulations
is given in Fig. 3.2. Given four data points $\overline{P}_i$, i = 1, ..., 4, connected by a defining polygon. The cross-hatched area represents the "convex hull" of the four data points. The interpolating curve $\overline{r}_1(s)$ tends
to "oscillate more" than the defining polygon in the sense that it does
not lie entirely within the convex hull and that there are straight-
lines like (g-g) which will intersect the curve more often than the
polygon. The faired curve $\overline{r}_2(s)$ can be constructed so as to lie entirely within the convex hull and to have no more points of intersection
with an arbitrary straight-line (g-g) than does the polygon. Fairing
in this sense tends to reduce the tendency of a curve to oscillate.

Generalizing these observations a little further, we may surmise that
curve (or surface) generation as a process with predominantly hard con-

straints will tend to be sensitive to incongruous requirements and hence apt to produce unfair shapes. Fairing, on the other hand, using few hard and many soft constraints, will tend to reduce oscillatory tendencies and thus to improve the quality of the shape.

It may be argued that it seems feasible to include capabilities for generation and fairing within a single software system so that a two-stage division need not be made. But within such a system functions must be provided to deal with hard and/or soft constraints so that two logical options are still present.

In summary, we have recognized two distinctly different problem types to be of importance in the development of shape descriptions, that is, generation as opposed to fairing. We have formulated these problems in a general way for curves and surfaces, and may now proceed to examine more closely the available solution techniques for each problem type.

3.3 FORM GENERATION

3.3.1 Curves

The generation of curves from given form parameters will be discussed first. A parameter notation is introduced for the curves to be generated:

$$\overline{Q}(t) = \begin{bmatrix} x(t) \\ y(t) \\ z(t), \text{ if appl.} \end{bmatrix} \quad (1)$$

The equation of the curve $\overline{Q}(t)$ is a vector valued function of the parameter t. The presentation will refer to planar or space curves simultaneously unless explicitly stated otherwise.

Parametric notation for curves (and surfaces) has become almost universal in computer-aided design for several reasons:

- Ambiguities caused by non-monotonic functions $y(x)$, $x(y)$
  etc. can be avoided since every parameter value t corres-

ponds to one and only one point on the curve.

- Picture generation by scanning the parameter range of
  t is straightforward.

- The treatment of space curves and planar curves can be
  unified readily.

We shall not deal with the generation of analytically representable
curves. Parametric representations of such curves, particularly conic
sections and other simple shapes are found in the literature [1] .

In accordance with the problem formulation of the preceding section
we will concentrate on the design of "free-form" curves from form parameter requirements. Two special situations are of primary interest:

- Only offset data points are given, or

- A mixed variety of form parameters is given.

In the first case the problem is reduced to an ordinary interpolation
problem. Offset data are frequently available from preliminary drawings,
reference designs,hand sketches etc. They will normally convey a relatively complete idea of the intended shape.

If on the other hand the concept of a shape is still being evolved and
modified, it is often advantageous to specify the curve in terms of
some global and some local shape characteristics such as area, centroid,
offsets, slopes etc. This facilitates well-coordinated, systematic
changes in the curve.

3.3.1.1 Form Generation from Offsets: Interpolation

Given (n+1) offset data points $\bar{P}_i$, i = o, ..., n, through which a curve
$\bar{Q}(t)$ is to be interpolated (Fig. 3.3). We will assume for simplicity
that the parameter values t_i associated with the $\bar{P}_i$ are also given.
(The issue of how to specify these parameter values, that is, how to
"parametrize" a curve, deserves its own discussion later. Suffice it
to say for the present purpose that there is no unique way of choosing
the values for the t_i and that any choice made will have an influence
on the shape of the curve. This problem does not arise, of course, if
the interpolation is performed with functions in explicit Cartesian

form). The t_i are called the <u>knots</u> of the function $\bar{Q}(t)$.

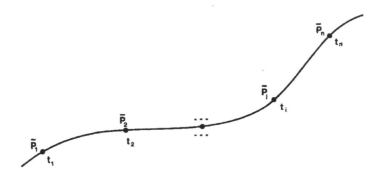

Fig. 3.3 : Interpolation problem

The interpolating function is subject to the constraints

$$\bar{Q}(t_i) = \bar{P}_i, \ i = o, \ \ldots, \ n \tag{2}$$

The problem can be solved by familiar <u>polynomial</u> <u>interpolation</u>. Polynomials are continuous and have continuous derivatives throughout their interval of definition, hence if desired, over the entire interpolated curve in $\left[t_o, \ t_n\right]$.

There exists one, and only one, polynomial of degree n that solves the interpolation problem (2), the <u>Lagrange</u> polynomial

$$\bar{Q}(t_i) = \sum_{i=o}^{n} \bar{P}_i \cdot L_{in} \ (t) \tag{3}$$

with

$$L_{in}(t) = \frac{(t-t_o) \ \ldots \ (t-t_{i-1}) \ (t-t_{i+1}) \ldots \ (t-t_n)}{(t_i-t_o) \ \ldots (t_i-t_{i-1}) \ (t_i-t_{i+1}) \ \ldots \ (t_i-t_n)}$$

$$\tag{3a}$$

In polynomial interpolation the degree of the function n is directly related to the number of given offset points (n+1). This causes one of the major drawbacks of polynomial interpolation for curve generation.

A polynomial of degree n has up to (n-1) extreme values and (n-2) inflection points, though not necessarily all real or in the interval of interpolation. Nevertheless in many practical problems accuracy requirements suggest using a substantial number of offsets which causes a tendency of the interpolating curve to oscillate. The curve will, in fact, oscillate if any of the given offset data are not compatible with a "smooth", that is, relatively low order character of the function. Thus it is often impractical to prevent undesired oscillations.

This difficulty can best be overcome by <u>piecewise continuous</u> interpolation of the curve. In many applications it is sufficient to require that the interpolating curve be continous at the knots only up to a certain order of its derivatives, say, the m'th derivative. Then the higher-order derivatives of adjoining spans of the curve need not to be matched up at the knots. So each span can be represented by its own polynomial of relatively low order, the order being selected so as to ensure continuity of the m'th derivative at the knots. For example, a piecewise third-degree polynomial (n=3, cubic spline) can be constructed to achieve C^2 (second derivative) continuity at the knots. The low order of the function reduces the likelihood of unwanted oscillations.

Many technical objects (cars, airplanes, ships) are deliberately designed so that their curves (and surfaces) are only piecewise continuous so that the use of piecewise continuous interpolating functions is not an unwanted restriction, but suggests itself naturally. In fact, the ability to produce derivative discontinuities of a certain type and order is part of the design objective in many applications.

The mathematical background to the problem of interpolation by means of polynomials with piecewise continuous derivatives is developed in the theory of splines. Mathematically a piecewise polynomial function S(t), scalar or vector valued, defined in the interval $\left[t_o, t_n\right]$, with $t_o < t_1 < \dots < t_i < t_{i+1} < \dots < t_n$, of order k (degree (k-1)) is called a <u>spline</u> if it has the following properties(Fig. 3.3):

1. S is a polynomial of degree (k-1) in each subinterval of span (t_i, t_{i+1}).

2. S and its derivatives of order 1, ..., k-2 are continuous throughout the interval $\left[t_o, t_n\right]$.

The vector T = $(t_o, t_1, \dots, t_n)$ is called the <u>knot vector</u>. It follows directly from the definition that a spline function of degree (k-1) is

C^{k-2} continuous at the knots.

The mathematical spline concept is a certain generalization of the behavior of an elastic spline, the drafting tool familiar in several industries. The elastic spline is a thin, elastic lath, usually made out of wood, metal or plastic, used in drafting to draw smooth curves through given points, much like in mathematical interpolation. The lath is held fixed in certain places by heavy weights, called ducks, constraining the curve to run through these points. The type of support may be regarded as hinged. Then the system of spline and ducks may be compared to a simply-supported, thin, continuous elastic beam. Assuming small slopes of the elastic deflection curve, at least relative to a local coordinate system for each span, and hence using linearized beam theory to analyze the spline deflection, one can show:

1. The deflection in each span can be represented by a cubic polynomial.

2. The curve, its slopes, and the bending moments, which are proportional to the second derivatives of the deflection, are continuous through the entire length of the spline, that is, the curve is C^2 continuous.

3. The third derivatives are discontinuous at the supports unless the supporting force happens to be zero.

It is evident that this behavior of the drafting tool can readily be simulated mathematically by a cubic spline, which has exactly the same three properties. This is one reason why cubic spline interpolation (and approximation) have found wide-spread application in practice.

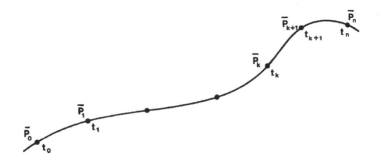

Fig. 3.4 : Cubic spline interpolation

The cubic spline interpolation problem in parametric form may be formulated as follows (Fig. 3.4): Given (n+1) offset points $\bar{P}_i$, i=o, ..., n,
and their associated knots t_i. Note that the choice of parametrization
is again reasonably free (possibilities: Integer step widths, chord
lengths, approximated arc lengths, ...). Find an interpolating piecewise
polynomial $\bar{Q}(t)$ for $\left[t_o, t_n\right]$ so that the function in each span is a
parametric cubic and $\bar{Q}(t)$ is C^2 continuous at the knots.

Consider the span $\left[t_k, t_{k+1}\right]$ and let $l_k = t_{k+1} - t_k$.

A cubic for this span can be expressed by the vector valued function

$$\bar{Q}_k(t) = \bar{a}_k + \bar{b}_k(t-t_k) + \bar{c}_k(t-t_k)^2 + \bar{d}_k(t-t_k)^3 \qquad (4)$$

$\bar{a}_k, \ldots, \bar{d}_k$ = vectorial coefficients

End points and tangent vectors may be used as boundary conditions to
the span.

$$
\left.\begin{aligned}
\bar{Q}_k(t_k) &= \bar{P}_k \\
Q_k(t_{k+1}) &= \bar{P}_{k+1}
\end{aligned}\right\} \quad
\begin{aligned}
&\text{end} \\
&\text{point} \qquad (5) \\
&\text{conditions}
\end{aligned}
$$

$$
\left.\begin{aligned}
\left(\frac{d\bar{Q}_k}{dt}\right)_{t=t_k} &= \bar{P}'_k \\
\left(\frac{d\bar{Q}_k}{dt}\right)_{t=t_{k+1}} &= \bar{P}'_{k+1}
\end{aligned}\right\} \quad
\begin{aligned}
&\text{tangent} \\
&\text{vector} \qquad (6) \\
&\text{conditions}
\end{aligned}
$$

Substituting (4) in these sets of boundary conditions we may solve for
the vector coefficients

$$\bar{a}_k = \bar{P}_k$$

$$\bar{b}_k = \bar{P}'_k$$

$$\bar{c}_k = \frac{3(\bar{P}_{k+1}-\bar{P}_k)}{l_k^2} - \frac{2\bar{P}'_k}{l_k} - \frac{\bar{P}'_{k+1}}{l_k} \qquad (7)$$

$$\bar{d}_k = \frac{2(\bar{P}_k-\bar{P}_{k+1})}{l_k^3} + \frac{\bar{P}'_k}{l_k^2} + \frac{\bar{P}'_{k+1}}{l_k^2}$$

These equations hold for each of n spans (k = o, ..., n-1). In eq. (7) we have 4n vector equations for 4n vector coefficients; however, on the right-hand sides only the end point offsets are initially given, the (n+1) tangent vectors remain still unknown.

We now introduce the continuity condition at the internal knots for the second derivatives of adjoining spans. For k = o, ..., (n-2)

$$\left(\frac{d^2\overline{Q}_k}{dt^2}\right)_{t\,=\,t_{k+1}} = \left(\frac{d^2\overline{Q}_{k+1}}{dt^2}\right)_{t=t_{k+1}} \tag{8}$$

Eq. (8) provides (n-1) further vector equations, which, with eq. (4), are of the form

$$6\,\overline{d}_k\,l_k + 2\,\overline{c}_k = 2\,\overline{c}_{k+1} \tag{8a}$$

This may be combined with eq. (7) to yield one equation, valid for knot t_{k+1}, in which the tangent vectors $\overline{P}_k$, $\overline{P}_{k+1}$, $\overline{P}_{k+2}$ are unknowns. Corresponding equations hold for all internal knots, k = 1, ..., (n-1), so that we obtain (n-1) vector equations for the (n+1) unknown tangent vectors. This system of equations is therefore underdetermined by two vector equations; in other words, in order to obtain a unique solution we must specify two additional vector quantities.

Physically this result means that the shape of the spline cannot be determined uniquely without applying two end constraints (or other constraints). The simplest choice is perhaps to specify the two end tangents $\overline{P}_o$ and $\overline{P}_n$. Another possibility is to let the ends be free of second derivatives (relaxed): $\overline{P}_o'' = \overline{P}_n'' = o$. Rogers and Adams [2] mention these and a few other possibilities and show how for each situation to set up a system of equations in matrix form and to solve this system recursively to obtain the complete spline function. Theilheimer [3] , who successfully introduced cubic spline interpolation to ship lines applications, determined the two missing constraints in such a way that the sum of the squares of the bearing reactions at the internal knots (k=1, ..., (n-1)), which are proportional to the discontinuities of the third derivatives at the knots, were minimized. This aims at a somewhat "more relaxed" shape of the spline.

However, despite possible precautions like these there is no general way to ensure that the interpolated curve will be free of unwanted oscillations, the smoothness of the result depending entirely on the quality of the input data points. In fact, any deviation from a smooth character in the offset data, for example, by reading errors, will tend to be amplified by the interpolation process. Another drawback of the cubic spline (elastic spline) concept is that changes made locally will propagate over the entire curve so that error corrections may cause undesired effects elsewhere. Cubic spline interpolation can, therefore, best be used with offset data of rather definitive quality.

A method of piecewise polynomial interpolation, which is enjoying increasing popularity, notably for interactive curve interpolation from graphical tablets and the like, is parabolic blending, first proposed by Overhauser [4] . A detailed description is also found in [2] .

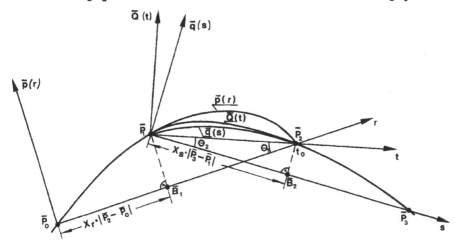

Fig. 3.5 : Parabolic blending

Consider a sequence of four given points $\overline{P}_i$, i = o, ..., 3 (Fig. 3.5).
To derive the equation of the curve $\overline{Q}(t)$ for the center span $(\overline{P}_1 - \overline{P}_2)$
two parabolas $\overline{p}(r)$ and $\overline{q}(s)$ are calculated, each parabola being defined by a three-point set. The two definition ranges overlap in the center span. Here the function $\overline{Q}(t)$ is defined as the weighted average of $\overline{p}(r)$ and $\overline{q}(s)$, using a linear function of t (local coordinate) as a weighting factor. This results in the curve (Fig. 3.5)

$$Q(t) = \overline{p}(r) \cdot (1 - \frac{t}{t_o}) + \overline{q}(s) \cdot \frac{t}{t_o} \qquad (9)$$

$$\text{for } o \leqslant t \leqslant t_o, \ t_o = \left| \overline{P}_2 - \overline{P}_1 \right|.$$

The individual parabolas are each given by three points:

For $\bar{P}_0 - \bar{P}_1 - \bar{P}_2$ (o $\leqslant$ r $\leqslant$ d$_r$) in the local r-coordinate system

$$\bar{p}(r) = \bar{P}_0 + \frac{r}{d_r} \cdot (\bar{P}_2 - \bar{P}_0) + \alpha \cdot r(d_r - r) \cdot (\bar{P}_1 - \bar{B}_1) \qquad (10)$$

and for $\bar{P}_1 - \bar{P}_2 - \bar{P}_3$ (o $\leqslant$ s $\leqslant$ d$_s$) in the local s-coordinate system

$$\bar{q}(s) = \bar{P}_1 + \frac{s}{d_s} \cdot (\bar{P}_3 - \bar{P}_1) + \beta \cdot s \cdot (d_s - s) \cdot (\bar{P}_2 - \bar{B}_2) \qquad (11)$$

where

$$d_r = \left| \bar{P}_2 - \bar{P}_0 \right| \; , \quad d_s = \left| \bar{P}_3 - \bar{P}_1 \right|$$

$$\bar{B}_1 = \bar{P}_0 + x_r (\bar{P}_2 - \bar{P}_0) , \quad \bar{B}_2 = \bar{P}_1 + x_s (\bar{P}_3 - \bar{P}_1)$$

$$x_r = \frac{(\bar{P}_1 - \bar{P}_0)(\bar{P}_2 - \bar{P}_0)}{(\bar{P}_2 - \bar{P}_0)^2} \; , \quad x_s = \frac{(\bar{P}_2 - \bar{P}_1)(\bar{P}_3 - \bar{P}_1)}{(\bar{P}_3 - \bar{P}_1)^2}$$

$$\alpha = \frac{1}{d_r^2 \cdot x_r \cdot (1 - x_r)} \; , \quad \beta = \frac{1}{d_s^2 \cdot x_s \cdot (1 - x_s)} \qquad (12)$$

The local coordinates r and s, respectively, can be calculated from t (Fig. 3.5)

$$r = x_r d_r + t \cdot \cos\theta_1, \quad s = t \cdot \cos\theta_2$$

$$\cos\theta_1 = \frac{(\bar{P}_2 - \bar{P}_1)(\bar{P}_2 - \bar{P}_0)}{t_0 \cdot d_r} \; , \quad \cos\theta_2 = \frac{(\bar{P}_2 - \bar{P}_1)(\bar{P}_3 - \bar{P}_1)}{t_0 \cdot d_s}$$

Substituting (12), (13) into (10), (11) and the latter into (9) gives the complete equation for $\bar{Q}(t)$ in the span $\bar{P}_1 - \bar{P}_2$. The curve is cubic in t because the quadratic functions $\bar{p}$ and $\bar{q}$ are each multiplied by a linear term. One can show by differentiation that the slope of $\bar{Q}(t)$ equals that of $\bar{p}$ at $\bar{P}_1$ and that of $\bar{q}$ at $\bar{P}_2$. That is, the slope at the knots of the span is governed only by the pertinent local three-point set. This ensures $\underline{c^1 \text{ continuity}}$ at the internal knots when dealing with a succession of connected spans. This is an important difference between parabolic blending and cubic spline interpolation.

Note further that each span is defined strictly by four offset points at its own ends and from the two neighboring spans, only the end spans are parabolas defined by just three points. The interpolation is _local_ rather than global, in contrast to the cubic spline method. This enables parabolic blending to be of particular advantage in interactive curve definition from a tablet or similar input device because curve segments can be added one by one and verified by inspection on a display without having to wait for a complete input data set and a much more time-consuming curve calculation.

a) Input data   b) Parabolic blending   c) B-spline interpo-
   polygon,   interpolation,   lation,
   c^0 continuous c^1 continuous c^2 continuous

Fig. 3.6 : Comparison of interpolation methods

Fig. 3.6 illustrates the results of parabolic blending interpolation. Part a) shows a set of input data, digitized on a tablet from a photograph, connected by a polygon, part b) displays the corresponding interpolation by parabolic blending. (Part c) is a c^2 continuous B-spline interpolation).

Input data points to this method have to be given in such a way that the base points $\overline{B}_1$, $\overline{B}_2$ (Fig. 3.5) lie inside the base line length because the parabola definitions (10) and (11) are subject to this premise. In practice, this can be arranged with a little caution. It is feasible, too, to parametrize the blending parabolas differently, replacing chord length as a coordinate basis, which allows to avoid the restriction cited [5].

The Bézier method [6] should be briefly mentioned although interpolation is not its proper purpose. It is principally intended for interactive curve approximation, but is has some attractive features of general interest. A Bézier curve is a parametric polynomial defined by

$$(\overline{Q}/t) = \sum_{i=o}^{n} \overline{P}_i \cdot J_{n,i}(t) \tag{14}$$

$$0 \leqslant t \leqslant 1$$

where

$$J_{n,i}(t) = \binom{n}{i} t^i (1-t)^{n-i} \tag{15}$$

The functions $J_{n,i}(t)$ are polynomials of degree n, called Bernstein polynomials. The $\overline{P}_i$, i = o,..., n, are vectors of (n+1) given data points, they form the vertices of a polygon $\overline{P}_o - \overline{P}_1 - \ldots \overline{P}_n$, the defining polygon of the curve. The Bézier curve has the following important properties:

- The shape of the curve $\overline{Q}(t)$ approximates the shape of the defining polygon by a smooth curve. The curve passes through the two end points of the polygon and is tangent to the first and last polygon sides.

- Moving the vertices $\overline{P}_i$ controls the shape of the curve; hence the usefulness of the Bézier method in interactive curve approximation.

- Moving one vertex affects the entire curve (elastic behavior!)

- It is possible to connect Bézier curves with continuous derivatives (like splines), thus interpolating through the end points. First and second derivative continuity can be achieved with reasonable effort [2] at the expense of some freedom in vertex control.

In summary, this method is far better suited for interactive curve manipulation than interpolation, but it is appealing by its ability to produce smooth curves controlled by a defining polygon. It was

Riesenfeld [7] who recognized these virtues and combined some features of the Bézier concept with a new type of polynomial function base, the B-splines, to obtain a new, general and powerful method applicable to curve design, interpolation, and fairing.

B-splines, the common abbreviated name for the basis splines first introduced by Schoenberg [8] , are a class of piecewise continuous parametric polynomials. They are splines as defined in the context of Fig. 3.3, that is, the B-spline of order k is a piecewise continuous polynomial of degree (k-1), continuously differentiable (k-2) times at the knots.

Given the knot vector $T = (t_o, t_1, ..., t_n)$. For simplicity, we will at present assume the knots to be normalized as integers; the resulting B-splines are called uniform B-splines. Then the B-spline basis function $N_{i,k}(t)$ can be defined in the interval $t_i \leqslant t \leqslant t_{i+k}$ by means of the recursion scheme of Cox and de Boor:

For k = 1

$$N_{i,1}(t) = \begin{cases} 1 & \text{for} \quad t_i \leqslant t \leqslant t_{i+k}, \\ 0 & \text{otherwise.} \end{cases}$$

and for k > 1

$$N_{i,k}(t) = \frac{t - t_i}{t_{i+k-1} - t_i} \cdot N_{i,k-1}(t) +$$

$$+ \frac{t_{i+k} - t}{t_{i+k} - t_{i+1}} \cdot N_{i+1, k-1}(t) \tag{16}$$

Fig. 3.7 shows the basis splines $N_{i,k}(t)$ for the special case of i = o and orders k from 1 through 4. Note that these functions vanish outside the interval $[t_i, t_{i+k}]$, that is, the "support" of the basis polynomials is local. This property is essential for obtaining local curve interpolation and modification methods. Each basis function has k spans with (k-1) interior knots, denoted by the dots in Fig. 3.7 (at the integers). The (k-2)nd derivatives are continuous at the knots. Thus the basis spline of order k = 4 is C^2 continuous just like a regular cubic spline. It would be called a cubic B-spline.

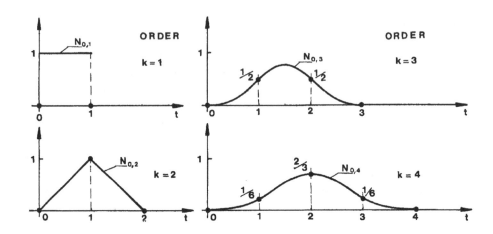

Fig. 3.7 : B-spline basis functions
$N_{i,k}(t)$ for i=0 and k=1, ..., 4

From these functions $N_{i,k}(t)$ as basis elements the equation of an
approximating (or interpolating) B-spline curve can be formulated using
Riesenfeld's approach, who introduced the principle of polygon vertex
control to B-spline curve generation in analogy to Bézier's method.
A B-spline curve is thus defined by

$$Q(t) = \sum_{i=o}^{m-1} \overline{P}_i \cdot N_{i,k}(t) \tag{17}$$

The order k of the curve and the number of vertices m may be chosen
independently of each other (m ⩾ k), an essential difference from
Bézier's method.

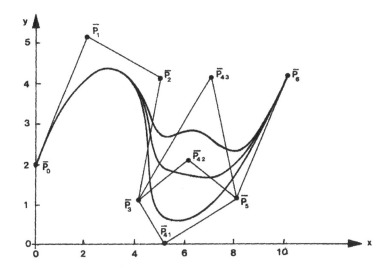

Fig. 3.8 : B-spline curve manipulation
(based on [2])

Fig. 3.8 illustrates the principle of curve control by polygon vertices.
A quartic B-spline curve (k-1=4) is here controlled by seven vertices
(m=7). It consists of m - k + 1 = 3 spans, separated by m - k = 2
interior knots. The knots at the ends of the curve are knots of multiplicity k = 5 so that the knot vector is T = $(t_o, t_o, t_o, t_o, t_o,$
$t_1, t_2, t_3, t_3, t_3, t_3, t_3)$ in order to have the ends of the open
curve collapse with the end vertices.

The shape of every span is affected by k successive vertices, for example, the span i by the vertices i through (i+k-1). Conversely, no vertex influences more than k spans. This property permits local changes
to be made, given an appropriate surplus of vertices (m> k), to some,
but not all spans of the curve. In the example of Fig. 3.8, moving the
vertex $\bar{P}_4$ has some effect on all three spans, whereas changing $\bar{P}_5$ or
$\bar{P}_6$ would not have altered the left-most span etc. The picture under-
scores the general resemblance between polygon and curve, which is
crucial in interactive curve design.

More details about B-spline theory can be found, for example, in [2]

$\begin{bmatrix} 7 \end{bmatrix}$, and $\begin{bmatrix} 9 \end{bmatrix}$.

Some of the most important properties of B-spline curves are in brief summary:

1. Local deformability, as discussed.

2. Variation diminishing property: A B-spline curve approximating a data set $\overline{P}_i$ has no more points of intersection with an arbitrary straight line than does the defining primitive (polygon), see Fig. 3.2, fairing context.

3. Convex hull property: Each span of a B-spline curve of order k lies within the convex hull of its k associated vertices (Fig. 3.9).

4. Collinear vertices: A straight-line span is produced by k collinear vertices, while with (k-1) collinear vertices the curve becomes tangent to the polygon.

5. Discontinuities at the knots, such as knuckles, curvature jumps etc., are obtainable using multiple interior knots; a knot of multiplicity p reduces the differentiability of the curve at this knot by (p-1) orders.

6. Limiting case: Choosing m = k vertices(without multiple vertices) reduces the B-spline curve to a Bézier curve. The knot vector then consists of k knots at either end, the curve has only one span. The local deformability is lost.

This brief survey demonstrates the extraordinary versatility of the B-spline method. It is capable of representing curves with specified orders of continuity of their derivatives at the knots, at the same time allowing discontinuities of well-controlled type to occur where needed. By virtue of its convex hull property it ensures a certain inherent smoothness of the curve. It permits local shape control, with global control as a limiting case.

While most of these properties are particularly useful in the context of approximation work, the method can readily be used for interpolation problems. De Boor $\begin{bmatrix} 9 \end{bmatrix}$ describes the theory and presents several useful algorithms.

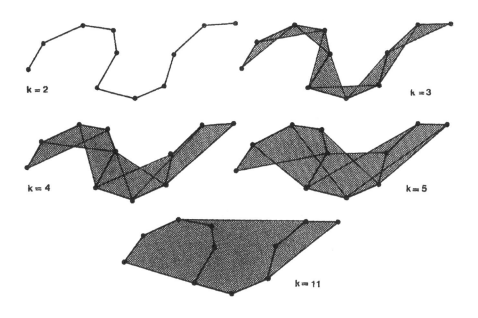

Fig. 3.9 : Convex hull property
        (based on [7])

A comment is in place regarding the initial choice of a uniform (integer) step width knot vector, resulting in <u>uniform</u> B-splines. This re-
lates to the general question of how to suitably parametrize a curve.
The choice of parameter values at the knots has, of course, some effect
on the shape of the curve. Further, if in the B-spline context the
(Euclidean) vertex spacing is very non-uniform, while the (parametric)
knot spacing on the curve remains uniform, there may result disparities
in local curve control (or resolution) in that many vertices would control short arc lengths, and few vertices long ones. Whenever this is
a problem of practical concern and a simple change in the vertex pattern is not desired, one may resort to a nonuniform knot spacing in the
knot vector. This necessitates the use of <u>nonuniform</u> B-spline curves
[10] . In practice, chord length distances of the knots may be a
good choice for the parameter increments for B-spline (and other)
curves, provided that the knots are placed within such spacing, also
in areas of great curvature, that chord length becomes a reasonably

commensurate measure of arc length between knots. The actual placement
of the knots is likely to remain a trial and error process. Moreover,
the nonuniform B-spline basis functions are no longer standard, but
a family of such functions must be computed individually, a heavy
price for usually a moderate gain.

3.3.1.2 Form Generation from Mixed Constraints

The design of curves is often based on a variety of geometrical requirements of different type, which we may call mixed constraints. Let
us confine the present discussion to the design of planar curves, the
most frequent practical application, though similar methods for space
curves can be derived without difficulty. Then the designer would normally specify the desired form parameters of the curve in familiar
Cartesian x-y-coordinates. The specifications may include any combinations of

Offsets

Pairs of (x_i, y_i), $i = o, \ldots, n$

Derivatives, e.g.,

$y'(x_j)$, $j = 1, \ldots, J$

$y''(x_k)$, $k = 1, \ldots, K$

etc.

Integrals, e.g.

$$A = \int_{x_1}^{x_2} y(x)\,dx \quad \text{(area)}$$

$$M_x = \int_{x_1}^{x_2} xy(x)\,dx \quad \text{(stat. moment about x=o, important for centroid)}$$

etc.

Note that these form parameter constraints result from linear operations on $y(x)$, except for the statical moment. In practical applications the nonlinear constraints can often be kept few; linear constraints are, of course, easier to contend with.

It is feasible to reduce this general problem to several subproblems
of standard type by subdividing the design curve into several segments
so that offset and derivative constraints are applied only to segment
ends. This may look impractical whenever very many constraints of this
type are present, but in such case methods of interpolation or approximation might be preferred anyway. In the presence of integral constraints it is rare that point constraints would be very numerous
because of the probability of conflicts. We may consequently concentrate on cases with relatively few point constraints and introduce a
standard subproblem with point constraints (offsets and derivatives)
only at the interval ends.

A special, but illustrative case was treated by Creutz [11], who
introduced a standard form parameter segment (Fig. 3.10) subject to
the following set of constraints:

> End offsets: (x_o, y_o), (x_1, y_1)
>
> End tangent angles: α_o, α_1
>
> End curvatures: K_o, K_1
>
> Area: $A = \int_{x_o}^{x_1} y(x)\,dx$
>
> x-coordinate of centroid : x_s

The designer may specify this complete set or any meaningful subset.
He is interested in the shape of the curve, $y = f(x)$ or, in parameter
form, $\bar{Q}(t)$. It is possible to solve this problem with many different
types of functions whose free coefficients must be determined from the
given constraints. In the event of only linear constraints the solution can be derived by matrix inversion. However, the centroid constraint is nonlinear. Further, if all constraints are applied a system
of equations with ten unknowns must be solved, hardly attractive in
interactive design work.

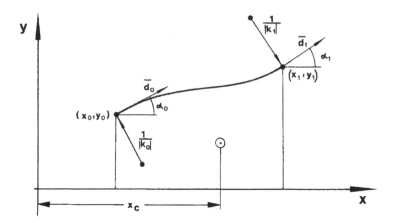

Fig. 3.10 : Form parameter segment

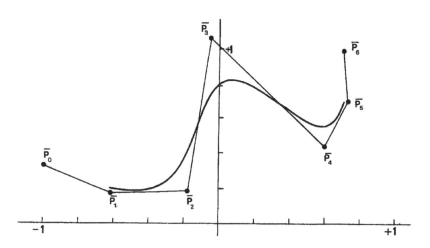

Fig. 3.11: B-spline curve for form parameter segment [12]

Creutz [11] developed a method based on B-splines avoiding these com-
plications by separating the resulting systems of equations. The local
property of B-spline curves permits introducing enough free vertices
for the end constraints at one end not to influence the form parameters
at the other end. The basic principle of the method is as follows:

A B-spline curve $\bar{Q}(t)$ with seven defining vertices (m=7) and of order
k=4 is chosen to represent the form parameter segment (Fig. 3.11).

The end knots and end vertices are not made to coincide. The vector co-ordinates of all seven vertices are thus free to be determined from the given constraints. When all ten constraints in Cartesian coordinates are specified, they can be converted to fourteen parametric constraints using the relations

at $t = t_o$ (left end)

$$\bar{Q}_o = \left[x(0), \; y(0) \right] = \left[x_o, \; y_o \right]$$

$$\dot{\bar{Q}}_o = \left[\left(\frac{dx}{dt} \right)_o, \; \left(\frac{dy}{dt} \right)_o \right] = \left[d_o \cos\alpha_o, \; d_o \sin\alpha_o \right] \qquad (18)$$

$$\ddot{\bar{Q}}_o = \left[\left(\frac{d^2x}{dt^2} \right)_o, \; \left(\frac{d^2y}{dt^2} \right)_o \right] = d_o^2 K_o \left[-\sin\alpha_o, \; \cos\alpha_o \right]$$

and six corresponding equations at the other end ($t = t_{max}$). Two further constraints result from area and centroid. In (18) d_o denotes the magnitude of the tangent vector at $\bar{Q}_o$, which is a free parameter resulting from the parametric notation (the same as d_1 at the other end).

The first three vertices of the B-spline curve depend only on the end constraints at $t = t_o$. It can be shown [11] that

$$\bar{P}_o = \bar{Q}_o - \dot{\bar{Q}}_o + \frac{1}{3} \ddot{\bar{Q}}_o$$

$$\bar{P}_1 = \bar{Q}_o \qquad - \frac{1}{6} \ddot{\bar{Q}}_o \qquad\qquad (19)$$

$$\bar{P}_2 = \bar{Q}_o + \dot{\bar{Q}}_o + \frac{1}{3} \ddot{\bar{Q}}_o$$

Analogous equations are obtained at the other end for $\bar{P}_4$, $\bar{P}_5$, $\bar{P}_6$.

The middle vertex $\bar{P}_3$ depends on the area and centroid constraint (as well as the other six vertices) via a small quadratic equation. It is therefore a straightforward matter to calculate the defining vertex set from the given constraints, and hence the B-spline curve. No trial and error procedure is required to meet all given constraints.

If fewer than the whole set of constraints are given the method can still be used with some default assumptions unless the remaining constraints are too fuzzy to define the shape of a curve.

This form parameter design method has been used as a basis for developing an interactive system for the initial design of ship lines [12]. It has been possible to design smooth lines meeting all constraints. By virtue of its resulting quality and limited computing effort the B-spline curve representation appears yet unrivaled for form parameter design with mixed constraints.

3.3.2 Surfaces

The design of free-form surfaces in engineering applications is generally performed from inputs as to

- Offset and perhaps derivative information at a set of given mesh points, or
- Positional and, where applicable, derivative information along a set of mesh lines in the surface.

Both types of problems can be treated as interpolation problems. Surface design from other types of parameters, especially integral form parameters, is rare.

We will concentrate on the case of quadrilateral mesh topologies. It may be necessary or useful in some technical applications to introduce other topologies, too. (See, e.g., Barnhill's work [13] on triangular meshes). But quadrilateral patches dominate in the applications, in part due to elegance and simplicity with which Coons [14] has been able to represent such patches.

In a notation similar to Coons·' we introduce curvilinear parameter coordinates (u, v) in the surface patch and normalize the ranges of these variables in the quadrilateral from zero to one (Fig. 3.12). The surface equation in vector form is given by

$$\bar{Q}(u, v) = \Big[x(u, v); \quad y(u, v); \quad z(u, v) \Big] \qquad (20)$$

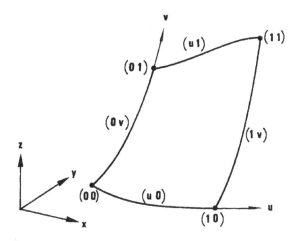

Fig. 3.12 : Coons surface patch

In surface design we are interested in a patch representation so that we may interpolate through given patch boundaries (or grid points) as well as meet certain continuity conditions across the boundaries.

We will first examine the more general case of interpolation through given patch boundary curves. For this purpose Coons has developed a patch representation (<u>Boolean sum</u> approximation, full Coons patch) of the following basic form:

In <u>vector</u> notation, using the abbreviations $\bar{Q}(u, v) = (uv)$ etc. (see Fig. 3.12):

$$(uv) = (0v) \cdot F_0(u) + (1v) \cdot F_1(u) +$$

$$+ (u0) \cdot F_0(v) + (u1) \cdot F_1(v) - \qquad (21)$$

$$- (00) \cdot F_0(u) \cdot F_0(v) - (01) \cdot F_0(u) \cdot F_1(v) -$$

$$- (10) \cdot F_1(u) \cdot F_0(v) - (11) \cdot F_1(u) \cdot F_1(v)$$

$$(0v), \ \ldots \quad = \text{boundary curves}$$
$$(00), \ \ldots \quad = \text{corner points}$$
$$F_0(u), \ \ldots \quad = \text{blending functions}$$

For the boundary curves to lie in the surface (<u>positional</u> continuity) it is easy to verify that the blending functions, both for u and v, must meet the conditions:

$$F_o(0) = 1, \ F_o(1) = 0, \ F_1(0) = 0, \ F_1(1) = 1 \qquad (22)$$

For <u>first derivative</u> continuity, in addition,

$$F_o'(0) = F_1'(0) = F_o'(1) = F_1'(1) = 0, \qquad (23)$$

where prime denotes differentiation with respect to u or v. Second derivative continuity would impose another set of conditions on the blending functions and so on.

The more compact <u>matrix</u> notation for the Boolean sum Coons patch is

$$(uv) = - \begin{bmatrix} -1 & F_o(u) & F_1(u) \end{bmatrix} \cdot \begin{bmatrix} 0 & u0 & u1 \\ 0v & 00 & 01 \\ 1v & 10 & 11 \end{bmatrix} \cdot \begin{bmatrix} -1 \\ F_o(v) \\ F_1(v) \end{bmatrix} \qquad (24)$$

Note that the boundary curves appear in the square matrix. They can be specified arbitrarily. However, one restriction of the Coons patch with only one set of blending functions F is that the surface has definite intrinsic values of its derivatives along its boundaries governed by the derivatives at the end points of each boundary. To be able to prescribe a desired arbitrary distribution of a derivative along the boundaries, additional terms must be added to the patch equation. For example, to achieve free control of the first derivatives we superimpose to (21) the vector expression

$$(uv) = (0v)_u \, G_o(u) \ + \ (1v)_u \, G_1(u) \ +$$

$$+ \ (u0)_v \, G_o(v) \ + \ (u1)_v \, G_1(v) \ -$$

$$- \ (00)_{uv} \, G_o(u) \, G_o(v) \ - \ (01)_{uv} \, G_o(u) \, G_1(v) \ - \qquad (25)$$

$$- \ (10)_{uv} \, G_1(u) \, G_o(v) \ - \ (11)_{uv} \, G_1(u) \, G_1(v)$$

$(0v)_u, \ \ldots$ = partial derivatives
$G_o(u), \ \ldots$ = blending functions

The blending functions G, for u and v, must be selected so that (25) will not affect the boundaries,

$$G_0(0) = G_0(1) = G_1(0) = G_1(1) = 0 \qquad (26)$$

and will produce the given first derivative distributions at the boundaries:

$$G_0'(0) = 1, \ G_0'(1) = 0, \ G_1'(0) = 0, \ G_1'(1) = 1 \qquad (27)$$

Equations (21) and (25) can be combined in compact matrix form like (24) (Coons [14]). The scheme of adding further corrective terms can be extended to any higher derivatives whose values at the boundaries are to be controlled.

We turn now to the special case that the boundary curves can be completely defined by information about their properties at the ends. Then mesh point information about offsets and derivatives will be sufficient to obtain the surface equation, hence we are interpolating in a grid of points. In this event the Coons patch representation can be simplified into a Cartesian product representation of matrix form, assuming blending functions of type F and G to be wanted,

$$(uv) = \begin{bmatrix} F_0(u) & F_1(u) & G_0(u) & G_1(u) \end{bmatrix} \cdot B \cdot \begin{bmatrix} F_0(v) \\ F_1(v) \\ G_0(v) \\ G_1(v) \end{bmatrix} \qquad (28)$$

where

$$B = \begin{bmatrix} 00 & 01 & 00_v & 01_v \\ 10 & 11 & 10_v & 11_v \\ 00_u & 01_u & 00_{uv} & 01_{uv} \\ 10_u & 11_u & 10_{uv} & 11_{uv} \end{bmatrix}$$

The boundary conditions at the patch corners are present in B. The principal difference from the Boolean sum approximation is that the boundary curves and their derivatives along the boundaries are no longer present in the surface equation. Otherwise the continuity and derivative matching properties at the boundaries of the Cartesian product patch are the same as before.

The choice of function type for the blending functions and boundary curves, where applicable, is arbitrary. Parametric Hermite polynomials (Coons [14]) and B-splines have frequently been used. The number of terms corresponds to the number of boundary conditions. For example, if first derivative continuity and control along the boundaries is desired, the blending functions F and G in (22), (23), (26), (27) are each subject to four boundary conditions so that a cubic Hermite polynomial or B-spline may be applied. The number of terms in the boundary curves depends on the desired derivative continuity in these curves. Cubics will do for curvature continuity of the curves at the grid points.

As an example, let us consider the popular Coons bicubic patch. This a a Cartesian product patch with cubic boundary curves and cubic blending functions of type F and G. This allows curvature continuity in the boundary curves, but only first derivative continuity and matching along boundaries due to the limited number of terms in the blending functions. This fact is sometimes overlooked. To connect patches with second derivative continuity a biquintic Cartesian patch (with six term blending functions and boundary curves) can be used.

To summarize this brief review of Coons surface interpolation we draw the following conclusions regarding the choice of the type of patch representation:

- Select a Boolean sum surface to interpolate given curves along mesh lines, a Cartesian product form if interpolation at mesh points is sufficient.

- Choose different levels of blending functions (F, G, H, ...) with corresponding vector terms according to the matching requirements along the boundaries for position, first, second derivatives and so on.

- Determine the number of terms in each blending function according to the continuity requirements across boundaries.

- Provide enough terms in the boundary curves to ensure their desired continuity at the ends, but no fewer terms than implied by the independent control level (matching) intended above, hence essentially at least as many terms as in the blending functions.

With these few rules in mind it is not difficult to set up an appropriate Coons surface interpolation.

3.4 FAIRING PRINCIPLES

3.4.1 Curves

Fairing aims at the refinement of a given preliminary shape design in the sense of some fairness criterion. Mathematical fairing techniques must be based on some objective measure of fairness in a curve or surface. Many definitions given for fairness are too subjective or qualitative to form the basis of a fairing method. Defining "fair" as "pleasing to the eye" is not uncommon, but thoroughly subjective. Our own earlier statement that "fairness is related to the absence of unwanted shape deficiencies, particularly oscillations", is also much too qualitative to be of practical use as a fairing principle. Besides, the absence of undesired oscillations is at best a necessary, but not a sufficient condition for fairness because a curve with a flat region between highly curved regions might well be rejected as "unfair" although it does not oscillate.

In a pragmatic sense we should be satisfied if we can describe how a fair curve or surface is produced. In many industries the free-form design of curves or surfaces is traditionally performed with the aid of elastic splines. A designer is willing to accept a result as fair if it corresponds to what he would be able to obtain with his fairing tool. We should, therefore, seek to analyze what it is that characterizes the spline fairing process and may, in our limited range of applications, equate "fairness" to what we might call "spline fairness". This is, of course, a property of both the fairing tool and the fairing process. The designer uses weights (ducks) to keep the spline in its deflected shape. Some of these weights may be kept "fixed" throughout the process to meet certain fixed constraints; all others are lifted successively to allow the spline to assume a relaxed, "fair" shape. (This is in contrast to an interpolation process). In its final position the spline should contain a minimum of potential energy, that is, internal strain energy, compared to all other positions it might have assumed within the given set of constraints and without deviating "too far" from the initially given curve. The last side condition inevitably requires subjective judgment.

This physically oriented description of the fairing process involves three important principles:

- A minimum strain energy objective,
- the presence of geometric constraints,
- and an accuracy requirement, that is,
  faithfulness to a given curve.

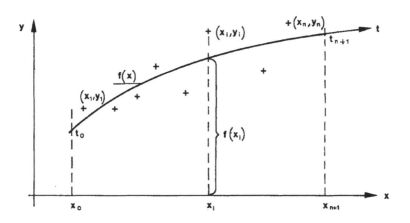

Fig. 3.13 : Curve fairing

Practical fairing methods must translate these principles into more
specific formulations. For example, for a thin elastic spline of constant cross section, the <u>fairness criterion</u> may be approximated by the
strain energy of flexure (Fig. 3.13)

$$U = EI \cdot \int_{x_o}^{x_{n+1}} \frac{y''(x)^2}{(1 + y'(x)^2)^{5/2}} \, dx =$$

$$= EI \cdot \int_{t_o}^{t_{n+1}} \left\{ \frac{\dot{x}\ddot{y} - \dot{y}\ddot{x}}{(\dot{x}^2 + \dot{y}^2)^{3/2}} \right\}^2 \, dt \qquad (29)$$

where primes denote x-derivatives, dots derivatives with respect to
the curve parameter t. In linearized (small deflection) beam theory
the first denominator is approximated by unity.

The accuracy measure, if the given curve is represented by a set of
its offsets $(x_1, y_1), \ldots, (x_n, y_n)$, may be expressed by the error
squares sum (Fig. 3.13)

$$A = \sum_{i=1}^{n} \left(f(x_i) - y_i \right)^2 = \sum_{i=1}^{n} \left(f(t_i) - y_i \right)^2 \qquad (30)$$

Many small variations of these two criteria are possible.

Geometric constraints of diverse types may be postulated. The softer
constraints can best be taken into account via the accuracy condition
(30). But it is important to be able to specify end constraints for
offsets and/or derivatives. This is because in many applications a
faired curve segment must meet certain continuity conditions at its
interval ends or, in fact, allow certain derivative discontinuities
to be produced at these boundaries, for example, for knuckles or flats.
In other words, many technical objects have features like curvature
or slope discontinuities deliberately designed into them in certain
places, which would tend to contradict the fairness criterion (29).
But these features may be treated as constraints at the ends of a fairing interval on the basis of a suitable segmentation of the curve.
Fairness is a global property of a curve (or surface), local unfair
features in this sense can nonetheless be applied as constraints.

With these remarks in mind we can now state the fairing problem in more
precise terms:

"In a given interval $\left[x_0, x_{n+1}\right]$ (or $\left[t_0, t_{n+1}\right]$ in parameter form) find a function $y(x)$ (or $\bar{Q}(t)$) that minimizes
the expression

$$E = A + s U \ (= min.) \qquad (31)$$

subject to any constraints present, particularly at the
interval ends."

The scalar s is a weighting factor used to control the degree of fairing relative to the accuracy objective based on the designer's judgment.

In its general form this is an extreme value problem of variational calculus with constraints. Some rather general conclusions have been drawn from this [15] , [16] , but most actual solution methods are based on simplified versions of this problem statement.

If, for example, eq. (29) is used in its linearized form, no special constraints are present, and the form of the function y(x) (or $\overline{Q}(t)$) is assumed, say, as a cubic spline ("cubic spline fairing"), then the coefficients a_j of this function can be determined from a linear system of equations resulting from the Ritz conditions

$$\frac{\partial E}{\partial a_j} = 0, \; j = 1, \ldots, J \tag{32}$$

Many practical fairing procedures make use of further simplifications in the underlying principles. Some of the more important schools of thought are the following:

- Different fairness criteria, often weakened substitutes for (29), e.g., the sum of the squares of the support reactions in a spline [3] , which is an indirect measure of its tendency toward unwanted oscillations. This criterion does not always produce satisfactory curves [17] .

- Least squares fitting, that is, discarding the fairness measure U and using only the accuracy expression A in (31) in conjunction with a function with fewer free coefficients J than given offset points n. This process does have a fairing effect compared to an interpolation, but lacks fairness vs. accuracy control and does not guarantee a "fair" result.

- Interpolation in place of fairing, using relatively few, but significant offset points and relying on the inherent smoothness of the function type chosen (cubic splines, Bézier curves, B-splines, ...). Success in this procedure is not automatic since it is sensitive to poor input data, so it needs a correction process. The latter can be provided very effectively by interactive graphical techniques.

3.4.2 Surfaces

The principles of surface fairing are much analogous to those for
curves. In practice many surfaces are faired indirectly by fairing a
mesh of curves in the surface. In computer-aided design this procedure
is often adopted, too. But any small car accident in a parking lot can
attest that fair boundary curves do not necessarily ensure a fair surface.

So it may be useful to look at the fairness definition for surfaces in
its own right. Seeking an analogy to curves we may examine the strain
energy of flexure (linearized) for a rectangular plate (size: a · b),
F(x,y) being its deflection:

$$U = C \cdot \int_0^a \int_0^b \left[\left\{ \left(\frac{\partial^2 F}{\partial x^2} \right) + \left(\frac{\partial^2 F}{\partial y^2} \right) \right\}^2 - 2 (1-\nu) \left\{ \frac{\partial^2 F}{\partial x^2} \cdot \frac{\partial^2 F}{\partial y^2} - \frac{\partial^2 F}{\partial x \, \partial y} \right\} \right] dx\,dy$$

(33)

Although this expression holds only for a special configuration, it does
suggest that surface fairness is somehow inversely related to the second derivatives ("curvatures") in the entire surface.

In practice the common approach to the construction of fair surfaces
is by interpolation to networks of faired curves. This approach relies
on the inherent smoothness of the surface interpolants. The results
should be examined for fairness in the interior of the network elements
and corrective action by trial and error is sometimes in place.

Two basic approaches to the interpolation of curve networks have been
taken. Coons' surface interpolation, discussed earlier, is local: For
each patch, information must be provided as to position, first, and
second derivatives along the boundaries (or at least at the corners)
in order to achieve corresponding continuity across the boundaries.
Gordon's [18] blending function interpolation method is global in the
sense that a given mesh of curves is interpolated simultaneously and
with automatically smooth transitions from patch to patch. The special
issues of curve parametrization in this context are discussed in [19] .

The preceding two methods of surface interpolation are independent of
the choice of function type for mesh line representation. Cubics, B-
splines, Bézier curves etc. may be used. More specific solutions,
which cannot be discussed here, result from the methods of Bézier
surfaces [6] and B-spline surfaces [20] .

Many systems for surface defintion are in practical use, especially in
the automotive, aircraft and shipbuilding industries. A few examples
are compared in Table I.

Table I: Surface Definition Systems:

System	Ref.	Curve Fairing (F) or Interp. (I)	Fair. Crit.	Curve funct. type	Surf. repr.
AUTOKON	[21]	F	Strain energy	Cubic spline	--
EUKLID	[22]	I	--	Cubic spline	--
SYSTRID 1	[23]	F + I	Least squares	gen. polyn.	Bézier surf. + ...
VIKING	[24]	I	--	Poly-nomials	Lofting
UNISURF	[6]	I	--	Bézier curves	Bézier surface

3.4.3 Interactive Fairing

Manual fairing is a highly interactive process, and current mathematical fairing methods similarly fall far short of being automatic. It
appears to be inherent in the problem formulation, as discussed, that

fairing requires human judgment at some crucial stages. This has motivated the development of several computer-aided interactive fairing
techniques.

Some of the basic causes for possible lack of fairness in curves and
surfaces are:

- Design deficiencies in initial shapes

- Reading or digitization errors in transferring
  data from drawings into the computer

- The fact that fair patch boundaries do not guarantee
  fairness in the interior of the patch

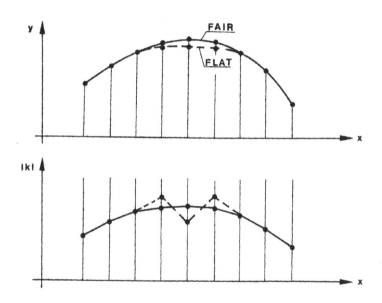

Fig. 3.14 : Curves and curvature distributions for
fair and flat curves (qualitative)

In interactive design we must devise visual tests to enable the designer
to detect where the shape is unfair so it may be modified. Just displaying sets of design curves on a display screen normally does not give
accurate enough information. Several more sensitive methods for visually testing the fairness of curves and surfaces have recently been

developed by Munchmeyer [25] , [26] ,[27] . These include:

- Inspection of the curvature distribution along a curve
  (Fig. 3.14), testing for absence of local oscillations
- Comparison of curvature distributions for sets of curves
  defining a surface, testing for resemblance
- Display of the orthogonal mesh of Euler's lines of principal curvatures in the surface, searching for irregu-
  larities
- Examination of the lines of constant, Gaussian curvature,
  which are highly sensitive to local unfairness

Techniques like these, which can guide the designer in interactive
fairing, should be further developed and incorporated in surface
design systems.

ACKNOWLEDGMENTS

The help received from U. Schumann-Hindenberg, P. Borchmeyer, and
Dr. K.-P. Beier in preparing the figures for this manuscript is gratefully acknowledged.

REFERENCES

1. S.H. Chasen, Geometric Principles and Procedures for Computer Graphic Applications, Prentice-Hall, Inc., Englewood Cliffs, New Jersey,
   1978.

2. D.F. Rogers, J.A. Adams, Mathematical Elements for Computer Graphics,
   McGraw-Hill Book Co., New York, 1976.

3. F. Theilheimer, W. Starkweather, "The Fairing of Ship Lines on a
   High-Speed Computer", David Taylor Model Basin Rept. No. 1474,
   Bethesda, Maryland, 1961.

4. A.W. Overhauser, "Analytic Definition of Curves and Surfaces by
   Parabolic Blending", Techn. Rept. No. SL 68-40, Ford Motor Co.
   Scient. Lab., 1968.

5. U.M. Waibel, "Procedures for Design and Manipulation of Surfaces in an Interactive Graphical Design System", in German, Diploma Thesis, Institut für Datenverarbeitung, Techn. Univ. Wien, Vienna, 1979.

6. P. Bézier, Numerical Control, John Wiley & Sons, London-New York, 1972.

7. R.F. Riesenfeld, "Applications of B-Spline Approximation to Geometric Problems of Computer-Aided Design", Rept. No. UTEC-CSC-73-126, Univ. of Utah, Comp. Science Dept., Salt Lake City, Utah, 1973.

8. I.J. Schoenberg, "Contributions to the Problem of Approximation of Equidistant Data by Analytic Functions", Quart. Appl. Math., vol.4, 1946, pp. 45-99 and 112-141.

9. C. de Boor, A Practical Guide to Splines, Springer Verlag, New York, 1978.

10. R.F. Riesenfeld, "Nonuniform B-Spline Curves", Second USA-Japan Comp. Conf., 1975.

11. G. Creutz, "Curve and Surface Design from Form Parameters by Means of B-Splines", in German, doctoral thesis, Techn. Univ. of Berlin, 1977.

12. G. Creutz, C. Schubert, "Interactive Curve Creation from Form Parameters by Means of B-Splines", Schiffstechnik, vol. 25, pp. 121-140, Hamburg, 1978.

13. R.E. Barnhill, "Smooth Interpolation over Triangles", Computer Aided Geometric Design, Barnhill and Riesenfeld, eds., Academic Press, 1974.

14. S.A. Coons, "Surfaces for Computer-Aided Design of Space Forms", Project MAC-Rept. TR-41, Massachusetts Institute of Technology, 1967.

15. E. Mehlum, "A Curve-Fitting Method Based on a Variational Criterion", Nordisk Tidskrift for Informations-Behandling, vol. 4, 1964.

16. L. Buczkowski, "Mathematical Construction, Approximation, and Design of the Ship Body Form", Journal of Ship Research, vol. 13, 1969.

17. W. Breitung, "About the Processing of Empirical Shipbuilding Data within the Scope of an Integrated Electronic Data Processing System", in German, Schiffstechnik, 1969.

18. W.J. Gordon, "Blending-Function Methods for Bivariate and Multivariate Interpolation and Approximation", SIAM Journ. Numer. Anal., 1971.

19. G.M. Nielson, J.A. Wixom, "Approximation Theory Techniques for Curve and Surface Description", Symp. on Comp.-Aided Hull Surface Definition, Society of Naval Arch. and Marine Eng., Annapolis, 1977.

20. W.J. Gordon, R.F. Riesenfeld, "B-Spline Curves and Surfaces", Computer Aided Geometric Design, Barnhill and Riesenfeld, eds., Academic Press, 1974.

21. E. Mehlum, P.F. Sörensen, "Example of an Existing System in the Shipbuilding Industry: The AUTOKON System", Proc. Roy. Soc. London, A 321, 1971.

22. H. Söding, "The Fairing of Ship Lines by Digital Computer", Hansa, 1967.

23. A.C. Massabo, Y. Moal, J. Stark, "An Introduction to SYSTRID.1", Batelle Geneva Research Centres, 1979.

24. N. Lidbro, "Analytic Form Definition of Ships", in German, Schiffstechnik, 1961.

25. F.C. Munchmeyer, G.K.H. Lau, "On the Interactive Design of Smooth Patched Surfaces", Proc. Int. Conf. on Interactive Techniques in Computer Aided Design, Bologna, 1978.

26. F.C. Munchmeyer, K.-P. Beier, "Designing Smooth Surfaces with DINAS", Proc. Int. Conf. on Graphical Data Processing, Vienna, 1979.

27. F.C. Munchmeyer, "The Gaussian Curvature of Coons Biquintic Patches", ASME Century 2 Int. Computer Technology Conf., August 1980.

Chapter 4

Modelling of Design Decisions for CAD

by

Horst Nowacki

Technische Universität Berlin
Institut für Schiffstechnik
Berlin 10, Salzufer 17-19

Chapter 4: Modelling of Design Decisions for CAD

4.1 INTRODUCTION

Engineering design is a decision process aimed at the concrete definition of a technical product. Every engineering discipline has developed
its own procedures and rules for design, which are not necessarily well
structured in the sense that a common denominator for the underlying
design logic in different applications is readily apparent. If the computer is intended to be used to support design decision-making, a clearly structured understanding of the design decision process is necessary in order to allow a well defined division of labor between man and
computer, to assimilate computer aids into design office organizations,
and to provide such aids in a sufficiently general, that is, relatively
problem-independent form. For this purpose a model of the design decision process, that is, a description of its general structure, should
be useful.

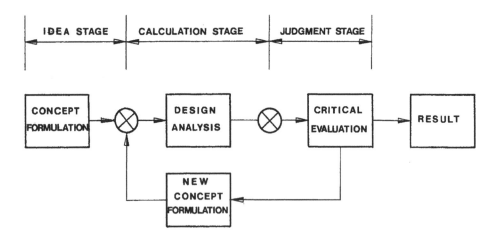

Fig. 4.1 : Design decision process

A natural division of labor in computer-aided design recognizes the
creative and critical abilities of man and the computer's superiority

in pure calculations. This is reflected in Fig. 4.1, where three stages
of the design decision process are distinguished: The idea stage, in
which a concept is formulated by the designer, the calculation stage,
where the proposed designs are analyzed, which can predominantly be performed by computer, and the critical judgment stage, which is man's
ultimate responsibility, although some more routine evaluations may
be delegated to computer programs. The evaluation will often lead to
new concepts being proposed so that the process generally is highly
iterative. On the basis of this subdivision, a CAD system must evident-
ly provide interfaces between man and computer, as indicated by the
circles with crosses in Fig. 4.1: An input interface to define design
concepts to the computer, an output interface to present calculation
results to the designer. The organization of these interfaces, not just
with respect to communication method, but chiefly also regarding the
design information content, is a cardinal task in designing a CAD system.

In the following we will concern ourselves further with the description
of models for design decision processes, mainly from the viewpoint of
design optimization. This is admittedly a special viewpoint, not necessarily prevalent in everyday manual design work. But it offers the
great advantage of allowing a unified approach to problem formulation
in design. Feasible design, in place of optimal design, which is a
common practical design objective, can be included in this discussion
as a specialized subcase of optimization.

We will emphasize the format of optimization as an aid in design problem formulation. It is also potentially an eminently useful tool in
design problem solution. However, our purpose is mainly an introduction
to the general potential of optimization in design, it is not intended
here to elaborate on numerical analysis aspects of optimization algorithms. There are many good textbooks available on this topic, some
are listed as [1 - 14] . Given the availability of such algorithms,
we rather wish to draw some conclusions as to their possible applications
in a CAD environment.

4.2 MODELLING OF DESIGN AS OPTIMIZATION

Design, after initial concept formulation, goes through a decision stage whose objective, from a general vantage point, is the following:

"<u>Given</u> the functional requirements (technical, physical, regulatory etc.) for a product or technical system. Among the proposed design alternatives meeting these requirements, <u>find</u> a best solution in the sense of some selection criterion!"

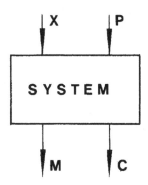

Fig. 4.2 : Technical system to be designed

Mathematical optimization in its general scope deals with a completely analogous type of problem so that we may model this particular stage of the design process according to the format of mathematical optimization (with constraints). The basic elements of an optimization problem, applied to a system or product to be designed, can be defined as follows (Fig. 4.2):

<u>Design variables:</u>

The design of the system can assume many different states characterized by variables. Those variables which are under the designer's control are called design variables (also free or decision variables). They are denoted by the vector

$$X = (x_1, \ldots, x_n) \tag{1}$$

Parameters:

Those variables which influence the state of the system design, but
cannot be controlled by the designer, are called parameters, P.

Constraints:

Those conditions which limit the free variation of the design variables
are called constraints, expressed by constraint functions C (X,P).
These functional relationships can be derived from functional and other
requirements which the design must meet. They can assume the form of
equality constraints

$$h_j (X,P) = 0, \quad j = 1, \ldots, J \qquad (2)$$

   or   inequality constraints

$$g_k (X,P) \gtreqless 0, \quad k = 1, \ldots, K \qquad (3)$$

For a well-posed problem, J must be less than n, but K can be arbitrary.

Measure of merit:

The merits of the design are judged on the basis of a criterion, called
the measure of merit function M(X,P) (or also object function, objective
function, return function).

In terms of these elements the mathematical optimization problem can
now be formulated, omitting the parameters P for brevity:

   "Find the set of design variables X that will minimize (or maximize)
   the measure of merit function M(X) subject to the constraints

$$h_j (X) = 0 \quad , \quad j = 1, \ldots, J$$
$$g_k (X) \gtreqless 0 \quad , \quad k = 1, \ldots, K" \qquad (4)$$

This formulation contains all essential features of the earlier definition of a design problem. Therefore it is possible to define a design
problem according to this format. To do so we must specify the meaning
of X, P, C, and M and their mutual dependencies in a given individual

case. The sum of the relationships among these quantities is the mathematical model of the system.

The choice of maximization can be disregarded from here on, because maximizing M is equivalent to minimizing -M.

We can now compare three different levels of design objectives:

- Feasible design
- Heuristic optimal design
- Algorithmic optimal design

The goal of feasible design is simply to find a design solution that does not violate any constraints. A measure of merit is not required for this purpose. Whenever it is difficult or impractical to define an explicit quantitative measure of merit this level of solution will be adequate.

In many everyday design applications, with or without computer aid, it is customary to use a measure of merit (like weight or cost) for comparison of designs, but changes to the design are made without resorting to formal optimizing strategies. This level may be called heuristic optimal design.

In CAD systems optimization strategies may be available to direct the redesign process, using measure of merit and constraint information. This corresponds to the level of algorithmic optimal design.

The last two levels of design require the same basis of information, that is, measure of merit and constraints; they differ only in the style of decision-making. Feasible design may be considered as the equivalent of optimal design with a constant measure of merit function. Thus the three levels of design are only different options under the same general problem formulation as given above. One can envision a single CAD system with all three options.

There is one important difference, however, between conventional heuristic design procedures and algorithmic design strategies: The former are frequently special purpose, that is problem-dependent, solution schemes, whereas in algorithmic optimization separation of "problem model" and "problem-independent strategy" is virtually a necessity. The model provides evaluations of M and C for any given X, the strategy in response to this information directs the changes in the design variables X (Fig. 4.3).

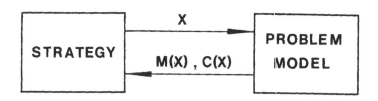

Fig. 4.3 : Interaction between strategy
and model

We have emphasized the general pertinence of the optimization format to design problem <u>formulation</u>. But, before discussing further details of the modelling process, the potential and limits of optimization as a method for design problem <u>solution</u> should also be clearly stated:

Optimization seeks a best solution in a proposed set of alternatives, based on a proposed criterion and in consideration of proposed constraints. For this purpose it will be a useful aid provided that the problem is so posed that a solution exists, which is either unique or one of several acceptable ones, and that a suitable solution algorithm is available. None of these prerequisites can be taken for granted. Optimization does not relieve the designer from the responsibility to submit sets of promising design alternatives, to choose relevant criteria and constraints, and to ensure the accuracy of the problem model.

Keeping these words of caution in mind we may proceed to examine the modelling process in more detail. A few simple rules are sufficient to describe the general modelling procedure:

- Enumerate the design variables
- List the constraints
- Choose a measure of merit
- Define the mathematical model $\left[M(X), C(X) \right]$

To review some basic modelling alternatives in connection with these steps several definitions must be discussed.

Design variables:

- Univariate vs. multivariate optimization:
  One vs. several design variables.

- Continuous vs. discrete design variables:
  Continuous design variables can assume any value in a specified range, which may be explicitly stated by upper and lower bounds. Discrete variables are limited to discrete states, for example, integer values, like the number of supporting bearings of a structure. Variables with only two states (Boolean variables) can be used to model the presence or absence of certain design features (members in a structure, ...).

- Lumped vs. distributed design variables:
  Most designs can be characterized by free variables of "lumped parameter" type, that is, variables assigned to discrete, scalar properties of the design. In some applications, particularly in optimum control, distributions of states (pressures, temperatures, ...) are treated as free variables (function optimization).

Parameters:

- Deterministic vs. stochastic parameters:
  If the parametric influences upon the design, which are not under the designer's control, are known in advance with certainty, the resulting model is deterministic. A stochastic model is obtained in the event of uncertainty in certain design parameters. Probability distributions may be given, or in some cases evaluated via the model by simulation methods. Decision theory provides rules for decision-making under uncertainty or risk.

- Single decision-maker vs. competition:
  One decision-maker, the designer, or sometimes several, including competitors, may influence the performance (measure of merit) of a design. Game theory provides certain methods for the latter case. The competitor's response can be entered into the model as a parameter.

Measure of merit:

- Unimodal vs. multimodal case:
  A measure of merit function is called unimodal if it has only one
  optimum (say, minimum) in its feasible range, that is, the range
  where no constraint is violated. Fig. 4.4, parts a) and c), illustrate this situation. The function is multimodal, Fig. 4.4, parts
  b) and d), if more than one local minimum exists in the feasible
  range; the smallest of these is the global minimum (or several
  in the case of ties).

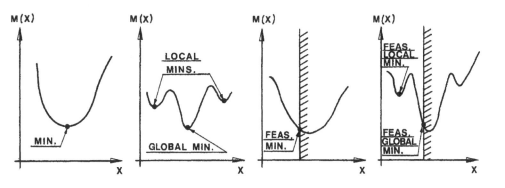

a) Unconstrained, b) Unconstrained, c) Constrained, d) Constrained,
   unimodal   multimodal   unimodal   multimodal

Fig. 4.4 : Types of optimization problems, univariate case

- Single-stage vs. multi-stage system:
  Fig. 4.5 shows a system that is so structured that several stages
  (subsystems) with separate contributions M_i to the measure of merit exist and such that the state of each stage (S_i, M_i) depends
  only on the vector of design variables of that stage X_i and information from the preceding stage S_{i-1}. Such a system is called multi-stage system (otherwise single-stage). The stage-wise structure
  of a system is exploited by the optimization methods of Dynamic
  Programming [10] .

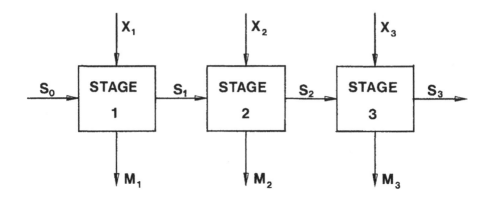

Fig. 4.5 : Multi-stage system

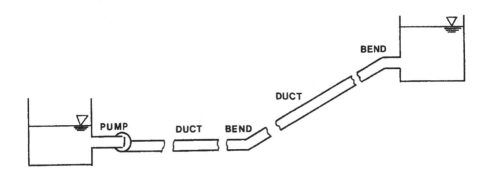

Fig. 4.6 : Hydraulic multi-stage system

An example of a multi-stage system is the hydraulic system shown
in Fig. 4.6. It consists of a pump and several ducts and bends to
pump liquid from one reservoir to another. Each element is characterized by a few design variables (diameter, shape, arc length
etc.). We may try to minimize the life cycle cost of the system,
that is, the sum of its acquisition and operating costs. Every
element contributes separately to this cost; the performance of
each stage (head loss etc.) for a given flow rate depends on the

output state (pressure, velocity) of the upstream element and the design variables of the element (stage) itself. The system may be optimized as a multi-stage system.

- Serial vs. non-serial systems:
  Multi-stage systems may be serial or non-serial (Fig. 4.7)

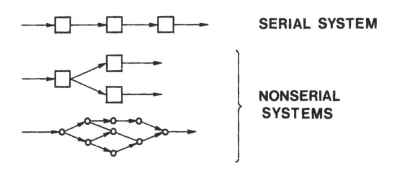

Fig. 4.7 : Serial and non-serial systems

- Single-mission vs. multiple-mission design:
  Some designs serve a single or very dominant, purpose, which can be reflected in the measure of merit. Others serve several objectives; to obtain a unique measure of merit the designer must assign priorities (weights, probabilities of occurrence of the operating states, etc.).

Constraints:

- Unconstrained vs. constrained optimization:
  The great majority of practical design problems involves one or several constraints.

- Equality vs. inequality constraints:
  Practical design problems usually involve both equality and inequality constraints. Hooke's law in contrast to a stress or deflection limit are examples of such different types in structural design. Depending upon what a particular solution method favors,

it is possible to convert inequalities into equalities, introducing slack variables, or vice versa.

This brief survey of possible modelling assumptions has indicated a great variety of available choices for describing practical design problems; the options presented, without being exhaustive, are rich enough to deal with a multitude of applications. Whether any such problem formulation is well-posed and amenable to effective solution by optimization methods is a different issue which must be carefully examined in the context of every new application.

A small and deliberately very simple example may serve to illustrate the modelling procedure and some of its consequences.

Consider a cantilever beam (Fig. 4.8) of length 1 with concentrated load F at its end. We seek a minimum weight design (material steel), assuming for simplicity a rectangular cross section (breadth b, height h), constant over the length of the beam. The formulation of the design problem is straightforward.

Design variables: b, h.

Measure of merit: $A = b \cdot h$ = cross sectional area, because the weight of the beam is proportional to A.

Constraints:

1) The maximum bending stress in the beam, σ_B, must not exceed the permissible bending stress, σ_{BP}:

$$\sigma_B = \frac{6 F \cdot 1}{bh^2} \leq \sigma_{BP} \qquad (5)$$

or in normalized form, introducing the constraint function g_1:

$$g_1 = g_1(b,h) = \frac{\sigma_{BP}}{\sigma_B} - 1 \geq 0 \qquad (6)$$

2) The maximum shear stress, τ, must be no greater than the permissible shear stress, τ_p :

$$\tau = \frac{1.5\ F}{b \cdot h} \leqslant \tau_p \tag{7}$$

$$\text{or} \quad g_2 = \frac{\tau_p}{\tau} - 1 \geqslant 0 \tag{8}$$

3) The deflection at the end of the beam, d_{max}, must not exceed a given limit, d_p:

$$d_{max} = \frac{Fl^3}{3EI_y} = \frac{4Fl^3}{Ebh^3} \leqslant d_p \tag{9}$$

$$\text{or} \quad g_3 = \frac{d_p}{d_{max}} - 1 \geqslant 0 \tag{10}$$

4) When the ratio of h/b becomes greater than a certain limit the beam develops an unstable condition with respect to twist about its longitudinal axis. The critical load for this insta-bility is:

$$F_{crit} = \frac{4}{l^2} \sqrt{\frac{GI_T \cdot EI_Z}{1 - \nu^2}} \tag{11}$$

$$\text{with} \quad I_T = \frac{b^3h + h^3b}{12}, \quad I_Z = \frac{b^3h}{12}$$

Applying a safety factor of 2 the twist instability constraint is

$$F \leqslant \frac{F_{crit}}{2} \tag{12}$$

$$\text{or} \quad g_4 = \frac{F_{crit}}{2F} - 1 \geqslant 0 \tag{13}$$

5) Finally we impose a limit on h/b for practical reasons, both because a high, thin beam may be impractical for our purpose and because beam theory analysis, which we have used, will not be valid beyond certain limits.

$$(h/b) \leqslant (h/b)_{max} \tag{14}$$

or

$$g_5 = \frac{(h/b)_{max}}{h/b} - 1 \geqslant 0. \quad (15)$$

Any further inequality constraints might have been introduced, if desired, to express physical or practical conditions the design must meet. Even in this very simple design application it is not possible to know in advance which constraint (or constraints) will be active, that is, govern the optimum design and which others are dominated. This depends on the numerical values assigned to the application.

Fig. 4.8 shows the design (or decision) space, that is, the dependence of measure of merit and constraint functions on the design variables, for the following numerical example:

$$F = 500 \text{ kp} \qquad l = 1500 \text{ mm}$$

$$\sigma_{BP} = 20 \text{ kp/mm}^2 \qquad \tau_p = 10 \text{ kp/mm}^2$$

$$d_p = 5 \text{ mm} \qquad (h/b)_{max} = 10$$

Plotting the results against h (mm) and $1/b$ (mm^{-1}) gives straight lines for constant measure of merit A. The constraints g_i are cross-hatched where they are active, that is, where they border the feasible space. The shear constraint g_2 is always inactive. Disregarding g_5 for the moment, the active constraints would be g_3, g_1, g_4 as we move from left to right. The lightest design would be governed by g_4 at unrealistically high values of (h/b). This is why a limit on (h/b) is necessary. If g_5 is applied, then the feasible optimum lies at the intersection of g_5 with g_3. Here the solution is

$$A = 2500 \text{ mm}^2, \ b = 15,8 \text{ mm}, \ h = 158 \text{ mm} .$$

We might have doubts in the lateral stiffness of this beam and, if so, introduce another constraint or reduce (h/b)$_{max}$. We may also consider a new type of design with a different cross section etc. In other words, having optimized a proposed concept the designer must critically evaluate the result and may have to modify the concept or problem formulation. Stages of optimization, evaluation, and reformulation are natural parts of the design process.

Note further that the optimum solution, which we have found by inspection of the design space, generally cannot be determined from equalities alone, for example, by equating $g_5 = g_3 = 0$, because it is not known in advance which inequality constraint or constraints will be active at the optimum. The optimum might also be governed by just a single active constraint or, in fact, none if the optimum should be located in the interior of the feasible space (rare case in design). Therefore, the designer can only be assured of the optimality of a solution by solving the optimization problem with its complete set of constraints.

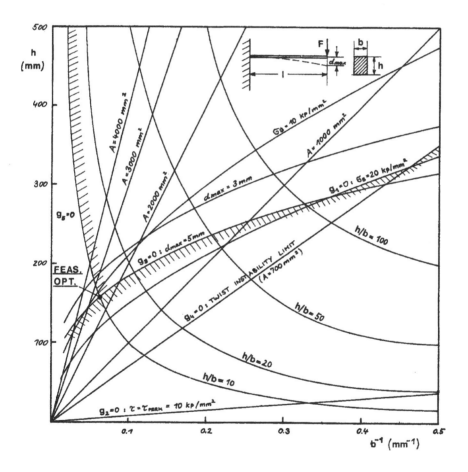

Fig. 4.8 : Design space of cantilever beam

4.3 OVERVIEW OF OPTIMIZATION METHODS

4.3.1 Classification of Problem Types

In the following a condensed overview of available optimization methods
will be given, mainly as background to their possible application in
computer-aided design. It is not intended to review any algorithms in
great detail; there is ample material in the literature about this topic (e.g. [1-14]).

The general nonlinear optimization problem with constraints, which corresponds to a general design problem as discussed in the preceding section, is of the form:

"Find the optimal solution vector $X = X^*$ so that

$$M(X^*) = min$$

subject to the constraints $\qquad$ (16)

$$h_j(X) = 0, \; j = 1, \; ..., \; J,$$

and $\qquad g_k(X) \geqslant 0, \; k = 1, \; ..., \; K"$.

The problem types and solution methods resulting from this formulation
can be classified according to the following possible assumptions:

- Linear vs. nonlinear case
- Optimization without or with constraints
- Continuous or discrete design variables (def. in 4.2)
- Univariate vs. multivariate optimization (def. in 4.2)
- Analytic vs. heuristic optimization methods

Those cases which are more important for design applications are under-
lined. The implications of the major distinctions must be examined more
closely.

In the general case any or all of the functional relationships $M(X)$,
$h_j(X)$, and $g_k(X)$ are nonlinear. If at least one of them is nonlinear,
then (16) is referred to as nonlinear programming problem, where pro-

gramming is used in the sense of "optimization with constraints". Most
practical design applications contain nonlinearities. Linear programming
deals with the special case where M(X) and the (inequality) constraints
are linear functions.

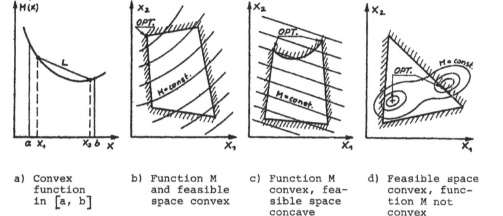

a) Convex
   function
   in [a, b]

b) Function M
   and feasible
   space convex

c) Function M
   convex, fea-
   sible space
   concave

d) Feasible space
   convex, func-
   tion M not
   convex

Fig. 4.9 : Convex and non-convex functions
and feasible spaces

It is of interest to discuss the question of uniqueness of optimal solutions for the general nonlinear programming case. Uniqueness depends
on the convexity of measure of merit function and feasible solution
space. These concepts are illustrated by examples in Fig. 4.9. A function is convex in a region, represented here by the interval [a, b] ,
if for any two points x_1 and x_2 in the region a straight-line L connecting the ordinates $M(x_1)$ and $M(x_2)$ does not contain function values at
any abscissa between x_1 and x_2 that are less than M(x) at the same abscissa (Fig. 4.9 a). For concave functions, replace "less" by "greater".
Linear functions are convex and concave. A convex space is defined similarly: A space (region, set) is convex if the straight-line connection between any two points in the space contains only points which
are also in the space (Figs. 4.9, b) and d): Spaces with crosshatched
boundaries).

It can be shown that a set of concave inequality constraint functions g_k forms the boundaries of a convex space. On this basis a uniqueness theorem for optimal solutions of the nonlinear programming problem with only inequality constraints can be stated:

If M(X) is a convex function to be minimized and the inequality constraints form a convex feasible space, then a local minimum, if one exists, is also the global minimum (case b) in Fig. 4.9).

It is unfortunately only under these restrictive assumptions that an optimum can be proven to be unique. In any other case, e.g., as in Figs. 4.9 c) or d), several local optima may exist, which complicates the search for a global solution.

Optimization problems without constraints are rare in design applications. We will nevertheless discuss some solution methods for this case because they can be adapted to be used in problems with constraints, too.

It is also rare in design that the problem model (measure of merit and constraints) can readily be expressed in closed analytic form. Analytical methods of optimization are therefore of limited use. Heuristic methods predominate because they do not require explicit analytic expressions and are liberal with respect to the function type.

4.3.2 Optimization Strategies

Table I give a survey of several kinds of methods and algorithms in use for different types of optimization problems. The unconstrained methods are subdivided into: a) Search methods, requiring only function values of M(X); b) Gradient methods, requiring function values and first partial derivatives; c) Methods requiring, in addition, the second partial derivatives. Other details will be explained in the following discussion of some of the major examples.

Table I: Optimization Methods

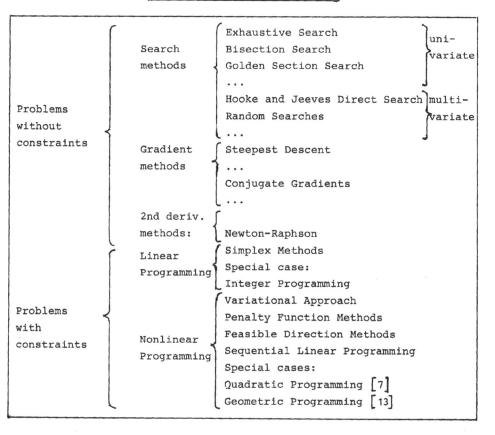

Exhaustive Search

This algorithm for univariate, unconstrained optimization requires function values M(X) as input. It does not depend on the function being unimodal, continuous, or differentiable.

The function is sampled at equidistant stations (Fig. 4.10), using N subintervals. The optimum is presumed to lie within the two subintervals bordering the "best" function value found. This is strictly true for unimodal functions, but not really certain in multimodal cases. However, with sufficiently small intervals the method will tend to find the global optimum.

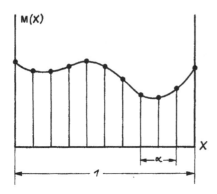

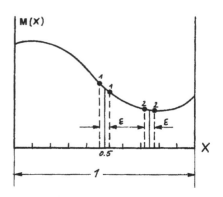

Fig. 4.10 : Exhaustive search   Fig. 4.11 : Bisection search

If the initial interval of uncertainty is 1 , it will be reduced to
α = 2/N at the end (Fig. 4.10). This requires 1 + 2/α function evaluations. The computing effort is high to achieve a reasonable accuracy
α (e.g.: 2001 function evaluations for α= 0.001).

Bisection Search

This is a search algorithm for univariate, unconstrained optimization
of unimodal functions M(X). However, the function need not be continuous or differentiable.

In every cycle of this search (Fig. 4.11) the interval of uncertainty
is approximately halved by calculating two sample values at interval
midpoint $\pm$ ε/2. The minimum of a unimodal function cannot lie on that
side which borders the greater of the two values. The remaining interval of uncertainty is thus

$$\alpha = \frac{1}{2} + (1 - \frac{1}{2}) \varepsilon , \qquad (17)$$

and after n steps

$$= \frac{1}{2^n} + (1 - \frac{1}{2^n}) \cdot \varepsilon . \qquad (18)$$

The search continues until α becomes less than a given end tolerance; the best solution found up to that stage is the final approximate optimum. The method is much more effective than the exhaustive search, using only

$$N = 2 \cdot \frac{\ln \frac{1-\varepsilon}{1-\alpha}}{\ln 2} \qquad (19)$$

function evaluations to reduce the interval of uncertainty from 1 to α: E.g. 20 samples for $\alpha = 0.001$.

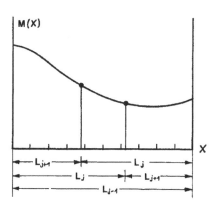

Fig. 4.12 : Golden Section search

Golden Section Search

This search is also intended for univariate, unconstrained optimization of unimodal functions, which need not be continuous or differentiable.

In this algorithm the sample points are placed so that the interval of uncertainty is reduced by a constant factor in each successive step (Fig. 4.12):

$$\tau = \frac{L_j}{L_{j-1}} = \frac{L_{j+1}}{L_j} = \ldots \qquad (20)$$

with

$$L_{j-1} = L_j + L_{j+1}$$

These two equations combined yield $\tau^2 + \tau - 1 = 0$, hence $\tau = 0.618$.

In each cycle this search discards one subinterval of length L_{j+1}, which cannot contain the minimum because it borders the greater of the two sample values. The remaining interval of length L_j will always contain one reusable sample point, which is already properly located a distance of $L_{j+1} = \tau \cdot L_j$ away from either the right- or left-hand boundary of the new interval. Thus only one new sample calculation is required per cycle except for the first cycle, which requires two. The number of function evaluations to reduce the uncertainty interval from 1 to α is consequently rather low:

$$N = 1 - 2.08 \ln (\alpha) \qquad (21)$$

The Golden Section Search belongs to the most effective univariate searches (together with the Fibonacci Search [7]). For $\alpha = 0.001$, N = 16.

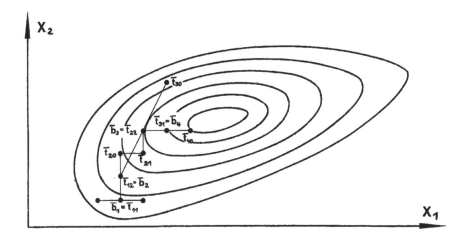

Fig. 4.13 : Hooke and Jeeves Direct Search

Hooke and Jeeves Direct Search

This algorithm is for multivariate, unconstrained optimization of unimodal functions.

The method has two alternating search patterns (Fig. 4.13). The local exploratory search samples the function at the currently active base point $\overline{b}_k$ and at neighboring points $\overline{b}_k \pm \Delta x_1, \overline{b}_k \pm \Delta x_2, \ldots$ in all directions parallel to the coordinate axes. The temporary best point moves on to any location with improved function value, and at the end of a local search cycle becomes the new base point $\overline{b}_{k+1}$. The <u>global</u> exploratory move attempts to double the progress made in the preceding local cycle $\tilde{t}_{k+1,0} = \overline{b}_k + 2 (\overline{b}_{k+1} - \overline{b}_k)$. If it succeeds, the next local search will continue from there $(\tilde{t}_{k+1,0})$, otherwise from $\overline{b}_{k+1}$, starting a new local/global cycle. Whenever $\overline{b}_{k+1} = \overline{b}_k$, the step widths Δx are reduced, and the search terminates when all Δx have become less than their tolerances. More details about the algorithm can be found in [7] , [15] .

The method is one of the most efficient multivariate search techniques. However, like most similar schemes, it is not entirely safe against functions with narrow "ridges", oblique to the coordinate axes, which may cause the algorithm to stop before the optimum is reached.

Other well-known methods of similar type are Powell's Direct Search [16] , and Rosenbrock's method [17] .

<u>Random Search Methods</u>

In random search methods the abscissa values where the function is sampled are drawn from random number generators (computer programs). Pure random methods have a uniform probability distribution for all variables in their ranges of variation. The purpose of a random distribution of sampling points is to safeguard against multimodalities. However, to reach a reasonable level of probability that a good approximation to the global optimum has been found the sampling density must be very high. The pure random search is thus very ineffective, and may result in prohibitive computing times with increasing number of design variables.

Random search methods with built-in learning can be applied to reduce this difficulty. Here the probability distributions, from which the random numbers are generated, are modified from time to time so as to increase the sampling density in the vicinity of the temporary optimum. But this is only a partial cure, particularly when the number of design variables is high.

Rechenberg's Evolutionary Strategy [11] is a very advanced form of random search with learning. It simulates the principles of biological evolution (mutation and natural selection), and adapts the standard deviation of its random design variable changes to its rate of success in sampling. This makes this search far more effective than other random methods, even under certain conditions competitive to deterministic methods.

Gradient Methods

Gradient methods rely on information on the objective function and its first partial derivatives, usually approximated numerically. The function is assumed to be unimodal and differentiable at least once.

The method of steepest descent is a classical gradient method. It follows the direction of the gradient of the objective function as a measure of the greatest possible improvement locally and makes a finite step of width h in this direction. The choice of step width is crucial for the effectiveness of the search, but also its final convergence to the optimum. The method has the tendency of overshooting the optimum for lack of a simple rule for adjusting the step width. The rate of convergence near the optimum consequently is slow.

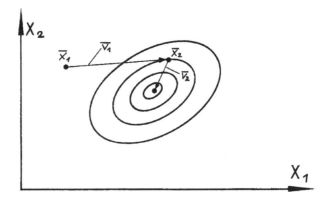

Fig. 4.14 : Conjugate gradient method

The modern Conjugate Gradient Methods avoid this dilemma by resorting to information about the global characteristics of the objective function. Consider the case of a quadratic measure of merit function

$$M(X) = Q - \bar{b}^T \cdot X + c \qquad (22)$$

where

$$X = (x_1, \ldots, x_n) = \text{Design variable vector}$$
$$\bar{b} = (b_1, \ldots, b_n) = \text{coefficient vector}$$
$$c = \text{a constant}$$

and   Q is a quadratic form

$$Q = X^T \cdot A \cdot X \qquad (23)$$

with

$$A = \begin{bmatrix} a_{11} & a_{12} & \cdots & a_{1n} \\ a_{21} & \cdots & & a_{2n} \\ \cdots & & & \cdots \\ a_{n1} & & & a_{nn} \end{bmatrix} \qquad \text{with } a_{ij} = a_{ji}$$

We postulate a positive semi-definite matrix A and hence form Q, which will ensure that Q remains non-negative for any X.

A positive definite quadratic form has a the property that a set of conjugate gradient directions, $\bar{V}_i$ etc., exists, which is defined by

$$\bar{V}_i \cdot A \cdot \bar{V}_j = 0, \quad 1 \leqslant i \neq j \leqslant n \qquad (24)$$

Fig. 4.14 illustrates the concept. In the set of contours of a quadratic function (ellipses) an initial starting point X_1 and an arbitrary direction $\bar{V}_1$ is chosen. A univariate optimization can be performed in this direction leading to X_2. At this point a conjugate direction $\bar{V}_2$ is determined, another one-dimensional optimization carried out, and so on until n conjugate directions have been completed. It can be proven that a sequence of n univariate searches for the quadratic form with n design variables will lead precisely to the extremum of the function. This is the basis of success for the conjugate gradient methods.

There are several possibilities for calculating the conjugate gradient directions, described in the literature. Two of the best-known conjugate gradient algorithms are by Fletcher and Powell [18] and Fletcher and Reeves [19] .

If the real objective function is not of quadratic form, the conjugate gradient methods may be used iteratively. The effectiveness of this approach depends on how close to quadratic the real function is.

Second Derivative Methods

The Newton-Raphson method and other so-called Newton type methods, explained in [7] , rely also on a local quadratic approximation of the function, but calculate this approximation using second partial derivatives, for example, via the Hessian matrix of the function. This promises to be very effective for nearly quadratic functions although the computing effort for accurately calculating many higher derivatives must be kept in mind, too.

In summary, there exists a reasonable variety of good optimization algorithms to choose from in any of the categories of search, gradient, and second-derivative methods. Their relative merits depend on the application and usually on the fine tuning of step widths, starting points etc. Many of the better algorithms perform rather equivalently under comparable tuning conditions. A thorough review of the effectiveness and reliability of numerous algorithms of this class is given by Himmelblau [7] .

Linear Programming

Linear Programming (LP) is the most important special case of constrained optimization. It deals with the optimization of a linear measure of merit function subject to linear inequality constraints. The problem may be normalized in different ways, for example:

$$\text{"Maximize } M(X) = \sum_{i=1}^{n} c_i x_i \qquad (25)$$

subject to

$$g_k(X) = \sum a_{ik} x_i - b_k \leq 0, \quad k=1, \ldots, K \qquad (26)$$

and

$$-x_i \leq 0, \quad i=1, \ldots, n \text{ (nonnegative design variables)"}$$

This LP problem has a concave objective function and a convex feasible space, since linear functions are convex as well as concave. Therefore any local optimum is also a global optimum. Moreover the optimum cannot lie in the interior of the feasible space, because for any interior point there is a point on some boundary whose function value is better (Fig. 4.15) due to the linearity of M. The optimum can only lie at one corner of the feasible space (intersection of constraints) or, in the event of a tie, at more than one corners simultaneously. This property greatly facilitates the solution of LP problems because the vertices of the feasible space are the only points to be examined in searching for the optimum. We refer to the literature for details about solution algorithms [2] , [6] . The LP algorithms are generally very effective and allow solving problems with many design variables and constraints.

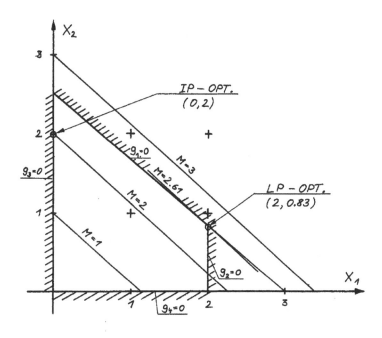

Fig. 4.15 : Linear and Integer Programming

An example may illustrate the properties of this problem type (Fig.4.15) Consider the following LP problem in two variables:

$$\text{Maximize} \quad M = \frac{8}{9} x_1 + x_2 \quad (27)$$

$$\text{subject to} \quad g_1 = 10x_1 + 12x_2 - 30 \leqslant 0$$

$$g_2 = x_1 - 2 \leqslant 0$$

$$g_3 = -x_1 \leqslant 0 \tag{28}$$

$$g_4 = -x_2 \leqslant 0$$

The feasible solution space (Fig. 4.15) is surrounded by four constraints; M increases toward top right. The optimum, by inspection, is at (2, 0.83), where M = 2.61. The other corners have lower values of M, so this optimum is unique.

LP has found many applications in engineering, notably in resource allocation problems, scheduling, network planning. But its applications to product design are relatively rare, because design is usually plagued by nonlinear relationships. However, in this context LP may be used in approximate, iterative methods (Sequential Linear Programming, see below).

Integer Programming

If we consider the LP-problem (25), (26) with the added restriction that only integer values of the variables x_i are feasible, we obtain the Integer Linear Programming (ILP), or briefly Integer Programming (IP), problem. Referring back to Fig. 4.15 we can discuss the following features of this problem type:

- The integer optimal point may lie on the boundary or in the interior of the feasible space. In Fig. 4.15 the integer optimum is M = 2 at (0, 2).

- The IP optimum is not necessarily the closest feasible integer point to the LP optimum, so that in general the IP solution cannot be obtained by simply rounding the LP solution point to the nearest feasible integers.

Several IP algorithms have been developed with the common purpose to find the solution without having to enumerate all feasible solutions, which may become very numerous. Some of the more successful methods are adaptations of LP algorithms or Branch and Bound methods [1].

The IP format is rather important for many types of technical applications. It occurs whenever a large number of discrete feasible solutions must be compared, sometimes also in the modified forms of nonlinear integer programming or mixed integer-continuous variable optimization. Many design decisions are of "Yes - no" (Boolean) type, hence
in the class of IP. The evaluation of decision trees, and the optimization of networks and graphs are also in this category.

Nonlinear Programming

The general form of the Nonlinear Programming problem (NLP) was defined
earlier in (16). NLP is probably the most frequent problem type in engineering design applications because of its very general scope. It has
also posed many special computational difficulties so that no single
best approach to all kinds of NLP problems has yet evolved, but several
different proposed solution methods have proven successful in their proper context. Some of these were listed in Table I and will be reviewed
in the following.

Variational Calculus Formulation

The complete NLP problem can have equality and inequality constraints.
Classical variational calculus deals with extreme value problems in the
presence of equality constraints. However, it is possible to remove the
inequalities from the NLP formulation by introducing nonnegative unknowns
s_k^2 , called slack variables, so that

$$g_k(X) \geqslant 0, \ k = 1, \ \ldots, \ K$$

becomes

$$g_k(X) - s_k^2 = 0 \qquad (29)$$

In variational calculus the extreme value of M(X) subject to equality
constraints is determined by introducing further auxiliary unknowns,
the Lagrange multipliers μ_k, and solving for the unconstrained minimum
of the modified function

$$H(X) = M(X) + \sum \mu_k \left\{ g_k(X) - s_k^2 \right\} = \min \qquad (30)$$

A nonlinear system of equations for (n+2K) unknowns is then derived from
the extremum conditions

$$\frac{\partial H}{\partial x_i} = \frac{\partial H}{\partial \mu_k} = \frac{\partial H}{\partial s_k} = 0 \quad \text{for} \quad \begin{cases} i = 1, \ldots, n \\ k = 1, \ldots, K \end{cases} \qquad (31)$$

The equation solving effort involved in this mathematically elegant solution is often a strong deterrent.

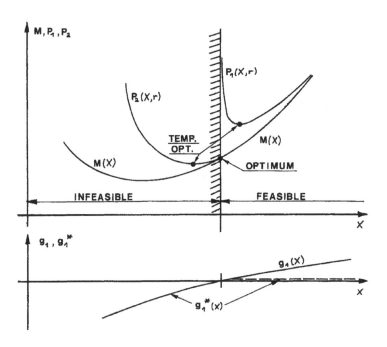

Fig. 4.16 : Penalty function techniques, univariate example

Penalty Function Methods

The objective of transforming the constrained NLP problem into an unconstrained problem leading to the same solution, which was one of the basic principles in the variational formulation, can also be achieved by a transformation akin to (30), but without any additional unknowns. This is the basis of the so-called penalty function methods [3] , [7] , [20].

The principle of these methods is to create an artificial objective function by adding a penalty term to the natural objective function of the given problem. The penalty term, which may be constructed in one form or another, allows for the presence of constraints by raising the objective function when a constraint is violated or nearly violated. There are two principal variants of this method, the _interior_ and the _exterior_ penalty function techniques. Both are illustrated for the univariate case in Fig. 4.16.

The _interior penalty function_ technique is also known under the name of SUMT (Sequential Unconstrained Minimization Technique [3]). It applies a penalty term to the function in the interior of the feasible space. This results in the penalty function

$$P_1(X,r) = M(X) + r \sum_{k=1}^{K} \frac{1}{g_k(X)} + \frac{1}{\sqrt{r}} \sum_{j=1}^{J} h_j^2(X) \qquad (32)$$

Preferably the equality constraints $h_j(X)$ are accounted for separately beforehand in calculating $M(X)$ and eliminating a few unknowns, so that the inequality penalty term is of main concern to us. Its magnitude is controlled by the parameter r. The method begins by minimizing the penalty function P_1 for some finite value of r. A feasible starting point must be chosen. The minimization of P_1 can be performed by any unconstrained method such as those discussed earlier. Under certain conditions it can be arranged that this method will not accidentally leave the feasible space, but keep a certain distance from its boundary due to the barrier effect of the penalty term. The solution provides a minimum of P_1 which serves as a temporary minimum in optimizing M. The minimization is now repeated with a reduced value of r, and so on for a few iterations, in order to let the temporary minimum approach the true minimum as r goes to zero. It is not to be recommended to begin with a very small value of r right off because the resulting penalty function would be highly nonlinear (nonquadratic) and the barrier effect would become too weak.

With proper tuning of all elements in this algorithm the method has given reliable results [7] .

In the _exterior penalty function_ technique the transformation is

$$P_2(X,r) = M(X) + \frac{1}{r} \sum_{k=1}^{K} g_k^*(X)^2 \qquad (33)$$

where $\qquad g_i^* = \begin{cases} 0 \text{ for } g_i(X) \geqslant 0 & \text{(feasible)} \\[2ex] g_i(X) \text{ for } g_i(X) < 0 & \text{(infeasible)} \end{cases}$

That is, a penalty is applied only if a constraint is violated, hence only outside the feasible space (Fig. 4.16). The penalty term may be assumed in different form, too. Its purpose here is to penalize against deviations from the feasible space.

The starting point in this method may be feasible or infeasible. Otherwise the solution procedure is the same as with SUMT. The temporary optimum of P_2 again approaches the true optimum as r goes to zero in successive iterations. Experience with this method has also been good [20]

Feasible Direction Methods

These methods deal with the NLP problem without any function transformations [14]. It is a straightforward matter to calculate M(X) and all constraints $g_k(X)$ (only inequalities allowed) and to test whether X is a feasible point. If no constraint is violated, this method seeks to improve the function M(X) as if it were unconstrained.

Generally one (or several) constraints will eventually be violated. When this happens the method seeks its new orientation in a so-called usable-feasible direction, that is, a direction that will improve the function value, but attempt not to violate a constraint. Figs. 4.17 and 4.18 illustrate the principle for a two-dimensional example. At any given point P_i at (or near) a boundary of the feasible space ($g_i=0$) the gradients of the measure of merit and "violated" constraint functions can be calculated. Together they define a sector, shown in Fig. 4.17, within which locally the function M improves whereas the constraint is not violated. This is the usable-feasible sector. A suitable direction in this sector, say, the median, is chosen for a uni-directional optimization, which will tend to roughly follow the boundary, at least locally. In fact, this search may find a unidirectional optimum P_{i+1} before reaching a new constraint (or the same one again), Fig. 4.17, or P_{i+1} may be located on such a constraint, Fig. 4.18. In the former

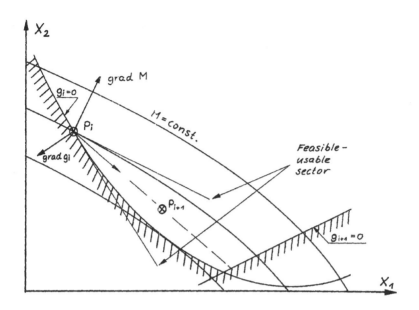

Fig. 4.17 : Feasible-usable sector (based on [22])

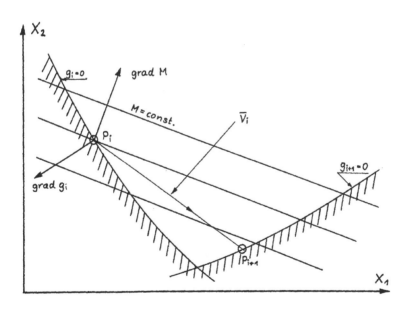

Fig. 4.18 : Feasible-usable direction and new
constraint violation (based on [22])

case the unconstrained strategy takes over again, in the latter the usable-feasible search.

If it succeeds the method will find a local optimum. It should be used from different starting points if it is necessary to test for multimodality.

Computing experiences with feasible direction methods have also been very satisfactory [21] .

Sequential Linear Programming (SLP)

The SLP method solves the NLP problem indirectly, replacing it by a sequence of linearized approximations. For a given NLP formulation as in (16), but with inequalities only, a linear approximation may, for example, be obtained by Taylor expansions about an arbitrary point X_o

$$M(X) \approx M(X_o) + \text{grad } M(X_o) \cdot \left\{ X - X_o \right\}$$

$$(34)$$

$$g_k(X) \approx g_k(X_o) + \text{grad } g_k(X_o) \cdot \left\{ X - X_o \right\} \geqslant 0$$

$$k = 1, \ldots, K$$

The resulting linearized problem is of LP type and can be solved by any of the effective LP algorithms. This is the major advantage of this method. The procedure is applied iteratively, using the optimum of each LP approximation as the base point for a new linearization. Special precautions are required to achieve convergence if the solution does not lie at a vertex of the feasible space [22] .

The SLP approach has been used with good success, particularly for problems with larger numbers of variables and constraints, where the efficiency of the LP algorithms is of special advantage.

Summary

We have seen in section 4.2 that it is possible to state design problems in the form of rather general optimization problems. We have learnt in this section that optimization theory provides a great variety of corresponding solution methods. The format of Nonlinear Programming, which is a very general form of an optimization problem, is particularly perti-

nent to design by virtue of its nonlinear merit functions and constraints. Our review has suggested that there exists a reasonable choice
of applicable NLP solution methods and algorithms. Methods of this rather general type are suitable for dealing with many different classes of
design problems. They should be among the first candidates to be used
in the context of CAD.

4.4 APPLICATION OF OPTIMIZATION IN CAD

Despite the rather general pertinence of the optimization format to
engineering design problems I believe it is fair to say that the status
of application of such methods in CAD has not yet measured up to its
potential. In some areas, of course, optimization methods have a well
established tradition so that computer-based optimization is enjoying
popularity and success. These areas include:

- Structural design [22]
    (Weight and cost minimization of structures in aerospace,
        civil, mechanical engineering etc.)

- Chemical process design
    (Optimization of chemical processing systems for many
        industries, also of nuclear processes)

- Economic optimization of technical systems
    (For example, cost minimization of manufacturing processes,
        optimization of transport systems and their components etc.)

- Resource allocation problems
    (Optimum capacity planning, scheduling, resource distribution
        in queuing systems, optimization of networks and graphs)

- Electrical and electronic system design
    (Optimization of power systems, circuits etc.)

- Optimum control
    (Control of dynamic systems)

Many of the examples cited involve the optimization of larger systems,
where computer aids are recognized as a necessity or at least as a valuable time-saving expedient. By contrast, in areas of medium and small
size design problems the acceptance of computer-aided optimization has
been relatively slow. The reasons for this situation should be discussed

a little more thoroughly. As background let us classify design problems
by their sizes into three somewhat arbitrary groups (Table II).

Table II: Size of Design Optimization Problems

Problem size	No. of design variables	No. of con- straints	Task time w.o. comp.	Task time w. comp.
Small	$\leqslant 5$	$\leqslant 10$	$\leqslant$ sev.hours	$\leqslant 1$ h
Medium	$\leqslant 20$	$\leqslant 50$	sev. days	$\leqslant 1$ day
Large	> 20	> 50	sev. weeks	a few days

Some of the major factors potentially inhibiting the introduction of
computer-based optimization in design, particularly in everyday design
work, are the following:

1. Problem size:

   Some problems are of such size that either the computing times and
   costs or the total task performance times become prohibitive. This
   is aggravated where access to the computer is slow and job turnaround
   time long. In this situation, feasible design, analyzed by computer
   or by hand, often becomes the reduced target.

2. Programming effort:

   Any major programming or program adaptation effort required prior
   to or during design tends to deter from the use of the method.

3. Data preparation effort

4. Variability of design tasks:

   If the design tasks are highly variable, frequent changes in the
   software may be necessitated.

5. Verification of results:

   The designer may have difficulties in verifying and judging the
   sometimes massive results of an optimization run. This is particularly serious if the system lacks graphical aids for output interpre-

tation and if intermediate calculation results cannot be inspected.

6. Lack of specialized knowledge on optimization

7. Wickedness of the design problem:

This refers to the elusive properties of some design problems to defy definitive problem formulation.

Closer examination of this list suggests that items 2 through 5 are principally related to properties of the computer software system, that is, these factors need not be considered as necessary evils, but can be brought under better control by suitable design of the CAD system.

4.5 INTERACTIVE OPTIMUM DESIGN

Computer use in design is considerably enhanced by interactive computing facilities for two major reasons: Human judgment and experience can be brought to bear immediately on the design process, and necessary response times in man-machine communication can be achieved to obtain economical performance times for the entire design task.

These reasons are obviously also valid for computer-aided design optimization. Human involvement is necessary in problem formulation, verification of intermediate and final results, and imaginative problem reformulation. If the designer chooses to optimize by algorithms, he is responsible for tuning the strategy with respect to step widths, starting points etc. If he prefers heuristic optimization (or feasible design), he further is in control of the changes in the design variables. A computer system for design should not limit itself to supporting design analysis, but it should also provide capabilities for the designer's immediate participation in design activities such as those just mentioned. This is the basis of the concept of "Interactive Optimum Design", which is advocated by many CAD practitioners.

In summary, a CAD system for interactive optimum design, whether at the levels of algorithmic or heuristic optimal design, or even feasible design, should provide support for the following design activities:

- Problem formulation
- Input data preparation and verification
- Test calculations
- Optimization runs
- Monitoring and control of such runs in progress
- Examination of intermediate and final results
- Problem reformulation

4.6 A DESIGN OPTIMIZATION SESSION

A sample design session performed with an existing design optimization software will help to illustrate how the requirements just discussed can be met and how the designer can perform his work in such a software environment. The example is based on the software system OSW (Optimization Software), developed at the Technical University of Berlin [23] .

This software system is a general purpose software system for optimization in design. It is structured into modules for strategies and user application programs. The strategies are collected in a bank of methods and can be invoked by the designer during a session. The user programs (in FORTRAN) are regular main programs working from an input data file into an output data file. The input data file must contain the design variables, the output data file contains information from which it must be possible to calculate measure of merit and constraint function values by means of FORTRAN-like artihmetical expressions. Strategy and user program are connected with each other during problem formulation in dialogue at the OSW command level. This permits to combine at execution time arbitrary strategies from the bank of methods with arbitrary application programs provided by the user.

The command level of the OSW also supports the formulation of design optimization problems by simple declarations in terms of variables occurring in the application program input and output data files. These variables can interactively be assigned names to address them at the command level. It is also possible to introduce command level names for quantities defines by arithmetical expressions with variables from the data files of the application program. All assigned command level names are called communication symbols, briefly "cosyms", and are stored in a system file (ZDAT) together with their definitions in terms of the associated variables or expressions. During problem formulation the designer declares by suitable commands which cosyms or cosym expressions play what role in optimization as design variables, constraints or measure of merit. The result of these declarations is stored in another system file (GDAT), whose status can be updated whenever desired. The OSW also provides commands to set up and monitor the optimization run and to print out (or display) its results.

For its general functions for command interpretation, data base management, and interactive execution control the OSW relies on the support of design executive system software. One version of the OSW uses the system core IST (Informationssystem Technik), the other the executive system DINAS. The following examples are based on the OSW version under DINAS [24] .

The bank of methods contains primarily NLP strategies, both of penalty function and feasible direction type, in addition to a number of unconstrained strategies.

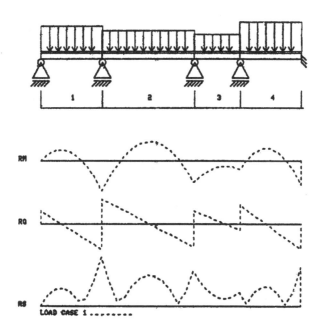

Fig. 4.19 : Continuous beam, initial design

The example chosen to illustrate a design session with the OSW is the minimum weight design of a statically indeterminate system, a continuous beam of four spans, supported as shown in Fig. 4.19 . We consider a single load case with distributed loads in each span. The span lengths and loads are given as (t = tonnes, metric):

$$l_1 = 4.0 \text{ m}, \quad l_2 = 6.0 \text{ m}, \quad l_3 = 3.0 \text{ m}, \quad l_4 = 4.0 \text{ m}$$

$$q_1 = 6 \text{ t/m}, \quad q_2 = 5 \text{ t/m}, \quad q_3 = 4 \text{ t/m}, \quad q_4 = 7 \text{ t/m}$$

The cross section of the beam is assumed to consist of a built-up I-girder section, constant in each span, but variable from span to span. Flange widths (B) and girder heights (H) are to be treated as free variables, flange thickness is assumed as B/7, web thickness as H/10. The bending stresses at the interior supports and at the wall are taken into consideration as potentially critical conditions and limited to permissible values of 20.000 t/m^2. No other constraints are applied.

A calculation program (DLTRGT) for the weight and stress of a continuous beam (general configuration) is available in the system. Its input data file, named /EINGABE/DLTRG/7/, is known (under DINAS) and has been filled with basic load case input data previously. The output data file /AUSGABE/DLTRG/7/, which is empty, is also available in the system.

The OSW design session, which is performed on a storage tube terminal, proceeds as follows:

Step 1:

The project is activated under DINAS, and the data files entered. The DISPLAY command can be used to verify the load configuration (upper part of Fig. 4.19). Next the OSW level is entered, and the system files ZDAT and GDAT are created by default if none are specified by the user. (User entry lines in the protocol are marked with arrows).

```
      ENTER PROJECT NUMBER
  ──▶  2
      READY-DINAS

  ──▶ ENTER /EINGABE/DLTRG/7/ A
      FILE ENTERED IN PART. A  BL.CNT.=  1
      READY-DINAS

  ──▶ ENTER /AUSGABE/DLTRG/7/ B
      FILE ENTERED IN PART. B  BL.CNT.=  1
      READY-DINAS
```

```
━━► DISPLAY /EINGABE/DLTRG/7/ 1
    READY-DINAS


━━► OSW
    LOESCHE ZEICHEN = #, LOESCHE ZEILE = &

    * ZDAT CREATION *
    ZDAT      ZDAT       0   PART.= C
    * GDAT CREATION *
    GDAT      GDAT       0   PART.= D
    READY-OSW
```

Step 2:

Command level names (cosyms) are introduced for any variables of interest in the input and output data files. This is done by the command
DKOSYM, which serves to define the position of the variable in its file.
After completing these declarations the verification command VKOSYM can
be used to display all cosym specifications.

```
━━► DKOSYM BREIT1 INPUT REAL*4 /EINGABE/DLTRG/7/ 0 7
    READY-OSW
    .  .  .  .  .
━━► DKOSYM SIGMA4 OUTPUT REAL*4 /AUSGABE/DLTRG/7/ 0 4
    READY-OSW


━━► VKOSYM *
    BREIT1    INPUT    REAL   *4   FI=EINGABE   DLTRG   7   GR= 0   EL=  7
    HOEHE1    INPUT    REAL   *4   FI=EINGABE   DLTRG   7   GR= 0   EL=  9
    BREIT2    INPUT    REAL   *4   FI=EINGABE   DLTRG   7   GR= 0   EL= 19
    HOEHE2    INPUT    REAL   *4   FI=EINGABE   DLTRG   7   GR= 0   EL= 21
    BREIT3    INPUT    REAL   *4   FI=EINGABE   DLTRG   7   GR= 0   EL= 31
    HOEHE3    INPUT    REAL   *4   FI=EINGABE   DLTRG   7   GR= 0   EL= 33
    BREIT4    INPUT    REAL   *4   FI=EINGABE   DLTRG   7   GR= 0   EL= 43
    HOEHE4    INPUT    REAL   *4   FI=EINGABE   DLTRG   7   GR= 0   EL= 45
    GEW       OUTPUT   REAL   *4   FI=AUSGABE   DLTRG   7   GR= 0   EL=  5
    SIGMA1    OUTPUT   REAL   *4   FI=AUSGABE   DLTRG   7   GR= 0   EL=  1
    SIGMA2    OUTPUT   REAL   *4   FI=AUSGABE   DLTRG   7   GR= 0   EL=  2
    SIGMA3    OUTPUT   REAL   *4   FI=AUSGABE   DLTRG   7   GR= 0   EL=  3
    SIGMA4    OUTPUT   REAL   *4   FI=AUSGABE   DLTRG   7   GR= 0   EL=  4
    READY-OSW
```

Step 3:

The optimization problem is formulated by declaring the design variables,
measure of merit, and constraints. We introduce eight design variables,
the widths and heights of the girders in the four spans (BREIT1 through
HOEHE4), using the command DXVECTOR. The object function (named GESGEW)
is declared by the command DOBJFN to be equal to the variable GEW (total
weight of beam), which is to be minimized. The inequality constraints

are declared by DCONSTR, naming each constraint (NEB1 etc.). Eight constraints require the design variables to remain positive, four others pertain to the stress limits at the critical supports. The command VCONSTR displays the status of the constraints for verification. (The results of steps 2 and 3 are stored in the files ZDAT and GDAT, respectively, which can be saved, so that these steps need not be repeated in future sessions dealing with the same problem form).

```
──►DXVECTOR = BREIT1 HOEHE1 BREIT2 HUEHE2 BREIT3 HOEHE3 BREIT4 HOEHE4
   READY-OSW
──► DOBJFN GESGEW = GEW = MIN
   READY-OSW
──► DCONSTR NEB1 = BREIT1 > 0.
   READY-OSW
   .   .   .   .   .
──► DCONSTR NEB12 = 1.-SIGMA4/20000. > 0.
   READY-OSW
──► VCONSTR *
   NEB1     = BREIT1       >   0.0                          ACTIVE
   NEB2     = HOEHE1       >   0.0                          ACTIVE
   NEB3     = BREIT2       >   0.0                          ACTIVE
   NEB4     = HOEHE2       >   0.0                          ACTIVE
   NEB5     = BREIT3       >   0.0                          ACTIVE
   NEB6     = HOEHE3       >   0.0                          ACTIVE
   NEB7     = BREIT4       >   0.0                          ACTIVE
   NEB8     = HOEHE4       >   0.0                          ACTIVE
   NEB9     = 1.-SIGMA1/20000. >        0.0      ACTIVE
   NEB10    = 1.-SIGMA2/20000. >        0.0      ACTIVE
   NEB11    = 1.-SIGMA3/20000. >        0.0      ACTIVE
   NEB12    = 1.-SIGMA4/20000. >        0.0      ACTIVE
   READY-OSW
```

Step 4:

The SET command allows assigning data to any cosyms. This serves here to define the initial design (unit is meters).

```
──► SET BREIT1 = 0.2          .   ..  .   .   .
   READY-OSW
                              ──► SET HOEHE3 = 0.5
──► SET BREIT2 = 0.2          READY-OSW
   READY-OSW
                              ──► SET HOEHE4 = 0.5
   .   .   .   .   .          READY-OSW
```

Step 5:

A test calculation is performed for the initial design, using COMPUTE. The results are printed out via PRINT. For this application program it is also possible to display the results graphically, showing the distributions of bending moments (RM), shear forces (RQ), and stress magnitudes (RS) in the beam (Fig. 4.19, lower part). Current results indicate that the beam is heavily overdimensioned (weight GEW in tonnes), the stresses being far below permissible levels.

```
——► COMPUTE
     READY-OSW

——► PRINT *
     KOSYMS :
     BREIT1    =   0.20000
     HOEHE1    =   0.50000
     BREIT2    =   0.20000
     HOEHE2    =   0.50000
     BREIT3    =   0.20000
     HOEHE3    =   0.50000
     BREIT4    =   0.20000
     HOEHE4    =   0.50000
     GEW       =    4.4801
     SIGMA1    =    3775.9
     SIGMA2    =    3775.9
     SIGMA3    =    2699.7
     SIGMA4    =    2979.1
     OBJECTFUNCTION AND CONSTRAINTS :
     GESGEW    =    4.4801
     NEB1      =   0.20000
     NEB2      =   0.50000
     NEB3      =   0.20000
     NEB4      =   0.50000
     NEB5      =   0.20000
     NEB6      =   0.50000
     NEB7      =   0.20000
     NEB8      =   0.50000
     NEB9      =   0.81121
     NEB10     =   0.81121
     NEB11     =   0.86501
     NEB12     =   0.85104
     XVECTOR :
     BREIT1    =   0.20000
     HOEHE1    =   0.50000
     BREIT2    =   0.20000
     HOEHE2    =   0.50000
     BREIT3    =   0.20000
     HOEHE3    =   0.50000
     BREIT4    =   0.20000
     HOEHE4    =   0.50000
     READY-OSW

——► $
     READY-DINAS

——► DISPLAY /AUSGABE/DLTRG/7/ 1

     READY-DINAS

——► OSW
     LOESCHE ZEICHEN = #, LOESCHE ZEILE = &
     READY-OSW
```

Step 6:

When the initial design is satisfactory, an optimization method is selected by MOPT, here the Tangent Search [21] , setting a limit to the
number of function evaluations (NMAX=1000). The run is started by

OPTIMIZE. The results are again printed out and displayed (Fig. 4.20).

```
——►MOPT = TANGENT (NMAX = 1000)
    READY-OSW


——►OPTIMIZE (TRACE)
    READY-OSW

——► PRINT *
    KOSYMS :
    BREIT1    =   0.15411
    HOEHE1    =   0.23636
    BREIT2    =   0.10964
    HOEHE2    =   0.29872
    BREIT3    =   0.10836
    HOEHE3    =   0.20749
    BREIT4    =   0.66946E-01
    HOEHE4    =   0.31957
    GEW       =   1.4008
    SIGMA1    =   19975.
    SIGMA2    =   19993.
    SIGMA3    =   19931.
    SIGMA4    =   19337.
    OBJECTFUNCTION AND CONSTRAINTS :
    GESGEW    =   1.4008
    NEB1      =   0.15411
    NEB2      =   0.23636
    NEB3      =   0.10964
    NEB4      =   0.29872
    NEB5      =   0.10836
    NEB6      =   0.20749
    NEB7      =   0.66946E-01
    NEB8      =   0.31957
    NEB9      =   0.12602E-02
    NEB10     =   0.36895E-03
    NEB11     =   0.34469E-02
    NEB12     =   0.33172E-01
    XVECTOR :
    BREIT1    =   0.15411
    HOEHE1    =   0.23636
    BREIT2    =   0.10964
    HOEHE2    =   0.29872
    BREIT3    =   0.10836
    HOEHE3    =   0.20749
    BREIT4    =   0.66946E-01
    HOEHE4    =   0.31957

    READY-OSW
```

The result obtained is not necessarily a definitive optimum, because the search was terminated after 1000 trials before reaching the specified tolerance limits. But is appears to be close to optimal since the design is nearly "fully stressed", that is, all stress constraints are nearly active. The beam is considerably lighter than the initial design. For verification of the global nature of this optimum a new search might be performed from a different starting point.

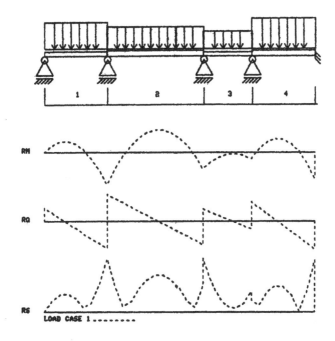

Fig. 4.20 : Continuous beam, final design

The OSW can also be used for heuristic optimal design, controlled by the designer by means of the SET and COMPUTE commands, or for feasible design with neutralized measure of merit.

Modelling of design decisions calls for a great variety of choices to be presented to the designer depending on application and design procedure. But it appears possible to find a common denominator in such diverse activities, based on such broad concepts as interactive optimum design, and to provide CAD software systems supporting the designer during both problem formulation and problem solution.

ACKNOWLEDGMENTS

The development of the software system OSW was supported by a grant of the Bundesminister für Forschung und Technologie, administered by the Kernforschungszentrum Karlsruhe.

The author also gratefully acknowledges the help received from W. Jonas, who performed the sample calculations and prepared the figures for this chapter.

REFERENCES

a) Books

1. R.E. Burkhard, Methoden der Ganzzahligen Optimierung, Springer-Verlag, Wien-New York, 1972.

2. G.B. Dantzig, Linear Programming and Extensions, Princeton University Press, Princeton, 1963.

3. A.V. Fiacco, G.P. McCormick, Nonlinear Programming: Sequential Unconstrained Minimization Techniques, John Wiley, New York, 1968.

4. R. Fletcher, ed., Optimization, Academic Press, New York, 1969.

5. R.L. Fox, Optimization Methods for Engineering Design, Addison-Wesley, Reading, Mass., 1971.

6. S.I. Gass, Linear Programming, McGraw-Hill, New York, 1964.

7. D.M. Himmelblau, Applied Nonlinear Programming, McGraw-Hill, New York, 1972.

8. H.P. Kuenzi, W. Krelle, Nonlinear Programming, Blaisdell, New York, 1966.

9. W. Murray, P.E. Gill, eds., Numerical Methods for Constrained Optimization, Academic Press, New York, 1974.

10. G.L. Nemhauser, Introduction to Dynamic Programming, Wiley, New York, 1966.

11. I. Rechenberg, Evolutionsstrategie, Optimierung technischer Systeme nach Prinzipien der biologischen Evolution, F. Frommann Verlag, Stuttgart-Bad Cannstatt, 1973.

12. D.J. Wilde, Optimum Seeking Methods, Prentice-Hall, Englewood Cliffs, N.J., 1964.

13. C. Zener, R.J. Duffin, E.L. Peterson, Geometric Programming - Theory and Application, John Wiley, New York, 1967.

14. G. Zoutendijk, Methods of Feasible Directions, Elsevier, Amsterdam and New York, 1960.

b) Articles

15. R. Hooke, T.A. Jeeves, "Direct Search Solution of Numerical and Statistical Problems", Journ. ACM, vol. 8, April 1962.

16. M.J.D. Powell, "An Efficient Method for Finding the Minimum of a Function of Several Variables without Calculating Derivatives", Computer Journal, vol. 7, 1964/65.

17. H.H. Rosenbrock, "An Automated Method for Finding the Greatest or Least Value of a Function", Computer Journal, vol. 3, Oct. 1960.

18. R. Fletcher, M.J.D. Powell, "A Rapidly Convergent Method for Minimization", Computer Journal, vol. 6, 1963.

19. F. Fletcher, C.M. Reeves, "Function Minimization by Conjugate Gradients", Computer Journal, vol. 7, 1964/65.

20. W.I. Zangwill, "Nonlinear Programming via Penalty Functions", Management Science, vol. 13, January 1967.

21. R.R. Hilleary, "The Tangent Search Method of Constrained Minimization", U.S. Naval Postgraduate School, Techn. Rept. No. 59, Monterey, March 1966.

22. G.G. Pope, L.A. Schmit, "Structural Design Applications of Mathematical Programming Techniques", Agardograph No. 149, AGARD, Neuilly - sur - Seine, 1971.

23. K.-P. Beier, H. Nowacki, C. Schubert, A. Weichbrodt, "A General Purpose Software System for Optimization in Ship Design", Proc. 2nd Int. Conf. on Comp. Appl. in the Automation of Shipyard Operation and Ship Design, eds. Jacobsson et al., North-Holland Publ. Co., Amsterdam, 1976.

24. K.-P. Beier, W. Jonas, "DINAS - - A Transportable Executive System for Interactive Computer-Aided Design", Proc. Int. Conf. on Interactive Techniques in Computer Aided Design, Italian Chapter ACM, Bologna, September 1978.

PART II

CAD SYSTEM ENGINEERING

Chapter 5

DATA BASE DESIGN

by

Ketil Bo

RUNIT, Computing Centre at
the University of Trondheim,
Norway

5.1 Introduction

All Computer systems of some complexity has data organization problems. The efficient structuring of the data is critical to both storage needs and execution speed.

This is expecially true in Computer Aided Design (CAD) because one usually deals with large volumes of data at high speed.

The Data Base is the heart of any CAD/CAM system, feeding information to all the activities in the production process.

But what is a Data Base? Even this basic question has a variety of answers if you read the literature. Ideally seen, it is like a Norwegian lunch table on an expensive mountain hotel: There is all kinds of food and you can walk up to the table (if you can afford it), pick out just what you want and don't care about the rest. If you look at the dishes of the different guests, you will find that everyone has composed his own very special dish from the same table of food.

The same approach should be possible on an ideal Data Base. Different people should be able to access the same Data Base and pick out just the data they need and don't be disturbed by the remainding data.

Unfortunately, it is not that easy, because our Data Base systems are not developed up to this kind of efficiency yet, but we are on our way.

From a more formal point of view, we can define a DATA BASE as:

> A collection of interrelated data stored together without unnecessary redundancy to serve multiple applications. The data is stored so that they are independent of programs which use the data. A common and controlled approach is used in adding new data and in modifying and retrieving existing data within the data base [1].

The information that describes a particular design project resides on a PROJECT DATABASE. It corresponds to the information that normally resides on drawings, specifications and engineering data. This database grows significantly over time and its structure must be fairly dynamic.

A convenient conceptual organization (as versus physical organization) of a project database is as a description of entities and their attributes. The attributes may be cost, axial load or other performance requirements, nominal text strings such as manufacturer or function (structural, acoustical, control etc.) and more complexely coded information, such as shape, location and colour.

A basic requirement of database systems is that the application programmer should be able to write application programs that are independent of the data stored in the database. Although this requirement has been known for some time, efforts to achieve it have been only partially successful.

Data used by an application program has four components:

1. The data itself
2. The syntax (format) of the data
3. The semantics (meaning) of the data
4. The access path to the data

Usually the second, third, and fourth components are implicitly incorporated into the program and the database only keeps track of the data itself. The format of the data, its meaning, and its access path must be known to the application program.

5.2 Retrospective Glance

In order to get a better understanding of a modern DATA BASE, it may
be worth while to look back into the short history of computer stored
data and see how the techniques and complexity have evolved from one
stage to another: [1].

FIRST STAGE: Elementary Data File (Predominant in the early 1960's):

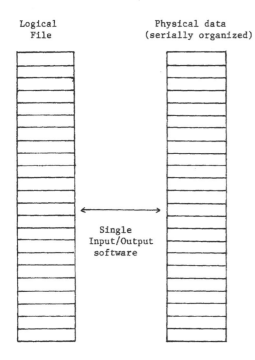

Logical
File

Physical data
(serially organized)

Single
Input/Output
software

. Files organized in serial
  manner
. Physical data structure
  essentially the same as logical file structure
. Several copies stored of the
  same file because previous
  generations of data are kept
. Software handles only input/
  output operations
. Application programmer designs the physical file layouts and embeds them in the
  application programs
. If the data structure or
  storage device are changed,
  the application program must
  be rewritten, recompiled,
  and retested
. Data is usually designed and
  optimized for one application
. High level of redundancy between data files

Fig. 5.1. Elementary Data Files

SECOND STAGE: File Access Method (Predominant in the late 1960's)

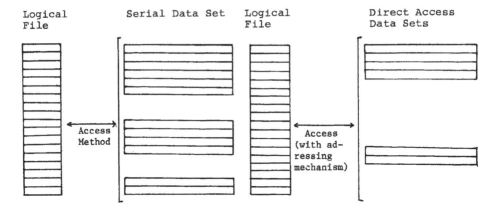

Fig. 5.2. File Access Methods

- Serial access or random access is possible to records (not fields)
- Logical and physical file organization are distinguished but the relationship between them is fairly simple.
- Storage units can be changed without changing the application program.
- Data structures are usually serial, indexed sequential, or simple direct access.
- Multiple-key retrieval is generally not used.
- Data security measures may be used (but are rarely very secure).
- Data still tends to be designed and optimized primarily for one application.
- Much data redundancy still exists.
- The software provides "access" methods but not "data management".

THIRD STAGE: Early Data-Base Systems (Predominant in the early 1970's)

Application
Programmer's
Logical Files

Physical Data-Base

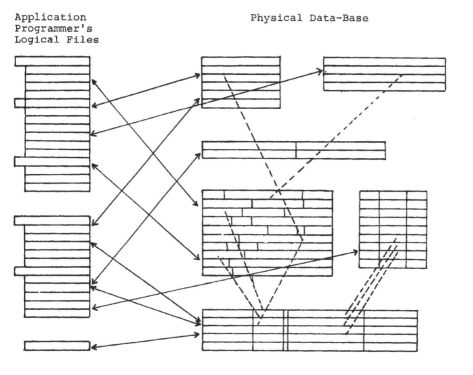

Fig. 5.3. Early Data-Base Systems

- Multiple different logical files can be derived from the same physical data
- The same data can be accessed in different ways by applications with different requirements
- Software provides the means to lessen data redundancy
- Data elements are shared between diverse applications
- Absence of redundancy facilitates data integrity
- The physical storage organization is independent of the application programs. It may be changed often in order to improve the data-base performance without application program modification
- Multiple-key retrieval can be used
- Complex forms of data organization are used without complicating the application programs.

232

FOURTH STAGE: Today's Requirement in Data-Base Systems

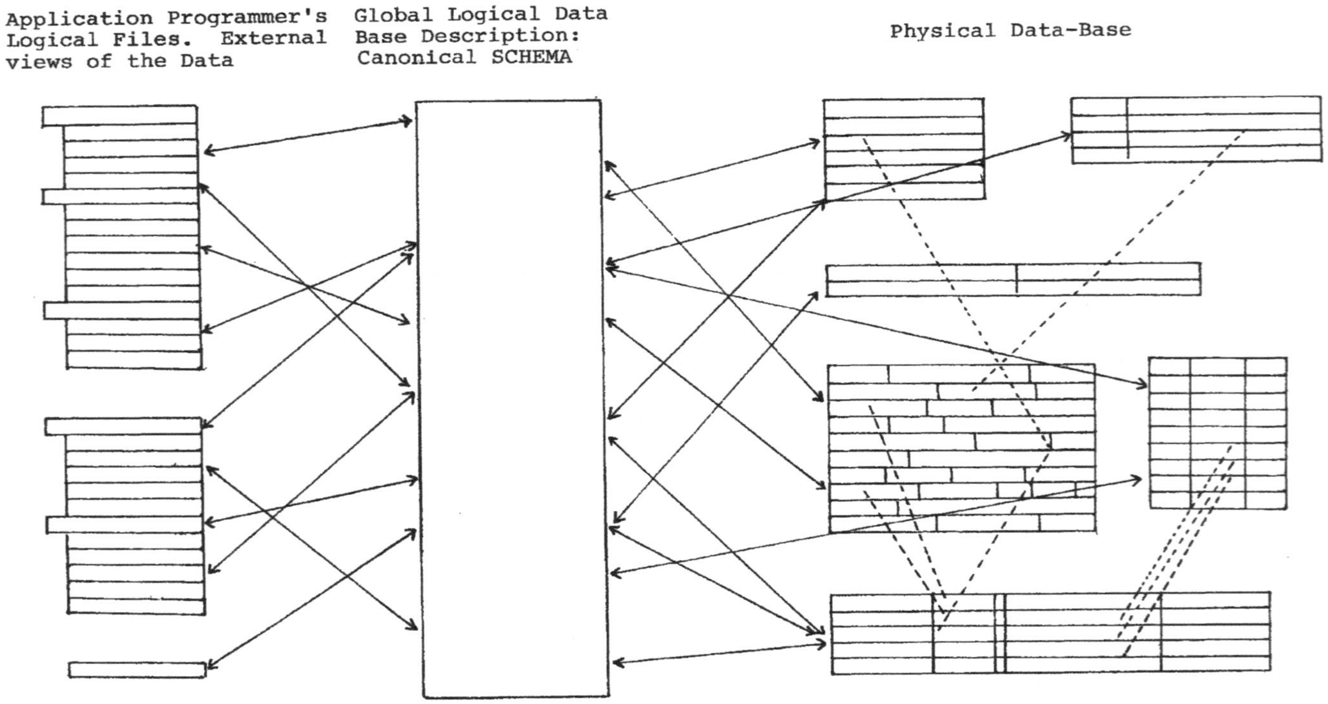

Physical Data-Base

Application Programmer's   Global Logical Data
Logical Files.   External   Base Description:
views of the Data   Canonical SCHEMA

Fig. 5.4.   Modern Data-Base

- Software provides logical as well as physical data independence, allowing a global logical view of the data to exist independently of certain changes in the application programs' views of data or the physical data layouts.

- The data base may evolve without incurring high maintenance costs.
- Effective procedures are provided for controlling the privacy, security, and integrity of the data.
- Inverted files are used on some systems to permit rapid data base searching.
- Data bases are designed to provide answers to unanticipated forms of information request.
- Data migration is facilitated.
- The software provides a data description language for the Data-Base Administrator, a command language for the application programmer, and sometimes a data interrogation language for the user.

The main trend during this period is to discriminate between the LOGICAL DATA-BASE (as the application programmer sees the data) and the PHYSICAL DATA-BASE (as the data actually is stored in the computer).

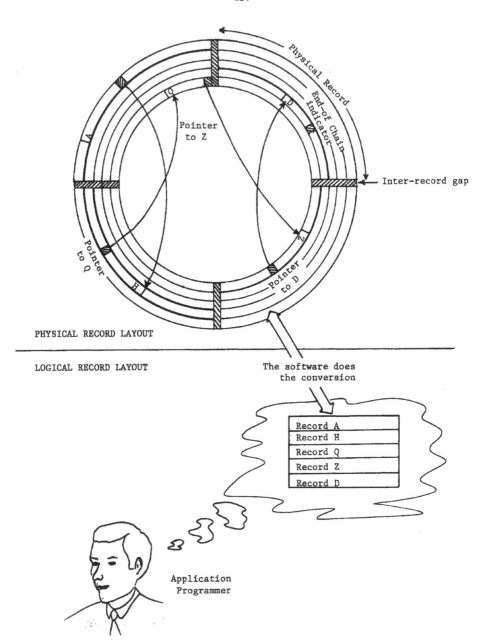

Fig. 5.5. Physical and Logical Record Layout

5.3 Logical And Physical Data Base Design

The important distinction between logical and physical databases provides logical as well as physical data independence.

Logical data independence means that the overall logical structure of the data may be changed without changing the application program.

Physical data independence means that the physical layout and organization of the data may be changed without changing either the overall logical structure of the data or the application program.

To achieve this goal we must design two types of data bases: The logical and the physical data-base and let the data-base software provides a means for mapping the application programmers logical data structure on to the physical data structure that is actually stored and <u>vice versa</u>. By doing this, the data-base can be designed to serve the enterprise without caring about the possible limitations imposed by the physical implementation.

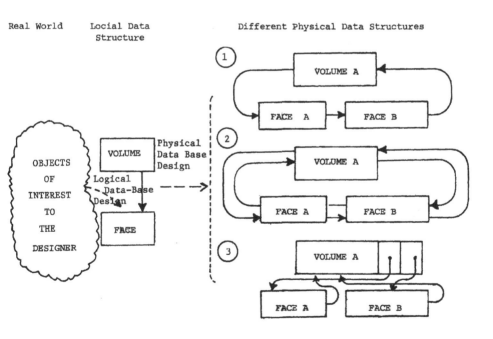

Fig. 5.6. Logical and physical data-base design

5.3.1 The Four-Level Model

A concept for mapping real-world information to the level of data
stored in the storage devices of a data base has been developed by
Senko [6] . This concept has also been applied to problems of CAD,
e.g. the digital representation of mechanical parts in an engineering
data base [7].

As shown in figure 5.7, four levels may be distinguished:

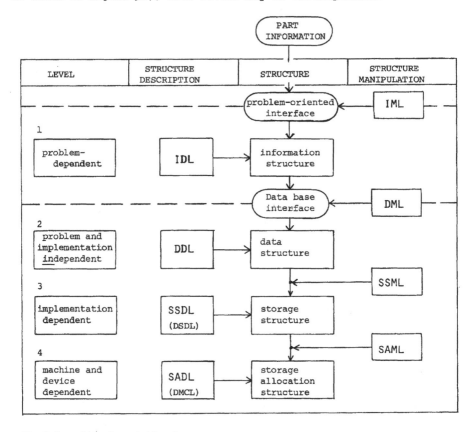

IDL Information Description Language
DDL Data Description Language
SSDL Storage Structure Description Language
SADL Storage Allocation Description Language

IML Information Manipulation Language
DML Data Manipulation Language
SSML Storage Structure Manipulation Language
SAML Storage Allocation Description Language

Fig. 5.7. Interface levels for the storing of information.

1. Information-Structure Level. This level is problem-dependent. The interface to the application program is a problem-oriented language, termed IML in this particular case. (Conceptual SCHEMA)

2. Data-Structure Level. At the data-structure level, elements of a problem-oriented structure of informations are described and handled in an abstract and formal manner. (Canonical SCHEMA/External SCHEMA)

3. Storage-Structure Level. At this level a given data structure is mapped on linear address spaces, physical records, and access paths like trees and chains. (Internal SCHEMA)

4. Storage-Allocation Level. The storage-allocation level corresponds to the physical storage of the data.

The last two levels are internal levels of application-independent data-base management systems.

The special characteristics of the first three levels are illustrated in a double-funnel diagram of figure 5.8. The funnels opening upward and downward indicate that one concept on the data-structure level will support a wider variety of applications on the information-structure level, while many storage structures may be supported for an efficient mapping on the internal levels of a data base system. Because of its application and implementation independence, the data-structure level is most suitable for standardization, and shows some similarity to the device-independent level of the graphical core system.

It turns out that the main reason for poor computer systems in most cases, can be traced back to a poor design of the Logical Data Base.

The logical Data Base is a conceptual model of the real world and is here referred to as the Conceptual SCHEMA when the data structure is not decided and the Canonical SCHEMA when also the data structure is included (such as CODASYL, Relational etc.).

While the programmers views of the data change and the physical storage and organization change, the conceptual model of the data should remain stable or grow to incorporate new data types.

To make it stable it must be designed to represent the inherent properties of the data.

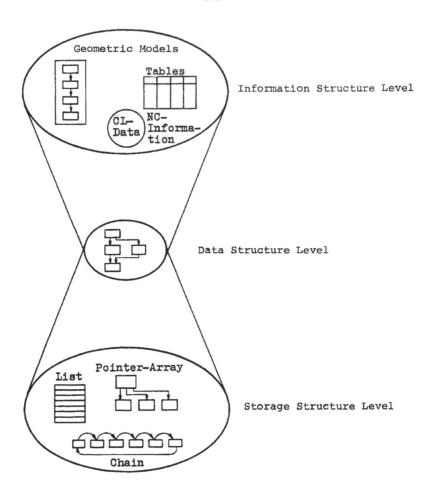

Fig. 5.8. Two-funnel model to display the application and implementation independence of the data-structure level.

Currently, there are insufficient tools to aid the logical data-base
design process. The data-base designer usually has to rely on intuition and experience. As a result, many data-bases existing today are
not properly designed.

5.3.2 THE ENTITY/RELATIONSHIP DESIGN METHOD

Let's look at one of the methods: The Entity-Relationship (E/R) approach [3], which is quite helpful in constructing a conceptual SCHEMA.
The conventional approach to logical data-base design have only one

phase: mapping the information about entities in the real world directly to the canonical SCHEMA.

The E/R approach consists of two phases:

1. Defining the Conceptual SCHEMA using the E/R diagram.
2. Translating the Conceptual SCHEMA into the Canonical SCHEMA.

The E/R diagram consist of only 3 types of symbols:

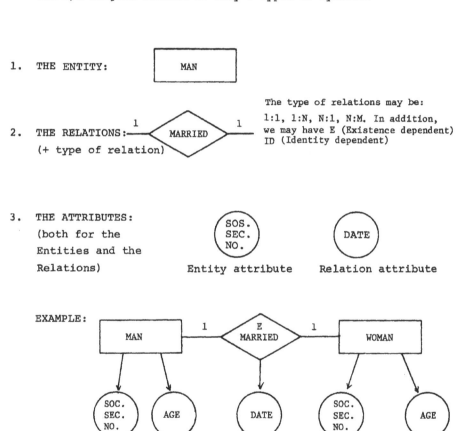

1. THE ENTITY:

2. THE RELATIONS:
   (+ type of relation)

The type of relations may be:

1:1, 1:N, N:1, N:M. In addition,
we may have E (Existence dependent)
ID (Identity dependent)

3. THE ATTRIBUTES:
   (both for the
   Entities and the
   Relations)

Entity attribute   Relation attribute

EXAMPLE:

Fig. 5.9.   A binary E/R relation

There are different ways of representing the information:

The previous example can also be expressed as a UNARY relation:

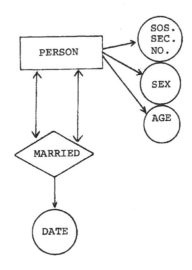

Fig. 5.10 A unary E/R relation

A systematic approach to the deisgn of the Conceptual SCHEMA is as follows:

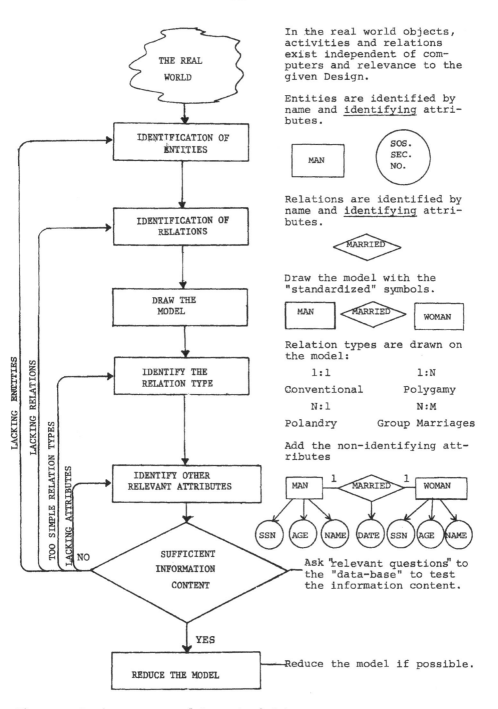

In the real world objects, activities and relations exist independent of computers and relevance to the given Design.

Entities are identified by name and _identifying_ attributes.

Relations are identified by name and _identifying_ attributes.

Draw the model with the "standardized" symbols.

Relation types are drawn on the model:

1:1	1:N
Conventional	Polygamy
N:1	N:M
Polandry	Group Marriages

Add the non-identifying attributes

Ask "relevant questions" to the "data-base" to test the information content.

Reduce the model if possible.

Fig. 5.11 Design process of Conceptual Schema.

The "relevant questions" asked to test the information content of each class in the data-base is usually of the following types, (or for more complex questions a combination of this):

Type:	Function:	Example:
$A(E) = ?$	Common attribute inquiry	What is the price of the ball bearings no 135
$A(?) \begin{smallmatrix}=\\\neq\\\leq\\>\end{smallmatrix} V$	Which entities have the given value?	Which ball bearings cost less than $50?
$?(E) \begin{smallmatrix}=\\\neq\\\leq\\>\end{smallmatrix} V$	List all attributes having a given set of values for a given entity.	Which firms has Pettersen worked with for more than 3 years?
$?(E) = ?$	Request for all information about a given entity	List all information stored about the ball bearing no. 97.
$A(?) = ?$	List the value of a given attribute for every entity	List the manufacturers of all ball bearings
$?(?) \begin{smallmatrix}=\\\neq\\\leq\\>\end{smallmatrix} V$	List all entity attributes having a given set of values	For every salesman list every month when his sales exceeded $ 50.000.

Six types of simple query. E means Entity, A means Attribute, and V means Attribute Value.

The questions we ask for testing the relations between the Entity classes is of course of the type "Which ball bearings are used in connection with shaft number 3?"

The task of translating the conceptual SCHEMA into the Canonical SCHEMA is now manageable even for very complicated cases.

REAL WORLD   CONCEPTUAL SCHEMA   CANONICAL SCHEMA

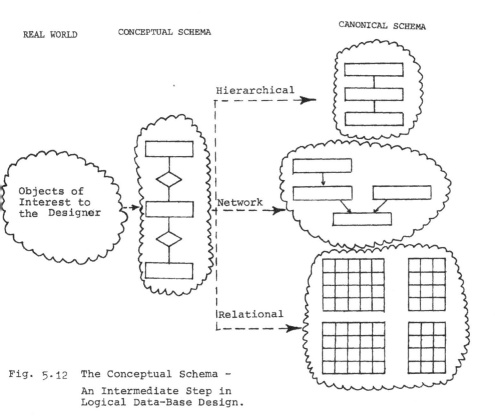

Objects of Interest to the Designer

Hierarchical

Network

Relational

Fig. 5.12   The Conceptual Schema –
An Intermediate Step in
Logical Data-Base Design.

5.4 Data Base Structures

For CAD systems we have basically three classes of Canonical SCHEMA. The Hierarchical, the Network and the Relational structure.

5.4.1 HIERARCHICAL STRUCTURE

A hierarchical structure is typically a tree structure composed of a hierarchy of elements called nodes.

The uppermost level has only one node and is called the root. A terminal node is frequently called a leaf.

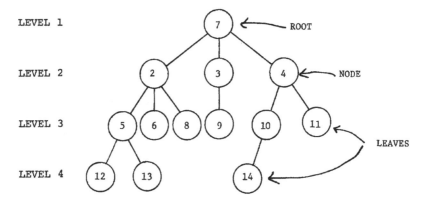

Fig. 5.13   A tree: No element has more than one parent.

Every node, except for the root, has one node related to it called its PARENT. Each node, except for the leaves, has one or more element related to it on a lower level called CHILDREN.

NO ELEMENT IN A TREE HAS MORE THAN ONE PARENT.

Hierarchical models originated from sequential storage structures are simple and fast, this is their advantage.

Their drawbacks are many and has usually to do with the fact that few relations in the real world are purely hierarchical.

To implement complex relations as hierarchical structures usually means duplicating data, this is creating redundancy and danger for inconsistency.

5.4.2 NETWORK STRUCTURE

If a child in a data relationship has more than one parent, the relationship cannot be described as a tree or hierarchical structure. Instead it must be described as a NETWORK structure.

ONE OR MORE ELEMENTS IN A NETWORK HAVE MULTIPLE PARENTS.

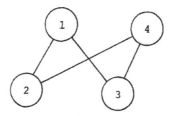

Fig. 5. 14 A NETWORK: One or more nodes have multiple parents.

Network structures are usually linked lists (rings), every ring is often referenced as a set and posess one owner and zero or more members. A set represents a one to many relation. To establish many to many relations one has to make use of socalled link nodes. Each link-node may be a member of two sets and this is how the network is constructed.

The lists of a network is usually represented by physical pointers, which avoids searching of tables and gives a direct access to a node.

A drawback is the experienced complexity of the programs that manipulate complex datastructures. The set operations are not natural tools for an end-user. Lists of members that are physically disjoint may require many disc-acesses. It is therefore to be recommended to store data that are logically grouped in the same physical area.

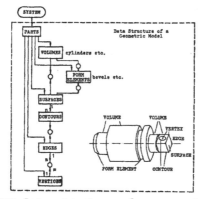

Fig. 5.15 A CODASYL-data structure of representations of mechanical parts in a data base.

5.4.3 RELATIONAL STRUCTURE

A RELATIONAL structure is a "flat" data representation:

> A relation R on sets S_1, S_2,....S_n, is a set of n-tuples each of
> which has n elements, the first from S_1, the second from S_2,....,
> and the nth from S_n, (i.e., R is a subset of the Cartesian pro-
> duct $S_1 \times S_n$). The set S_i is called the ith domain of R. A rela-
> tion with n domains has degree n and is called a n-ary relation.
> Each domain can be given a name; these names are then attributes
> of the relation. A relation can be represented conveniently as an
> array in which each row is a n-tuple and each column is a domain.
> The ordering of rows and columns assuming unique domain names is
> immaterial. An exaple is shown in Figure 5.14 [9].

SUBASSEMBLY:

PNAME	NPOS	TRANSF.	ELEMENT	V1	V2	COLOR
PART1	X_1,Y_1	T1	DEF.1	10	1000	RED
PART2	X_2,Y_2	T2	DEF.3	2	10000	BLUE
⋮	⋮	⋮	⋮	⋮	⋮	⋮
PART6	X_6,Y_6	T6	DEF.1	3	1000	RED
⋮	⋮	⋮	⋮	⋮	⋮	⋮

Fig. 5.16 A relation.

This relation can be written as a relation structure:

SUBASSEMBLY(PNAME,NPOS,TRANSF.,ELEMENT,V1,V2,COLOR,.....)

where PNAME uniquely identify the subassembly and is called the KEY.

The great advantage of the relational model is that it is at all times
consistent. Also the stringent notation of relational calculus is very
valuable in semantic data modelling and in theoretical work on datastructures in general.

A relational model is also very flexible with respect to user manipulation of relations and data. The user may directly operate on the
tables and create relations between the tables as need arises.

One big drawback is that operations tend to take long time, e.g. the
two operations of relational algebra, join and project, are based om
comparing tuples and building new tables. For tables with many attri-

butes and tuples (columns and rows) this process is very timeconsuming.

Another drawback is that relational algebra and calculus are not all that easy to apply in datastructures typical of CAD.

It should be noted that all these Data Base types may be derived from each other by introducing (or reducing) redundancy in the data.

5.5 Design And Implementation Of Data Bases

Suppose an Enterprise is going to design, manufacture and marketing a certain article. A fraction of the Conceptual Schema describing the integrated Data Base may be designed as follows:

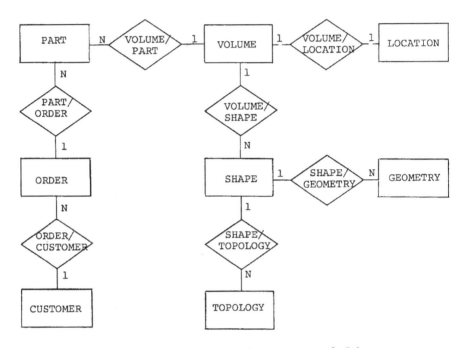

Fig. 5.17 A Fraction of a Conceptual Schema.

Most spatial data bases for design are traditionally built up as Tree or Network structures, but the Relational Data Base is also convenient, because it is general and provides a clear way to talk about the Data Base. It incorporates also more information about functional dependencies than other Schemas.

Based on the conceptual schema the Data Base administrator decide to use a RELATIONAL SCHEMA for this Data Base:

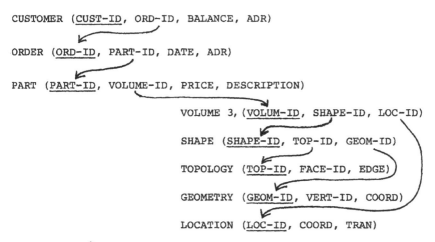

CUSTOMER (<u>CUST-ID</u>, ORD-ID, BALANCE, ADR)

ORDER (<u>ORD-ID</u>, PART-ID, DATE, ADR)

PART (<u>PART-ID</u>, VOLUME-ID, PRICE, DESCRIPTION)

VOLUME 3, (<u>VOLUM-ID</u>, SHAPE-ID, LOC-ID)

SHAPE (<u>SHAPE-ID</u>, TOP-ID, GEOM-ID)

TOPOLOGY (<u>TOP-ID</u>, FACE-ID, EDGE)

GEOMETRY (<u>GEOM-ID</u>, VERT-ID, COORD)

LOCATION (<u>LOC-ID</u>, COORD, TRAN)

Fig. 5.18 A Relational Schema mapped from the Conceptual Schema.

As we can see, the relational SCHEMA is no more than a framework into which the values of the data items can be fitted:

VOLUM:

VOLUM-ID	SHAPE-ID	LOC-ID
ELEM1	TRUC	5
ELEM2	TRUC	2
ELEM3	MACHIN	3
ELEM4	MACHIN	4
ELEM5	CHOSE	2
ELEM6	CHOSE	1

TOPOLOGY:

TOP-ID	FACE-ID	EDGE
TETRA	1	1 2
TETRA	1	2 3
TETRA	1	3 1
TETRA	2	1 2
TETRA	2	3 4
TETRA	2	5 1
TETRA	3	3 3
TETRA	3	4 4
TETRA	3	5 2
TETRA	4	1 3
TETRA	4	3 4
TETRA	4	4 1
PRISM	1	1 2
PRISM	1	2 3
PRISM	1	3 1
PRISM	3	4 5
PRISM	3	5 6
PRISM	3	6 4
PRISM	4	1 2

SHAPE:

SHAPE-ID	TOP-ID	GEOM-ID
TRUC	TETRA	1
MACHIN	TETRA	2
CHOSE	PRISM	3

GEOMETRY:

GEOM-ID	VERT-ID	COORD
1	1	X3 Y4 Z5
1	2	X1 Y2 Z2
1	3	X3 Y1 Z3
1	4	X2 Y5 Z1
2	1	X5 Y4 Z6
2	2	X6 Y1 Z4

LOCATION:

LOC-ID	COORD	TRAN
1	X10 Y27 Z36	0 36 180
2	X67 Y09 Z26	90 90 90
3	X24 Y70 Z18	180 0 180
4	X48 Y32 Z16	90 110 45
5	X50 Y17 Z62	0 110 80

Fig. 5.19 Values in the Relational Data-Base.

Different application programmers do not need to know about the entire canonical SCHEMA. It is ofteh highly complex and the programmer doesn't want to be concerned with problems outside his particular application.

The application programmers needs therefore access only to a particular part of the Data Base. This particular part i described by a subschema called the EXTERNAL SCHEMA.

The external SCHEMA is the application programmer's view of his part of the Data Base.

ALL EXTERNAL SCHEMAS MUST BE DERIVABLE FROM THE CANONICAL SCHEMA.

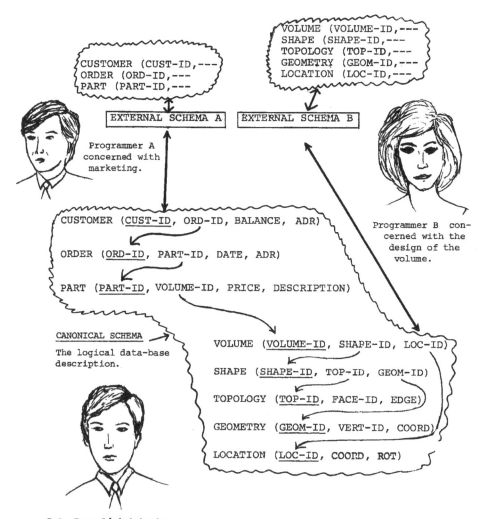

VOLUME (VOLUME-ID,---
SHAPE (SHAPE-ID,---
TOPOLOGY (TOP-ID,---
GEOMETRY (GEOM-ID,---
LOCATION (LOC-ID,---

CUSTOMER (CUST-ID,---
ORDER (ORD-ID,---
PART (PART-ID,---

EXTERNAL SCHEMA A

EXTERNAL SCHEMA B

Programmer A concerned with marketing.

Programmer B concerned with the design of the volume.

CUSTOMER (CUST-ID, ORD-ID, BALANCE, ADR)

ORDER (ORD-ID, PART-ID, DATE, ADR)

PART (PART-ID, VOLUME-ID, PRICE, DESCRIPTION)

CANONICAL SCHEMA

The logical data-base description.

VOLUME (VOLUME-ID, SHAPE-ID, LOC-ID)

SHAPE (SHAPE-ID, TOP-ID, GEOM-ID)

TOPOLOGY (TOP-ID, FACE-ID, EDGE)

GEOMETRY (GEOM-ID, VERT-ID, COORD)

LOCATION (LOC-ID, COORD, ROT)

Data-Base Administrator
Concerned with the complete Data Base.

Fig. 5.20   TWO different programmers need different files. Both EXTERNAL SCHEMA are derived from the CANONICAL SCHEMA.

When the Canonical SCHEMA is designed and tested, we are ready for the third step: The _physical_ data base design and implementation.

"Physical data-base design" is the process of selecting a physical data structure for a given logical structure.

The physical data structure is described in the INTERNAL SCHEMA.

There are at least 3 possible physical structures within a data-base system which is able to support the same logical structure, each with its own advantages and disadvantages:

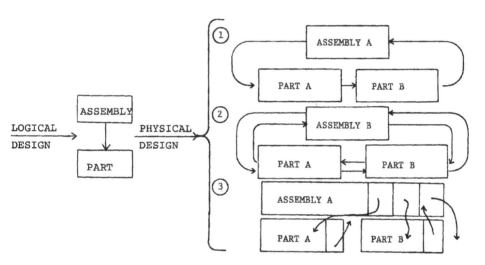

Fig. 5.21 Logical and physical design.

At this stage, the system designer is faced with tradeoffs between different desirable features as shown in figure 5.22 [1].

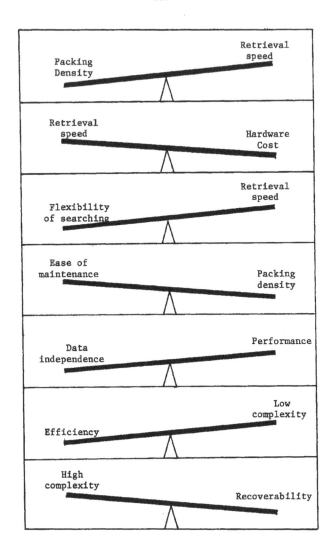

Fig. 5.22 Trade-Offs in Physical Data-Base Design.

Another important aspect is the utilization of the storage structure
which will grow more and more important as time goes by:

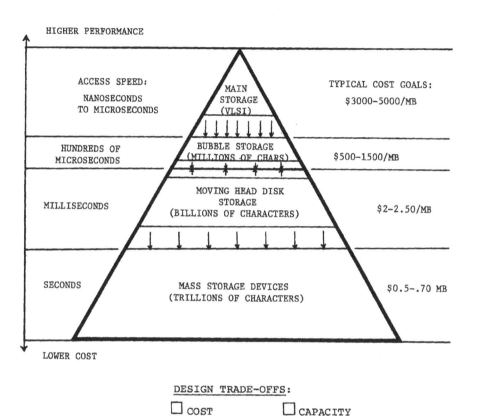

Fig. 5.23   The Expected Hierarchical Storage Structure.

5.6 Conclusion

What all this means is that we actually have four views of the data organization:

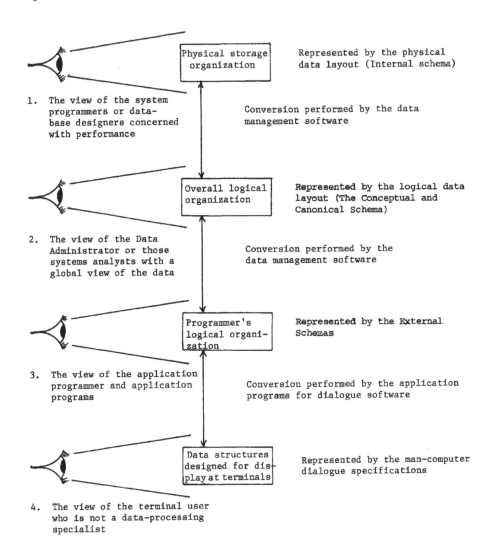

Physical storage organization — Represented by the physical data layout (Internal schema)

1. The view of the system programmers or data-base designers concerned with performance

Conversion performed by the data management software

Overall logical organization — Represented by the logical data layout (The Conceptual and Canonical Schema)

2. The view of the Data Administrator or those systems analysts with a global view of the data

Conversion performed by the data management software

Programmer's logical organi-zation — Represented by the External Schemas

3. The view of the application programmer and application programs

Conversion performed by the application programs for dialogue software

Data structures designed for display at terminals — Represented by the man-computer dialogue specifications

4. The view of the terminal user who is not a data-processing specialist

Fig. 5.24   Four view of the data.

And, the resulting modern data base will have the following structure:
[1]

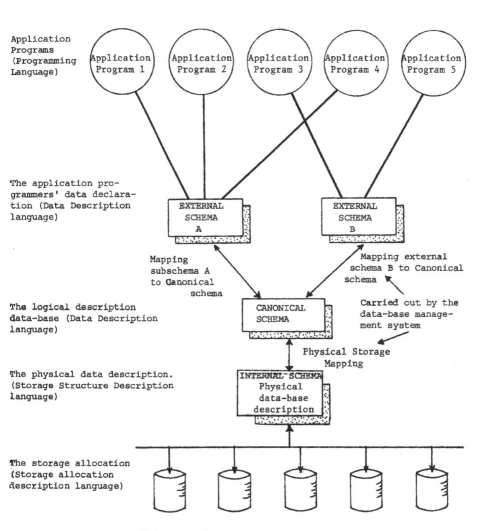

Fig. 5.25 A Modern Data-Base Structure.

The main events that occur when an application program reads a record
by means of the data base system are shown on fig. 5 . 26.

A number of other events also occur, depending on the details of the
software but they are outside the scope of this paper.

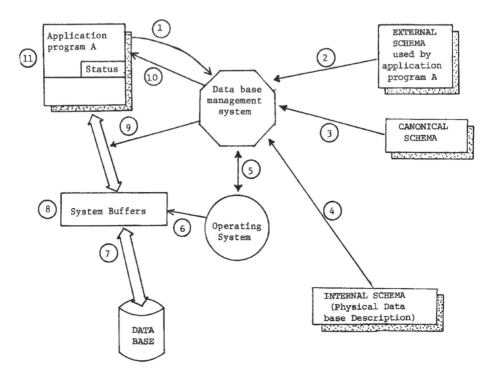

Fig. 5.26 The sequence of events when an application program needs
a record, using a data-base management system (DBMS).

1. Application program A issues a call to the data-base management
   system to read a record. The program states the programmer's name
   for the data type and gives the value of the key of the segment or
   record in question.

2. The data-base management system obtains the external schema that
   is used by application program A and looks up the description of
   the data in question.

3. The data-base management system obtain the canonical schema and
   determines which logical data types are needed.

4. The data-base management system examines the Internal Schema (the
   physical data-base description) and determines which physical record or records to read.

5. The data-base management system issues a command to the computer
   operating system, instructing it to read the requisite record(s).

6. The operating system interacts with the physical storage where the data are kept.

7. The required data are transferred between the storage and the system buffers.

8. Comparing the External schema and the Canonical schema, the data-base management system derives from the data the logical record needed by the application program. Any data transformations between the data as declared in the External schema are made by the data-base management system.

9. The data-base management system transfers the data from the system buffers to the work area of application program A.

10. The data-base management system provides status information to the application program on the outcome of its call, including any error indications.

11. The application program can then operate with the data in its work area.

5.7 Future Trends

5.7.1 DATA BASE MACHINES

The size, complexity and data independency of modern data-bases tends to slow down the response time to an intolerable level for inter-active CAD. The advance in hardware technology and prices have now made it possible to use special purpose DATA BASE MACHINES (DBM) to take care of the data management which traditionally has been done by software and thus speed up the response time considerably.

The System utilizing DBM may be organized differently dependent on the task which is to be performed [5]:

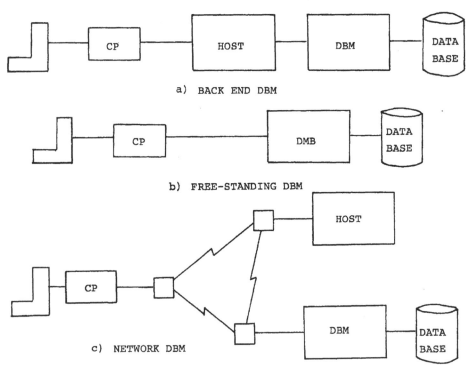

a) BACK END DBM

b) FREE-STANDING DBM

c) NETWORK DBM

CP - COMMUNICATIONS PROCESSOR
DBM - DATA BASE MACHINE

Fig. 5.27 Future Trend 1: Data base Machine.

5.7.2 INTEGRATED DBMS AND TELECOMMUNICATION

The idea of integrated data-bases has created the need for remote accessing of the data-base which means that telecommunication management software will become an important part of the Information System.

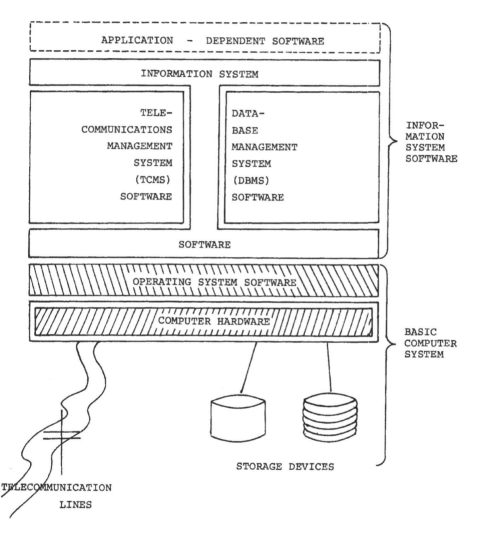

Fig.5.28 Future Trend 2: Telecommunication management as
part of the Information System.

5.7.3 DISTRIBUTED DATA BASES

However, the data-base designers have also realized that access to all the data is not needed at all places simultaneously. In fact, in most cases, each site will use a particular part of the data-base most of the time and only occassionally access other data. This has lead to the idea of distributed data-bases which are a rapidly growing sub-field of data-base technology.

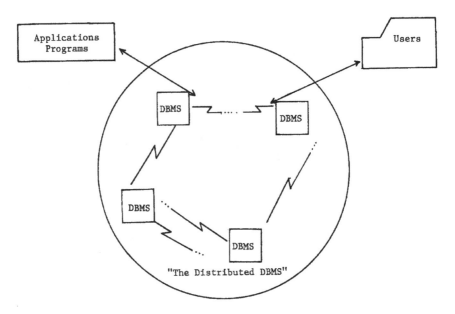

Fig. 5.29 Future Trend 3: Distributed Data-Bases

Distributed data-bases are an attractive approach to solving the data management needs of many organizations because it permits the data-base system to act conceptually as a centralized system, while physically mirroring the geographic distribution of organizations in today's world.

REFERENCES

[1]   Martin, J.: "Computer Data-Base Organization", Prentice-Hall, Inc.
      Englewood Cliff, New Jersey, 1977.

[2]   Bø, Ketil; "Data Bases in CAD". Tutorial at SIGGRAPH-78, Atlanta
      1978.

[3]   Chen, P.: "The Entity-Relationship Approach to Logical Data-Base
      Design", Q.E.D. Information Scienc, Inc., 1977.

[4]   Lafue, G.: "Design Data-Base and Data-Base Design", Proceeding of
      CAD78 pp 254, IPC Science and Technology Press.

[5]   Hsiao, D and Stuart, E.: "Database Machine Architecture in the
      Context of Information Technology Evaluation", Proceedings
      Very Large Data Bases 1977, Tokyo, Japan, October, 1977.

[6]   Senko, M.E., E.B. Altman, M.M. Abraham, P.L. Fehder: Data Struc-
      tures and Accessing in Data-base Systems, IBM Syst. J,
      No. 1 (1973), pp 45-93.

[7]   Fisher W.E. "The interface between CAD/CAM Software and CODASYL
      Data Base Management Systems" Proceedings EUROGRAPHICS 79,
      Bologna 1979.

[8]   Ulfsby, S.: "Datastructures and databases in GPM" SI-internal
      report. SI, Aug. 1979.

[9]   Williams Robert: "On the Application of Relational Data Structures
      in Computer Graphics" Data Structures, Computer Graphics,
      and Pattern Recognition. Academic Press, Inc. 1977.

Chapter 6

CAD Data Base Requirements and Architectures

by

Thomas Neumann

Technische Hochschule Darmstadt
Fachgebiet Graphisch-Interaktive Systeme
Institut für Informationsverwaltung und Interaktive Systeme
Darmstadt, Steubenplatz 12

6 CAD DATA BASE REQUIREMENTS AND ARCHITECTURES

6.1 COMPONENTS OF A CAD SYSTEM

Modern CAD systems consist of the following components:

* graphical input and output system

* method base

* applications programs

* dialogue system

* data base management system (DBMS)

The subcomponents of the system communicate via a common data base. The data base management system manages all the data in the system. The nature of data can vary from data structure representing some graphical objects to tables representing costs of various parts. The data management system provides a data model and a language to manipulate it. All other components represent their information in terms of this model.

Isolation of data management from the rest of the system offers several advantages:

* application programs are easier to write

* application programs are portable

* data can be shared without having to re-format it

* the system can ensure data consistency

* performance aspects can be shifted from the application programmer

It seems to be preferable to use some established DBMS rather then to develop special ones for CAD systems. Two major reasons are:

* benefiting from the developments in commercial DBMS

* easy integration of design activities with other data such as accounting, project supervision etc.

6.2 THE DATA BASE MANAGEMENT SYSTEM

6.2.1 The Responsibilities of a DBMS

The software responsible for the management of the data base is called the Data Base Management System.

The major role of this system is to allow its users (programs and people) to handle data in abstract terms.

Other responsibilities of DBMS are:

* provision of different views of the information

* maintaining data consistency

* maintaining data security

* synchronization of concurrent access

* crash protection and recovery

The role of presenting data in abstract form is accomplished by introducing a model of data and several levels of abstraction.

DBMS based on a relational model of data seems to be the system of the future. We shall therefore dwell a little longer on this model and only skim the surface of other two major models.

6.2.2 Levels of Abstractions in a DBMS

As the user deals with objects such as 'wing', 'transistor', etc and the computer handles bit strings, the abstract objects have to be mapped to the internal representation. Different users have different perceptions of the same data. Some users cannot be granted access to sensitive parts of the information. During the design process new data objects can be created, they should not affect the programs for which these new objects are irrelevant. So it is reasonable to have two levels of mapping:

- User or also called external view is mapped onto central conceptual model of information.

- The conceptual model is mapped onto some physical representation.

Note that physical data base can be decomposed into several levels of abstraction.

6.2.3 Data Independence.

The two levels of abstraction provide two levels of data data independence.

The physical data structure can be altered without affecting the conceptual scheme. This is referred to as physical data independence. Of course reorganization of the physical database can effect efficiency. In fact the advantage of the physical data independence is, that it allows 'tuning' of the physical database for better performance.

The mapping between views and conceptual database provides logical data independence. For example adding additional information to the conceptual scheme does not effect the programs for which this information is irrelevant.

6.2.4 Different Interfaces of a DBMS.

A DBMS supports two kinds of interfaces.

1. programming interface

    The DBMS provides a language (frequently called the data sublanguage) which can be imbedded in a procedural high level language such as PL/I or Pascal. It serves for data definition and manipulation. The data language statements must be precompiled to produce procedure calls in the host language. Some data languages provide support for ad-hoc queries which are not known in advance and hence cannot be precompiled.

2. interactive user interface

    The data sublanguage can be used as a stand-alone language at an interactive terminal.

6.3 INFORMATION MODELLING

6.3.1 Entity - Relationship Model

In order to capture information in a data base we have to introduce some means of information modelling.

Let us introduce a model called "Entity - Relationship Model"

Information can be represented in terms of facts about things and in terms of relationships between things

For more formal definition let us introduce the following concepts:

entity   represents anything that can be described by properties and is distinguishable.

property an association of an attribute with an attribute value

attribute any characteristic to which a value can be assigned

attribute value is a state of an attribute

entity set a set of entities having the same attributes

key   property or a set of properties uniquely identifying an entity.

relationship relationships among entity sets is an ordered list of entity sets.

> if there is a relationship REL among entity sets $E1, E2, \ldots Ek$ then a set of k-tuples $(e1, e2, \ldots ek)$ exists. We shall call such a set a relationship set.

The relationships can be of type:

one-one for each entity in either set there is at most one associated member of the other set

many-one one entity in set $E2$ is associated with zero or more entities in set $E1$ but each entity in $E1$ is associated with at most one entity in $E2$

many-many one entity in set $E2$ is associated with zero or more entities in set $E1$ and each entity in $E1$ is associated with zero or more entities in $E2$

As an example consider following entity sets:

- ASSEMBLY with attributes ANO (Assembly number), ANAME (assembly name)

- PARTS with attributes PNO (Part number), PNAME (part name), WEIGHT, COLOUR

- SUPPLIER with attributes SNO (Supplier number), SNAME (Supplier's name), LOCATION

and following relationships:

- IS PART OF: many-many relationship between ASSEMBLY and PARTS

- SUPPLIED BY: many-many relationship between PARTS and SUPPLIER

The model can be shown diagrammatically as follows:

Entity set are represented by rectangles, attributes by elipses and relationships by diamonds (Fig. 6.1)

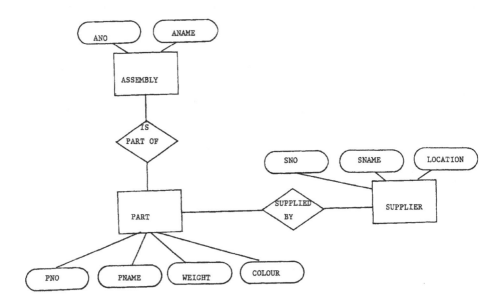

Figure 6.1 Entity-Relationship Diagram

6.4 DATA MODELS

A DBMS provides a data definition language to specify the conceptual scheme. The data definition language describes the conceptual scheme in terms of a data model.

There are three major data models that have been developed for data base systems:

Relational model

Network model

Hierarchical model

6.4.1 The Relational Model

6.4.1.1 Definition

The mathematical concept underlying the relational model is the set - theoretic relation, which is a subset of the cartesian product of a list of domains. A domain is a set of values.

The cartesian product of domains D1,D2,...,Dk is the set of all k-tuples (d1,d2,...,dk) such that d1 is in D1, d2 is in D2 and so on. The members of a relation are called tuples.

A relation can be viewed as a table where each row corresponds to a tuple. The columns are given names called attributes. The number of columns is called the arity of the relation.

Example of a relation:

```
PARTNO|PNAME|QTY
_____|_____|_____
  p1 |bolt |100
  p2 |wing | 2
```

The list of attribute names for a relation is called the <u>relation scheme</u>.

The scheme of the above example is

PARTS(PARTNO,PNAME,QTY)

<u>6.4.1.2 Representing Information in the Relational Model</u>

We have seen how information can be represented in terms of the entity-relationship model. Now we shall show how the entity-relationship model can be translated into relational model.

1. An entity set can be represented by a relation whose scheme consists of all the attributes of the entity set. Each tuple represents one entity.

2. A relationship among entity sets E1,E2...,Ek is represented by a relation whose scheme consists of the keys for each of E1,E2,...,Ek. A tuple denotes a list of entities e1,e2,...,ek. The presence of tuple t in the relation indicates, that the entities are related.

For illustration consider the example in the section 6.3.1: Following tables can be used to represent the information:

The entity sets are represented by :

    ASSEMBLY(ANO,ANAME)

    PART(PNO,WEIGHT,COLOUR)

    SUPPLIER(SNO,SNAME,LOCATION)

The relationships are represented by:

    IS_PART_OF(ANO,PNO)

    SUPPLIED_BY(PNO,SNO)

6.4.2 The Network Data Model

6.4.2.1 Model Definition

The network model is essentially the entity-relationship model with the relationships restricted to be binary many-one. This allows us to represent data as simple directed graph.

The basic concepts are:

logical record type corresponds to an entity set

logical record corresponds to an entity

logical record format corresponds to the relation scheme

binary many-one relationships called links

The nodes of the directed graph (network) represent the logical records type, the arcs represent the links.

6.4.2.2 Entity Sets and Relationships in the Network Model

1. Entity sets are represented by logical record types. Attributes are fields of the logical record format.

2. Binary many-one relationships are represented directly by links.

3. Arbitrary relationships can be represented as follows:

    Say we have a relationship R among entity sets E1,E2,...,Ek. We create a new logical record type T representing k-tuples (e1,e2,...,ek) of entities that stand in the relationship R. Second we create links L1,L2,...,Lk. Link Li is from record type T to the record type Ti for entity set Ei. The intention is that the record of type T for (e1,e2,...,ek) is linked to the record of type Ti, so each link is many-one.

6.4.3 The Hierarchical Model

6.4.3.1 Model Definition

A hierarchy is a forest (collection of trees) in which all links point in the direction from child to parent.

6.4.3.2 <u>Representing</u> <u>Many-Many</u> <u>Relationships</u> <u>in</u> <u>the</u> <u>Hierarchy</u>

Suppose we have entity sets El and E2 with many-many relationship R between them. We can represent R in a hierarchy by selecting either El or E2 to be the root of a tree. We give the root a child logical record of type T consisting of

1. a serial number, to identify records and

2. attributes forming a key for E2.

We create logical record T2 for E2 and place it somewhere in the the hierarchy. Similarly we can include as child of E2 record type a new record type consisting of the key fields of El.

6.5 <u>DATA</u> <u>MANIPULATION</u> <u>LANGUAGES</u>

Two classes of data languages can be distinguished:

•   procedural languages

•   non-procedural languages

Procedural languages access a record at a time. Thus the programmer has to "navigate" through his data model. Languages of this type have been developed for the network and hierarchical models. As an example consider a simple hierarchical database consisting of the following logical record types: LOCATION, ACCOUNTS, INVOICES A Location has its accounts as children and an account has its invoices as children. To find all invoices for an account at a certain location one might write the following program:

```
Set cursor1 to location=Darmstadt
Set cursor2 to account=01277741
Set cursor3 before first_child(cursor2);
while (not end_of_children) do
   Fetch(cursor3) next child; Process;
end;
```

Non-procedural languages access multiple records at a time. The access path is completely hidden from the interface and it is left to an "optimizer" to select the most efficient path to access the record. Languages of this type have been developed for the relational model.

6.5.1 The DBTG Proposal

The DBTG Proposal is based on the network model. The links are called set in DBTG proposal. When we have a many-one relationship form records of type R2 to records of type R1 and the relation is called S, then R1 is the owner of the set S and R2 is the member. A record of type R1 together with all the records of type R2 associated with it is called a set occurrence. The basic construct of the language is the FIND statement. The FIND statement locates a particular record by some designated strategy. In brief the FIND statement can be used in the following ways: (This is not a complete list)

1. find a record given its data base key

2. find a record given its calc key (hash function applied to some record fields)

3. scan the file records of given type

4. scan all the members of set occurrence

5. find the owner of a given record in a given DBTG set

6.5.2 Data Languages for the Relational Model

One appealing feature of the relational model is the fact that the set algebra can be extended deal with relations. In fact query languages for the relational model can be broken down to two classes:

1. Algebraic languages

2.   Predicate calculus languages

Algebraic languages express queries by applying specialized operators to relations.

Predicate calculus languages describe the queries in terms of a desired set of tuples by specifying a predicate the tuples must satisfy.

6.5.2.1 The Relational Algebra

The relational algebra can be defined by introducing 5 basic operations.

Union   The union of relations R and S is the relation consisting of tuples that are in R or in S or in both

Set difference The difference of relations R and S are is a relation with tuples that are in R but not in S

Cartesian product Let R be of arity k1 and S of arity k2. Then the cartesian product is a relation with (k1+k2)-tuples whose first k1 components form a tuple in R and whose last k2 components form a tuple in S

Projection This operation removes some domains and/or rearranges others, and discarding duplicate tuples.

Selection This operation selects those tuples whose components satisfy some formula. Thus Select(R) where 1=Smith and 2=Blue selects those tuples whose first component has the value Smith and the second component has the value Blue.

One other useful operation which can be derived using the basic operations is Join. It is defined as follows

Join   The theta-join of R and S on columns i and j, where theta is an arithmetic comparison operator is Select i theta (r+j)(RxS) if R is of arity r. In other words it yields those tuples in the cartesian product of R and S whose i-th component of R stands in relation theta to the j-th component of S. If theta is '=' the operation is called equijoin.

Some Retrieval Examples

Consider the following relations:

S(SNO,SNAME,CITY)
P(PNO,PNAME,COLOUR)
SP(PNO,PNAME,SNO)

1. get supplier members for supplier who supply part p2

    Select SP where PNO='p2' giving TEMP

    Project TEMP over sno giving result

2. Get supplier numbers for suppliers who supply at least one red part

    Select p where colour='RED' giving TEMP1

    equijoin TEMP1 and SP over PNO giving TEMP2

    project TEMP2 over SNO giving result

Since the relational algebra is closed system (operations on relations yield a relation), the expressions can be nested. Thus example 1 can be represented as:

project(select SP where SNO='S2')
over SNO giving result

6.5.2.2 The Relational Calculus

As we mentioned before the relational calculus describes the tuples which should appear in the result relation.

It uses the existential, the universal quantifier and logical operators to express the qualification of tuples.

get r(SP.PNO,S.CITY):SP.SNO=S.SNO

The term within brackets defines the columns of the result relation.

The colon stands for 'such that', the term following the colon is a qualification or predicate representing the defining property of the relation.

Examples:

1. Get supplier names for supplier who supply part p2

> range SP X
>> get W (S.SNAME): X(X.SNO=S.SNO and X.PNO='p2')

A variable X of type SP has to be introduced. The query can be paraphrased as follows: get sname from tuples in S such that there exists a tuple in SP with the same SNO and PNO equal to p2.

2. Get supplier names for suppliers who do not supply part1

> range X SP
> get W (S.SNAME):V X(X.SNO=S.SNO or X.PNO='p1')

or paraphrased: get all SNAME from S such that for all X SNO is different from the current SNO or the PNO is not equal to p1

6.5.2.3 The Data Language Sequel

6.5.2.3.1 General Description: Sequel is the data language developed at IBM San Jose Research Laboratories as the Data Language for System R . The acronym Sequel stands for Structured English Query Language. In system R Sequel may be used both at an on-line terminal as an interactive stand-alone language and in a host language such as PL/I. Sequel stands somewhere between a pure algebraic language and a language based on relational calculus. The basic construct of the language is the select statement:

> select <column>*,from R where <search condition>

A simple sequel statement includes the selection and projection operators of the relational algebra. Referring to our relations S,P and SP we shall now formulate some queries to exemplify the language.

1. Simple retrieval

```
select *
from S
```

2. Qualified retrieval

```
select SNO
from   S
where  CITY='Paris'
```

3. Join

```
select SNAME
from   S
where  SNO is in (select SNO from SP where PNO='p2')
```

4. Retrieval from more than one table

```
select unique PNO,CITY
from   SP,S
where  SP.SNO=S.SNO
```

6.5.2.3.2 Programming Interface in Sequel: Sequel statements may be imbedded in a host
language. This is a very important feature in CAD environment where complex computations may be performed on retrieved data.

If the host program wishes to execute a Sequel query and fetch the result, it does so by
means of a "cursor". The cursor is defined by a Let statement which associates the
cursor name with a particular query:

```
Let <cursor name> be <query>
```

The cursor is readied for retrieval by an open statement which binds the value of the host variables appearing in the in the search condition of the query. Then a Fetch statement is used repeatedly to fetch rows from the answer set into the designated program variables, as in the following example:

```
let C1 be
 select name,salary into $x,$y
 from emp where job=$z;
$open cl;
$fetch cl;
$close cl;
```

Support for ad-hoc queries

Queries as described above must be known at compilation time. (Sequel statements have to pre-processed to produce call to access modules.) In an interactive environment, however queries cannot be always predicted. Consider a hidden line elimination problem where the user defines a window and invokes the appropriate procedure. A sequel query must be generated at run time. To speed up the things Sequel provides a Prepare statement:

```
Prepare<statement name> as <variable>
```

For example, a programmer might write: "prepare s1 as Qstring". Qstring may contain any kind of Sequel statement and may have parameters indicated by question marks, such as:

```
Update emp set salary=? where empno=?
```

The prepared statement may be executed by stating:

```
open s1 using $a,$b;
fetch s1 into $x,$y;
 .

 .
close s1;
```

Input variables may be included in an open statement, and the target variables are listed in the fetch statement.

6.5.2.3.3 View Definition in Sequel: External data model or a view can be defined in terms of a Sequel query. As a matter of fact a view is a named query. It is defined as follows:

```
define newview view as
select (c1,c2) from t1 where c3='k1'
```

Once a view has been defined any subsequent updates to the original (base) relations will be reflected in the view.

Three major reasons for defining views are:

• Logical data independence giving programs a logical view of data thereby isolating them from data reorganisation.

• Data isolation giving programs exactly that subset of data they need.

• Authorisation hiding sensitive information from a program (user).

Typical reorganisations include:

• adding columns to tables

• splitting tables (attribute migration)

• combining records

• adding or dropping access path (see section)

Immunity of programs against logical data reorganisation is especially needed in such a dynamic environment as design. Logical data structure may change frequently due to imprecise specifications or newly discovered dependencies.

6.6 FOCUSING ON CAD APPLICATIONS

In this section we shall look at some properties of of information specific to CAD applications and the types of queries.

6.6.1 Properties of CAD Information

The type of relationships among entities is many-many. The simplest example is a border line that belongs to several surfaces. In modelling of electrical circuits one element belongs to more than an one subcircuits.

Ordering is an important concept in graphical applications. Consider a curve consisting of curve segments. The ordering of segments is important.

Structures in CAD systems can be hierarchies of varying number of levels. Consider an electrical circuit consisting of subcircuits and subcircuits consisting of subcircuits etc. If a single program should display circuits of varying complexity it must be able to traverse a hierarchy of arbitrary depth.

Data consistency. In a CAD data base derived (secondary) data may exist. Consider an electrical circuit. Primary data is the circuit description itself as entered by drawing it using a light pen at an interactive terminal. The derived data may be printed board diagram. Such derived data must be invalidated whenever the primary data changes. Updates of secondary data should not be allowed directly. It must be possible to state such consistency rules.

6.6.2 The User

An engineer (designer) is involved in a creative process and tends to pose a large number of queries against the data base each of them rather infrequently. Ad hoc queries must be supported at the programming interface. (The retrieved data is going to be used in some computations and not only looked at.)

People of diverse skill are often involved in a design process. (In a building consruction there are architects, draftsmen, mechanical engineers, accountants involved. Each group is interested only in the information relevant to their work. As a matter of fact they can interpret the same information differently. Clearly a concept of an external model of data (or a view) is an important one.

6.6.3 The Design Process

The design process is an interactive procedure. It often happens, that the conceptual data model must be reorganized as a result on newly found dependencies among entities and attributes. We again arrive at the concept of an external model of data.

6.6.4 Graphical Structures in a Relational Data Model

We have mentioned that a graphical subsystem forms a part of the CAD system. Data produced by the graphical system (say as a consequence of a drawing action at an inter- active terminal) should be directly accessible for inspection or modification using the available data language. Conversely it should be possible to store a relation using the standard data language and to display it using some graphic interpreter.

We shall observe one possible way how to store graphical data using the relational mod- el.

A graphical object can be represented as a relation. For example a triangle can be represented by a relation containing three tuples, each representing a line. The relation scheme may look as follows:

triangle(x1,y1,x2,y2,operation)

To display such a relation a program like following can be written:

```
let c1 be
select * into x1,y1,x2,y2,command
from triangle;
open c1;
for i:=1 to 3 do
  begin
  fetch c1;
  if command='line' then line(x1,y1,x2,y2);
  end;
```

A graphical meaning can be ascribed to each domain. It can be stored as another relation:

domains(domain-name,data-type,semantics)

A domain can have a graphical meaning "relation" meaning a reference to another relation. In this way a hierarchical structure which is often required to represent a picture can be simulated. Take for example a shape consisting of two triangles:

shape

relation	xshift	yshift	rot
triangle	0	0	0
triangle	2	2	180

The above relation invokes the relation triangle twice. The triangle will be displayed using different display transformations.

6.7 THE STORAGE STRUCTURES

6.7.1 Storage Representation of Relations

The data base resides on secondary storage consisting of direct access devices. Phys ical storage space is divided into fixed-size blocks called pages which are units of secondary storage allocation. A (data) page contains tuples of a relation. A page may contain tuples from more than one relation. Each tuple in the data base has a unique identifier called the Tuple Identifier (TID). A TID allows direct access to tuples. A segment is a large address space containing one or more relations. Each stored tuple in a segment contains the name of the relation of which it is a member.

6.7.2 Access Pass Structures

To obtain all the tuples of a relation, the segment can be scanned by fetching pages one by one and checking every tuple in the page for membership in the desired relation. Such a scan is called a segment scan. A segment scan is potentially slow and other access path are desirable.

Index A single domain index on a domain D1 of a relation R consists of pairs whose first component is a value from domain D1 of R and whose second component is the TID of a tuple having that value. An index is stored in a special way to provide rapid access to it. One of the structures that can be employed is a B-tree. To find a TID, the number of index pages referenced is equal to the height of the tree. An index on domain D1 permits rapid access to a single tuple that has desired value in column D1. An index also per- mits all tuples to be retrieved in sorted order. The utility of an index in evaluating a query depends on whether the relation is clustered with respect to the index. If the relation is clustered each data page is accessed at most once.

Link A link is designed to support many-one relationships (In any data model). A link permits more tuples (children) in a relation R to be linked to a tuple (parent) in another relation. The children linked to a parent are ordered. Links can be implemented as a ring structure: storing in each child the TID of the parent and the TID of the next child and storing the TID of the first child in the parent. Again clustering can consid- erably affect performance. A relation can have parent-child clustering or twin-clustering

6.7.3 Performance Tuning

The performance can be tuned to a particular application by dynamic defining and dropping of indices and links according to the types of queries. Note that this performance tuning does not affect the application programs in any way (except hopefully the performance).

6.8 THE QUERY EVALUATION

As we have seen a high level data language such as Sequel provides a high degree of data and access path independence. It places however a burden of finding the most efficient access path on the DBMS. A typical query involves selection, projection and a join. It has the following form: Apply a selection to a relation R, yielding R', apply a selection to S yielding S'. Join R' and S' to form a relation T and project columns from T.

Depending on the existence of indices and links, the above query can be evaluated in different ways affecting considerably the performance.

As an example consider two methods:

Method 1

Assume indices exist on join columns of R and S. Indices exist on the selection columns of R and S. Using the selection column indices, the TIDs of tuples that satisfy the predicates are obtained, the result TIDs are sorted and stored in files R' and S'. Sorting the join column indices, TIDs of tuples that participate in the unconstrained join are found. As they are found each TID pair (TID1,TID2) is checked to see whether TID1 is present in R' and TID2 is in S'. if these conditions are met, the tuples are fetched and joined and the subtuple of interest is obtained.

Method 2

By contrast consider a case where indices exist on two irrelevant columns X of relation R and Y of relation S. Indices are used to scan the tuples of a relation and the files F1 and F2 are created. File F1 (F2) contains subtuples corresponding to tuples of R (S) that satisfy the predicate, and consists of columns of R (S) that are in the output or the join predicate. Files F1 and F2 are sorted on the join column values. The resulting sorted files are scanned and the join is performed.

We can conclude that in order to determine the cheapest access path (in terms of page transfers) a number of parameters must be taken into account. The system has to keep some statistics so as to be able to estimate the number of tuples to be retrieved. For illustration following is the (incomplete) list of parameters involved in query optimization:

cardinality of relations

average number of tuples in a data page

total number of data pages in the segment that contains the relation

effectivness of the join filter

average number of (key,TID) pairs in a leaf page of an index

6.9 DATA CONSISTENCY

We can think of the data base as being a collection of entities. The entities are usually related and satisfy some consistency constraints. If all constraints are satisfied the data base is said to be in a consistent state. The system undergoes actions due to actions performed on the entities. An action is considered to be atomic. Read and write are examples of atomic actions. After some actions have completed the data base might be in an inconsistent state. A transaction is a sequence of actions which transforms the data base from a consistent state to a new consistent state. The DBMS is responsible for maintaining the consistency. The user has merely to indicate the beginning and the end of the his transaction. In fact all Sequel statements must be imbedded within the Begin Transaction and End Transaction statements.

The system must preserve consistency in view of three factors:

* concurrently executing transactions

* possible system crashes

* possible abortion of transactions

6.9.1 PROBLEMS DUE TO CONCURRENCY

Three forms of inconsistency can occur due to concurrency:

* Lost Updates: If transaction T1 updates a record previously updated by transaction T2, then undoing T2 will also undo the updates of T1.

* Dirty Read: If transaction T1 updates a record which is read by T2, then if T1 aborts, T2 will have read a record which never existed.

* Un-repeatable Read:If transaction T1 reads a record which is then altered and committed by T2 and if T1 re-reads the record then T1 will see two different committed values for the same record.

An output of a transaction is said to be committed when the transaction abdicates the right to 'undo' the writes, thereby making the new value available to all other transactions. Outputs are said to be uncommitted or dirty if they are not yet committed by the writer.

A transaction T sees a consistent state if:

* T does not overwrite dirty data of other transactions.

* T does not commit any writes until it completes all its writes.

* T does not read dirty data from other transactions

- Other transactions do not dirty any data read by T before T completes.

Consistency can be enforced by abiding to certain lock protocols.

Locks can be shared or exclusive. A transaction T observes the consistency lock protocol if

- T sets an exclusive lock on any data it dirties

- T sets a share lock an any data it reads

- T holds all lock until end of transaction (EOT)

6.9.2 LOCK GRANULARITY

The choice of lockable units presents a tradeoff between concurrency and overhead due to multiple locking. Example of lockable units are segments, relations (files),tuples (records),fields. On the one hand, concurrency is increased if a fine lockable unit (for example a record) is chosen. On the other hand a fine unit of locking would be costly for a complex transaction which accesses a large number of records. Such a transaction would have to set and reset a large number of locks. From this discussion it follows that it would be desirable to have lockable units ot different granularities in the same system. In the next section we introduce a hierarchical system of locks.

6.9.2.1 Hierarchical Locks

Assume following hierarchy of resources:

Data Base

|

Segments

|

Relations

|

Tuples

Each node of the hierarchy can be locked. If one requests exclusive access to a particular node, then when the request is granted, the requestor has exclusive access to that
node and to all its descendants. Similarly for shared lockes. In order to lock a subtree
rooted at node R in share or exclusive mode it is important to prevent locks on the
ancestors of R which might implicitly lock R in an incompatible mode. Intention mode is
used indicate that locking is beeing done at a lower (finer) level. The procedure to
lock a subtree rooted at node R in exclusive or shared mode is to first lock all ancestors of R in intention mode and then to lock node R in exclusive or share mode.

6.10 RECOVERY MANAGEMENT

The system must preserve data consistency in view of undesirable events. Examples of
undesirable events are system deadlock or system crash. The system preserves consistency of data by implementing atomic transactions. A transaction is atomic in the sense
that once it has completed its updates will become permanent. If it is aborted (due to
explicit user's desire) or due to some system malfunction (software or hardware) none
of its updates are visible to other transactions.

The storage is blocked into fixed length units of allocation and transfer (between primary and secondary storage). The primary storage is volatile that is in case of a failure its contents are lost. Any page transfer can have one of three possible outcomes:

• Success - page gets new value

• Partial failure - page is a mess

- Total failure - page is unchanged

The recovery manager must detect these errors and correct them.

The partial failure can be eliminated by repeated writes and subsequent reads, the old copy is discarded only after the new copy has been successfully written. So we can assume that a single write action is either successful or it is a total failure.

There are several strategies to preserve atomic behaviour of a transaction. We shall look at one possible.

The system maintains a buffer pool in the volatile memory. The pages are swapped on an LRU basis. Depending on when then pages are forced onto disc several strategies can be devised. LRU algorithm implies that some uncommitted updates may migrate to the disc. To be able to undo these changes if the transaction aborts the system maintains a log of changes. Before a page is written on the disc the log records are forced. If the transaction is subsequently aborted all updates which have been writen to the disc can be undone using the log records. Notice that if the system crashes after the log has been forced there is no way of telling whether the page has been written or not. It implies that the undone procedure must be repeatable. The procedure of writing the log before the page is called the Write-Ahead Log Protocol. To be able to redo updates of committed transactions the system writes the commit log record and then forces all the transaction's log to disc. A transaction is considered to have committed its updates once its commit record appears on disc. If the system subsequently crashes all updates can be restored using the forced log records.

BIBLIOGRAPHY

Section 6.1

1. J. Encarnacao und E.G. Schlechtendahl, "Konzepte, Probleme und Moeglichkeiten von
    CAD-Systemen in der industriellen Praxis" Proceedings GI-Jahrestagung, Berlin
    1978, Forschungs- und Arbeitsberichte des Fachgebietes "Graphisch-Interaktive
    Systeme" Herausgeber: Prof.Dr.J.Encarnacao, Prof.Dr.W.Strasser, Nr.GRIS 78 -3,
    Technische Hochschule Darmstadt

Sections 6.2, 6.3, 6.4, 6.5

2. Jeffrey D. Ullman, Principles of Database Systems, Computer Science Press,1980

3. C.J.Date, An introduction to Database Systems, Second Edition, Addison-Wesley Pub-
    lishing Company, 1977

4. M.M.Astrahan,et.al.,"System R: A Relational Approach to Database Management", ACM
    Transactions on Database Systems,
      June 1976, p.97.

Section 6.6

5. J.Encarnacao and T.Neumann, " A survey of DB-requirements for graphical applica-
    tions in engineering", Proceedings of the Int.Conf.on Data Base Techniques for pic-
    torial applications ,Florence, 1979

6. A. Blaser, U. Schauer, "Aspects of Data Base Systems for Computer Aided Design", in
    Informatik-Fachberichte, Band 11; 1977 pp.78 -119

7. R.Williams and G.M.Giddings " A Picture-Building System" IEEE Transactions on Soft-
    ware Engineering, Vol. SE-2.No.1, March 76 pp.62-66

8. Dan Weller and Frank Palermo, "Database Requirements for Graphics" Proc. of Int.
    Conf. on Data Base Techniques for Pictorial Applications, Florence, 1979

9. J.L.Becerril, R.Casajuana, R.A. Lorie "GSYSR: A Relational Database Interface for Graphics" Proc. of Int. Conf. on Data Base Techniques for Pictorial Applications, Florence, 1979

Sections 6.7, 6.8

10. M.W.Blasgen and K.P.Eswaran, "Storage and Access in Relational Databases", IBM Systems Journal, No.4,1977, p.363.

 Sections 6.9, 6.10

11. J.N. Gray, "Notes on Database Operating Systems" in Operating Systems: An Advanced Course, (edited by Goos and Hartmanis), Springer-Verlag, 1978, p.393

Chapter 7

Hardware for Computer Graphics
and Computer Aided Design

by

Ketil Bo

RUNIT, Computing Centre at
the University of Trondheim,
Norway

7.1 Introduction

Computer graphics is potentially the most powerful and convenient means of man/machine communication for a very wide range of applications, but only recently has the necessary hardware become sufficiently cheap, and the software problems sufficiently mastered, for the breakthrough in graphics to become a reality. The eye is man's most efficient data-channel - over 70 % of all information received by the brain comes from visual input. Many complex problems become simple when translated into graphic images, and the ability to manipulate such images easily and accurately can enormously enhance man's problem-solving abilities. In many applications, computer graphics have for many years promised tantalising rewards in terms of the creative productivity of designers, engineers, and managers. Why has the pay-off so far been so meagre, except in very specialised areas?

High hardware costs, the exceptionally complex software and datahandling problems imposed by graphics systems have been to blame for the slow penetration of graphics into mainstream data processing.

But now is the technology getting available because of the rapid decrease of hardware cost. The basic graphics software standardization is about to make it possible to start the system development on a relatively high level and the users requirements for graphic tools are getting strong.

However, computer graphics requires more different equipments than most branches of computer science.

According to Frost & Sullivan [1], there are 163 different graphic suppliers in business today. And very few of the graphic products on the marked are in any way standardized.

This variety of equipments may make the utilization of computer graphics work consuming and expensive, unless one from the very beginning prepare for an integration which gives room for growing both in hardware, software and functionality.

7.2 Classification

There are several ways of classifying graphics hardware, dependent on what the classification are to be used for.

One way is to classify according to the type of graphics the hardware are to support:

TYPE:	CHARACTERISTICS:	TYPICAL HARDWARE:
1. Passiv Graphics	No interaction or image movement	Plotters
2. Static Graphics	Interaction but no image movement	Storage tubes
3. Dynamic Graphics	Interaction and image movement	Refresh CRT
4. Animation	"Real time" motion	Film/Video

Another way is to classify according to the technical characteristics of the hardware:

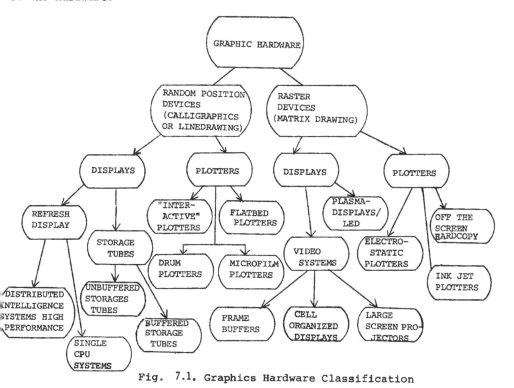

Fig. 7.1. Graphics Hardware Classification

7.2.1 LINE DRAWING VERSUS RASTER

Althrough computer-graphics displays incorporate many diverse techno-
logies, two techniques are fundamental to all graphics-display devices.
They are known as raster and random position devices.

Random positioning offers high resolution, as would typically be required in engineering and scientific applications. Its drawbacks include limited color capability and low flicker-free information content. In comparison, raster devices offers excellent color presentation and high flicker-free information content. For raster displays, the
limitation is resolution - typically one half to one fourth that of
random position. Television, the most common raster display system, em-
ploys a 512 by 512 element display, whereas a typical random-position
system uses 1024 by 1024 upto 4096 by 4096 element display.

In broadcast TV, the scanning spot moves horizontally across alternate
lines of the entire frame during one downward sweep, then returns to
the top in a continuous, regular pattern. Lines alternate from frame
to frame in a bandwidth-conserving process known as interlacing - which
is not always applied in digital TV.

The random-position technique simultaneously moves the CRT beam in an
arbitrary X and Y direction. The beam is moved directly to the point
at which the graphics element is to be displayed - with the beam off -
and then the beam is deflected to trace the desired graphics element -
with the beam on. This technique is often referred to as random scanning, beam steering, or calligraphy. Function generators driving a
random-position system must provide X- and Y-axis analog deflection
waveforms and Z-axis intensity waveforms. The amount of information
that can be displayed before the picture appears to flicker depends on
both the speed with which the beam may be deflected and the display's
phosphor characteristics. [10]

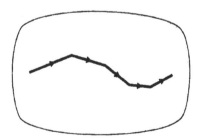

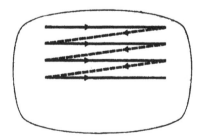

Fig. 7.2. Random position   Fig. 7.3.   Raster scan

7.2.2 GENERAL COMPARISON OF RASTER AND VECTOR GRAPHICS[11]

	Raster system	Random system
Addressability for X, Y positions	Lower	Higher
Resolution of display image	Lower	Higher
Line smoothness	Lower	Higher
Color potential	Good	Limited
Shaded areas	Yes	No
Flicker limits	None	Exist
Motion dynamics	Limited – can be jerky	Unlimited
Update/delete	Slower	Faster
Cost	Lower entry price	Generally comparable
Cost trend	Sharply lower	Lower

7.3 Random Positioning Devices

Random Positioning Devices (sometimes known as Line drawing or Calli-
graphics Devices) generates the pictures by tracing out dots, lines
and text in an arbitrary sequence. The displays are mostly used for
interaction and temporary display of the images, while the plotters
are used for intermediate hardcopy or permanent precise drawings.

7.3.1 RANDS POSITIONING DISPLAYS

The Random Positioning Displays can be divided into two main classes'
the Storage tubes with no picture movement or selective erase and the
dynamic Refresh displays:

7.3.1.1 Storage Tubes

I think it's fair to say that the breakthrough of interactive Computer
Graphics started with the direct-view storage tube which has dominated
the low cost graphics marked since Tektronix introduced the 4010 in
1972.

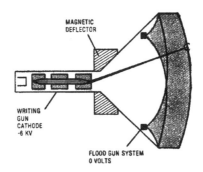

Fig. 7.4   Direct view Storage tube.

The direct view storage tube contains a writing gun, a flood-gun system, and a phosphor collector target. Flood electrons continuously
bombard the phosphor. In the absence of writing-gun electrons, flood
electrons maintain the phosphor at the flood-gun cathode potential of
0 volts. When writing-gun electrons strike the phosphor, the phosphor
is charged past a threshold to maintain a stored charge image. [2]

Fig. 7.5   Storage tube with typical output. The input tools are:
            Keyboard and crosshair with thumb wheels.

Characteristics for storage tubes:

Positive   Negative

- Large size (up to 45.4x34 cm) - No picture dynamic
- High resolution (up to   - No selective erase
  4096x4096)   - Enoying blinking when the
- Relatively low price   picture is erased
- Flickerfree even with very
  high information content
- Clean vectors

Some of the storage tubes are equipped with a small display buffer
which allows it to refresh a limited part of the picture. This feature
is frequently used for menue handling in order offer a more dynamic
system.

Typical input tools for the storage tube are: keyboard, crosshair and
tablet.

7.3.1.2 Refresh Display

The Refresh Displays are the currently most powerful devices for dynamic Computer Graphics and is therefore specially suitable for man/

machine communication in for instance Computer Aided Design (CAD).

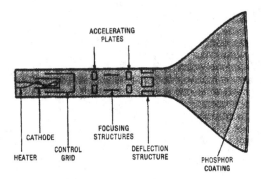

Fig. 7.6   The Cathod Ray Tube (CRT) in a Refresh Display.

The CRT consists of seven general structures: The heater, with an applied voltage, heats the cathode and causes a "cloud" of electrons to
be emitted. The control grid determines the number of electrons allowed to escape. Since the control grid is at a negative voltage, it will
repel many of the electrons. The applied voltage on the grid controls
the brightness of the displayed image. The accelerating plates raise
the velocity of the electrons to a sufficient value to cause a visible
spot on the phosphor coating when it is bombarded by the electron
stream. The focusing structures create a fine beam from the incoming
stream of electrons. The displayed spot may be controlled so that it
ranges from a very fuzzy, broad one, to a small, confined dot-like one.
The deflection structure aims the beam dictating where it will strike
the phosphor coating. The phosphor coating, on the inside faceplate of
the CRT, acts as a target which may have regions illuminated when
struck by a sufficiently energetic stream of electrons. [3]

The Refresh display works by continously (30-50 Hz) executing a sequence of drawing instructions stored in the display file.

The Refresh display systems range from single CPU systems to powerful
workstations with several Refresh displays connected as satellites to
a host computer in a Distributed Intelligence System:

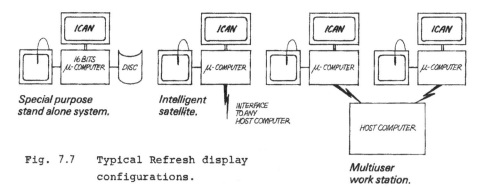

Fig. 7.7   Typical Refresh display
           configurations.

The distributed intelligence system try to exploit the advantages without suffering the disadvantages of dedicated stand-alone systems and
of large time-shared computers that directly support one or more display consols.

Two basic software techniques are used today with these systems:
"fixed-function" and "programmable-satellite".

In fixed-function systems a fixed set of general purpose graphical
functions is chosen and implemented on the satellite by the graphics
installation's software programmer. The application program is totally
hostresident and controls the satellite by subroutine calls to this
fixed set.

This approach relieves the application programmer of the burden of
programming two computers. But because the application program runs
exclusively on the host computer, a lot of user interactions have to
be reported to and serviced by the host. These so-called "significant
events" include many decisions at a very low level which have to be
done by the application program and cannot be predetermined or
are not supported by the satellite-resident set. Each time, a
message has to be sent from the satellite to the host, and the host
computer's operating system has to activate the application program
which takes a - perhaps trivial - decision and sends a message back to
the satellite - some delay will obviously occur.

Nevertheless, the fixed-function approach is useful in a lot of cases,
expecially in those where only a low interaction rate between graphics
system and user is required.

Programmable-satellite systems, on the other hand, allows the application programmer to directly program the satellite computer. Thus, the strong connection between satellite and host can be relaxed, and the application programmer can try to find a division of labor optimized for this particular application. On the other hand, this might consti-tute a danger if the satellite has enough computing power and suffici-ently background memory: it can favor and induce a software pendant of the "wheel of reincarnation" [4].

Fig. 7.8   Refresh display with typical output. The input tools are: con-
            trol dials, function buttons, joystick, keyboard and tablet

Positive	Negative
- Highly dynamic	- Limited information content on
- High resolution	the screen (flickering)
- Good contrast	- Relatively expensive
- High vector quality	
- Possibilities for colour	

Refresh displays are delivered with litterly any kind of input devices such as: Light pen, joystick, tracker ball, tablet, function buttons, keyboard,. touch panel, hit mechanism, control dials etc. (See chap.7.5)

7.3.2 RANDOM POSITIONING PLOTTERS

Even if the Product Model in the CAD/CAM systems are supposed to take over the role of the work drawings, hardcopies and plotts will play a dominant roll in Computer Graphics and CAD for a long time.

Small plotters are often used together with a graphic terminal to take hardcopies of drawings presented on the screen. They are manually controlled by the user and connected to the computer like any other terminal.

Large plotters are expensive and needs usually an operator, they are therefore mostly used as a central resource for many users.

Drum plotters are in general more compact and less expensive than large flatbed plotters, while flatbeds offer better accuracy and resolution plus the ability to plot/cut on a variety of materials.

7.3.2.1 Drum Plotters

The paper for the drum plotters is fed from a roll which can be moved back and forth, while the pens moves in the perpendicular direction.

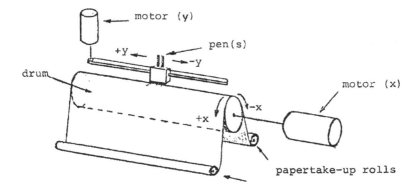

Fig. 7.9 Basic principle for a drum plotter.

These offers an in principle unlimited size of the drawing in one direction.

The width of the paper is limited from under 50 cm up to 200 cm.

Because most drum plotters are incremental, the vectors appears more or less jaggied dependent of the step size.

Drum plotters are now offered with three colours.

 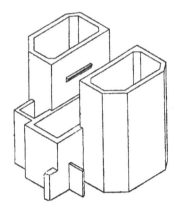

Fig. 7.10 Drum plotter with typical output.

Characteristics for drum plotters:

- Reasonable price
- Easy to operate
- Middle speed and accurency
- Colour
- Standard paper
- Jaggied lines
- Large plotts (long)
- High load on host if no function generators are available
- High output capacity

7.3.2.2 Flatbed Plotters

Flatbed plotters range from small cheap hardcopy devices up to very large sophisticated drafting machines.

Typical for both classes is that the paper (or other materials like transparencis, plastic etc.) are fixed to the flat drawing surface and the pen (or other tools like photoheads, tangentially controlled engraving tools, scribing tools etc.) are moving both in the X and Y direction.

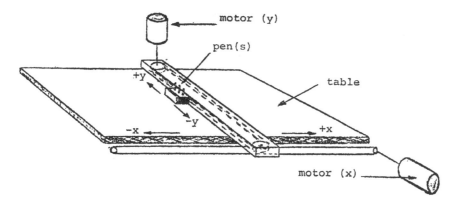

Fig. 7.11   Basic principle for flatbed plotters.

The flat, fixed drawing surface makes it easy to use all kinds of drawing materials like maps, preformatted forms and drawings which contains standard information.

Colours are also available. Some of the plotters have even multicolour penholders which makes it possible to control the colours directly from the program.

7.3.2.2.1 Hardcopy Flatbed Plotters

These plotters are mostly used for fast, high quality hardcopies on the operators desk.

Fig. 7.12   Hardcopy flatbed plotter with typical output.

Characteristics for small flatbed plotters:

- Cheap   - Automatic paper advance

- Reliable
- Easy to operate
- Colours
- High quality hardcopy

- Useful for transparency preparation
- Easy to interface

7.3.2.2.2 Large Flatbed Plotters

The large flatbed plotters or drafting machines are expensive, but sophisticated line drawing devices with very high speed and accuracy. They are mostly used for high quality drawing or specialized operations like filmcutting etc.

Fig. 7.13 Drafting Machine with typical output.

Characteristics for large flatbed plotters (Drafting machines)

- High speed (15-50 m/min) and accuracy ($\sim$ 75 μm)
- Large drawing area (up to several meters)
- Large number of tools
- Expensive
- High line quality
- Operator needed
- High load on host unless use of intelligent controller
- Frequently run off-line
- Colours available
- Convenient to use different "drawing material"

7.3.2.3 Microfilm Plotters (COM)

For large amount of drawings such as work drawings, maps etc. it may be convenient to use Microfilm plotters.

A common photographic technique images the output of a CRT onto a photosensitive paper. Often the "paper" is ordinary camera film, in which case the arrangement is called computer-output-to-microfilm or COM. If material such as 3M's Dry Silver is employed, it is possible to develop the image by a heating process rather than by chemicals, as in conventional photography.

7.3.2.4 Interactive Plotters

In addition to the output capabilities of the Interactive plotters, facilities for input of data are also provided.

The data input is performed by "inverting" the plotter, and moving the plotting head around by means of joystick, function buttons etc.

Most of the interactive plotters are small hardcopy devices (see fig. 7.9) but large combined drafting machines/digitizers are also available.

7.4 Raster Graphics Devices

Raster Graphics Devices present the picture as a matrix or raster of dots.

The raster display differs from the random line-drawing display chiefly in how displayed data are represented. A display file for a line-drawing display contains only information about lines and characters to be drawn; the void areas of the screen are ignored. The raster display, however, controls the intensity of each dot, or pixel, in a rectangular matrix, or raster, of dots that covers the entire surface.

7.4.1 RASTER DISPLAYS

The raster displays can be divided into two distinct classes [5]:

1. Video devices. These devices, of which the TV monitor is the most common, do not have any inherent image-storage capability. The displayed image must therefore be passed repeatedly to the device, at a high enough refresh rate to prevent flicker. The image is therefore passed as a video signal, a continuously fluctuating voltage that specifies the intensity variation along each scan line of the display. Colour video devices can be fed with three separate video signals, one for each of the primary colours, or with a single signal in which the three colour components are encoded together.

2. Matrix-addressed storage devices. The plasma panel is the best known of these devices. The screen is divided up into a matrix of cells, each one of which can be individually turned on or off to produce the desired image. Once turned on, the cell remains lit until turned off. Cells are addressed by row and column.

These two classes of displays are similar in the sense that they use a rectangular array of pixels to generate images.

7.4.1.1 Frame Buffer Systems

Most raster displays use video display devices based on the use of a large digital memory, or frame buffer, to store the displayed image. Many different kinds of memory have been used in frame buffers: drums, disks, integrated-circuit, shift registers, and core stores. The number of bits assigned to each pixel may be as few as 1 or as many as 24. Nowadays most frame buffers are constructed from random-access integrated-circuit memories, with between 1 and 16 bits assigned to each pixel.

The frame buffer consists of three main components:

1. The frame buffer itself, a large random-access memory in which the intensity of each pixel is stored as a binary intensity value;

2. A TV-moniator, on which the image is displayed;

3. A display controller, whose purpose is to scan repeatedly through the matrix of intensity values stored in the frame buffer and to produce from them a signal that can be fed to the TV-monitor.

In addition the advanced frame buffer systems contains also a colour look-up table for fast changing of colours without rewriting the content of the frame buffer.

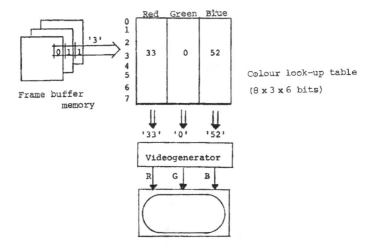

Fig. 7.14 Basic principle for a frame buffer with a colour look-up table.

The pixel value (between 0 and 2^N-1, where N is the number of planes in the frame buffer) is used as an index into the colour look-up table.

The bit combination from each of the primary colours found in the look-up table decides the colour of the corresponding point on the screen. However, even if the look-up table increase the number of colours available, the number of colour displayed simultaneously on the screen are limited by the number of planes in the frame buffer.

The frame buffer is one of the most versatile display devices. Given
8 or more bits of intensity precision, it can produce colour and mono-
chrome images whose quality and complexity are limited only by the
performance of the TV monitor on which they are displayed. For applications that involve shading, solid areas of colour, and high-quality
text. For any type of image processing, the frame buffer offers the
only satisfactory form of display.

The frame buffer is not without its problems, however. It does not
offer the most compact way of representing an image; the large amounts
of memory it uses make it expensive, and the time taken to fill this
memory or change its contents makes interactive response slow at times.

Another problem is the staircase effect on slanting vectors. That problem is tried solved partly by software (Anti-aliasing) and partly by
hardware (higher resolution).

Fig. 7.15 Raster display with typical output and a TV-digitizer
and keyboard as input tools.

Characteristics for frame buffers:

Positive	Negative
- High quality "life like" pictures	- High price - Medium dynamic

- Full range of colours
  available
- Polygon filling
- Mixing of real images with
  synthetic images
- Combine Graphics with image
  processing

- Large amount of data
- Medium line quality

7.4.1.2. Plasma Displays

The demand for flat panel television have stimulated a steady growth
in the development of gas discharge displays or plasma displays.

The essential picture element (pixel) in the plasma display is an electrical gas discharge that develops between two electrodes when the
applied voltage exceeds a critical level. In the simplest display, an
on-off indicator, there is only a single discharge site, but also high
resolution matrix displays are now available. (512x512)

An interesting feature with the plasma panels is the transparent screen
which allows superposition of computer generated displays with optical
projected images.

Fig. 7.16 A Plasma panel with keyboard and touch panel as
input devices.

Characteristics for plasma panels:

Positive	Negative
- Flat Panel	- Medium resolution
- Selective erase	- Slow writing speed
- Transparent screen	- Limited interactive properties
- Flicker free	

7.4.1.3 Cell Organized Displays

The cell-organized display constructs images out of strings of square
characters, each one either blank or containing one or more short line
segments. Each character is composed by a number of pixels grouped in
a cell. The number of pixel pr. cell varies from device to device (ex.
Tektronix 4025 uses 8 x 14 pixels). The characters are chosen from a
standard set or from a dynamically created set to allow display of
arbitrary graphics.

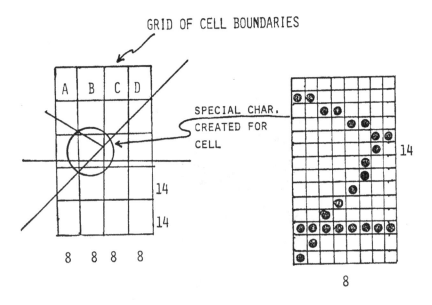

Fig. 7.17 Drawing by means of character cells.

Each cell (in T4025) is represented by two bytes: The character set
(max 16) and the character code (128 per set).

Individual pixels cannot be manipulated, the cell is the primitive
element in the system.

7.4.2 RASTER PLOTTERS

Similar to the raster displays, the raster plotts are built up from a matrix of points each one with a given symbol, intensity or colour.

The raster plotters utilize well known mechanical, electrostatical or electrodynamic prinsiples. The simplest and most available raster plotter is the Line Printer. Even if the resolution is very poor, the Line printer is a useful tool for prevewing etc.

7.4.2.1 Electrostatic Plotter

The electrostatic writing process is entirely electronic. The only movements are in the paper transport and toner supply. With few moving parts, the plotter is quiet and reliable.

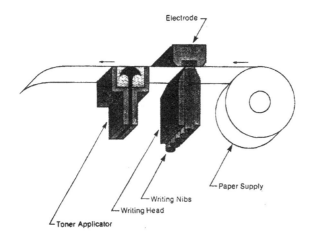

Fig. 7.18   Basic principle for electrostatic plotter.

Programmed voltage is applied to an array of densely spaced writing nibs embedded in a stationary writing head. Upon digital command the nibs selectively create minute electrostatid dots on the paper passing over the writing head. The paper is then exposed to a liquid toner, producing the image or text.

The drawing speed is independent of the complexity of the image, but the process implies a heavy load on the computer. Electrostatic plotters are therefore often run off-line. The raster plotters are frequently a combination of a plotter and printer.

The image generation process is frequently very resource demanding unless special purpose line to raster converters are used.

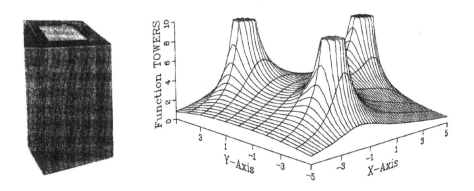

Fig. 7.19   Electrostatic plotter with typical output.

Characteristics for electrostatic plotters:

Positive	Negative

- Reliable
- Drawing of shaded images
- Quiet
- Combined printer/plotters
- Fast drawing independent of image complexity
- High resolution (4-8 points/ mm)

- High load on host
- Jagged lines and characters
- Special, expensive paper
- No colour

7.4.2.2 Colour Ink Jet Plotter

Due to the excellent ability of the human eye to extract relevant information from a complex picture, mechanical and electrostatic plotters are used increasingly to present computer data in the form of graphs and pictures. However, these plotters mostly generate black and white pictures only and thus do not make use of the special property of the human eye to perceive colours.

Since colours are adding a further dimension to the pictorial type of information presentation, a colour hardcopy display has been developed which allows the presentation of computer-based information in the form of coloured graphs, maps or pictures.

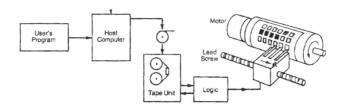

Fig. 7.20   Basic principle of the colour ink jet plotter.

The writing head of the plotter consist of three nozzles, one for each
of the primary colours. A stream of ink is forced through the nozzles
under high pressure and forms a narrow stream drawing a point on the
paper which is fixed to a rotating drum as the writing head moves
perpendicular to the drum.
The ink stream passes by a charge electrode. If a voltage is applied
between the charge electrode and the ink stream, an electrostatic
charge is induced into the ink drops which will break away from each
other and turn the ink stream into a spray which prevents the ink from
reaching the paper.

The electrostatic charged drops in the spray are then captured by an
electronic field and lead back to the ink reservoir.

The total information content in an A4 size image drawn on the Appli-
con plotter is $3.7 \cdot 10^6$ bit which implies that the plotter is usually
run off line.

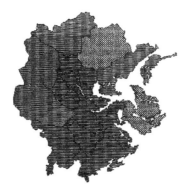

Fig. 7.21 Typical output from a colour jet ink plotter.

7.4.2.3 "Off the screen" Hardcopy Devices

Fast "off the screen" hardcopy devices are very useful tools for people working with computer graphics and CAD. People want something to scribble on, something to discuss around, something for simple information communication to the colleagues and customer and something to take home.

The supply of suitable "off the screen" hardcopy devices are not satisfactory, but new products are on their way.

The products on the market today are based on the scanning-, video- or photographic-principles.

7.4.2.3.1 Scanning based Hardcopy Devices

The Scanning hardcopy devices work on storage tubes and actually scans the content on the CRT screen.

Fig. 7.22 "Off the screen" hardcopy device based on scanning.

Emulators for electrostatic plotters are also available.

7.4.2.3.2 Videobased Hardcopy Devices

The video hardcopy devices converts the video signal directly into raster data. Separate controllers for converting videosignals into standard formats for raster plotting is also available, permitting use of standard electrostatic plotters as "off the screen" hardcopy devices (see fig. 7.19)

7.4.2.3.3 Photographic based Hardcopy Devices

The advantages of photographic hardcopy for the majority of colour computer graphic applications are widely recognized. But, until now, the poor quality of images made directly from colour video displays has prevented the general adaption of video display photography.

Recently, however, some companies have developed new photographic systems that produces accurate, high fidelity colour images directly from a video display.

The techniques used by colour raster displays and colour photography to reproduce the colours found in nature are each distinctive. Colour television uses an additive colour process: it combines phosphors of the three primary colours of light (red, blue, green) to reproduce the full range of natural colours. A banana on a television screen appears yellow because red and green primary colours are produced and are "mixed" by the eye to create the sensation of yellow.

Colour film, on the other hand, uses a subtractive process: complementary dyes selectively absorb and reflect the spectra of real objects to produce a range of colours. The dyes are Cyan, which is "minus" (absorbs) red; Magneta, which is "minus" green; and Yellow, which is "minus" blue. Yellow dye, by absorbing blue and reflecting the red and green components of light makes the banana in a photograph appear yellow. [6]

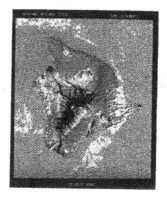

Fig. 7.23 "Off the screen" hardcopy device based on photography.

7.5 Input Devices

The input devices supported on a CAD system are the portals through
which the user enters information about his model, drafts, makes inquiri-
es for output, and controls the operation of the system. The user comes
in contact with these devices more often than any other part of the
system. The interplay of input device and display feedback must match
the user's design thought process to ensure the success of the system.
[8]

7.5.1 LIGHT PEN

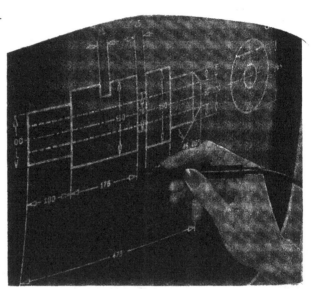

Fig. 7.24   Light pen

The light pen is a narrow tube meant to be grasped by a hand and used
like a pen on the surface of the display to point to an object or location. At the pen's tip is a light sensitive detector which generates
a signal when placed over a lighted portion of the display screen. The
lighted portion causing the "hit" can then be identified by specialized
software. The light pen's advantage is its direct hand to object natural style usage in the user's line of sight.

There are two disadvantages. Arm fatigue can result from heavy continued use since the pen is usually brought to seated eye level with the
elbow out of reach of the station's tabletop. Sinking the display into

the tabletop can solve this problem. The second problem arises from the light to electrical signal link in the light pen's feedback loop. Ambient light noise, inadequate display intensity, user positioning error, and interrupt software preemption can all cause a "hit" to be missed. The light pen is used with refresh displays. The input device on a large number of successful CAD turnkey and in-house developed systems is the light pen.

7.5.2 TABLET

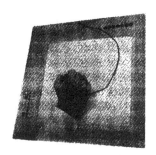

Fig. 7.25 Tablet.

The tablet is an input device consisting of a flat plane over which a stylus is moved. The tablet surface is usually mapped to correspond to the display screen surface with a cursor on the screen representing the position of the stylus on the tablet's surface. The tablet can be used as a pointer to an object by bringing the cursor near the desired object and depressing the stylus. Software then determines the object of nearest proximity.

A refresh system with a tablet and program controlled "hit window" (comparator) is also available.

When a line crosses through the "hit window", there will be generated a report identifying the line by means of a name stack which may be used by the application program to make changes in the corresponding data base [9].

Since the position of the cursor is always known, the tablet also makes a good positioning device. Many systems also implement a virtual menu on the tablet's surface which functions much like a set of predefined keys or switches. Menus on the tablet leave the display screen free for viewing. Large tablets (more often called digitizers) can be used as a drafting board on which an existing drawing may be placed and traced. Care must be taken in this application, however, since any inaccuracies in the drawing will be replicated. These inaccuracies do not occur when the data is inputted geometrically.

7.5.3 JOYSTICK

Fig. 7.26   Control dials, joystick and function buttons.

The joystick is a device which allows the user to specify X and Y screen positions via two orthogonal analog-to-digital converters. As with the tablet, a cursor on the display screen, is used as the visual hand to screen feedback cue. The joystick may be designed with a button on the top of the shaft for a finger actuated event trigger. Support software for the joystick can implement it as a X-Y displacement positioning device or a spring-returned-to-center velocity or acceleration control.

7.5.4 FUNCTION BUTTONS

A menu driven command structure can be implemented with a set of function buttons also called switches or keys. The definition of the function of each key can be user specified. Some turnkey vendor systems have a selection of button function overlay templates, each representing functions most often performed in a particular application. (See fig. 7.26)

7.5.5 KEYBOARD

Fig. 7.27   Refresh display with keyboard and light pen.

The alphanumeric keyboard is an input device that is used with all CAD systems regardless of which other input devices are present. Every design project has a need to include alphanumeric non-graphical information on the drawing or design and such information is tedious to input through a menu. The keyboard can also be used when the system is driven by a command language of sufficiently concise syntax to limit the number of keystrokes necessary for an advanced user to perform a task.

7.6 Configuration Of Graphics Hardware

Graphics hardware may be provided for solving a particular class of problems, where one single device is sufficient. But in most cases this is not the case, the user may want to work on a fast display with powerful interaction tools and access to one or more hardcopy devices.

7.6.1 SIMPLE CONFIGURATION

One of the simplest multitask graphics systems on the marked is combining all the mentioned facilities in one single device. The desk top computer combines interactive keyboard, expandable memory, graphics CRT display, a central processing unit, hardcopy device and dual tape drivers into one single unit.

Fig. 7.28 Single Graphics device combining multiple function.

7.6.2 WORKSTATION CONFIGURATION

The hardware in a CAD workstation consist of a processing unit, and a variety of input and output devices put together to serve the designer in performing his tasks:

Fig. 7.29 A typical CAD configuration.

1. Central Processing Unit (CPU): - which manipulates data and transfers information between the other units. This is normally a mini-computer.

2. Magnetic tape input and output device.

3. Disc units providing multi megabytes of random access storage.

4. A console display for text input and operating feedback.

5. Hard copy printer.

6. A graphics terminal work station which would normally include:

        a) a Storage, raster or refresh tube
        b) a CRT monitor
        c) a function keyboard
        d) an alpha numeric keyboard
        e) a data tablet
        f) a joy stick, light pen, cross hair, tracker ball etc.

7. A digitizing table.

8. A flatbed plotter (High quality plotter).

9. A fast hardcopy device is also usually included.

7.6.3 GROWING GRAPHICS CONFIGURATION

7.6.3.1 Step One

Besides of a personell computer, the easiest and cheapest way to get started in computer graphics is to get a direct view storage tube or some equivalent priced hardware, connect it to an existing computer with available graphics software either directly or via a telephone line and start working:

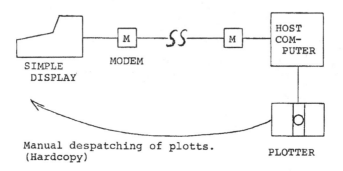

Fig. 7.30 Step one: Simple graphics system (Display and modem).

This "testconfiguration" is cheap enough for a trial and error periode after which the whole investment can be written off if one don't find the tool profitable enough.

7.6.3.2 Step Two

If it turns out profitable, the next step will normally be to provide a mini/micro computer if no suitable inhouse computer are available.

To make the transition smooth it may be useful to have a switch for utilization of both the remote computer and the new inhouse computer.

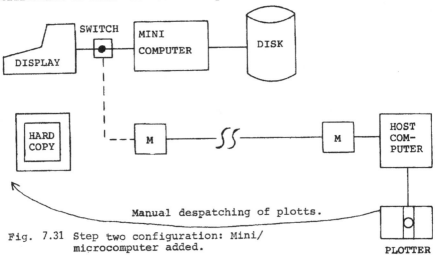

Fig. 7.31 Step two configuration: Mini/microcomputer added.

To increase the power of the configuration the mini-computer may be connected to the Host computer as a simple network. The question is now: Is the graphic software portable enough to be moved to the mini-computer in order to achieve an efficient resource sharing?

By portability we mean the ability to transport graphical application programs from one installation to another with minimal program changes.

7.6.3.3 Step Three

As the use of computer graphics increase, new equipments such as plotters, displays etc., will be added to the mini-computer.

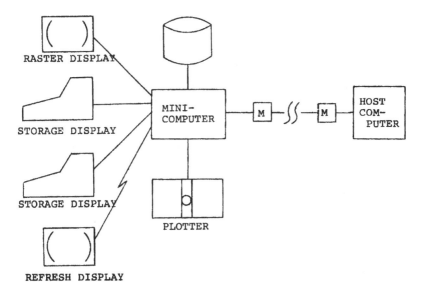

Fig. 7.32   Step three, Configuration: Additional graphics devices.

The question is now: Is the software device independent enough to support all the different devices?

By device independence we mean the capability of switching from one device to another without rewriting the programs, or to include new devices without a substensial rewriting of the basic graphics software.

7.6.3. 4 Step Four

As new devices and functions are added, the load on the computer will increase and degrade the minicomputer system such that the throughput

and response time is not acceptable any longer. Then it is time for
getting another computer and dedicate the old one as a special purpose
graphics computer for handling the most resource demanding devices.

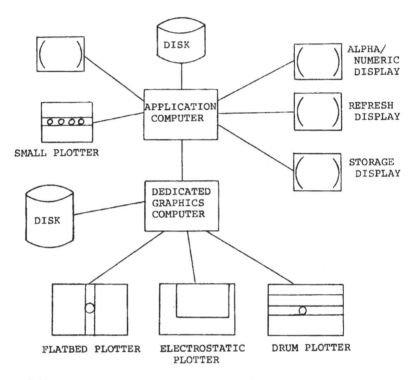

Fig. 7.33   Step four configuration: Dedicated graphics computer.

The question is now: Is the software powerfull enough to support graphics network?

In the simplest case "networking" may be achieved by generating the
complete picture on the application computer in device independent
compressed code which is sent to the graphics computer for drawing.

7.6.3.5 Step Five

If the software and the interfaces are modular and powerfull enough,
a number of functions such as digitizing, image processing voice in-
put/output etc. can be added to the system and several independent
systems can be connected to an operated special purpose graphics computer for producing resource demanding drawings or drawings on specialized expensive hardware.

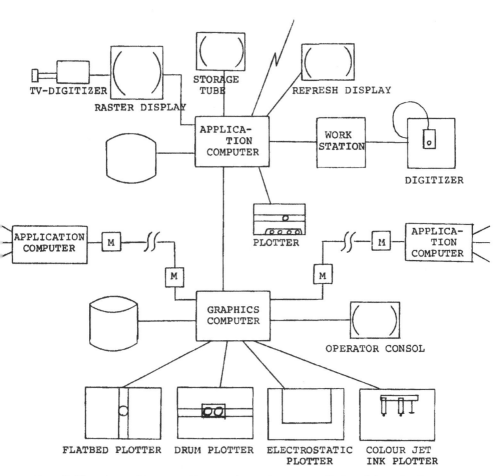

Fig. 7.34   Step five configuration: Integrated Graphics System.

Besides that the system is integrated and modular, it may also be fully
distributed. One may for instance sit in Oslo on a display, generate a
picture on a computer in Trondheim and get the result plotted on the
colour jet plotter in Lund. [7]

REFERENCES

1   Computer Graphics Software & Service Market. Report ≠ 653 Frost
    and Sullivan, New York, Feb. 1979.

2   Preiss, R.B.: "Storage CRT Display Terminals: Evolution and Trends"
    Computer, November 1978.

3   Lucido A.P.: "An Overview of Directed Beam Graphics Display Hard-
    ware" Computer, November 1978.

4   Myer, T.H., Sutherland, I.E.: On the Design of Display Processors.
    Comm. of the ACM, Volume 11, No 6 June 1968.

5   Newman, W.M. and Sproull, R.F.: "Principles of Interactive Com
    puter Graphics", McGraw-Hill Computer Science Series 1979.

6   Gruber, L.S.: "Imaging Colour Computer Graphics. The Dunn Camera
    and the Polaroid instant 8x10 Photographic solution.

7   Bø, K.: "IGS, Integrated Graphics System", RUNIT, Trondheim 1980.

8   Dearing, M.P.: "CAD Tutorial Introdction" SIGGRAPH'79, Chicago
    1979.

9   Lillehagen, F.: "Real Intelligence in CAD Workstations" CAD tuto-
    rial at SIGGRAPH'80, Seattle 1980.

10 Machover, C.: "Graphics displays", IEEE Spectrum, August 1977.

11 Foley, J.: "Introduction to Raster Graphics Concept", Tutorial
    SIGGRAPH'79, Chicago 1979.

Chapter 8

Basic Graphics for Data Representation

by

E.G. Schlechtendahl

Kernforschungszentrum
Karlsruhe

8.1 Graphical Kernel Systems

8.1.1 Purpose of Graphic Kernel Systems

Graphic data processing is an essential part of CAD in two respects: It is required for both modelling (generation of geometrical design information) and for presentation of numerical results. For driving graphic input and output peripherals a great number of software packages has been made available by manufacturers of graphic hardware and by software producers. These packages, however, are insufficiently compatible. Portability of the application programs is not guaranteed. The incompatibilities are not merely of a syntactic nature, but considerable reprogramming is often needed for adaptation of a program to another graphic hardware and software environment. Since about 1975 several attempts for standardization are underway. The state of these activities is documented in [1] for the CORE system and in [2] for GKS.

8.1.2 The Graphical Kernel System GKS

GKS is the result of a long process of evolution [3,4] and the present version has been influenced by international discussion and parallel activities. GKS features two-dimensional ouput to and input from single or multiple workstations. Besides basic line drawing primitives (POLYLINE, POLYMARKER, STRING) raster primitives (FILL_AREA, PIXEL_ARRAY) are supported for output. The input primitives LOCATOR, VALUATOR, CHOICE, PICK and STRING may be obtained from the workstation in three input modes: REQUEST, SAMPLE and EVENT. The first corresponds to a FORTRAN read, the last allows for asynchronous operation. Output primitives may be grouped in "segments", which may be addressed later in the process for modification and deletion. GKS is a language independent specification and leaves the syntactical definition open for definition of a language dependent layer (fig.8.1).

The conceptual model of the processes coexisting in a GKS application is shown in fig.8.2. The application program creates and deletes a GKS process via OPEN_GKS and CLOSE_GKS. Once this process exists, it may be requested to create workstation processes, change their operating state and delete them (OPEN_WORKSTATION, ACTIVATE_WORKSTATION etc.). Various input processes corresponding to the input devices of each workstation may be ENABLEd and DISABLEd. Only one output process per workstation is under control of GKS, even though the graphical terminal associated with the workstation may provide different output surfaces. We consider segments as processes (for definition see chapter 11.1.1), which communicate permanently with those workstations that were active at the time of segment creation. The segment storage may be used for reuse of the graphical information defined in a segment, the GKS metafile serves for longterm saving.

The visualization of segments on a graphical terminal is performed in two stages as shown in fig.8.3. From the application program "world" the graphical information is mapped onto a workstation independent picture within GKS. From there it is mapped onto each workstation separately. This two-stage procedure is applied to both the geometrical size of the picture and to visualization of individual parts (linestyle, colour, text font etc.). The application program has, via GKS, access to a workstation description table, that describes the functional capabilities of the workstation (e.g. whether it supports colour or not). Thus the application program may perform an optimum adaptation of the graphical output to the available resources.

8.1.3 Significant Differences between GKS and the CORE System

Three conceptual differences between GKS and the CORE system should be pointed out [5]:

- Dimensionality
  CORE treats two-dimensional graphics as a special case of
  three-dimensional graphics, while GKS deals with two-dimensional
  graphics only.
- The workstation concept
  CORE treats individual input and output devices as individual and
  independent processes, while GKS groups them into workstations.
- The two-stage visualization
  We consider graphical information as geometrical information with
  visualization information added. CORE associates these two types
  of information on the intermediate level (between the application
  program and the graphical terminal), while GKS defines the
  visualization information in a parametric way first, leaving the
  mapping onto the workstation capabilities open to a second stage.

8.2 Data Presentation Techniques

8.2.1 Introduction

The application of powerful numerical methods to the analysis of design objects generally produces huge amounts of data. In order to make these results useful for interpretation and evaluation, they need to be presented in a form which is suited for this purpose. Long lists of printed data are totally unsuited for comprehension by man. Graphic repesentations are the appropriate solution. Thus computer graphics is closely related to numerical methods and has been included in this chapter for that reason. The benefits of graphic data presentation stems from two facts:

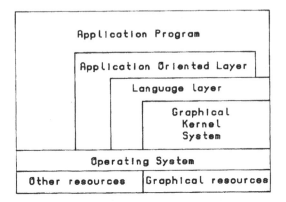

Fig.8.1: The layer model of GKS

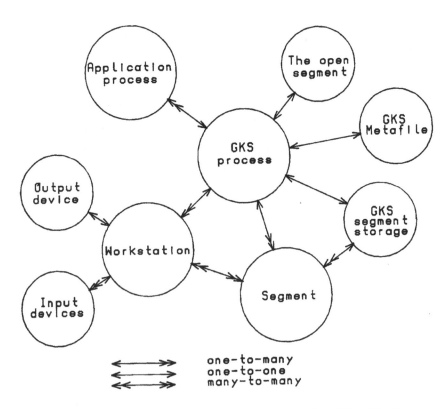

Fig.8.2: Relationships between the processes of a GKS application

- Informations contained in graphical representations are perceived
  by man in a parallel fashion while lists of printed data must be
  parsed more or less sequentially. "One picture is worth a thousand
  words".
- The graphic representation can produce evidence of structures like
  "peaks" or "waves" or "shock fronts". Such structures are often
  essential for the evaluation. Note that finite difference or finite
  element techniques do not intrinsically treat such structures, but
  the results may be expressed most effectively in these terms.

To a great deal graphic representations are used for the following purposes:

- immediate presentation of result to the engineer who is responsible
  for the analysis
- reporting results to a customer or supervising authority
- publications, presentations
- longterm documentation.

The requirements regarding turn-around time and prettiness of the representations
is quite different. For the analyst fast response has the highest priority. Thus
either graphic displays or fast plotters (e.g. electrostatic plotters) are
appropriate. For reports and publications aesthetics aspects become more important,
which makes line plotters (particularly table plotters) more attractive.

For presentations and longterm documentation the space requirements for the display
medium can be minimized by utilizing graphic output on microfilm, microfiche or
videotape. Output of analysis results on a display or plotter medium is only part
of the task. In most cases (except for the immediate result presentation to the
analyst himself) the representation of the data must be edited. Axes must be added
to diagrams, annotations, sketches or scaled-down drawings of the design object
must be included with the data representation. This is a typical task for
interactive graphics.

8.2.2 Functions of one Variable

8.2.2.1 Diagrams

The standard technique of representing a function of one variable is a diagram.
Various forms of diagrams (for a single functions) based on the same data points
are shown in fig.8.4 through fig.8.7 with increasing degree of continuity. When
the data are available at discrete intervals only, as for all numerical
simulations, then the difference between the linear interpolation and a smoothed

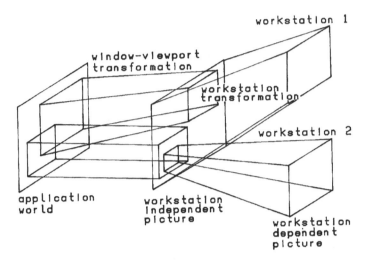

Fig.8.3: The two-stage transformation in GKS

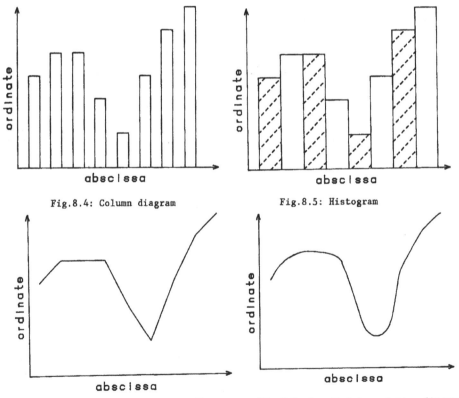

Fig.8.4: Column diagram

Fig.8.5: Histogram

Fig.8.6: Linear interpolation diagram

Fig.8.7: Smooth interpolation diagram

representation is merely an aesthetic one. The smooth curve looks nicer - but the linear interpolation is more truthful, as it does not pretend a higher accuracy of the analysis than was actually achieved. Furthermore, the linear interpolation is cheaper and faster than smoothing. Thus for technical communication fig.8.6 is preferable, while for commercial or advertisement presentations the smooth curve of fig.8.7 will be the better choice.

8.2.2.2 Representations of several functions in a diagram

The representation of more than one function of only one variable does not pose great problems. We may distinguish between the different curves by using different linestyles or colours, by adding markers or by shading, hatching or colouring the area below the curve. Fig.8.8 through fig.8.9 show various possibilities depending on whether the functions are continuous and whether they have the same ordinate axes.

8.2.3 Functions of two Variables

With the growing capability of the numerical computer programs, the detail analysis of design objects has shifted from one-dimensional to two-dimensional or even three-dimensional problems. Graphical representations, however, are at first sight limited to the two dimensions of a display screen or a plotter. Thus, while the representation of a function of one variable is a simple task, representations of functions of more variables may require rather sophisticated methods.

8.2.3.1 Marker Clouds

In order to present a single <u>scalar</u> function of two variables one may map the value of this function on to the reciprocal distance of markers. Thus the apparent density of the displayed markers indicates the the variations of the function. As an example, the function sin(x)*sin(y) over a 2π range in either direction is shown in fig.8.11. In this case the markers are distributed regularly within small rectangles for which some average value was computed. An alternative is to use a pseudo random number generator to make the representation look smoother. Choice of different size (fig.8.12), shape or colour for the markers provides further options.

The applicability of the marker cloud technique depends upon the hardware which is used for visualisation. The technique is unsuited for drum or table plotters because it may require many hours to draw so many markers. For electronic displays (particularly storage tube and raster displays) as well as raster plotters (electrostatic or ink jet) and microfilm plotters the technique is useful.

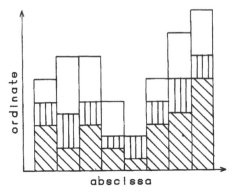

Fig.8.8: Simultanuous representation of several discontinuous functions with the same ordinate

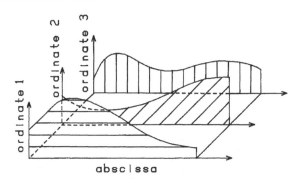

Fig.8.9: Pseudo-perspective view of several function with different ordinates

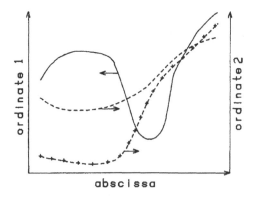

Fig.8.10: A diagram with two ordinates for three functions

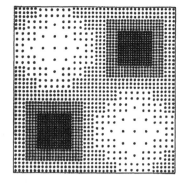

Fig.8.11: Marker density plot of a two-dimensional function

8.2.3.2 Hatching, Shading and Colouring

A different technique to represent a single scalar function of two variables is based on hatching, shading or colouring areas. The hatching technique can be used on vector oriented hardware (line plotters and storage tubes). For refresh displays hatching may soon exceed the refresh capacity and lead to flicker. On raster oriented hardware (plotters as well as displays) shading is preferred because it may produce a smoothly looking picture (as opposed to hatching which is always restricted to discontinuous steps in the representation). Fig.8.13 shows the same function as fig.8.11 with finer raster and 16 levels of shading. Colour is even better suited for showing both discontinuous and smooth variations of a function.

Hatching, shading and colouring are less suited to represent more than one function in a single picture. A combination of colouring, marker clouds and contour plots, however could be used to display a small number of functions in a single picture. But care should be taken not to overload one picture with too much information.

Coloured images for representation of computer results of structural mechanics programs have been published already in the early 70's [6]. But the breakthrough of colour is yet to come. Despite the advantages of colour data presentations this technique is not widely spred. A major problem with colour is the cost of reproduction which is significantly higher than for black and white line drawings or gray shaded pictures. (Note, that this book, too, refrains from colour reproduction for this reason.) Even though colour pictures can now be produced much more easily and cheaper than years ago (due to the progress in colour display and instant colour photography), the reproduction problem is likely to persist for a longer time.

8.2.3.3 Contour Plotting

A widely spred technique for representing a scalar function of two variables is the contour plot (or isoline plot). Fig.8.14 is a contour plot of the same function as in fig.8.11. The advantage of contour plot is that it is suited for vector oriented hardware (line plotters, vector tubes) which is (as yet) more common than area oriented graphic hardware. The hardware has even an influence upon the algorithm that is best used to produce contour plots. On electronic displays it does not matter whether a contour is plotted at once or as many separate edges of a polygon. A mechanical plotter would spend too much time in latter case and, hence, requires contour following algorithms.

The example used above is particularly easy because the data which represent the surface are arranged in a regular rectangular pattern. A slightly more general problem has the same degree of complexity: if the positions x and y of the data points do not form a rectangle but may be arranged in two-dimensional arrays $X(I,J)$ and $Y(I,J)$, very simple algorithms may be used. The same is true for data resulting from finite element analyses as long as the topology of the finite element net (Which nodes form an element? Which elements are adjacent on each node?) is available. In all these cases the "neighbourhood" of the data points is either explicitly or implicitly known. The problem becomes more difficult when only a vector of data $X(I),Y(I),Z(I)$ is given. The problem now resembles the task of constructing a solid body based on the information about the vertices alone without any knowledge about the topology of faces and edges. Nevertheless contour following algorithms have been developed for this task (e.g.[7]. Such algorithms are often based on implicit assumptions of the following type:

- the surface does not overlap,
- the projection of the surface onto the x-y-plane is convex or has a predefined boundary,
- the surface is spanned by triangles between the data points; the edges of the triangles represent shortest connections between the projections of the data points in the x-y-plane.

Isolines are well suited to indicate a small number of pronounced structures like peaks and wave fronts. They become less suited if the function does not show such pronounced structures or too many of them. It is impossible to perceive hills and valleys from isolines alone. They give no indication of the direction of slope. Additional visualization aids should be used to supply the missing information:

- annotations,
- different line style at different levels (in fig.8.14 lines corresponding to positive/negative values are solid/dashed),
- different markers added to the lines

8.2.3.4 Pseudoperspective View

Another way to represent two-dimensional functions applies techniques which are known from the representation of curved surfaces. The function values are mapped onto a third spatial coordinate and the resulting surface in space may be treated in just the same way as a real curved surface in space. The same techniques for hidden line removal or smoothing are applicable. Fig.8.15 shows the same function as used previously in pseudoperspective view. Pseudoperspective views are very helpful for data presentation because

- they are equally applicable for line oriented and area oriented hardware

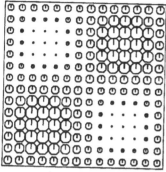

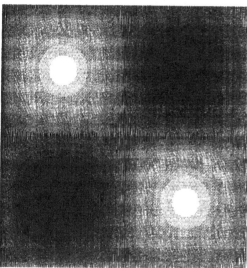

Fig.8.12: Markers of different size representing a two-dimensional function

Fig.8.13: Shaded picture representation of a two-dimensional function

Fig.8.14: Contour plot of a two-dimensional function

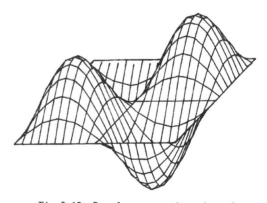

Fig.8.15: Pseudo-perspective view of a two-dimensional function

- they provide an excellent perceivability of the general shape of
the function, even provide gross quantitative information.

Problems arise when the function values pass through several decades or if hills in
the front part of the view hide relevant information (as fig.8.15, where a hill in
the background is hidden).

8.2.3.5 Vector Plots

The above mentioned techniques are applicable to the representation of scalar
functions. Vector functions (such as velocity field) may be represented as vector
plots. The vectors are represented starting at the points of interest and pointing
in the vector direction. The arrow length is taken proportional to the vector
length (or in the case of extreme variations: proportional to its logarithm). Care
must be taken to avoid overlapping of the vectors which would obscure the
information. Two vector fields may be represented in the same plot by using
different arrow heads, as in fig.8.16, or different colours.

8.2.3.6 Two-dimensional Functions on Curved Surfaces

Often the need arises to represent two-dimensional functions on the curved surface
of a body. A typical example is the temperature or stress distribution on the
surface of a technical component. Pseudo-perspective views are not applicable in
this case; hatching is not advisable (hatching lines would have to be curved), but
other techniques (marker clouds, shading, colouring, isolines and vector plots) are
applicable. Obviously different techniques should be used to represent the
three-dimensional shape of the surface and the behaviour of the function. If curved
lines are used to represent the surface, shading or colouring is well suited for
function representation. If the surface is represented in different shades (or
colours), isolines are best suited to visualize the function.

In summary, none of the techniques described here is best in all cases. The
available hardware has a significant influence upon the best choice, but for
successful and fast design analysis there is no alternative to providing several of
these techniques in an interactive graphics environment such that the user may
select between the various options according to his needs.

8.2.4 Functions of more Variables

Three-dimensional functions (stresses, temperatures etc.) result from static
three-dimensional analysis or two-dimensional transient analysis (where time is the

third dimension). When we represent a three-dimensional function on a two-dimensional display surface, we actually loose two dimensions (the dimension of the function value itself and one space or time dimension). Thus, we must look for techniques to simulate these two missing dimensions. Three methods may be used to overcome this problem:

- Clouds of markers in 3D-space with different size or colour (according the function value) may be projected from different view points (possibly with some scissoring applied). Human perception must reconstruct the full three-dimensional information from these views. As an alternative to several static projections, interactive display techniques may be provided to rotate the domain of interest under user control. As a compromise, the image may rotate in a predefined way. This technique is applicable for computer generated movies and video tapes. 3D vector fields may be represented in this manner too.
- Stereoscopic projection of marker clouds (in different colours or sizes) requires the overlay of two projections from appropriate view points. Because of the problems associated with the separation of the two images (each one must be seen with one eye only) the technique has not become very popular. Wearing special glasses to separate light of different colour or polarization is too much of a burden for the user.
- The most successful way to represent three-dimensional functions is the use of techniques for two-dimensional functions (see above) with time to simulate the third dimension. Computer generated movies or video tapes are an excellent tool for representing three-dimensional behaviour.

8.2.5 Graphical Editing

The editing operations for data presentation usually comprise the following functions

- Generation of coordinate axes
  Care must be taken to assure the consistency of the displayed axes with the corresponding data display. In particular, when linear transformations (shift, rotate, scale) are applied to an already generated data display, the associated axes must be submitted to the same transformations.
- Annotations
  Descriptive text must be added to most data displays.
- Viewing transformations and picture combinations.
  For diagrams quite often data curves from different sources must be combined into a single diagram. Analysis data are to be shown together with scaled drawing or sketches of the objects to which they relate.

Thus graphics for data presentation and graphics for geometric
modelling need to be interfaced in an appropriate way. A suitable
method is a standardized data schema for both applications.

Fig.8.17 shows a concept for an editing system [8] which is based on two
standardized data formats:

- the PLOTCP format for data vectors and matrices[9]
- the AGF-plotfile format for graphic information[10]

Graphic information can be produced from

- the geometrical description of objects (3D or 2D) with the
  graphical programming language GIPSY[11,12] or from interactive
  display terminals;
- the results of various simulations;
- the results from corresponding experiments.

Batch and interactive processors are available to combine information from these
sources, to edit it and to display it on various hardware. Since the output format
of the graphic editors is again the standard AGF-plotfile, edited pictures may be
used for editing other pictures e.g. by inserting them.

8.3 References

[1]   "GSPC79":
          ACM-SIGGRAPH Graphics Standards Planning Committee,
          Special Issue on GSPC 79, Computer Graphics 13(1979)3

[2]   "GKS":
          Proposal of Standard DIN 0066252,
          Graphical Kernel System, Functional Description, Berlin(1979)DIN

[3]   R.Eckert F.-J.Prester E.G.Schlechtendahl P.Wisskirchen:
          Functional Description of the Graphical Core System GKS as a
          Step towards Standardization,
          Informatik Fachberichte 11,Berlin(1977)Springer P.163:176

[4]   R.Eckert G.Enderle K.Kansy F.-J.Prester:
          GKS 79 - Proposal of a Standard for a Graphics Kernel
          System, Proc. Eurographics 79 Bologna(1979) P.2:17

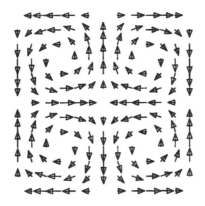

Fig.8.16: Two-dimensional vector plot

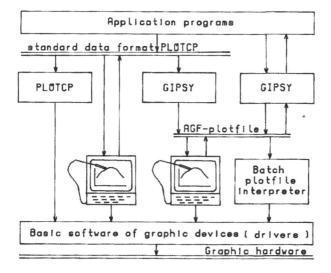

Fig.8.17: Standard data formats for graphic data presentation

[5]   J.Encarnacao G.Enderle K.Kansy G.Nees E.G.Schlechtendahl J.Weiss
       P.Wißkirchen:
       The workstation concept of GKS and resulting conceptual
       differences to the GSPC core system,
       7 th Annual Conf. Computer Graphics and Interactive Techniques
       Seattle(1980)

[6]   H.N.Christiansen:
       Application of Continuous Tone Computer Generated Images in Structural
       Mechanics,
       In:Pilkey,W.,Saczalski,K.,Schaeffer,H.: Structural
       Mechanics Computer Programs
       Charlottesville(1974)Univ. Virginia Press P.1003:1015

[7]   M.R.Patterson:
       CONTUR: A Subroutine to Draw Contour Lines for Randomly Located Data,
       Report ORNL/CSD/TM-59
       Oak Ridge(1978)UNION CARBIDE CORP,NUCLEAR DIVISION

[8]   K.Leinemann P.Royl W.Zimmerer:
       Integration graphischer Systeme für Darstellungszwecke,
       KfK-Nachrichten, Karlsruhe(1980)Kernforschungszentrum

[9]   W.Zimmerer:
       PLOTCP - Ein FORTRAN IV-Programm zur Erzeugung von Calcomp
       Plot-Zeichnungen,
       Report KFK 2081, Karslruhe(1975)Kernforschungszentrum

[10]   G.Enderle I.Giese M.Krause H.-P.Meinzer:
       The AGF-Plotfile - Towards a Standardisation for Storage and
       Transportation of Graphics Information
       Computer Graphics 12(1979)4, P.92:113

[11]   R.Schuster:
       System und Sprache zur Behandlung graphischer Information
       im rechnergestuetzten Entwurf,
       Report KfK 2305, Karlsruhe(1976)Kernforschungszentrum

[12]   G.Enderle K.H.Bechler F.Katz K.Leinemann W.Olbrich E.G.Schlechtendahl
       K.Stölting:
       GIPSY-Handbuch, Report KfK 2878, Karlsruhe(1980)Kernforschungszentrum

Chapter 9

Utilization of Graphics Resources

by

Ketil Bo

(Merged into Chapter 7)

RUNIT, Computing Centre at
the University of Trondheim,
Norway

Chapter 10

Man Machine Interaction

by

Ketil Bo

RUNIT, Computing Centre at
the University of Trondheim,
Norway

10.1 Introduction

The success of most computer systems seems to be closely connected to their ability to interact with the user.

Despite the internal quality of the programs, it is the user's acceptance or rejection of the system which decides its position and life span in the working environment.

The human user and the computer are to complement each other successfully and in particular without stress being applied to the user.

Computers have considerable powers of data manipulations, but no creative ability. The speed and accuracy of performing well defined operations is extremely high compared to the human, but he has the intuition and experience which is very difficult to build into a computer.

If the data base is built effectively, the computer can store, manipulate and retreive huge amounts of detailed information, but the human is usually far superior when extracting the significant information is concerned.

The problem therefore, is one of matching the attributes of the human with those of the computer system.

Unfortunately, the interaction used to be one of the more neglected parts of many computer systems for several reasons:

1. System builders have been more concerned about making the system work, than the fact that it is supposed to be used by a human being as a tool for problem solving.

2. Man/Machine interaction is a fairly poor understood aspect by system builders, because it involves so many factors which he can't pin down by an algorithm.

3. The human factors involved in communication has not yet been studied sufficiently.

4. Necessary techniques for utilizing all the human resources in communication has not been available.

In fact, not very much has changed in principle since E. Sutherland presented his "Sketchpad" with CRT and lightpen in the early 60's. Many of the clever emergency solutions for the early systems due to lack of technology, are unnecessarily repeated for the present systems and creates both problems and constraints which could be avoided because of advance in knowledge and technology.

A simple example is cards and papertapes which is still hunting computer people a long time after it should be out of this world.

10.2 Classification of interaction

To identify the problems, it may be convenient to divide Man/machine communication into three main subgroups:

1. Input of initial data for processing and manipulation (data capturing)

2. Manipulation of the data and results as "real time" interactions between the user and the computer

3. Output of bulk data and results

At the present time, data capturing is far behind the interaction and output when elapsed time is concerned. It may take days to prepare input data to a program which takes only minutes or seconds to solve the actual problem and present the results.

As far as "real time" interaction is concerned, the major problem is to utilize all the user's abilities to communicate. The output is far the most developed and understood part of the interaction, seen from a technical point of view, but there may be a lot to gain in studying human perception. It is not obvious that a detailed message (in some form) which demands broad bandwidth or a long time frame, communicates the ideas better than one with low data content presented in the right way.

Most interactive graphics system are geared to rapid interaction, not to initial input of large amounts of data, which frequently is the basis for the interaction.

Fig. 10.1. On-line terminal with preformatted screen layout.

The selection of a programmable data terminal largely depends on the
cost of errors by the operator and in the source document. In either
case, the intelligent terminal minimizes errors by "cleaning" or vali-
dating inputs. In cases where the host computer cannot accept high load,
or when the cost of on-line connection to the host are critical the
programmable data terminal can preprocess the data and save the user
time and money.

Any additional functions outside of the immediate application may further
justify the added expense of an intelligent terminal. But before jump-
ing to the benefits a programmable terminal offers, be sure the programming resources are available to write and maintain the software.

It is obvious that the closer to the source we can capture the data --
the faster we can get the data into the computer and the less error
will be introduced.

This means that the one who is extracting the data also should enter
the data directly into the computer. By eliminating the coding form,
the user not only saves time and introduction of unnecessary errors,
but he is also able to capture the primary errors where it is cheapest

- close to the source. He can then use his system knowledge (which key-punch personal is normally lacking) to immediately correct the errors.

There are several ways of entering the data directly into the computer, the most used is the alpha/numeric terminal. The usability of these terminals can be considerably increased by utilizing portable terminals acoustic transmission which means that the data can be entered from anywhere a telephone is available.

Fig. 10.2 Portable terminal with memory and acoustic transmission.

Off-line hand-held data entry systems with reasonable amount of storage capabilities are also available.

Fig. 10.3. Hand-held data entry system with up to 48.000 character memory size.

10.3 Data Capturing of Available Data

Bulk input data has traditionally been prepared on rigid preformatted coding forms, then punched on cards or papertape and submitted to the computer.

This input procedure is slow and error prone, because of the rigidity and number of steps, each one with the possibility of introducing new errors into the data.

Surprisingly enough, this procedure is still quite popular. In fact, if we look into the average computer department, we will find it a major method for data capturing.

A simple way of improving this procedure is to get rid of the cards and use terminals for on-line or key-to-disc entry of the data.

This change does not only increase the through-put but it also seems to reduce the number of errors introduced to the data.

The rigid fixed data format which usually is used for card input, may now be replaced by free format or preformatted layout of the screen which reduces the error rate and increase the speed dramatically.

The question is now how much assistance, if any, should be built into the terminal? In other words, do we need a programmable terminal or not?

This decision is usually dependent on the application because there are both advantages and disadvantages with both types.

TYPE TERMINAL	ADVANTAGES	DISADVANTAGES
Nonprogrammable	• Low cost • Simple to operate • Interactive or batch • More reliable (less down time)	• Relies on host to detect errors • No preprocessing of data
Programmable	• Validates data on entry • Fewer keystrokes • Preprocessing of data • Lower burden on host • Very flexible	• Higher equipment cost • Requires Programming resources • Requires more training

10.3.1 DIGITIZING

The other main tool for direct inputing of data is the digitizer.

A digitizer is a tool that converts positional information of a stylus, etc., into a data format usable by the computer.

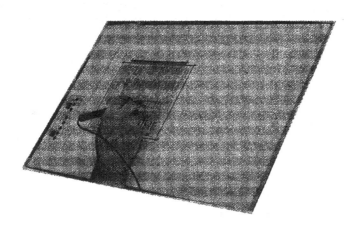

Fig. 10.4   A digitizer with stylus and control panel.

Early digitizers used beams, wires, sheels, cams and gears. Later digitizers uses sound, pulse trains and magnetic methods for determining the position. The resolution of a modern digitizer is usually better than 0.1 mm.

Digitizers are available in a number of sizes, surfaces and positioning tools.

Most of the digitizers use moveable or fixed menues which may be user definable.

Some of the newest digitizers have also incorporated microprosessors for local processing of the digitized data.

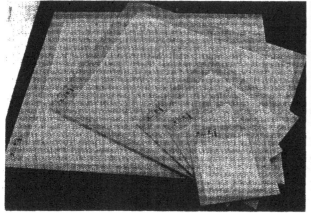

DIFFERENT SIZES OF SOLID SURFACES

REAR PROJECTED

BLACK LIGHTED

STYLUS

CURSOR

Fig.10.5 Digitizers with different sizes, surfaces and positioning tools.

10.3.2 AUTOMATIC DATA INPUT

The next major step is to eliminate the human also from the data extraction process, because he is slow and inaccurate compared to a computer. He cannot measure coordinates of a point without the assistance of a tool, he cannot discriminate between specific shades of grey or colours and he has a high error rate in recognizing even slightly complex patterns, especially when he gets tired.

Only by making the computer itself, aided by a human, able to capture the data at the source, are we able to entre bulk data in a speed and reliability which is compatible with the other operations.

Using the computer in collecting its own data has been used successfully in process control, etc.:

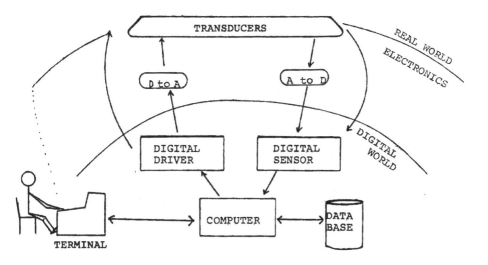

Fig.10. 6.   Real time process control.

Optical Character Recognition (OCR) is another well-known example.

Data capturing to CAD systems can in general, be divided into two main
categories:

1. Information which already is available, but has to be transformed into computer readable form. Such as drawings, photo-
   graphs, blueprints, maps, real world scenes, etc.

2. Information which is being created by the designer, such as
   sketches with associated alpha/numeric attributes (dimensions,
   connectedness, prices, etc.) or spoken words.

The humans input bulk data of category 1 mainly through the visual
system utilizing tremendously effective sensors and mechanisms for
selecting only the significant information but of the huge amount of
data which is brought into the system. Our present input methods are
expensive, slow and inefficient compared to this system, so we need to
investigate image processing, parallel processors, etc., to perform
this task in a reasonable time frame comparable with the speed to
interaction, processing and output of the data.

10.3.2.1 Image Processing

The currently most used data entry tool for imaging processing is the video digitizer which converts standard television signals into digital data for computer processing.

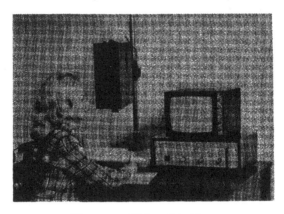

Fig. 10.7 Video Digitzer

Thi   of image processing for digitizing, etc,. has not yet been fully developed, but let me give you an idea how it can be done. [8]

The objectives of computer assisted image processing fall into the following categories: the removal of known image degradations, a procedure called "image restoration"; the exaggeration of interesting details called "image enhancement", and the location or measurement of specific details, a process called "information extraction".

Suppose we want to input a logic diagram. Normally, diagrams are drawn on paper which is bigger than we can represent in the computer with reasonable resoluation (a 420 x 297 mm logic diagram with 0.1 mm resoluation would require 12.5 M-bit of memory), so we need to process a part at a time.

Lines cannot be recognized correctly without getting a good replica of the original image. This requires a method of distinguishing lines from the background noise originated from the section paper grids, discoloration on the diagram surface or ununiformity in illumination for opto-electro conversion. Conversion from a multi-leveled image obtained by an image input device, to a binary pattern is necessary for the subsequent line recognition process.

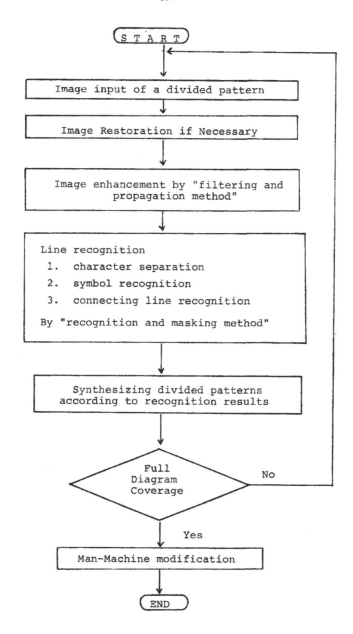

Fig. 10. 8.   Flow chart for recognizing large diagrams.

Two threshold levels are frequently employed to get a ternary pattern.
The higher threshold level defines the "black areas" which belong to
the lines. This means that the level is selected as the grayscale value
of the lowest limit of the black area.

The lower one is selected as the grayscale of the highest limit of a
"white area" which belongs to a background. The area between these two
threshold levels consists of "gray points" that cannot directly be defined as either black or white and more elaborate methods must be applied in order to make a decision.

10.4 Direct input of created data

In the latest year, we have also begun to see a break through for computer input of handwritten characters and sketches, which is an important step against our goal of capturing the data of category 2 as close
to the source as possible.

Drawings and sketches have usually been the designer's language by
which they can express their conceptual models on a sheet of paper by
defining the shapes, dimensions, functions, constraints, materials and
manufacturing methods. As the engineering drawing is made by a sequentially defining process of the object, it can be described by an appropriate command sequence.

10.4.1 HANDWRITTEN INPUT

This can be done by directly using the designer's drawing action as
input to the system. [2]

The designer do the wiring and sketching on a sheet of paper placed on
a tablet. First he divides the paper into four regions: three of the
regions are used for the three views projection drawings. The fourth
region is used for auxiliary information.

360

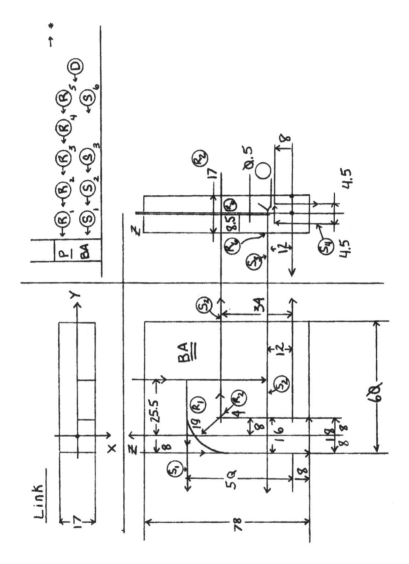

Fig. 9. Definition of the shape with dimensions

By the information entered, the internal model of the object is constructed.

This model can now be manipulated and displayed from any point of view
with perspective and shading:

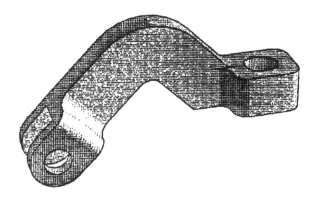

Fig.10.10.   Prospective Projection With Shading.

The recognition process consists here of a main and a back-up step. The
main recognition process comprises the initial filtering and local processing of measured data, the rough feature extraction, and the decision making. The back-up step includes the refining and correction of
the previous extracted features and it is used when the previous decision making step cannot give a definite answer.

362

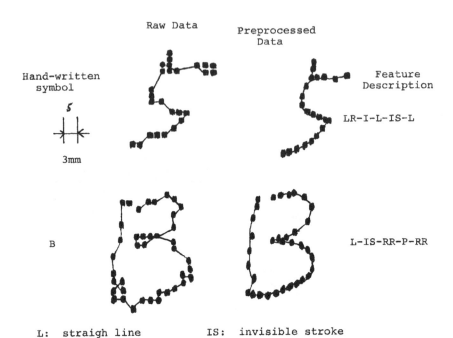

Raw Data

Preprocessed Data

Hand-written symbol

Feature Description

LR-I-L-IS-L

3mm

B

L-IS-RR-P-RR

L: straigh line   IS: invisible stroke
LR: left rotation   P: cusp
RR: right rotation   I: inflection point

Fig. 10. 11. Feature descriptions of hand-written symbols.

10.5 Man/Machine Dialogue

Initial data may also be entered into the computer by a dialogue between the system and the operator. The computer is here assisting the
operator by asking questions, indicating which data is to be entered
next, catching inevitable errors which will occur during a session and
helping the operator to make the necessary corrections.

The problems of designing this kind of system is pretty much the same
as for designing the "real time" man/machine interaction for manipulating the data, so let's discuss this two together.

The man/machine communication process is in principle quite simple [3]:

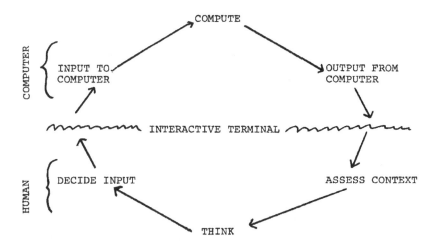

Fig. 10.12.   The Principle of the Man/Computer Communication process.

However, if we break the different components down we will find a very
complicated picture:

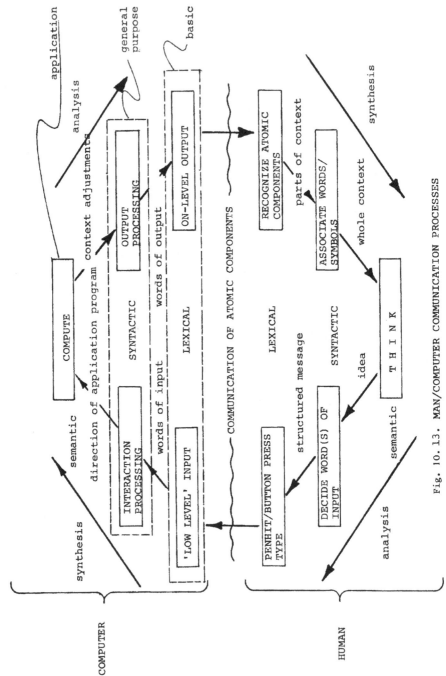

Fig. 1O. 13. MAN/COMPUTER COMMUNICATION PROCESSES

The main problem is how to design a dialog environment where the user can feel safe and comfortable and the misunderstandings between the user and the system is reduced to a minimum.

This is best achieved if the way the computer communicates is as much like the way humans communicate as possible.

The condition for a symetric dialogue is access to equally powerful tools for handling interaction on the lexical, syntactic and semantic level both for input and output.

The lexical level is related to the binding of specific hardware capabilities to primitive components of the input and output "languages". For input this means associating actions or sequences of actions using input devices as words of the "language". For output the primitive elements such as lines and characters as well as attributes such as line style and colour are used to encode the context.

The syntactic level is related to the way "words" are put together to form "sentences".

For input this means decisions of the action sequence. For output it means the display layout such as how the primitive elements are organized on the display surface, prompt posission, error messages and menue control.

The semantic level is related to the meaning of the "language".

For input it has to do with the selection of information which the user conveys to the computer. In output it is concerned with how the information will be displayed to the user examplified by the presentation form of geometrical objects (wire frame, hidden surface, shading etc.).

Symmetry is one of the important parameters for an effective, natural and unambiguous dialogue. The distinction between knowing and doing is another important parameter: [12]

> "The flavor of interaction is to achieve agreement on what to do (knowing), then pass the control to task performance (doing). When the task is completed, or when disagreement occurs in task performance (errors, unexpected events etc.), then control is returned to knowing, so that agreement may be reestablished before doing is resumed."

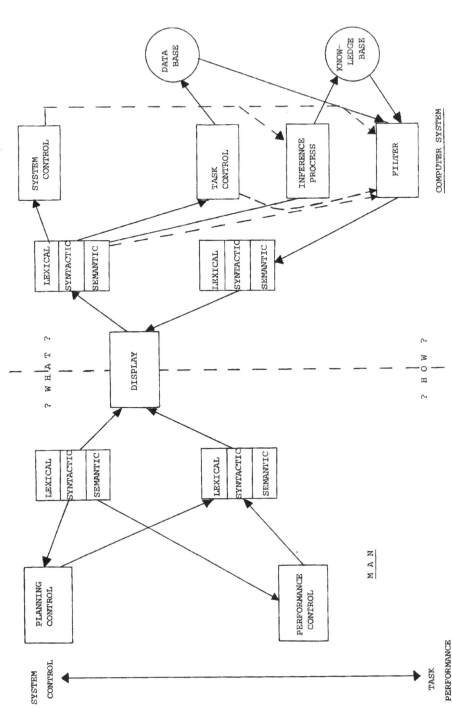

Fig. 10.14. Levels of Control in a Man/machine communication session.

10.5.1 COMMAND LANGUAGE

The classical interaction device is the keyboard which is a fairly
artificial way of communication for a human being. However, the keyboard has developed considerably, from a plain typewriter keyboard to
a very sophisticated multi-task keyboard.

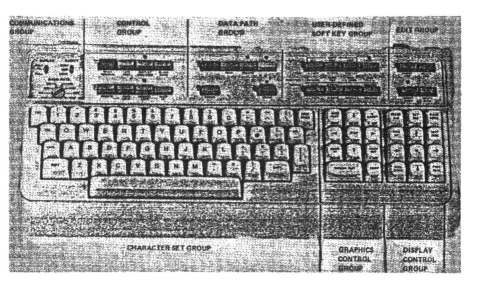

Fig.10.15. Multi-task keyboard.

Despite the keyboard, has been around for a long time, no one has yet
come up with a really user-friendly, flexible command language which
is able to adapt to the single users need, skill and pecularity [7].

It is true that many languages have been developed with English words
and near English syntax, but they never seem to fulfill their designer's
claims. A training course, or a big thick manual beside one at the
terminal, always seems to be necessary. The reason for this is maybe
that the language is only a covering despite its sophistication.
Underneath is still a system with the characteristics of mathematics,
namely:

- One-to-one correspondence between symbols and their meanings
- Nothing assumed except what is expressly stated
- Deductions made from an absolute invariant frame of reference

Everyday thought and conversation have very different characteristics:

- Many words with the same meaning
- Innumerable unstated and even unconcious assumptions
- Meaning strongly dependent on immediate context

Artificial Intelligence people are working on this and they will eventually solve these problems, but not for a long time.

In the meantime, we must utilize what is available as far as possible by finding principles, concepts, standards and notations which form an essential frame work against which ideas can be created, and communication and criticism made.

Let's try to illustrate some of the problems that dialogue designers have to tackle and how they actually are solved in existing systems:

Example A - Error BB No Environment Present For Return

Here is a classic piece of jargon totally incomprehensible to the nonspecialist. There is always a language barrier between the specialist and the nonspecialist and it is almost impossible for the systems programmer to drag himself out of the little world of code which he is creating deep inside the operating system and to see the situation from the point of view of a nonspecialist user sitting at the terminal.

Example B -

QUIT?	NO
QUIT?	YES
QUIT?	YES
QUIT?	NO
QUIT?	NO
QUIT?	N
QUIT?	Y

(Here the user gives up in desperation)

This is a little better. The user is confronted with English. Unfortunately the programmer has, quite rightly, assumed that the user has read the manual recently where it explains that the correct answer are "Q" (for quit) or "C" (for continue).

Example C -

DO YOU WISH TO MONITOR TEMPERATURES?
YES
HOW MANY POINTS DO YOU WISH TO MONITOR?
2
PLEASE ENTER POINT NO. 1
123
PLEASE ENTER POINT NO. 2
43
TYPE C FOR CONTINUOUS OR S FOR SINGLE SHOT
C
PLEASE GIVE MONITORING INTERVAL IN MILLISECONDS
500
DO YOU WISH TO MONITOR PRESSURES?
YES
HOW MANY POINTS DO YOU WISH TO MONITOR?
3
PLEASE ENTER POINT NO. 1
345
PLEASE ENTER POINT NO. 2
678
PLEASE ENTER POINT NO. 3
987
TYPE C FOR CONTINUOUS OR S FOR SINGLE SHOT
V
******ERROR 27 ILLEGAL CHARACTER
DO YOU WISH TO MONITOR TEMPERATURES?

Now the user is questioned in clear English and the legal replies are obvious. The slightest error, however, sends him back to square one. The pain is really excruciating when done on a 10 character printer by an inexperienced hunt and peck operator.

Example D - RETRIEVE FOR TOWN EQ BEDFORD UNDEFINED FIELD NAME

Here we have it all --- natural-language commands and a diagnostic message in clear English which shows exactly where the parser had a problem. Unfortunately, the diagnostic is completely mystifying.

What is the explanation? The parser interpreted is as "Retrieve all

records in which the contents of the TOWN field equalled the contents
of the "BEDFORD field" and naturally could not find the BEDFORD field.
The user should have put BEDFORD in quotes indicating a textstring
constant. Natural English does not distringuish between an object and
its name.

What went wrong? Although there was no language mismatch between programmer and user, there was a conceptual mismatch. His view of the
situation did not tally with the user's view so that the message did
not relate to the user's view at all and so was of no help.

The important thing to notice about these examples is that none of the
difficulties would have been avoided by sophisticated hardware or software. They are all "people problems". In the first case, the programmer
was in a dilemma. Should he be comprehensible to the nonspecialist and
be inaccurate to the specialist or be accurate to the specialist and
incomprehensible to the nonspecialist? In the second case, a manual
was needed but the user either did not realize that it was needed or
did not have it to hand. In the third case, the programmer assumed
that errors were so exceptional that he did not have to think about
the consequences. Finally, in the fourth case, the programmer could
not see ahead into the state of the user's mind at the time the error
occurred sufficiently well to provide a helpful message.

Four major principles of man/computer dialogue has been identified [4]
to avoid such problems.

1. Expectation and prediction

    The user's expectations of performing a dialogue with the com-
    puter should be met in such a way that he can utilize his ex-
    perience in communicating with other humans.

    This is only possible if the dialogue is made reasonably pre-
    dictable.

2. Context

    At any point in time, there is a selected set of previous ex-
    periences which we are currently using to interpret the mess-
    ages and to generate our expectation of the next experience.

3. Experimentation

    For some reason or another, the designers of man/machine dia-

logues tend to assume that a user can learn once and for all
a sequence of correct patterns of activity and from then on-
wards never make a mistake. But this is not the case, humans'
nature is to experiment. The system must therefore be able
to handle trial and errors without letting the penalty of
making errors become excessive.

4. <u>Motivation</u>

The computer dialogue sould do everything it can to generate
confidence. This may be done by making the user feel that his
commands will be obeyed and that the machine is going to help
him.

10.6 Computer Graphics

Up to recently, we have only utilized a limited part of the human resources for man/computer communication. The ability to extract significant information from a picture is far superior to the ability of reading alpha/numeric information.

From ancient time, the humans have used graphics for communicating their ideas. We can find it on stones, in caves and on papyrus:

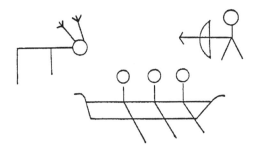

Fig.10.16. Rock Carving

Even if the information content in these carvings are very low, must humans get the messages.

That's one of the reasons why Computer Graphics has become one of the most powerful interaction tools.

Another reason is the human ability to integrate and almost instantly grasp the content of fairly complex visual scenes.

If we look at an interactive design process, we will find that is consists of a design loop which the designer repeats until the product is satisfactory.

Characteristically, each time a pass is made through the design loop, the design approaches closer to the optimum. Computer Graphics makes it possible for the designer to rapidly view the results of his hypothesis, enables him to introduce the desired changes much more quickly and thus be able to carry out more design cycles. Hence a superior design should result within the budget and time constraints.

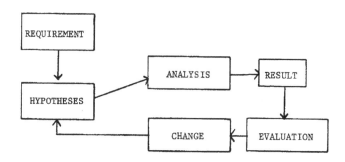

Fig. 10.17. Simplified Interactive Design Process

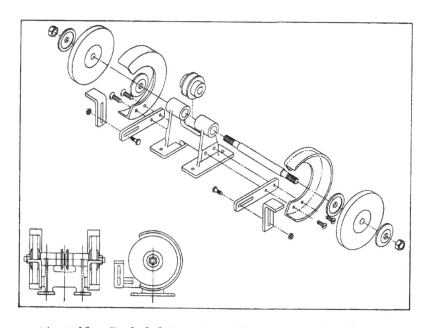

Fig. 10.18. Exploded Isometric View of a Mechanical Part

10.6.1 CLASSIFICATION

Computer Graphics can be classified into four major categories, dependent on the characteristics.

TYPE	CHARACTERISTICS	TYPICAL HARDWARE
1. PASSIVE	No image movement or interaction	PLOTTER

2. STATIC	No image movement	STORAGE, TUBES
3. DYNAMIC	Interaction and image movement	REFRESH, CRT, VIDEO
4. ANIMATION	"Real time" motion	FILM, VIDEO

Fig.10.19. Classification of Computer Graphics

The choice of graphics system is application dependent, but one thing should be kept in mind: If you start up with a relatively cheap/low performance system, make sure that you can expand it into a higher performance system without starting from scratch again. Because experience shows that the demand to graphic systems increase with use.

Unfortunately, in the early stage there was very little order or organization amongst the program developers, the suppliers and the users of interactive computer grahpics terminals. Methods of defining hardware/software specifications of many facilities varied so widely, very little of the programs for one application could be used in other application and even simple use of Computer Graphics became quite expensive. During the early growth years, these factors coupled with premature propaganda on the cost-effective benefits that one could receive from using computer graphics inhibited the serious use of interactive computer graphics as a production tool.

10.6.2 GRAPHICS STANDARDIZATION

However, today there is an intense activity in standardizing graphics software. Let me just mention: ACM SIGGRAPH [1], IFIP W.G. 5.2, DIN [9], ANSI, NORSIGD [10] and ISO.

The strongest single justification for the development of a standard is the promotion of program portability, i.e., the ability to transport graphics applications from one installation to another with minimal program changes. The two major qualities in a portable system is device and machine independence. By a device independent graphics software system (package) we mean a system that can be used in conjunction with two or more different graphics terminals (such as two different displays with different graphics input devices) without the need to modify the application programs that use the system.

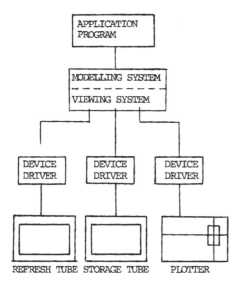

Fig.10.20.   Device Independent Systems

By <u>machine-independence</u> we mean the ability of a software system to run
on a variety of different computers without major implementation problems. This is normally achieved by using commonly available machine-
independent programming languages.

10.6.3 INCREASING CAPABILITIES

The first programs in computer graphics required that each figure was
defined in terms of lines specified by X-Y coordinates. The programmer
had to visualize how the 3-D figure would look like in two dimensions,
and enter the view in the computer as X-Y coordinates. For even simple
objects, many such lines had to be generated.

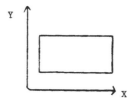

Fig.10.21.   X-Y Coordinate Figure

Programs were next refined through addition of a Z-axis. The programmer no longer had to translate the view into two dimensions. Given the
three Cartesian coordinates, the computer program can take the data
that fell within the "view-pyramid" of an observer, and map it into a
two-dimensional perspective view. The object, represented in the computer as a series of points and lines, can be multiplied by a matrix
that incorporates rotations, translations and scaling to generate the
perspective view on the display. The lines of the transformed objects
are terminated at the view-pyramids plane boundaries.

The output of such programs look like wire frames, with all lines in
the object visible.

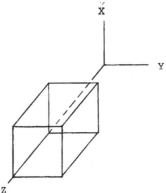

Fig. 10.22.   Wire frame figure.

In the next step of development, lines that were hidden by intervening
surfaces were removed. In this process, lines were defined as edges of
polygonal surfaces. Solid objects were constructed from these polygons.

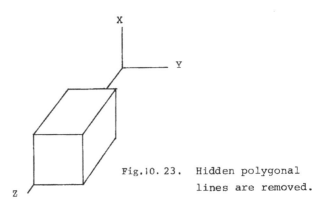

Fig. 10. 23.   Hidden polygonal
               lines are removed.

Once surfaces are defined, lighting effects can then be simulated, yielding the shaded and surfaced views attainable today. Light intensity and reflectivity are defined by the programmer for each polygon surface in the data base as a vector normal to the plane of each polygon. The amplitude of the vector denotes the amount of light reflected from the polygonal surface. The dot product between reflectivity vectors and the position of an illuminating source defines an intensity value for each polygon. Thus, through variation in the amplitude to the reflectivity vector, surface shading can change.

The object now appears as a many-faceted solid, with the edges of polygons forming the facets. Smoothing routines simulate curved surfaces by making the transitions between polygons less abrupt. These routines manipulate the reflectivity vectors of the polygons.

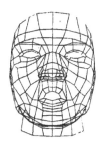 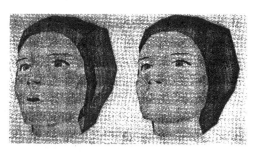

Fig. 10.24

Framework model   Many-faceted solid   Smooth solid

To generate a smooth, solid figure, surface-description graphic systems start with a framework model. Surfaces are stretched across the framework through specification of reflectivity vectors for each surface. The reflectivity vectors are computed in conjunction with the position of an illuminating source to yield light and dark shading. Finally, smoothing routines blur the edges of the faceted surfaces by blending and integrating reflectivity vectors to provice smooth transitions between surfaces.

By this technique, we are now able to produce full-color, three dimensional images with a fidelity approaching that of high grade colour photography.

10.7 Voice Input/output

Another of the human resources for communication which has not been utilized yet is the voice.

When communication is concerned, no media is more natural to a human than speech.

Because we now begin to be able to recognize and synthesize speech by computer, even at the moment in a very simple way, we must begin to recognize its potential in the man/machine communications and find out how it can be utilized in the future.

Already now, we can see a lot of advantages using speech as a communication tool.

It is human's most natural modality and requires little or no training. It permits simultaneous communication with the computer and other humans at the same time as the hands and eyes are free for other duties.

Fig. 10.25. Voice input

10.7.1 VOICE RECOGNITION

Voice recognition is the process through which an individual's voice is recognized by a machine. The speaker's commands are then put into effect by a computer. The technology can be used as a substitute for other means of interacting with the computer.

The key to voice recognition lies in the ability of the machine to recognize individual characteristics of voice patterns - or phonemes - without fail, regardless of vexations like background noise, post-

nasal drip, and mumbling. The technology has also been used to identify an individual, with so reliable results that the method is under
evaluation as the security key for military purposes.

10.7.2 VOICE SYNTHESIZING

Speech synthesizing equipment is now available which is able to give
the computer output in a very human like voice.

The speech is first broken down into voiced and unvoiced sounds. Voiced
sounds, like l, 0 and m, have a definite pitch and include vowels and
fricatives that can be represented by low-frequency, high-amplitude
signals. Unvoiced sounds, like s, f, and sh, are mostly rushing air
and are represented by low-amplitude, random high frequency signals
similar to white noise.

Linear Predictive coding (LPC) defines speech by determining the characteristics of a time-varying digital filter that is directly related
to the characteristics of the vocal tract determined by the lips, ton-
gue, teeth, and so on. LPC gets its name from the way the coefficients
characterizing the digital filter are predicted from a linear combination of previous coefficients. LPC is widely used in narrow bandwidth
communications.

TI's "Speak and Spell" [5] uses in all, 12 parameters to determine the
sound created in any 20 ms period: the first is the energy or amplitude; the second is the unvoiced or voiced signal, which includes pitch
information; and the other 10 are the filter coefficients.

10.7.3 NATURAL LANGUAGE

Work is also in progress on man/machine communication in natural language, but because the fundamentals of languages are not yet fully
understood this belongs far into the future, except for very specialized and well defined applications.

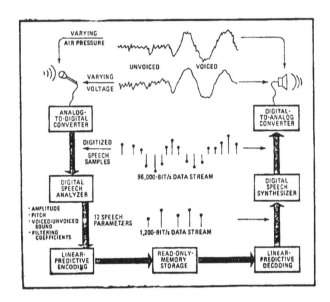

Fig. 10.26

Elements in a speech synthesizer chip which
recreate speech from data placed in ROM by
equipment that analyzes components of a human
voice.

10.8 The Time-factor

In "real-time" interaction there is one more factor which has to be taken seriously. This is time.

The meanings of various lengths of elapsed time do not vary widely from one individual to another. Less than 1/3 s is 'instantaneous'. Less than 1 s is 'fast'. Less than about 5 s is a 'pause' and greater than 10 s is a 'wait'. Designers of interactive systems must be aware of these characteristics in relation to response times, otherwise, he will not be able to obtain a fully user accepted man/machine dialogue.

1o.9 Bulk Output

Bulk output of information and results have traditionally been easy to produce and consequently easy to misuse. How often haven't we seen piles of listing with only one or two lines circled as significant data?

This could easily have been avoided by writing a simple processor for on-line looking at the print files on the CRT.

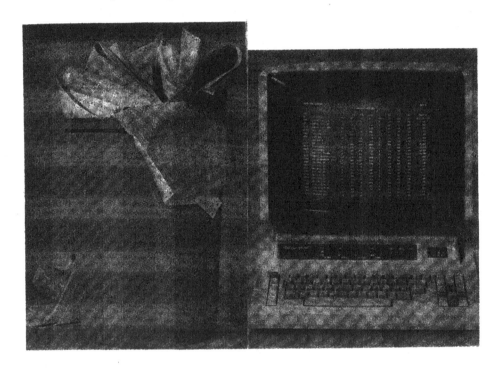

Fig.1o. 27. Different ways of looking at output.

This is only one example. You can find as many such examples as you want to because the variety of output devices is so large, the speed of output so high and the work put into detailed designing of the output is frequently so insufficient.

First of all, the type of output which will communicate the message in an optimal way, listing, drawing, curves, voice, ND-tapes, DNS, etc. must be decided. Secondly, the detailed layout of the output must be designed in such a way that redundancy is avoided and the message is easy and fast to grasp.

The system should also be able to present the information and problems in such a way that the idea is communicated in a user dependent way, i.e., the methods for communication may be differently dependent on if Charlie or Paul is operating the system.

10.10. Artificial Intelligence In Interaction

Maybe more important than what we have discussed up to now is the introduction of artificial intelligence into the interaction. It may be
equally important for a system to decide what is to be communicated to
the user rather than how to communicate it.

If we look at the interaction process in a computer session
today, a lot of the messages are redundant or conventional which could
be taken care of by an intelligent system utilizing a knowledge data-
base and a problem solving system. [4]:

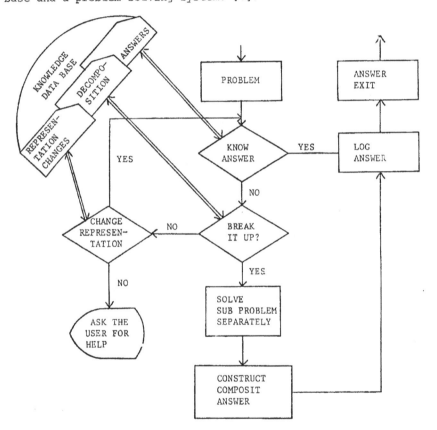

Fig.10.28. Use of knowledge database

The system should also be able to know the context in which the interaction takes place, in order to make the input easy and to prevent
erroneous interpretation of the data.

10.11 . Future Work Stations

We are now approaching an integrated interactive environment which is
utilizing all the human senses and devices for communication in a
natural way.

My model of the future Work Station will contain a number of special
purpose microcomputers and what I will call an "Interaction Machine"
for handling the different interaction devices and serve as a "Simultaneous Interpreter" between the user and the host system. The Host
System will most probably be a distributed multiprosessor system.

We can envision this future work station as a flexible pilot's cockpit
which is combining effectiveness and pleasure of work because it provides a natural way of working with the computer.

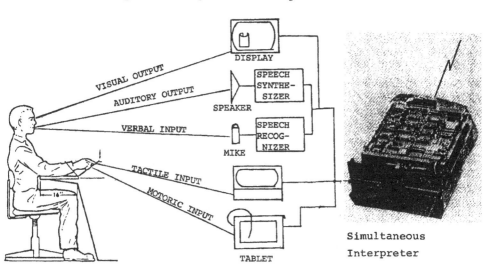

Fig. 10.29.   Future Work-Station

Such a work station demands also that a lot of effort are put into human
engineering. to make them as attractive and efficient as possible also
seen from a physiological point of view.

REFERENCES

[1] Status Report of the Graphics Standards Planning Committe of ACM/
    SIGGRAPH, Volume 13, Number 3, August 1979.

[2] Hosaka M. and Kimura F: "An Interactive Geometrical Design System
    with Handwriting Input". Proceedings IFIP 77, North- Holland.

[3] Butlin, G.A.: "Techniques for Processing Interactions in Fortran
    CAD Systems." IFIP W.G. 5.2 North-Holland 1977.

[4] Jones P.F.: "Four Principles of Man-Computer Dialogue" Computer
    Aided Design Journal, Volume 10, number 3, May 1978.

[5] "Single Cilicon Chip Synthesizers Speech in $50 Learning Aid"
    Electronics/June 22, 1978.

[6] Bø, K.: "Man/Machine Interaction" CAD Tutorial, SIGGRAPH '78,
    Atlanta Georgia 1978

[7] Bø K.: "A text Analyzer and Text Generator for Interactive Command
    Languages in CAD" CAD Systems - North Holland 1977.

[8] Kakumoto S., Fugimoto Y., Kawasaki J.: "Logic Diagram Recognition
    by Divide and Synthesize Method" Artificial Intelligence and
    Pattern Recognition in CAD. North Holland - 1978.

[9] Graphical Kernel System (GKS) Verion: 5.0 1979. Proposal of
    Standard DIN 0066 252.

[10] Bø K.: Interactive Device Independent Graphics System (IDIGS)
     version 2.0. Proposal of Graphics Standard, NORSICD 1980.

[11] Sussman G.J.: "The Engineering Problem Solving Project" Artificial
     Intelligence adn Pattern Recognition in CAD, North Holland -
     1978.

[12] F.R.A. Hopgood et.al.: SEILLAC II. Workshop on Man-Machine Inter-
     action. To appear on North- Holland 1980.

PART III

CAD SYSTEMS
(Architecture, Design, Justification)

Chapter 11

CAD Process and System Design

by

E.G. Schlechtendahl

Kernforschungszentrum
Karlsruhe

CHAPTER 11

CAD PROCESSES AND SYSTEM DESIGN

11.1 CAD Processes

11.1.1 Design as a Process

Since we will use the term "process" frequently in this chapter, let us define the characteristics that we associate with this term:

A process is an item, that
- can be identified,
- has a lifetime (a beginning and an end),
- has a certain state,
- uses resources either shared with other processes or exclusively,
- may communicate with other processes,
- may create new processes, and delete them at a later time,
- may allocate part of its own resources to other processes.

CAD provides computer support for the design process [1]. Hence, if we want to talk about CAD we must first talk about the design process. Design processes are quite different and depend on the product (a bycicle versus a chemical plant), on the company size and its organisation (a large architect engineer versus a specialized engineering buro) and on the type of design (variation of a basically fixed design versus completely new design of a new product). Nevertheless we need at least a crude model for the design process, so that the designer of a CAD system and a potential user can both agree on a description of the interfaces of the computer aided part of the design process with the remaining part of the process.

Fig.11.1 represents items which we find in all design processes:

- the design goal is set from outside the design process and
  remains fixed for at least some time;
- various resources, in particular the designer's knowhow, are
  required to perform the design;
- the design process produces information (the "design") which in
  one way or another can be documented and used for production.

The design process is not a once through sequence of actions. It is most often iterative. Decisions on certain product characteristics are made in a heuristic way at an early design stage on the basis of incomplete knowledge about their consequences with respect to the design goal. We call this the "synthesis" part of the design process. As a result, the "design" must be analysed and evaluated in the light of the design specification. If the goal is not met, appropriate design decisions must be corrected.

Fig.11.2 reflects these points. It shows the design process as a control loop. The inner loop operates on a fixed design "specification" and consists mainly of the operations "synthesis", "analysis" and "evaluation". The results are "presented" as achievements to the higher level process which had issued the specification. The deviation of the preliminary design from the specification is fed into the synthesis operation. A second loop is closed not within the design process itself but rather in the higher level process. The design specification is thus a moving target in particular for long-running, large projects, such as a chemical or nuclear power plant or the space shuttle. For the economy the design process it is essential that due to appropriate specification methods the rate of change of the target is minimized. The control loop character of design becomes most evident when the specification can be formalized as a "measure of merit" function in terms of the design parameters. In this case "design" is equivalent to "optimization" and we may try to apply appropriate optimization techniques (see e.g. [2]).

Fig.11.2 illustrates additional important aspects. The design process does not only generate the information for production of the product. A complete model of the object must be developed that represents all information for the analysis part of the design process and for all other processes which may follow. Testing, marketing and maintenance e.g. need information produced in the design process. The model which is generated by the synthesis and checked against the specification via analysis and evaluation thus becomes the central point of all subsequent operations. The model actually consists of two parts:

- a conceptual model [3] in the mind of the designer and
- a formal model (the schema), represented in machine readable form.

It is for this central role, played by the formalized model in CAD processes, that literature on CAD/CAM emphasizes the importance of the data base. Another point reflected in fig.11.2 is the fact that the design resources may change during a design process as well as the specification. Knowhow is probably the most valuable resource, but computer hardware and software are essential design resources, too. The resources needed for performing the design task must be supplied by the design environment. The environment may itself be considered as a process, which existed already before the start of the design and will continue to exist afterwards.

11.1.2 Man-Machine Cooperation

Design is mainly information processing. With CAD part of the information processing is delegated to the computer. The information processing capabilities of computers are, however, limited when compared to those of a person. The most critical limitations appear to be:

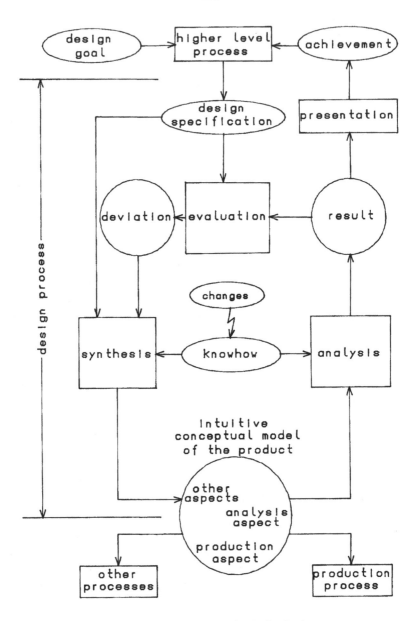

Fig.11.2: A refined model of the design process

- the inability of computers (or the programs which run of them) to "recognize situations";
- the inability to work with rules directly. Instead, all rules must be formulated as algorithms (programs);
- the unsatisfactory efficiency in handling model changes in the synthesis task (as compared to the excellent capabilities in working on fixed models in the analysis task).

These deficiencies may become less important if artificial intelligence methods are more widely introduced into CAD [4,5]. However, nowadays CAD methods generally call for an operation of the two main design activities with

- synthesis preferably associated with a person,
- analysis preferably associated with the computer.

In the cooperation between a design process and a subordinate CAD process we may often distinguish various degrees of interaction in different phases. These phases are illustrated in fig.11.3 . The first phase consists of the transmission of a prepared task specification to the CAD process. This "primary input" includes often a considerable amount of information which has to be checked with respect to completeness and correctness before it is processed any further. The next step is usually a highly interactive communication between the two partners involving validation and correction of the input. The next step is the actual execution of the task. Interaction is often less predominant in this phase. Finally, the presentation of results usually requires again a high degree of communication until the user is satisfied (see chapter 8).

These phases may be more or less pronounced in a particular environment so that they do not always show in the architecture of CAD systems. Besides the two highly interactive phases of a CAD process mentioned above there are two more situations which are associated with a high degree of interactive communication:

- information retrieval,
- synergetic cooperation of a person and computer
        (as is typical for computer supported drafting).

11.1.3 The Design Environment

The design environment is generally taken for granted simply because it exists in all organisations doing design work. The environment is, however, of more concern when we introduce the computer for part of the design process. Standards and codes that were perfectly acceptable for person-to-person communication, are no longer suitable when the computer is introduced. The introduction of a CAD system into a previously conventional design environment causes problems, not because the CAD system might be unsuited for the design task but rather because the environment is not yet adapted to the CAD system. CAD knowhow and computer knowhow must first be established, design procedures may have to changed, the standardization needs more formalization. Even such details as the different appearance of plotter written text on design drawings as compared to text that was written by a draftsman, influences the acceptance of the new CAD system.

11.1.3.1 The Organisation

Considerable variety may be found with respect to the organisational embedding of CAD. This depends not only on the size and organisation of the company but even reflects differences in attitude towards CAD between the U.S. and Europe. As Allan [6] pointed out, U.S. companies have a tendency to use CAD as a technical service whenever the need arises. Responsibility for CAD is directly associated with the design departments which will make use of the CAD systems. In Europe CAD (or CAD/CAM) is regarded as "an extension of management". Responsibility for introducing and using CAD methods and CAD systems is associated with higher level management. This latter attitude may reflect the fact that application of CAD is often accomponied by an increasing trend to formalization and standardization both in the products and in manufacturing. Full benefit will be gained from CAD and its side effects only if not the design aspect alone, but also work planning and manufacturing is envolved.

11.1.3.2 The Human Environment

The human factor is dominant in the early phases of introducing of CAD into an organisation. The spectrum of skills which is required to do a certain design task will change. The most obvious change is that a certain amount of knowledge about computers and how to deal with them will be required. Exactly know much computer knowledge is necessary in the design environment will depend mainly on these factors:

- access to a central data processing department versus installation of one or more computers in the design department;
- use of black-box ("turn-key"[7]) CAD systems versus development or modification of CAD systems;
- complexity and amount of the knowledge required to perform the design task.

Another change in skill requirements, however, is of much greater concern for the poeple working in the design office: Since computer based systems are so well suited for performing analytical work along prescribed algorithms (programs) but so ill suited for the actual "design" work (which is basically decision making), introducing CAD will cause a change in job content as pointed out in [8]. High-level designers will be able to increase their productivity and the quality of the product by using CAD, however, they may be subject to more stress during their work because they may miss certain periods of relaxation which were caused by the more or less routine work prior to introduction of CAD. On the other hand, low level designers whose capabilities are limited to routine work may no longer be needed.

The introduction of CAD in general requires

- additional skills (computer oriented);
- higher level skills (planning and decision making rather than
                execution and analysis).

11.1.3.3 Computer Resources

In a CAD environment mainly three computer configurations may be found:

- the local CAD computer;
- the CAD terminal attached to a remote computer;
- the local satellite of a remote host computer.

Any one of these configuration may be found in the different operational modes

- batch mode only;
- interactive mode only;
- both batch and interactive mode.

Three of the many variations of CAD computer configurations are shown in fig.11.4 through fig.11.6. Fig.11.4 indicates most primitive case: a local CAD computer. It is used in batch mode with some means of program and data input (the punched card version is just one of the many possibilities) and with text output on a printer and plot output on a plotter. Fig.11.5 shows a configuration with a local terminal (both alphanumeric and graphic) attached to a remote computer center. Fig.11.6 shows what is generally considered as the most powerful configuration: a local computer with all alphanumeric and graphic input and output capabilities, backed up by a powerful remote computer.

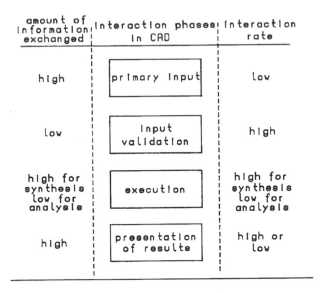

amount of information exchanged	interaction phases in CAD	interaction rate
high	primary input	low
low	input validation	high
high for synthesis low for analysis	execution	high for synthesis low for analysis
high	presentation of results	high or low

Fig.11.3: Man-machine interaction in CAD

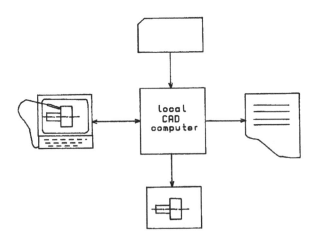

Fig.11.4: The local CAD computer in the design office

The decision which configuration and which operational mode is "best", very much depends on the individual situation. This is particularly true for the first ~ say five or eight years - of introducing CAD into a company. Organisations which make significant use of a large general purpose computer for non-CAD applications will likely start using CAD batch programs and proceed by attaching remote terminals to the central computer. Organisations with less computer background will likely increase the computer capacity of the design office from desk calculators to one or more special purpose CAD computers until they find it advantageous to connect some of the individual CAD computers to a bigger background computer. The final configuration will often have the structure shown in fig.11.6 (Note, that the background computer may be a network of computers instead of a single machine).

11.2 The Resource Aspect in CAD

11.2.1 Resource Availability and Conflicts of Resource Requirements

In the previous paragraphs we have mentioned "resources" several times as something which is indispensable for a process. Examples of such resources are

- time, money, manpower, storage capacity, a processor or
- a certain piece of hardware, a certain file, a certain compiler, a name.

The difference between the two groups of resources mentioned above is their ability of being substituted by other resources. Substitutable resources may be treated differently than non-substitutal ones. At this time we will deal with their common aspect: a resource is

anything which may have limited availability in its environment [9].

The resource problem is less evident if only one process exists (or can exist) within the environment. In this simple case, all the resources of the environment are available to the process. However, when several processes coexist, conflicts may arise already due to the fact that the resources which represent the process state cannot be shared. More conflicts arise when the processes are executing (not merely existing). Computer science has developed several constructs like semaphores [10] and others, which deal with the problem of resolving conflicts [11]. However, to the authors' knowledge these techniques have not yet been introduced to CAD systems. CAD could so far disregard this problem since CAD systems, which support several CAD processes in parallel and in real time, are uncommon. Furthermore, the notion of a "process" is usually associated with a "job" or a "run" on a computer, not which the longer lasting design task itself. Finally, constructs for coordination of concurrent processes have found their

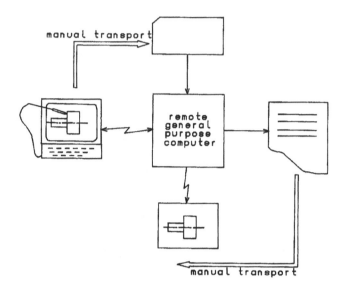

Fig.11.5: The CAD terminal attached to a remote host computer

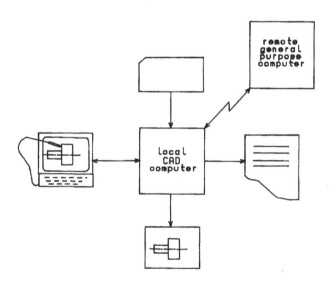

Fig.11.6: A local CAD computer with remote support

representation in programming languages [11,12,13] which are as yet unfamiliar to the CAD community.

Names are a special kind of resources. Names are used in processes as substitutes for objects which are represented by some lower level process. The action of replacing the name by its actual meaning is called binding [14]. Resource problems with names may arise in two ways:

- the use of identical names for different objects may cause an inconsistency,
- during binding of the resources which represent the named object it may turn out that the required resources are not available.

The aspect of resource availability is important for CAD systems. CAD systems which are designed to operate on a large central computer may not be applicable in an environment which does not provide sufficient memory capacity. On the other hand, an interactive CAD system which is used successfully on a small computer may be unacceptable when operated from a remote terminal on a large central computer where it has to share resource (central processor time, communication channels) with other processes. Software resources such as compilers for certain programming languages, certain data base systems or subroutine packages may as well constitute resource requirements which restrict the applicability of CAD systems. The same applies even to human resources,e.g., when a certain knowhow for operating the CAD system is required. As a consequence a CAD system is fully described only if in addition to its functional capabilities also its resource requirements are spelled out. It is not surprising that several CAD systems exist which are quite similar in functional respect but differ in their resource requirements.

11.2.2 Resources and Efficiency

Besides the functional aspect of availability of resources, efficiency of their utilization is also an important point in CAD systems. Efficiency is related to cost and, hence introduces a commercial aspect. We always have to realize that CAD is an engineering discipline, not a science. Hence, the functional aspect is only one part of the game. A CAD system that operates efficiently in one environment may operate unsatisfactorily in another. In the early years of CAD the size of primary computer memory was limited because of high costs. For this reason CAD systems were developed which could operate with a minimum of primary memory by storing all but the most actual data on peripheral devices. The tremendous decrease in primary memory cost [15] caused a shift in optimum use of resources towards larger memories while ,on the other hand, time becomes more valuable. Thus recently a trend may be noticed to utilize more primary storage while minimizing the time consuming accesses to secondary storage. We note that the economical aspects related to resources may have a considerable influence upon CAD systems.

11.3 Tools for CAD Design and Implementation

In an established CAD environment it is unlikely to find a CAD system being developed from scratch. Generally one finds certain components in other systems which (at least in principle) could be used beneficially in the new CAD system. Considerable economic savings are possible if for a new CAD task either an existing CAD system can be used (eventually with some adaptation) or - if a new development cannot be avoided - the development work can be reduced by utilising available tools. The needs for and the benefits of such tools were pointed out by Hatvany [16]. Two categories of such tools may be distinguished:

- tools which become part of the CAD system and will be used during the system execution. We will call these tools "software machines";
- tools which are used during the CAD system development.

11.3.1 Tools for CAD System Application

Typical components which one would like to take from the rack to put them together into an operable CAD system are on a low level:

- a data base system;
- a file management system;
- a data structure handling system (for primary memory storage);
- a command interpreter (for string type command and graphic input);
- a graphic package;
- mathematical subroutine packages etc.

Similarly, software machines are conceivable on a higher level:

- finite element analysis;
- computer supported drafting;
- smooth surface design;
- three-dimensional design of solid bodies.

It is a well known problem in the CAD world that even if such machines are available (and quite often they are indeed available) it is a major task to put them together into a satisfactory or merely operational system. They just do not fit together. This is one reason for the continuous rewriting of programs all over the world.

11.3.2 Tools for CAD System Development

An environment which is specialized on the development of CAD systems, will likely maintain special software systems for this work. Tools of this kind are:

- specification aids and documentation aids;
- precompilers and program generators.

Although the specification is (or should be) completed before the development of a CAD system is started, while the documentation is performed in parallel with development, specification aids are often suited for documentation purposes as well. This applies particularly to more unformal methods like SADT [17] or PSL/PSA [18]. Such systems are already used for production purposes. Formal specification methods based on abstract data types as in [19] or on similar concepts [20] are still under development. For a survey on specification and planning methods see [21].

Precompilers and program generators usually serve two purposes. They guarantee the consistency of data declarations in various programs which are intended to operate on the same objects. For this purpose data declarations are retrieved from a data base and inserterd into the programs (in the most simple case by including a piece of declarations text or by expanding macros). The second purpose is to permit the algorithms to be written in a language that is either better suited to express the operations or simply shorter than the available programming language. The higher level program text is then compiled into a language for which standard compilers are available (e.g. FORTRAN, PL/1, etc.).

11.3.3 The Concept of a CAD System Nucleus

Since about 1965 a number of systems has been developed with the specific aim to support the development of CAD systems. We call them CAD system "nuclei", although the term "integrated system" was originally used by their authors [22]. Pioneering work was done at the MIT starting in the mid 60's. The ICES system [23] (ICES stands for "Integrated Civil Engineering System") is still the most widely used CAD system nucleus. Other systems followed the same philosophy with emphasis placed on different aspects (portability, efficiency, ease of subsystem development, interactivity). The systems

DINAS [24], GENESYS [25], IST [26], REGENT [27].

belong to this class of CAD system nuclei. CAD system nuclei envelope the basic computer (hardware and manufacturer supplied software) and hide it behind a higher level software machine (fig.11.7):

- the facilities of the nucleus are used by the CAD system
  developer for providing new CAD capabilities (e.g.
  three-dimensional modelling). The term "subsystem" is
  used for such new CAD capabilities. If the subsystem is
  useful for solving problems related to a large class of
  objects (a finite element or a line drawing subsystem e.g.)
  it is called a "problem oriented" subsystem.
- the capabilities of one or more problem oriented subsytems are
  combined by an application programmer to formulate
  the design tasks for specific design objects (e.g.welding
  machines). Due to the fact that all subsytems belong to
  the same family (being based on the same nucleus), they
  may be combined freely without the danger of conflicts.
  Subsystems on this level are generally "product oriented";
- a product oriented subsytem may still leave some parameters
  open. The parametric user may specify such parameters and
  perform variations of a basically fixed design.

We will discuss REGENT as a representative of the system nuclei in some detail.
Every implementation of the REGENT system consists of

- the nucleus;
- a number of subsystems for general purpose use such as
  * DABAL [28] for easy access to the REGENT file
    management system,
  * GIPSY [28,30] for graphic data processing;
- any number of application oriented subsystems.

The nucleus itself consists of software machines for support of

- subsystem development (see fig.11.8):
  * definition of a schema for the subsystem data structure; The
    subsytem data structure is global with respect to the
    subsystem and, hence, accessible from everywhere within the
    subsytem, but not from other subsystems.
  * generation of modules;
    A module may be considered as a subprogram on a logical
    level. However, modules are not bound into the application
    program before they are actually needed. Modules reside in a
    module library and are loaded into primary memory when

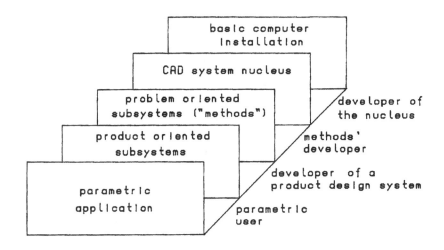

Fig.11.7: The levels of the CAD system nucleus concept

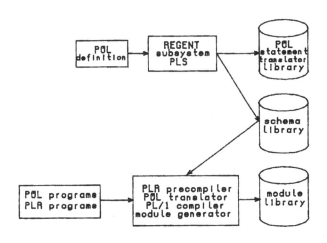

Fig.11.8: The generation of a REGENT subsystem

requested. Thus modules differ from normal subprograms in
their resource aspect.

* definition of a subsystem language (POL = "problem oriented
language" or "product oriented language"); The REGENT
subsystem PLS [31] generates statement drivers for
compilation of the POL statements of the new subsystem
language;

- subsystem execution:

* generation of an executable application program; The
application program that is written in one or more subsystem
languages is first translated into PL/1 and then into machine
code by the standard PL/1 compiler. REGENT subprograms that
are used frequently in this application are statically bound
into the program (see fig.11.9);

* execution monitoring;

At execution time the REGENT nucleus performs the function of
an executive system for the application program. Run-time
facilities for support of the special REGENT capabilities are
provided. Resource management, program flow control and
message management is performed. The application program may
be executed in batch or interactive mode (see fig.11.10).

None of the system nuclei mentioned above provides computer based tools for
documentation support and interactive user guidance. The reason for this is
historical. When the system nuclei were developed, computer power was not yet as
readily available as it is today. The system nuclei, though oriented towards
interactive data processing, found their dominant application in batch processing.
More recently the concept of a methods' base has been proposed [32]. This concept
is very similar to the concept of a nucleus, but documentation support and
interactive user guidance is inherently included in the methods' base concept.

11.4 CAD Schema Planning

11.4.1 A Sample Problem

Fig.11.11 represents a hammer-like object. The drawing contains

- structural information:
  the object consists of two subobjects (head and shaft);
- geometrical information:
  the geometrical shape of head and shaft, except that the actual
  dimensions are given as names instead of numbers representing

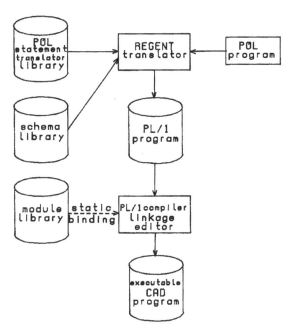

Fig.11.9: The generation of a CAD program with REGENT

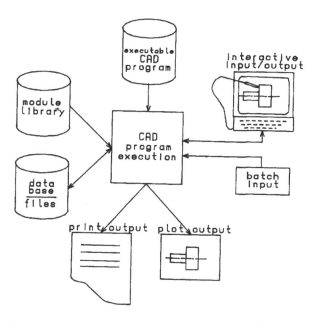

Fig.11.10: The execution of a CAD program in the REGENT environment

millimeters; the geometrical position of these two pieces after
assembly;
- information regarding manufacturing:
  the material information will (probably together with the
  geometrical data) influence the selection of the raw material
  for both pieces. The tolerance data will influence the
  quality control.

We will use this example to illustrate important aspects of CAD schema planning in
the next paragraphs.

11.4.2 Naming of Entities

A fundamental difference between a design drawing and a schema which is suitable
for computer application is the naming requirement. While on the design drawing
entities may be pointed at ("this length is 140 mm"), the entities in a schema must
have names assigned to them [3]. Two steps are required:

- selection of those entities that we want to include in the schema;
- assignment of names to them.

In our example we consider the dimensions of the two parts as essential for a first
schema. Assigning names produces fig.11.11. Programs that know this schema are
definitely "product-oriented". A different attitude might lead us to a more general
"problem-oriented" approach: We could have considered the drawing itself (the
points and lines) as essential, or perhaps the elementary forms (prisms, cylinders)
that constitute the geometrical shape of the whole object. Names must be unique in
the environment where they are used. In fig.11.11 we select DO and L for two
entities each. Nevertheless the names are unique if we prefix (or qualify) them by
the name of the object to which they belong. HEAD.DO and SHAFT.DO are two unique
names.

11.4.3 Alternative Schemas

We now represent the information of fig.11.11 in a Pascal-like notation:

```
TYPE    MEASURE = RECORD
          NOMINAL, TOLERANCE : REAL
                  END;
TYPE    HEAD_SCHEMA=RECORD
        ANGLE, H, W, OFFSET, L : REAL:
                  DO        : MEASURE
                  END;
TYPE    SHAFT_SCHEMA= RECORD
                  D1, L1, L : REAL;
                  DO        : MEASURE
                  END;
TYPE    HAMMER_SCHEMA=RECORD
                  GAP       : REAL;
                  HEADPART  : -> HEAD_SCHEMA;

                  SHAFTPART : -> SHAFT_SCHEMA

                  END;
```

We can now define objects of these types:

```
VAR   HAMMER : HAMMER_SCHEMA;
      SHAFT  : SHAFT_SCHEMA;
      HEAD   : HEAD_SCHEMA;
```

and address individual values of these objects, for instance:

```
HAMMER.GAP       := 0.0005;
SHAFT.DO.NOMINAL := 0.015;
HEAD.DO.NOMINAL  := 0.015;
```

However, there are alternatives to the above schema. One of them is:

```
TYPE ALTERNATE_HAMMER_SCHEMA=RECORD
                  GAP : REAL ;
                  DO : REAL ;
              SHAFT : RECORD
                DO_TOLERANCE : REAL;
                  D1, L1, L : REAL
                        END;
              HEAD : RECORD
                DO_TOLERANCE : REAL;
        ANGLE, H, W, OFFSET, L : REAL
                        END
                  END;
```

The question might arise: which one of these alternatives is correct? We emphasize that correctness is not an appropriate criterion at this stage of schema planning. Suitability is the criterion that we should apply: Which of the alternatives is better suited for the operations to be performed?

If we never intend to treat the constituents of the hammer (head or shaft) by themselves, then the ALTERNATIVE_HAMMER_SCHEMA is preferable. It is less complex, will be easier to implement, and it is safer: it eliminates the redundancy in

DO.NOMINAL. Separate treatment of the parts, however, calls for the first schema version.

11.4.4 Subschema Transformations

11.4.4.1 The Need for many Subschemas

Both schema versions proposed in the previous paragraph are suited for input of objects into a data base and for queries. Most likely, we want to perform other operations, too: produce design drawings and perform weight analyses. Product oriented programs can do this with the above schema. Since drawing and weight analysis are very common operations, we should try to apply problem-oriented systems for this purpose instead of writing new ones. A drawing program needs another schema (points and lines), a weight analysis program certainly a third one (elementary three-dimensional bodies). Thus we should consider each of these schemas as subschema of a complete schema as shown in fig.11.12. It would be nice, of course, if we could derive all data for the graphical schema from data contained in the input and query schema by applying a transformation. In general, this is not possible. Subschema transformations will in most cases require additional information as indicated in fig.11.13. For our example, additional input information is needed for positioning the part drawings on the paper sheet, for defining line styles, annotations etc.

The use of generally applicable "problem-oriented" systems instead of the development of special purpose "product-oriented" systems introduces the need for subschema transformations. The combination of many (say n) general purpose systems requires more and more subschema transformations, as the number of connections between them grows as $n*(n-1)$. It is advisable not to treat all subschemas as equivalent, but to select one "preferred" subschema [3] as a common basis for most transformations (fig.11.14).

11.4.4.2 Input/Output Transformations

Transformations take place, e.g., between the actions performed by the operator of a CAD terminal and data representations of these actions. The transformations will have to be different, when different hardware is used for the same set of functions (see Table 11.1).

For illustration of this point we assume that in a given situation the system is ready to accept a command like CREATE PUMP(<pump data>) or another "create"-command. We wish to identify the newly created object in subsequent actions. In a

409

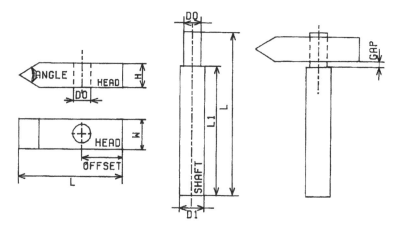

Fig.11.11: A design drawing interpreted as the
graphical representation of a schema

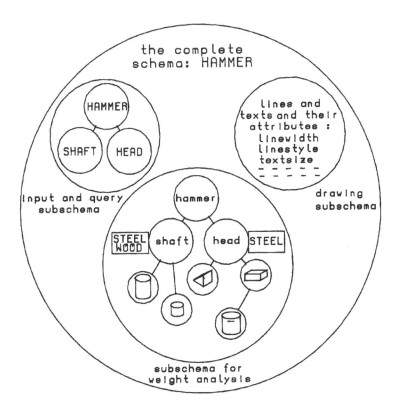

Fig.11.12: Subschemas of a complete schema for different operations

Table 11.1:
Use of available hardware for man-machine communication

available hardware	message visualization	result presentation
printer	printer	new page before and after results
printer + plotter	printer	plotter
teletype + display	teletype	display
display	display	erase display before presenting results
display	restricted area on display surface (message window)	remaining area of display surface
two displays	one display (alphanumeric)	one display (graphic)

command language we would use a name (of say up to 32 characters), with an interactive graphics terminal we would prefer to use graphic techniques for identification: picking with a lightpen or approaching the position of the object with a cursor. The command schema for the operator thus appears in three different forms depending on the available communication medium:

case A: keyboard (or a command file for batch operation)
    enter CREATE PUMP(<pump data>) <identification> <terminator>
    where
      <pump data>   := INTEGER,REAL,REAL (for example)
      <identification> := up to 32 characters
      <terminator>   := end_of_line or ";"

case B: storage tube display with function keys
    press a function key (say number 2); a cursor will appear;
    move the cursor to the desired position;
    enter <pump data> with the keyboard; terminate with <end> key.

case C: refresh display with lightpen
    pick <create> command on the command menu;
    pick <pump> symbol on the object menu; a pump symbol will appear;

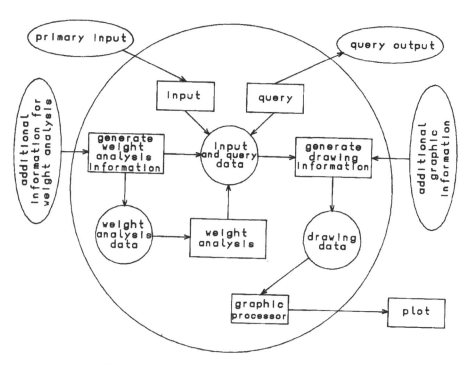

Fig.11.13: The relationship between subschemas, operations
and transformations

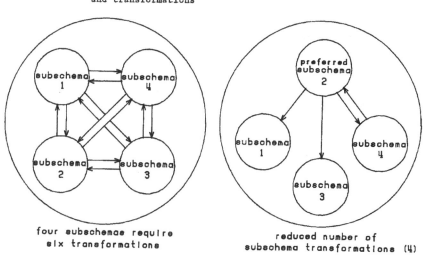

Fig.11.14: The n-square problem of subschema transformations

> track the symbol to the desired position with lightpen;
>
> enter <pump data> with the keyboard; terminate with <end> key.

The various ways to enter the command should not influence the whole CAD system. The "CAD execution programs" represented by a box in fig.11.15 should not depend on the communication medium. This can be achieved by appropriate transformations of the command subschema. While the input/output message subschema for the command would be different for the three cases, the internal command subschema can be identical. The main task of the communication processor is to perform the necessary transformations.

11.4.5 Flexibility versus Efficiency, a Measure of Prudence

CAD experts are quite familiar with a very serious problem: after some effort has been put into the planning of a CAD system (maybe even after implementation) suddenly the goal changes. There are many reasons for such changes:

- technical development calls for a design change of the objects;
- economical development sets different priorities;
- increased insight into the effect of introducing the CAD system opens a
  door to new wishes.

It is therefore good policy of CAD system developers to anticipate such new wishes and to clarify beforehand possible problems. It is often useful to plan for goals which are somewhat beyond what is actually requested and to classify wishes, which arise during the development time, into

- options which should immendiately be included in the plan even if they
  are not actually required;
- options which may be added later at low cost provided that such future
  modification is taken into account in early planning,
- options which would require more or less a new approach and which should
  definitely be refused.

11.5 Implementation of a Schema in a Programming Language

11.5.1 Mapping

The conceptual model defines the objects to be treated as abstract data types [19] in an abstract space. For implementation, these abstract data types must be mapped onto the data types of the implementation language. In a similar way, the algorithms and the comunication schema (see chapter 11.4.4.2) must be mapped onto

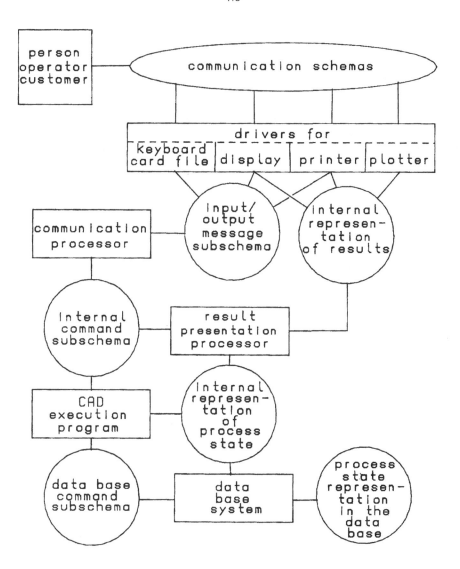

Fig.11.15: Interfaces between CAD system components

the operations that can be formulated in the implementation language (fig.11.16). From the language level an additional mapping onto the computer hardware is performed by the computer's language processors (the compiler,e.g.). In the ideal situation one would have to deal with the mapping between the conceptual level and the programming language level only. The mapping from this level to the hardware level would be hidden in the language compilers and the operating system. In reality the ideal situation is rarely found. This is particularly true when FORTRAN is considered as the main (perhaps only) available high level language. Since FORTRAN is by far the most common programming language for CAD we cannot simply ignore the deviations from the ideal.

A most peculiar situation arises if the high level language is totally unsuited for mapping of certain objects but adequate support could be provided on a lower level (assembler language and hardware). The system designer is then tempted to map around the language level in order to achieve what he needs despite the properties of the high level language. Fig.11.16, e.g., illustrates the mapping of characters onto the hardware and back up onto the language level for a programming language, that does not support characters. All FORTRAN programmers are familiar with this situation when they use EQUIVALENCE statements or treat INTEGERs or LOGICALs as character strings. Such inadequate mappings are avoided, when a more appropriate language is used (PASCAL or PL/1,e.g.). PASCAL and its derivatives in particular provide a powerful tool for mapping abstract data onto user defined data types.

11.5.2 Binding

According to [14] the term binding stands for the substitution of a name of an object by its actual representation. Examples of binding actions are:

- the inclusion of subprograms from a library into a program module in a process which is called binding, mapping or linkage editing (depending on the computer manufacturer's terminology);
- the establishment of a connection from a terminal to the main computer (by telephone dialing for instance);
- the opening of an actual data file by a CAD program;
- the substitution of a computer memory address for a programming language variable name during compilation.

In the design of a CAD system it is essential to pay attention to the time at which such binding occurs (the "binding time"). The following times may be distinguished:

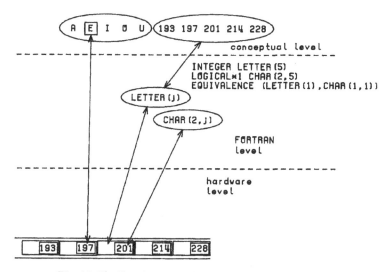

Fig.11.16: Mapping around the language level

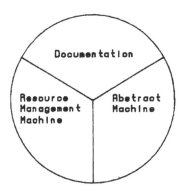

Fig.11.17: The components of a CAD software machine

- Case 1 : Binding at programming time

 (the time when the program is written in a programming language);
- Case 2 : Binding at module binding time

 (the time when the program and all its subroutines are bound

 together to form an executable module);
- Case 3 : Binding at job preparation time

 (the time when a job is prepared for execution);
- Case 4 : Binding at job execution time

 (the time when a process is executing).

These different times are often not identified as being separate. For instance, if we write a simple FORTRAN program which reads some data, performs certain calculations and prints results, then only the programming time and the run time are obvious. It is obvious that the flexibility introduced in cases 3 and 4 cannot be considered as an advantage in many applications. The security given by the first two options is often more important than flexibility. With respect to binding the designer of a CAD system will have to choose between the criteria of flexibility (enhanced by late binding) and safety (enhanced by early binding) as well as efficiency (enhanced by early binding).

It is important to realize that this decision has a very great influence upon the architecture of a CAD system. Two CAD systems may look quite different even if they perform the same fundamental tasks, depending on the choices made with respect to binding time. The following example shows the binding of an equation of state which computes pressure p as a function of density rho and enthalpy h for various materials (using a PL/1-like programming language):

- Case 1 : Binding at programming time combined with a selection

 between predefined options at execution time.

```
DECLARE P ENTRY(DECIMAL,DECIMAL) RETURNS(DECIMAL) VARIABLE;
P1: PROCEDURE(rho,h) RETURNS(DECIMAL);
  /* program code for material 1 */
  RETURN( p );
  END P1;
P2: PROCEDURE(rho,h) RETURNS(DECIMAL);
  /* program code for material 2 */
  RETURN( p );
  END P2;
P3: PROCEDURE(rho,h) RETURNS(DECIMAL);
  /* program code for material 3 */
  RETURN( p );
  END P3;
  ...............
SELECT (material) ;
  WHEN (mat1) P=P1;   WHEN (mat2) P=P2;   WHEN (mat3) P=P3;
  END;
any statement using P(rho,h);
```

- Case 2 : Binding at module binding time

      DECLARE P ENTRY(DECIMAL,DECIMAL) RETURNS(DECIMAL) EXTERNAL;
      any statement using P(rho,h);
   /* the operating system language is used to assure that the
     desired version of the function P (corresponding to the
     desired material) is bound into the load module */

- Case 4 : Binding at job execution time

   /* The following programming language is an extension of PL/1
     provided by the CAD system REGENT [27]   */
       BEGIN;
          DECLARE P ENTRY(DECIMAL,DECIMAL) RETURNS(DECIMAL)
          DYNAMIC MODULE(material);
          any statement using P(rho,h);
       END;

11.5.3 Algorithmic Modelling

So far we have dealt with models which could be mapped relatively easily onto a data schema. The representation of an object was always considered to exist, though it might be undefined or defined at a given instant. Such a data representation of objects consumes resources. In many cases these resources are too valuable to be spent. As an example: when graphic information is displayed at a remote terminal, the transport of the information accross the connecting line consumes manpower (the time of the operator who has to wait until the transport is complete). In order to save part of the resource one would like to condense the information. For graphic text, for instance, a data representation of the letter strokes consumes more storage space and transport time than a character string plus the information how the character string should be expanded into line strokes. In general, a data model may be condensed into

      - the identification of an algorithm;
      - a set of (condensed) data which will be used by the
        algorithm to generate the complete data model.

We call such a condensation an "algorithmic model". The prerequisite is of course that the algorithm is properly implemented and that the mapping from the condensed data to the expanded form has been agreed upon among all users of this "shorthand" model. Similar algorithmic models are implemented in conventional programming languages. Arithmetic functions like SIN or COS are not supplied as tables of data but rather as algorithms. A graphical system for two- and three-dimensional objects, which is completely based on algorithmic modelling, is described in [29]. In an algorithmic model data are not stored but they are evaluated whenever they are needed. The question arises:

- When should a model be represented as data?
- When should algorithmic modelling be used?

The answer cannot be given on the basis of abstract operations which the system should perform. With either approach a particular operation may be implemented. The answer must be derived from resource considerations as indicated in Table 11.2.

Table 11.2: Aspects for deciding between data models and algorithmic models

```
---------------------------------------------------------
|                     |The preferred modelling is        |
|      aspect         |data model | algorithmic model|
|---------------------|-----------|------------------|
|storage capacity     |   high    |      low          |
|processing costs     |   high    |      low          |
|usage rate of data   |   high    |      low          |
|change rate of model |   high    |      low          |
|processing rate      |   low     |      high         |
|time to retrieve and |   low     |      high         |
|   transport data    |           |                  |
|change rate of data  |   low     |      high         |
---------------------------------------------------------
```

In the wide range of practical situations the choice is a matter of judgment based on experience more often than on objective criteria. A particular problem is posed by the fact that the "best" solution is a function of how the system is used. In the early design phase of three-dimensional bodies the rate of change of the model is probably so high that a graphical representation (and dependent data such as weight) are used only once before the next change is made. Thus it is preferable to use an algorithmic model for the projection of the body (and other data). When a display is requested the projection lines may be evaluated and displayed on a plotter or a storage tube line by line with a minimum of storage requirements. At a later stage in the design process modifications of the body become rare, but editing of the twodimensional picture of the body may be required. Now it is advantageous to store the projection of the body as data in order to avoid the unnecessary repetition of the projection operation.

11.6 Software Machine Design

The architecture of a particular CAD system depends on

- the task to be solved by the system;
- the computer resources available for its implementation;
- the experience of the CAD system designer;
- rules established on a company basis or larger basis which restrict the freedom of the system designer.

Schematic representations of CAD systems always reflect the intention of their author to emphasize one or the other aspect. Fig.11.15 is a model of a CAD system during execution. The model concentrates on the interface between the main functional components. We have to deal with many kinds of interfaces in a CAD system: not only the interface between the operator and the system, but also the internal interfaces between system components.

> ! An interface between two components represents the use of a shared
> ! resource according to an agreed upon schema.

The components of the CAD system perform a certain function: The functional aspect of the CAD system is summarized by the term "abstract CAD machine". All processes within the executing CAD system, however, need support by a number of utility functions which are often related to resource management. Designers of CAD systems tend to hide them from the users. This is a short-sighted strategy, since the users must be aware of the resource aspects in order to use the system successfully and economically.We will discuss this in the subsequent paragraphs in more detail. The resource management in the CAD system provides the necessary environmental conditions for successful operation of the "concrete CAD machine" [33].

11.6.1 Basic Considerations

As noted in previous paragraphs CAD systems are composed of subsystems whose functions are fairly similar in most realizations. Such functions are required on different levels: command interpretation on various input devices, data management, three-dimensional and two-dimensional graphics etc. An obvious idea is: Couldn't we implement these elementary functions as "software machines" in such a way, that we may combine them as needed, without running into interfacing problems? When we study existing software machines, we generally note that they obey special rules for using certain resources. Examples of such standardized use of resources are: a filing system (rules for naming and structuring external data storage, most often used in chains of main programs), the COMMON-block technique (probably the most widely used CAD system basis of the FORTRAN oriented world, with rules for naming and structuring shareable internal memory), subroutine packages (based on rules for naming the procedures and structuring their argument lists). Such systems work fine as long as they are used just by themselves. However, when put together into a bigger system conflicts usually arise either because some of the "subsystems" do not allow sharing of certain resources with others or because they use shared resources according to conflicting rules.

Let us illustrate this point by a few examples:

- Obviously one cannot use two independent subroutine packages in one
  program, if both together allocate more memory than is available
  (even if they could share it).
- However, if each of the packages has its own dynamic memory
  allocation facility (as some FORTRAN packages provide by means of
  Assembler extensions) they may not be usable in combination
  either. Each of them must be limited to a maximum amount of memory:
  the authorisation to use a resource must explicitly or implicitly
  be passed from some higher level or organisation.
- The same is true if the resource to be used is not of a
  quantitative nature (such as memory space) but of a qualitative
  nature. Software machines cannot be used in parallel if they make
  independent use of certain global names such as program names, file
  names, common block names. This conflict becomes evident if one
  thinks of using two graphics packages in a single program, one for
  data presentation and one for geometrical design. The chances that
  both of them use different subroutines with identical names like
  OPEN, CLOSE PLOT, are rather high.

It is not sufficient that the required resources are available: some of these
resources, namely those which represent the state of a process, must be reserved
for exclusive use by this process. Other processes must be inhibited from modifying
such resources. The design of portable software machines will have to deal with the
following questions:

- What is the function of the software machine?
- Which resources does it need?
- How are these resources to be supplied? How must they be initialized?
- How do we guarantee that certain parts of these resources
  remain unchanged as long as needed?

The rules formulated in the subsequent paragraphs shall help to design portable CAD
software machines.

11.6.2 The Abstract Machine

A user can use a software tool intelligently only if he has a clear understanding
of its functional capabilities. For this reason we formulate the first rule

(R1) The functional documentation of a software machine must give a precise
definition of the type of process which is driven by this machine.

This means

- a complete description of the state in terms of the underlying
  conceptual schema;
- a complete description of all functions that modify the state
  or produce output.

This rule should require no particular explanation. However, it is violated quite often with respect to completeness. Most often, the system response to incorrect input is inadequately described. The second rule applies to software machines which are to be used to drive several processes in parallel.

(R2) Whenever a software machine may conceivably drive more than one
     process in parallel, caller and software machine should agree upon
     a unique identification of each newly created process in order to
     be able to communicate about this process at later time.

There are many ways how the agreement about the identification of the new process (its name) may be achieved. The caller may pass a name to the software machine or the software machine may determine the name. In the first case conflicts may arise if more than one caller wants to use the same name; this conflict may be removed if the name is prefixed by the callers name. In the second case it may happen that a process is created and terminated at a later time and and another process is then given the same name by the software machine. If the caller erroneously refers to the name of the already terminated process, a misunderstanding would result without the possibility of detection; this problem may be removed if the creation time (date and time) is made part of the process name. In either case at least one of the partners (either the caller or the software machine) must maintain a table which associates the name which was fixed in the other's environment with a private name of its own environment. A very efficient way of communication between caller and software machine may be achieved when both agree to use a combination of their respective private names.

11.6.3 Process State Representation

We may characterize a process by the fact that its state is modified only by the process itself. The process state -after mapping onto the language and hardware level respectively- is represented by the actual state of certain resources (values of variables, position of a magnetic tape on its unit, existing connection to a certain terminal etc.). If we have more than one parallel process, then the problem may arise that one process modifies the state representation of other processes. In order to avoid this we formulate the rule:

(R3) A software machine should be designed and implemented such that the
state representations of processes which it creates cannot be modified
by other software machines.

It is not always easy to implement this rule in a strict sense. Systems implemented
in FORTRAN usually map the process state onto a COMMON block. This technique is
applicable when the software machine drives only one process. If it drives more
processes at a time, two techniques are recommended: The use of special access
routines to store or retrieve data from the state representation, or passing the
resources, that represent the process state, as a parameter with each call to the
software machine.

11.6.4 The Concrete Machine

Software machines not only use resources for representing the state of a process.
They use resources also for operational purposes. Examples of such resources are:
Primary memory, working files, names of files in communication with the operating
system, names of subroutines. Some of these resources are merely a certain quantity
out of a larger pool (memory as an example). Other resources, however, are well
identified and must be reserved for exclusive use (such as the names of the
subroutines). In either case problems may arise whenever more than one software
machine is used in a CAD system.

With respect to quantitative resources conflicts may arise if one process
monopolizes a resource. (CAD nucleus systems as ICES tend to make optimum use of
primary memory by using as much as possible. This will cause failure if combined
with another package which itself provides a dynamic storage management facility).
Hence we state the rule

(R4) If a software tool is able to obtain certain quantities of a resource
for its operational purposes, the father process should authorize it
to allocate up to a certain amount of that resource. Otherwise the
necessary resources should be supplied by the father process. In any
case the documentation must include a list of the resources from which
the software tool needs a certain quantity.

With respect to qualitative resources (those which can be identified as individuals
such as all names) we state the following rule

(R5) Qualitative resources should be obtained from the father process. If
this is not possible (such as for the names of subroutines) the
description of the software machine must identify which qualitative

resources are used and how the software machine could be modified to substitute qualitative resources.

It is worth noting that the potential of resource conflicts with respect to names has been realized in the proposal of the graphical kernel system GKS [35]. This proposal of a standard for graphic systems suggests that GKS implementations should provide a "name converter", which allows to replace any global name in the package during the process of installation in a computer environment where otherwise name conflicts would arise.

11.6.5 Resource Management Strategies

Sometimes the amount of quantitative resources needed by a process depends heavily on certain process parameters. The buffer area for a graphic display file is a well known example. The particular requirements may also grow and shrink considerably with time. The design of software tools depends heavily on the resource management strategy followed:

A) During the whole process a maximum amount of resource is allocated to the process, no matter whether it is really needed (This is typical for local FORTRAN working arrays in subroutines). If many processes follow this strategy the resource may soon be exhausted.

B) The process obtains resources when needed and returns them when they are no longer needed. Although this strategy makes "optimum" use of the resource it may cause considerable overhead and may lead to storage fragmentation, unless the sequence of allocate and free requests is issued on a last-in-first-out basis [33].

C) The process provides a resource estimate algorithm. The father process usually has sufficient information available to produce good estimates of the relevant process parameters for a certain period of time. With these parameters an estimate of the amount of resource needed may be generated such that the father process can supply this resource to the process. Similar problems as in case B above may arise but their probability is significantly reduced.

Each of these strategies has its advantages and disadvantages and we do not dare to recommend one as being superior in all cases. We should not be surprised that software machines which perform the same function may appear totally different in the implementation depending on the resource management strategy is essential. Hence, we formulate the rules

(R6) The documentation of the software machine must contain a complete list of the resources which are needed for successful operation.

(R7) The documentation of a software machine must include a description of
the resource management strategy of this machine in particular
for case A: The limitations on the relevant process parameters
and the amount of resources needed at all times;
for case B: An estimate of the amount of a resource needed as
a function of relevant process parameters;
for case C: Same as for case B. In addition information should
be given about the consequence of providing more
or less than the estimated amount of a resource.

It is suggested that the resource estimate algorithms should not only be documented
in the user's manual but also be provided as callable subroutine within the
software machine itself.

In some cases a certain amount of one resource may be replaced by another. As an
example: external storage may be used instead of primary storage. In such a case
the software machine itself is unable to determine the global optimum balance
between these resources because it does not know how this would influence other
processes. Hence, if the software machine has the capability to adapt itself to
different resource configurations, strategy C is the only one which allows for a
global optimum.

In any case the software machine should provide information about the actual amount
of resources used for a particular process so that the user may be able to learn
from previous applications in order to make profitable use of the software machine
in futureapplications.

11.6.6 The Components of a Software Machine

Let us combine the functional aspect of a software machine with its resource aspect
in the following schema, which is illustrated by fig.11.17.

    software machine: = (abstract machine function,
                          resource management machine,
                          documentation);

The abstract machine performs the desired functions in terms of the abstract
objects. The resource management machine manages the necessary resources. It
consists of two components:

```
resource management machine: = (management state,
                                management functions);
```

The resource management state includes a list of the authorizations (or limitations) obtained from a higher level resource management process and list of the resources which have actually been allocated by the various processes of the abstract machine part of this software machine. The resource management functions are either operational functions which authorise or limit the use of resources by the software machine or which deliver information about resource requirements (estimated or actual).

Note that while the abstract machine part may drive several processes in parallel, there is only one resource management process associated with a software machine.

The machine is completed by its documentation:

```
documentation: = (documentation of the abstract machine,
                  documentation of qualitative resource
                  requirements, documentation of resource
                  management strategy);
```

The development of CAD systems is a task comprising planning and implementation of a software machine for specified operations in a given design environment in a way that makes optimum use of the available resources. It is the importance of the resource aspect and its influence upon the CAD system architecture that we wanted to emphasize in this chapter.

11.7 References

[1] J.Encarnacao E.G.Schlechtendahl:
     Computer Aided Design - Fundamentals, Systems, Applications
     New York(to be published)Marcel Dekker

[2] J.Hatvany W.M.Newman M.A.Sabin:
     World Survey of Computer-Aided Design,
     Computer Aided Design 9(1977)2 P.79:98

[3] G.M.Nijssen:
     Modelling in Data Base Management Systems, Amsterdam(1976)North-Holland

426

[4] E.A.Warman:
      The Possibility for the Automatic Production of Command Languages,
      In:Allan III,J.J.:CAD Systems Amsterdam(1977)North-Holland P.219:240

[5] J.-C.Latombe:
      Artificial Intelligence and Pattern Recognition in Computer Aided
      Design, Amsterdam(1978)North-Holland

[6] J.J.Allan III:
      CAD in the U.S. and in Europe,
      Report GRIS 78-3, Fachgebiet Graphisch-Interaktive Systeme
      Darmstadt(1978)Techn.Hochschule

[7] J.Hatvany W.M.Newman M.A.Sabin:
      World Survey of Computer-Aided Design,
      Computer Aided Design 9(1977)2 P.79:98

[8] J.Hatvany W.M.Newman M.A.Sabin:
      World Survey of Computer-Aided Design,
      Computer Aided Design 9(1977)2 P.79:98

[9] E.G.Schlechtendahl:
      Rules for Designing CAD Software Machines,
      Proceedings of the International Conference "Interactive Techniques in
      Computer Aided Design" Bologna,Italy(1978)

[10] E.W.Dijkstra:
      Cooperating Sequential Processes,
      In:Genuys,F.:Programming Languages, New York(1968)Academic Press

[11] P.Brinch Hansen:
      Distributed Processes:A Concurrent Programming Concept,
      Computing Surveys 5(1973)4 P.223:245

[12] "PEARL":
      Full PEARL Language Description,
      Report KfK-CAD 130, Karlsruhe(1977)Kernforschungszentrum

[13] P.Brinch Hansen:
      The Programming Language Concurrent Pascal,
      IEEE Trans. on Software Engineering,Vol.SE-1 (1975)2 P.199:207

[14] J.H.Saltzer:
       Naming and Binding of Objects,
       In:Goos G. Hartmanis J.:Lecture Notes in Computer Science 60:
       Operating Systems, Berlin(1978)Springer P.99:208

[15] C.Schuenemann:
       Speicherhierarchie-Aufbau und Betriebsweise,
       Informatik-Spektrum 1(1978)1 P.25:36

[16] J.Hatvany:
       Trends and Developments in Computer-Aided Design,
       In:Gilchrist,B.(ed.):Information Processing 1977
       Amsterdam(1977)North-Holland P.267

[17] D.T.Ross K.E.Schoman:
       Structured Analysis for Requirements Definition,
       Proc. IEEE/ACM 2nd Int. Conference on Software Engineering
       San Francisco(1976)

[18] D.Teichrov E.A.Hershey III:
       PSL/PSA: A Computer-Aided Technique for Structured Documentation and
       Analysis of Information Processing Systems,
       IEEE Transactions on Software Engineering,Vol. SE-3 (1977)1 P.41:48

[19] J.V.Guttag:
       Abstract Data Types and the Development of Data Structures,
       Communications of the ACM 20(1977) P.396:404

[20] W.Bartussek D.L.Parnas:
       Using Assertions about Traces to Write Abstract Specifications for
       Software Modules,
       In:Bracchi,G.G.;Lockemann,P.C.:Proc. Information Systems Methodology
       Berlin(1978)Springer

[21] J.Ludewig W.Streng:
       Ueberblick und Vergleich verschiedener Mittel fuer die Spezifikation
       und den Entwurf von Software,
       Report KfK 2509, Karlsruhe(1978)Kernforschungszentrum

[22] "Integrated Systems":
       Integrierte Programmsysteme,
       Report KfK-CAD 2, Karlsruhe(1975)Kernforschungszentrum

[23] D.T.Ross:
      ICES System Design,
      Cambridge(1976)MIT Press

[24] K.P.Beier W.Jonas:
      DINAS - A Transportable Executive System for Interactive Computer
      Aided Design,
      Proc.Int.Conf. Interactive Techniques in Computer Aided Design,
      Bologna(1978) P.393:403

[25] Alcock,Shearing and Partners.:
      GENESYS Reference Manual,
      Loughborough(1971)The GENESYS Centre

[26] P.J.Pahl L.Beilschmidt:
      Informationssystem Technik. Programmierhandbuch Siemens System 4004,
      (1975)Siemens

[27] E.G.Schlechtendahl et.al.:
      REGENT-Handbuch,
      Report KFK 2666, Karlsruhe(1978)Kernforschungszentrum

[28] K.Leinemann:
      Dynamische Datenstrukturen des integrierten CAD-Systems REGENT,
      Angewandte Informatik (1977)1 P.26:31

[29] R.Schuster:
      System und Sprache zur Behandlung graphischer Information im
      rechnergestuetzten Entwurf,
      Report KfK 2305, Karlsruhe(1976)Kernforschungszentrum

[30] G.Enderle K.H.Bechler F.Katz K.Leinemann W.Olbrich E.G.Schlechtendahl
      K.Stölting:
      GIPSY-Handbuch,
      Report KfK 2878, Karlsruhe(1980)Kernforschungszentrum

[31] G.Enderle:
      Problemorientierte Sprachen im REGENT-System,
      Angewandte Informatik (1976)12 P.543:549

429

[32]   K.R.Dittrich R.Hüber P.C.Lockemann:

Methodenbanksysteme : Ein Werkzeug zum Maßschneidern von
Anwendersystemen,

Informatik-Spektrum (1979)2 P.194:203

[33]   D.E.Knuth:

The Art of Computer Programming, Vol 1/Fundamental Algorithms (2nd ed.)
Reading Mass.(1969)Addison-Wesley Publ.

[34]   E.G.Schlechtendahl:

Rules for Designing CAD Software Machines
Proceedings of the International Conference "Interactive Techniques in
Computer Aided Design" Bologna,Italy(1978)

[35]   "GKS":

Proposal of Standard DIN0066252,
Graphical Kernel System, Functional Description, Berlin(1979)DIN

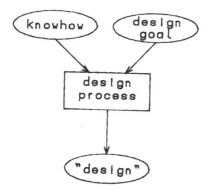

Fig.11.1 A crude model of the design process

Chapter 12

Infrastructure Approach to Integrated

CAD Systems

by

Hugh A. Tucker

CAD Center
Technical University of Denmark

TOWARDS A DESIGN METHODOLOGY

12.1 INTRODUCTION

Computer Aided Design is today an important issue, not only as a research topic, but also as a relevant and beneficial working tool in industry the world over. It is the link between the human innovator and the automatic computer system and although one of the oldest concepts of the computer community, it is still in its infancy of development. Progress in software and hardware have allowed CAD systems to become commercial products but there remains still a lot of work to be done before they can be called finished products. The area of CAD systems which is pressing most for development at this time is the topic of man-machine communication. This subject becomes more and more critical as users demand better and easier to use interfaces to their CAD systems. The problem for the system architect who faces a design project is, how can he be certain that the users will accept his system when he is finished with the implementation? The answer is that he will probably never be 100% certain, but by following certain rules and conventions he can considerably improve his chances of creating a success.

In the following sections I shall introduce some of the terminology and accepted concepts that one uses to discuss the design process of software and hardware systems, with particular interest in the CAD system and its interactive processes. As well, I present a framework which gives a guideline for the system architect to follow as he proceeds through the construction. This framework and its associated components are the results of discussions and observations from designers and system architects and are presented with the idea that potential designers may profit from these remarks.

12.2 THE USER INTERFACE

The user interface is that part of the interactive system that comes is contact with the user (physically, perceptually, and conceptually). The most direct contact will be through such physical facilities such as input and output devices, command languages, etc. but system capabilities such as prompting, help modules, and data layout will also form part of the user interface. As it is through this interface that all communication takes place, the user interface thus creates the environment of interaction. One can also say that:

> "Interaction is the process through which information is
> passed back and forth through the user interface."

The complete and detailed description of the user interface can be said to define the architecture of the system. (see later section on design specifications)

12.3 THE USER MODEL

Each user has a conceptual model of the environment which is called the user model and which contains a model of the system (its architecture) and a model of the task environment.

The user model is affected by the system only through the user interface as this is the only part of the system which he comes in contact with. It is through association with the user interface that the user model of the system is formed and perhaps influenced to change with time. For example, we can say that the user model is susceptible to training methods as they can change the user's perception and usage of the system, so in this respect the training methods form part of the user interface. Previous experience and the variability of the users themselves are examples of other influence that can affect the user model.

The user model includes a model of the user's task environment - the tasks to preform, available materials, and the methods used to effect the tasks.

Effective use of the system depends on the user knowing the model of architecture and being able to interact with it.

> "The user model is a basis for communication.
> - What makes two people that know each other communicate well?
> - They know each others models!"

It is the system architect's job to create a user interface through which the user can come to know and to communicate with the system.

12.4 THE DESIGNER'S MODEL

The designer of the system also has a model of the environment, though quite different from the users' models. The designer's model encompasses not only the model of the system and the task environment but also the target environment that is to be created.

> The designer's model is the list of criteria based on the designer's conception of the pre-design and post-design environment.

As it is the designer's model that will eventually be implemented as the target environment, the designer must be well aware of the influence of the user interface. It is the designer's influence through the user interface that makes the user model "good" or "bad" and which eventually determines the acceptability of the system.

> The user interface has a certain degree of "control" over the process of interaction. It is this degree of control which reflects the designer's "style".

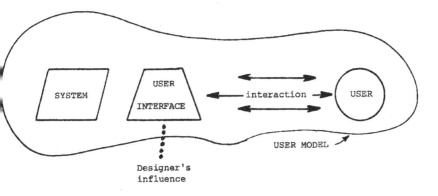

Fig. 12.1:   The designer influences the user model through the user interface.

12.5 THE DESIGN PROCESS

The design process consists of several milestones which the designer must pass during
his construction of the system. These major milestones which can be seen in Fig. 12.2
are as follows:

1. The ECONOMIC CONSTRAINTS imposed by the justification analysis.
2. The list of DESIGN CRITERIA produced by the task analysis.
3. The creation of the DESIGNER'S MODEL.
4. The documentation of the DESIGN SPECIFICATIONS.
5. The construction of the TARGET ENVIRONMENT.

The creation of these various constructs is dependent upon the tools and materials
available to the designer and the design methodology he follows. There exist no tools
or methodology that can ensure that the system architect can produce a successful
interactive design, as the success of a system is still largely a matter of good style
However, I believe that the following design process, if followed, can help to lead
to the consistant design of better systems.

In the following sections we can look at some of the working tools that the system
architect can employ for the formation of the above milestones.

12.6 THE DESIGNER'S TOOLS

Again refering to the diagram of Fig. 12.2, we can see the major working tools which
the designer can use to effect the construction milestones.

a. The JUSTIFICATION ANALYSIS which produces a list of economic
   constraints.
b. The TASK ANALYSIS used to produce the design criteria.
c. The EVALUATION TECHNIQUES used to valuate the "goodness" of
   the designer's model based on the design criteria and the
   economic constraints.
d. The DOCUMENTS that the designer can use as working tools, in
   particular the production and maintenance of the design specificatio
e. The DESIGNER'S CAPABILITY to combine design principles and
   experience to produce the design specifications.
f. Producing USER CRITIQUE during the design and construction
   of the system.
g. Some of the SOFTWARE TOOLS that can be used.

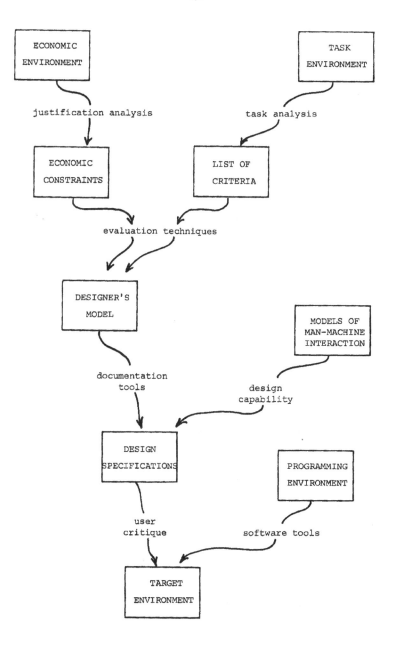

Fig. 12.2: A framework for the design process

12.6.1 Justification Analysis

It is not always certain that the system architect will be allotted this part of the design process but it is recommended that he be included as soon as possible, as the decisions made at this level have consequence throughout the design. The initiative for the start of this procedure, the justification analysis, will usually come from some economic or managerial source and will probably also be largely carried out by members of this group.

There are basically two reasons for acquiring a new system such as CAD; either it (1) produces an economic benefit surpassing the present manual methods or, (2) it provides new facilities, such as organizational aids which help to manage a product line.

The usual economical benefits a firm realizes from a new automation system is an increase in production due to quicker throughput, but it can also be an advantage by helping to put the product more quickly on the market. The latter reason is particularly important in the electronics branch where developments occur rapidly but lag-time in production can be several years. CAD systems can reduce this lag-time significantly thereby justifying their acquisition by a company. Other benefits worthy of consideration are (1) maintaining a high company quality product and (2) complianc with international standards. In-house CAD systems can provide these benefits by having standard symbols and drawing procedures locked into the software.

Justification analysis will, of course, be based upon the most relevant benefits the firm can expect to achieve. However, it can often be that a major expected benefit (such as speeded-up throughput) cannot justify the new system in itself and the actual deciding gain will come from another feature (such as an organizational aid). Thus the justification analysis must consider all facits of the task environment as it is a cumulative effect upon which the decision will be made.

One of the most used methods for analysis is the comparison of the various techniques available, manual, automatic, semi-automatic, etc. -these can be made into reference values for later evaluations and are usually given the name benchmark tests. However a word of warning here, benchmark tests can often be misleading, particularly when preformed by a biassed party, such as a manufacturer, and they should be controlled with the strictest of supervision. An independent consultant who is familiar with the proposition at hand can be of large benefit at this point. Justification of new facilities, particularly those in the organizational area are extremely difficult to evaluate objectively, and are often best left to managerial experts.

12.6.2 Task Analysis

Task analysis generates and maintains a set of criteria based on the candidate user's task environment. Through the task andlysis techniques, the designer determines the necessary facilities of the system and ascertains the interactive techniques of the user interface so that bhe user tasks may be effected in an easy and natural way. The designer begins the task analysis by deriving, from the user's working methods, which tasks are to be automated and from this creating a list of design criteria. Examples of design criteria which have wide application are: task completion time, difficulty of mastering the system, and the range of tasks that the system can preform.

The list of design criteria should be based as much as possible on actual observations of the user's task environment. Subjective valuations can also be used but are subject to misunderstandings, personal interpretations and prejudices which make later eval- uations of the user interface difficult.

Once the system architect has decided upon the list of design criteria, he must derive the constraints for the system. These, for example, can be: the necessary response times, memory capacity, abilities to handle simultaneous tasks, etc.

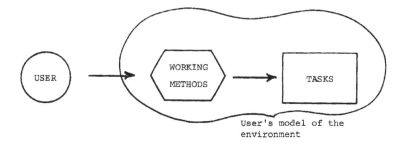

Fig. 12.3: User's Task Environment (pre-design)

Proper task analysis will describe the target environment in which the system will be used. It is the system architect's responsibility, at this point, to communicate to the potential users, completely and categorically, the target environment as he anticipates it. It is the all-important feedback from the candidate users that can insure that the design goal will be an acceptable one; therefore the users must under- stand thoroughly the part that the system plays in the proposed target environment.

One of the few ways that is known to be a successful and effective means of communication between the candidate users and the system designer is for them to work as closely as possible together on defining the target environment. This will require a certain amount of technology transfer from the system architect to the potential users about the proposed facilities and capabilities of the user interface. One might call this the first shaping of the user model.

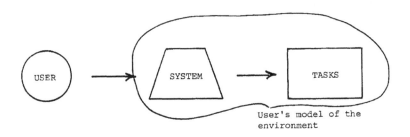

Fig. 12.4:   Target Environment (post-design)

There are some situations that the designer may encounter during the task analysis:

. the user may expect facilities which are not possible with todays technology, at least within a reasonable price range.

. the user may wish to maintain traditional working methods which are perhaps not the best suited for the tasks at hand.

. the user may wish unessential facilities which would require a considerable design and implementation effort.

It is quite likely that the target environment will include possibilities of preformin tasks not previously considered by the users. This makes the task analysis a more complex process as evaluation of these new tasks will envolve estimating their value rather than using observed valuations. These will cause the model of the target envi onment to flucuate during its creation.

The major handicap the system architect faces today in task analysis is the lack of adequate descriptive techniques for user environments, which not only makes the analy sis difficult, but is a constant source of misunderstanding between the the designer and the user.

12.6.3 Evaluation Techniques

During the design phase, the system architect will be constantly reviewing and modifying his model. The modifications will be based on evaluations of the system and the user interface using data from the lists of design criteria and constraints. Through the evaluations the system architect will settle upon a final model which he can then use to discuss with the candidate users.

A complete evaluation of the user interface involves assigning a priority to each criterion or set of trade-offs. This priority will vary according to the context, economy, system, and task environment under consideration. In the event that the evaluation is dependent upon some special hardware characteristics, the system architect must find some method of defining and explaining these characteristics in the design specifications. Without some type of definition a complete evaluation of the user interface is unobtainable. Likewise, evaluations dependent upon specific commands and display techniques will be less accurate in the absence of precise definitions of these components.

The best method of evauation during the construction of the design specifications is to have a community of real-world users with which the designer can interact. This is also a useful tool to have during the building of the system - see section 12.6.7 on User Critique.

The system architect must not only be prepared to change his model and design specifications but he must be ready to accept the fact that change will be a modus operandi during the whole design procedure. As Frederick P. Brooks points out in his excellent book, "The Mythical Man-Month" - the only constancy in system design is change itself and that the designer must deliver satisfaction of a user need which will change as the actual need and the user's perception of that need (the user model) changes.

However, not all user wishes and objectives can be met and the evaluations of the design criteria must be aimed at a threshold. This threshold must be established at the beginning of the project and raised as the project progresses or no product will will ever be completed.

As a last step, before any code exists, the design specifications must be given to an outside group to be scrutinized for completeness and clarity. The system architect and the candidate users cannot themselves do this as they themselves will not admit that they don't understand it (even to themselves) and they will be happy to invent their way through the gaps and obscurities.

12.6.4 Documents as Design Tools

The specification of the system architect's model is a working document in the form
of words, pictures, code, etc., which describes how the available materials are to
be utilized to effect the target environment. The preparation of this document serves
to focus and crystalize thoughts and discussions that the potential users and the
system architect have had during the task analysis and evaluation phases. By constant
maintenance of these design specifications, the designer can maintain control of the
consistancy of the target environment as well as having a checklist over the status
of the project. The design specification document is perhaps the most important tool
the system architect has to lighten the load of communication to the users and other
team members.

The design specifications usually tend to consist of a "user manual" of the system
plus preformance documentation. The user manual, as a written specification, is a
necessary tool, though not a sufficient one. The manual is often referred to as the
External Specification and as such it describes and prescribes every detail of what
the user sees, it describes that part of the user interface that interacts directly
with the system. Quite different are the Internal Specifications, which are strictly
meant for the implementors of the system and have little to do with the users. The
Internal Specifications include definitions of all module interfaces, effects of hardware, influences upon other programs, etc.

The design specification documents should be supplimented with other tools and I would
suggest that mock dialogues and "quick and dirty" implementations are needed at this
level to convey to the candidate users a real perception of the target environment.

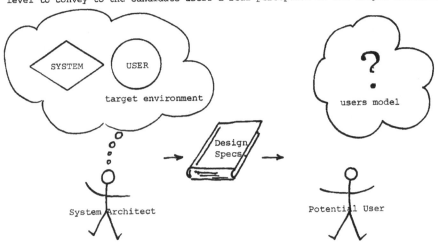

Fig. 12.5: Design specifications form a communication media

12.6.5 Design Capability

The "style" a designer imparts to the system and particualrly the user interface governs the acceptance that the system will receive. The designers capability is supported by his experience and exposure to various models of man-machine interaction.

> The style a designer bestows to the user interface will
> always be a matter of <u>art</u> - designers can learn about style
> but how well they apply it will affect the degree of accept-
> ance ·from the users.

Methodologies of man-machine communication are, as yet, based upon the principles and practices of interactive computer techniques. These principles and practices today are largely gathered by designers or system architects through their personal encounters with good (and bad) existing systems and can roughly be classed as "rules of the thumb". Written material on this subject is hard to come by and I know of no "bible" that is available as such, however, general principles of practice can be found scattered throughout software journals. There are also several projects underway by psychologists researching and trying to interpret the physical and psychological laws which govern man-machine interaction.

A contributing factor to the lack of documents is this area is no doubt due to the want of good descriptive techniques. This is particularly unfortunate for this phase of the design procedure as the description of the target environment must be clearly and unambiguously conveyed to the candidate users. Only if the users have a thorough understanding of the design specifications can they be expected to give relevant and constructive criticism. The designer can well be considered as part of the user interface during this phase as he helps to build up the users' models of the target environment.

12.6.6 User Critique

Creative activity has been described as occurring in three stages: the idea, the implementation, and the interaction. Most people will intuitively consider this activity as a sequence; for example, the writing of a book which progresses from a concept of the author, is realized in printed form, and then is read by someone thereby interacting with the mind of the author. However, I advocate that building a computer system should definitely not progress sequentially but rather in an atmosphere of interaction where the end user can influence not only the implementation but also the first conception. The reason for this is that contrary to most works of art, where the "beauty" is in the eye of the beholder, a computer system <u>must</u> please the users. And what better way to please someone than to build just the working tool he himself desires. Thus, by surrounding himself and the implementation group with a set of real-world users, the designer can give himself a valuable and useful tool.

It is the system architect however, who must make the decisions as to what is to be included in the design and what is to be left out. And in this respect, he must follow the maxim that no matter how good the new ideas are, if they don't integrate with the systems basic concepts, it gets left out! Under all circumstances the conceptual integrity of the system must be maintained as this will ultimately determine its ease of use.

> Conceptual integrity of the specifications makes the system
> not only easier to use, it also makes it easier to build
> and less subject to bugs.

If there appear to be many such important but incompatible ideas then the only thing to do is to scrap the system and restart from scratch with other basic concepts i.e. restarting from the task and economic analysis as there must exist some basic incon-sistances. Another trap to watch out for is what Brooks calls the "Second-System Effect", where a designer who has successfully completed his first system, tends to over-design the second system, using all the bells and whistles he conservatively left off the first system. The answer to both of these pitfalls is that the system architect must have a large degree of self-discipline and he must exercise it frequent-ly.

12.6.7 Software Tools

It is recognized that a good programming environment is essential for the implementa-tion of any sizable software project and CAD systems can be said to fall nicely into this category. It has been suggested that the programming and designing environments ought to be set up similar to the environments of other engineering design disciplines such as for example mechanical engineering. There one has two categories of facilities - a list of component parts, and a collection of previous designs. The hypothesis is that rarely are new designs constructed from scratch but are rather always minor perturbations of some already exsisting design.

If we accept this arguement then we must have a programming environment that supports more than just a programming language; we must have methods of examining previous designs and ways of inserting new components, just as in mechanical design. The

emphasis in software design is of course somewhat different and here, particularly
with interactive programs, and in this case it is not so much the components that are
important as is the structure of the system and its control functions. By establishing
a good interactive programming environment which can provide frameworks of successful
programs for modification into new systems, one can help to provide the elements of
style. Not only will this approach provide better (or in any case more consistant)
style, but it should make programming, debugging, and testing more constrained and
thereby more effective.

The programming environment should support tools for the viewing and editing of the
program library so that new components can be added to a framework and assembled into
a functioning system. Here is a list of some of the basic requirements for a good
programming environment:

- a programming language with the ability to describe ABSTRACT
  DATA TYPES.
- EDITORS for entering, updating, and modifying both programs
  and data.
- BROWSERS for viewing quickly through libraries and programs.
- DOCUMENTATION TOOLS for automatically cross-referencing,
  indexing, type-setting, etc.
- DEBUGGING AIDS such as backtracking mechanisms and structuring
  abilities for manipulation purposes.
- a HIGH-LEVEL PROGRAMMABLE COMMAND LANGUAGE in a suitable
  interactive environment (with filing capabilities) so that
  modules can be quickly improvised for users to play with.
- TEST-CASE GENERATORS to help to find bugs and simulate a real
  world situation.

12.7 SUMMARY

This paper is an introduction to the concepts and terminology now relevant in what
may be called design methodology. I have not tried to say what is good or bad with
specific designs but rather have tried to give general comments and rules of the
thumb which experienced designers have found to be useful and successful. The framework which is proposed can be used to follow during the design process and to incorporate the aforementioned ideas and observations.

One of the aspects of system design that is conspicuously lacking from our toolbox
is the ability to adequately and unambiguously describe the various facilities within

a system, particularly with user interfaces and interactive programs. The lack of these descriptive techniques hinders the development of another important working tool: the ability to evaluate the intrinsic interactions that take place in man to machine communication.

REFERENCES

Throughout this paper, I have drawn heavily upon the discussions which took place during the Seillac II meeting on Methodology of Interaction. As well, I have used many of the thoughts and ideas from the book by Frederick P. Brooks Jr., The Mythical Man-Month.

1) Guedj R.A., Hopgood F.R.A., ten Hagen P.J.W., Tucker H.A., Duce D.A.,
   Methodology of Interaction , SEILLAC II, North-Holland Publ. Co.,
   to be released 1980.

2) Brooks F.P.Jr., The Mythical Man-Month, Addison-Wesley Publ. Co.,
   1975.

Chapter 13

Choice of Turnkey Systems

by

Ketil Bo

RUNIT, Computing Centre at
the University of Trondheim,
Norway

13.1 Introduction

Computer Aided Design (CAD) and Manufacturing (CAM) are now being accepted as the keys to increased industrial productivity.

In the early fifties, numerical controlled machines (N/C) kindled a hope of a new industrial effectivity.

The minicomputer and computer graphics arrived in the sixties and gave promises of more effective design.

But, it is not until now the early eighties that these hopes actually can be realized by coupling CAD and CAM together to an integrated system.

Unfortunately, not all suppliers of turnkey CAD-systems have realized this as yet.

CAD can be described as a complex of hardware, software, and people, put together to execute a certain design function.

Naturally, such a system will have various qualities dependent on what is to be constructed.

There are after all principle differences from designing a boat to designing a computer system.

Several system vendors seem to have ignored this simple facts and attempt to solve all problems with one "box".

On the other hand, there the undoubtedly a number of similarities in the various design systems, which should imply that it is possible to deliver flexible application systems tailored to specific tasks. Such systems can be built on standardized modules, both of hardware and software.

Other than specialized systems developed in the automotive and aerospace industries, the first successful commercial penetration of CAD was in the printed circuit, integrated circuit and hybrid circuit design and production areas. To-date, these PC/IC applications have accounted for about 75 % of the installations. Outputs from these systems include artwork masters and automated machine controls. The applications are generally 2D, although the data bases associated with multilayer boards and IC chips must be able to handle and display information about numerous levels (2½ Dimension).

13.2 CAD Task Force

When a company decides to employ CAD as a tool to increase their competitiveness, there are several approaches which can be used:

1. Develope one's own tailored CAD system, more or less from scratch.
   (e.g. Boeing, Lockheed)

2. Bay a pure software system, and implement it on one's own equipment.
   (e.g. Autokon, AD2000)

3. Provide a tailored CAD system based on existing modules of hardware
   and software. (e.g. ICAN)

4. Purchase a turnkey CAD system. (e.g. Computer Vision, Auto-Trol)

All of these solutions have strong and weak points and should be evaluated in each case based on the company's economy, structure and the
character of the tasks to be performed.

Let us suppose that a company, in this case, choose to go for a turnkey system, (a corresponding discussion to the following should be
accomplished for all of the above alternatives).

The most important point is not to ask the likely candidates among the
system vendors the right questions (which can be difficult enough),
but to ask oneself the necessary questions (which is usually more
difficult).

It is therefore profitable to set up a small CAD task force (3-4
persons) with the following qualifications:

1. Detailed knowledge of the design and production problems within the
   company

2. Data processing knowledge

3. Experience in financial analysis

The CAD task force have to:

1. Identify the problem areas within the company:

   - personell resources
   - "know-how" problems

- "lead-time" problems
- quality problems
- bottlenecks
  etc.

2. Analyze the problems by quantifying each of the problem areas:
   - 3 persons with data processing experience
   - an average of 3 weeks longer "lead-time" for the design-phase than that of the competitors
     etc.

3. Decide which of the problems the turnkey system are supposed to solve, and quantify the value of these solutions (economy, competitiveness, work environment, etc.):
   - shorten the design-phase
   - improve quality
   - decrease the work costs
   - faster generation and updating of production support material
   - improve production planning
   - support for the tender-phase
     - faster
     - safer
     - modifiable
   - possibility for customer-modification
     etc.

4. Estimate capital investment and operating cost of the system

   Justify an eventual procurement from point 3 and 4 alone (don't include in the justification possible other utilizations of the system in the future).

Make sure that the task force are given sufficient time and resources to do a profound job. If necessary hire an experienced consultant to join the task force.

13.3 The Turnkey Vendors

If the conclution of the task force is to provide a turnkey CAD system, the time is due to approach the system vendors.

Then the simple questions arise: What is a turnkey CAD system and who are the vendors?

Traditionally we have two principally different views on what a turnkey CAD system is:

The first originates from activities around automatic drafting where the CAD system is regarded as a minicomputer based drafting/design aid with "stand alone" possibilities.

The second view originates from activities around problems which require greater resources of computer power for analysis and calculations. The CAD system is in this case looked upon as a terminal linked to a large host computer with possibilities of executing design, drawing and large calculations.

The current trend in the market is a synthesis of the two views: "stand alone" systems are continually upgraded to enable communication with a host computer in a flexible way, and the "terminal" systems are continually upgraded by adding more capabilities and programs for making the terminals more intelligent.

Which questions should then be asked to the turnkey vendors? It is clear that several of the questions will be of a general character (price, screen type, word length, etc.), while other questions are of a more specific character dependent on the company that undertakes the evaluation, and the task that has to be carried out. When we carried out our survey of CAD systems in 1978 [1], we started out with about 120 general questions to each of the vendors.

This number was then reduced to 68 questions which, from our point of view, gave a fairly good general picture of the systems.

Let us, as an example, look at some representative systems to get a feeling of which questions may be posed, and what the vendors have to offer:

Mechanical design applications account for about 15 % of the current installations. Included in these areas are schematic, logic and wiring diagrams plus conventional mechanical drawing and detailing. Mechanical design in particular requires a true 3 dimensional data base. The prospect is that once such true 3D CAD/CAM systems with well designed man/machine communication tools are available, the mechanical design installations will increase dramatically.

Cartography, accounting for about 5 % of current applications, is another projected high growth area, with growth depending on the availability of adequate digital geographic data bases.

The rest of the CAD systems are used in architecture, engineering and general research areas. Again, growth in these applications depends on establishing adequate data bases, attractive interaction tools development of suitably specialized software, and recognition of the economic benefits.

The continued growth of CAD systems is assured because return-on-investment - management's touchstone - has been demonstrated to be substantial. Reports of equipment amortization within 18-24 months are not unusual.

COMPUTERVISION

Fig.13.1. Typical COMPUTERVISION configuration.

TYPE: Stand alone CAD-SYSTEM

PRICE: Min. Configuration   150 000
                             Average Configuration   300 000 (3 workstations)

FIRST SYSTEM: 1970

COMPUTER: CGP 100 COMPUTERVISION

WORD LENGTH: 16 BIT

DISPLAY: Storage or raster

PRODUCTIVITY: 4:1 → 6:1

DIMENSIONALITY: 3D (wireframe & Math. surfaces)

SIZE OF PROGRAM: 70 M bytes

SOURCE CODE AVAILABLE: Yes

N/C TAPE DIRECTLY: Yes

SOFTWARE: CADDS 3/CADDS 4

SPECIALIZED APPLICATIONS: Mechanical Design, Circuit Design, N/C etc.

AUTO-TROL

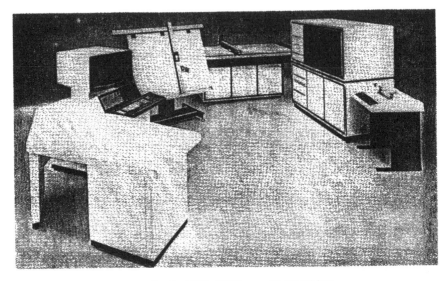

Fig.13.2. A typical AUTO-TROL configuration.

TYPE: Stand alone CAD-system

PRICE: Min. configuration ~$ 200 000
                               Average configuration ~$ 275 000 (5 workstations)

FIRST SYSTEM: 1971

COMPUTER: UNIVAC U-77-600

WORD LENGTH: 16 Bit

DISPLAY: Storage (standard or modified)

PRODUCTIVITY: 4:1 → 12:1

DIMENSIONALITY: 2D & 3D (wire frame & geometric)

SIZE OF PROGRAM: 64 K bytes

SOURCE CODE AVAILABILITY: Optional

N/C TAPE DIRECTLY: Yes

SOFTWARE: AD/380
                               GS2000

SPECIALIZED APPLICATIONS: Piping, Architecture, Circuit Design,
                           Mechanical Design

Potential customers of these systems will, in most cases, underestimate what is required of resources to identify and evaluate available systems. Not because the systems are so difficult to evaluate, but because:

1. The customer has not sufficient understanding of the present (manual) work operations which he is trying to improve.

2. The customer can't find a turnkey system which exactly suits his needs and therefore uses a great deal of time to find out (together with the vendor), how a system eventually shall be modified to meet his needs. If he finds out how the system should be modified, does he have the sufficient expertize to undertake the modifications. If not, will the system vendor take care of it? If so, is he able to do a satisfactory job within a given time frame?

   This is one of the real serious problems with turnkey systems and a source of uncontrolled expenses.

3. Development and running of "benchmark" tests often provide doubtful results because the success of CAD systems is greatly dependent on the people who operate the system, and of the company itself.

13.4 Selection Criterias

An evaluation of a CAD system should cover all aspects of hardware, software, service, support and management. The important factors in the evaluation are given below. [4]:

Hardware characteristics

- machine characteristics, capacity and performance
- peripheral characteristics, capacity and performance
- suitability of machine for CAD
- possible upgrades of processor and core
- peripheral enhancements possible
- further peripherals that can be supported

Company characteristics

- applications area experience
- job mix
- research, development, production bias
- future plans and support policy
- rental and purchase arrangements
- delivery delay times

Communications and interfaces

- terminal and peripheral hardware supported
- interfaces for other computers
- direct and dial-up lines
- transmission characteristics and speeds

Operational characteristics

- service availability
- speed of response
- reliability
- ease of access
- back-up available
- operational requirements (air conditioning, temperature etc.)

User support

- quality of available documentation
- dissemination of information (bulletins, updates etc.)
- staff support available (advisory, consultancy)
- maintenance contracts and arrangements
- training courses offered

Cost

   - purchase, rental and time hire costs
   - support staff costs
   - maintenance costs
   - charging algorithms and accounting procedures
   - discounts offered

Command system

   - ease of use
   - consistency of syntax
   - power (macro-command definition etc.)

Man/machine communication

   - types of input devices
   - organization of input devices
   - organization of menues etc.
   - prompts and echoes
   - error messages and recovery
   - error handling

Programming languages

   - compiler available
   - adherence to standards
   - degrees of code optimization available
   - quality of compiled code
   - quality of diagnostics
   - library routines available
   - operating systems functions available within the language

Development software

   - editors available
   - debug packages available
   - user-defined libraries
   - file maintenance and manipulation
   - other development aids

File store

   - dise storage available
   - secondary storage available (magnetic tape etc.)
   - files supported (random access, sequential etc.)
   - disc-core transfer block size

- disc-core transfer rate

Applications software

- type of CAD programs or packages available
- other programs or packages available (management, statistics etc.)

Graphics packages

- packages supported and their characteristics

Other facilities

- batch submission
- disc to tape archiving system
- system generator

Compability with other CAD groups and systems

- other research and development projects using such a machine or service
- other production systems operating on such a machine or service

13.5 Hidden Cost and Benefits

One must neither forget the "hidden" costs that are connected with the installation and introduction of a CAD system in a company such as:

- training

  After the equipment is installed a learning period will be required before the system will result in the productivity level upon which the initial justification was based. While the operation of a typical CAD system can be learned in a few weeks, the operators <u>productivity</u> cannot be expected to reach the peak level until about 6-8 months after the user learns how to operate the system (see the learning curve in fig. 3).

- motivation of the operators and the managers

- introduction/information (management, etc.)

- restructuring of the company

- interfacing with other systems

  etc.

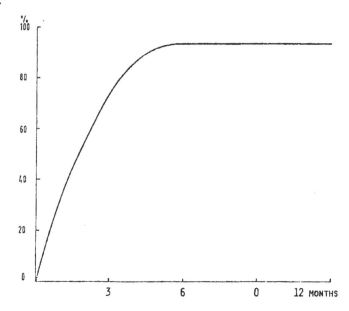

Fig.13. 3. Learning Curve for a new installation to reach 95 % efficiency.

But, there are of course also a number of "hidden" benefits that come
on top of the estimated such as:

- Improved drawing quality

- Improved compliance with standards

- Improved internal communication between the different departments

- Solving problems which could not be tackled without a computer

- Greater design capacity

- Provide better cost control

- Save materials and machining time by optimization algorithms

- Minimize transcription errors

- Lead to easier customer modification

  etc.

13.6 Conclusion

Last, but not least, CAD systems seems to have a sort of "narcotic" effect on most companies. If a company gets the taste of this tool, new application areas are continously detected and the need for expansion will appear at a constantly growing rate.

Two important questions should therefore be asked:

Is the system powerful enough to grow as the requirements of company increase? If not, can it be justified that the system are kept during its lifetime to execute a certain task without consideration of what is happening in the surroundings?

The answer to one of these questions should be a definite YES.

I hope these reflections do not frighten anyone from attempting to use CAD in his company, because surveys show that after the first frustrating "surprise" period (½-1 year) companies who have done a relatively sensible analysis come out with very positive results. Moreover for many companies the conversion to CAD is necessary to be able to at all continue to be competitive.

REFERENCES

[1]   J.J.Allan, K.Bø: "A Survey of Commercial Turnkey CAD/CAM Systems", PI, 1978.

[2]   Material from the CAD/CAM System Vendors.

[3]   Carl Machover: "Management Considerations in Buying Graphics Equipment", Seminar at Eurographics 79, Bologna, Italy 1979.

[4]   G.T. Webster and C.W. Johnson: "The evaluation and selection of a computer system for interactive design." Computer Aided Design Volume 8, Number 4, October 1976.

Authors' Addresses

Ketil Bø
RUNIT Computing Center
at the University of Trondheim
Sem Saelandsv. 2

N-7034 Trondheim-NTH - Norway

Tomas Neumann
Technische Hochschule Darmstadt
FG Graphisch-Interaktive Systeme
Steubenplatz 12

D-6100 Darmstadt - W.-Germany

Horst Nowacki
Technische Universität Berlin
Institut für Schiffstechnik
Salzufer 17-19

D-1000 Berlin 10 - W.-Germany

Aristides Requicha
Production Automation Project
University of Rochester

Rochester, N.Y. 14627 - USA

Tom Sancha
Quayside Cambridge

Cambridge CB5 8AB - U.K.

E.G. Schlechtendahl
Kernforschungszentrum Karlsruhe
Postfach 3640

D-7500 Karlsruhe - W.-Germany

Hugh Tucker
Northern Europe University
Computing Centre
Technical University of Denmark

2800 Lyngby - Denmark

M.A. Wesley
IBM Watson Research Center
Box 218

Yorktown Heights, N.Y. 10598 - USA

Lecture Notes in Computer Science